The BOOK of LIFE

PAUL, LIFE AND LETTERS

Paul's Ship

Painted by Edwin John Prittie; expressly for The
Book of Life

"And when they had taken up the anchors,
they committed themselves unto the sea,
and loosed the rudder bands, and hoisted
up the mainsail to the wind, and made
toward shore." Acts 27:40.

VOLUME 8

PAUL,
LIFE AND LETTERS

THE

BOOK of LIFE

ARRANGED AND EDITED BY

NEWTON M. HALL, A.M., D.D., *Pastor and Christian Educator,*
Author of Civic Righteousness and Civic Pride

IRVING F. WOOD, Ph.D., D.D. *Professor of Religion and Bible,*
Author of The Spirit of God in Biblical Literature

Joint Authors of The Bible Story; Early Days of Israel; Days of the Kings
of Israel; Adult Bible Classes and How to Teach Them

JOHN RUDIN &
COMPANY, INC.
Chicago

ACKNOWLEDGMENTS

We gratefully acknowledge our indebtedness to the following for valued editorial counsel and assistance: V. Raymond Edman, Ph.D., L.L.D., President, Wheaton College; Paul E. Kretzmann, Ph.D., D.D.; the late George L. Robinson, Ph.D., D.D.; Merrill C. Tenney, Ph.D.; the late Professor Robert L. Cooke, Ed.D.; John Luchies, Th.D.; Professor Kenneth S. Kantzer, Ph.D.; all distinguished and devout Biblical scholars, teachers and authors; Louise Rock, Children's Religious Book Editor; Moody Press for *Stories of Hymns We Love;* Dr. Wm. S. McBirnie; Lewis Bayles Paton, D.D., Hartford Theological Seminary; Edgar J. Goodspeed, Ph.D.; Elihu Grant, Ph.D., Professor of Biblical Literature, Haverford College; Henry Thatcher Fowler, D.D., Professor of Biblical Literature, Brown University; Mr. and Mrs. W. A. Pottenger; Mr. Charles F. H. Crathern, Jr.; the American Passion Play of Bloomington, Illinois, and Bess Hibarger for helping to assemble Passion Play pictures; The Pilgrim Press; Edwin Markham; Houghton, Mifflin and Company; Fleming H. Revell & Company; The Abingdon Press; British Broadcasting Corporation, Copyright, London, W. 1.

We make grateful acknowledgment to the following Art Galleries for permission to use their pictures: Metropolitan Art Museum of New York; British Museum of London; Boston Museum of Fine Art; National Gallery, London; National Tate Gallery, London; The Louvre, Paris, France; National Museum, Naples, Italy; National Gallery, Dresden, Germany; Galleria Ambrosiana, Milan, Italy; The Art Institute of Chicago; Curtis & Cameron, Incorporated.

For special contributions by Professor Robert Seneca Smith; Clara Bodman Hawks; Mrs. Louise Hall Tharp; Cecilia Rudin; Helen Rudin; and Frances Olcott; and many others for their help, the publishers here wish to extend grateful and sincere appreciation.

The pictures by James J. Tissot are reproductions of original paintings of the "New Testament" at the Brooklyn Museum, New York, and of the "Old Testament" at the Jewish Museum, New York. Permission for use by John H. Eggers Publications, New York, who have exclusive publication rights. These photos, and others, were taken by Three Lions, Inc., New York. Other photos in color are used by permission of International Publishing Co., Ltd., Jerusalem, and Wide World Photos.

PREFACE

THE apostle Paul was one of the greatest men of all time. He was providentially chosen and set apart to be the great captain of the new faith, in all the wide extent of the Roman Empire. His adventures by land and sea have all the interest and color of romance, truth far more interesting than fiction. He was beaten, stoned, cast into prison, shipwrecked, yet he continued with undaunted courage and unshaken faith, until the good fight was fought, the long course finished, the great task done. He was a conqueror, though he never drew a sword. Under Christ, the Captain of his Salvation, Paul went forth to proclaim the gospel to the world. The story of his life as he followed the commands of his Lord stands as one of the greatest epochs of the Christian faith. A knowledge of Paul, the apostle, is absolutely necessary to the intelligent understanding of human history.

Here will be found also in full the letters, inspired and full of inspiring thoughts, which Paul and others wrote to the early churches, together with the Book of Revelation. It is believed that the pictures illustrating the life and religion of the great Greek and Roman civilizations and the notes, introductions, and maps will be especially interesting and valuable to the reader.

ON MARS HILL

Walk up stone stairs to the top of yonder curved rock (middle of photograph) and, while sitting there, gaze over the city of Athens. St. Paul was here; and here on Mars Hill, the Areopagus, he preached to the pagan philosophers. From this hill he could see nearby on a flat hill-top the magnificent pagan temples of the Acropolis, dedicated to Athen's gods.

Said St. Paul, in his sermon, "Ye men of Athens, I perceive that in all things ye are too superstitious; for as I passed by, and beheld your devotions, I found an altar with this inscription, TO THE UNKNOWN GOD. Whom therefore ye ignorantly worship, him declare I unto you."

To find out what he declared to these pagan Gentiles, read Acts 17, pages 62-73.

CONTENTS

VOLUME EIGHT

PAUL, LIFE, LETTERS

9

Head of Paul—Detail from St. Cecilia

By Raphael Sanzio (1483-1520)

From a Steel Engraving in the Vatican Gallery

THIS wonderful study of Paul is a detail from the large altar piece, ST. CECILIA, which hangs in the Municipal Gallery, Bologna, Italy. An account of the life, letters and influence of the great apostle is given in this volume. It is truly said that wherever the church throughout all the world acknowledges God and his Christ, there Paul of Tarsus is revered as the great teacher of a redemption freely offered to all men.

Here we see the inspired leader rapt in silent meditation. In this head the strength of mind and nobility of purpose which characterized the life of Paul exist for us as never before. Thus does the painter capture the inner beauty of the outward form, the reality of the spirit, which few of us could fashion for our own mind's eye with such indescribable clarity and beauty.

In Raphael's short life of thirty-seven years, he may be said to have swept away the Middle Ages in art. The beginning of the great change in the general style of painting was brought about by Leonardo da Vinci and Michelangelo. However, Leonardo's analytic and poetic temperament and Michelangelo's intense individuality restricted the range and influence of their art. If Raphael's spirit was not so penetrating as theirs, his sympathies were wider. To Raphael, the world was a place filled with beautiful things which had only to be brought together and touched by the talisman of his art to fall into harmony with each other and the rest of humanity. Raphael was necessary to the spreading of the freedom first discovered by Leonardo and Michelangelo. Through him the best and fairest in Italian painting was given its final stamp, and Raphael's name remains the most famous and most beloved in modern art.

Another of his pictures is on page 67.

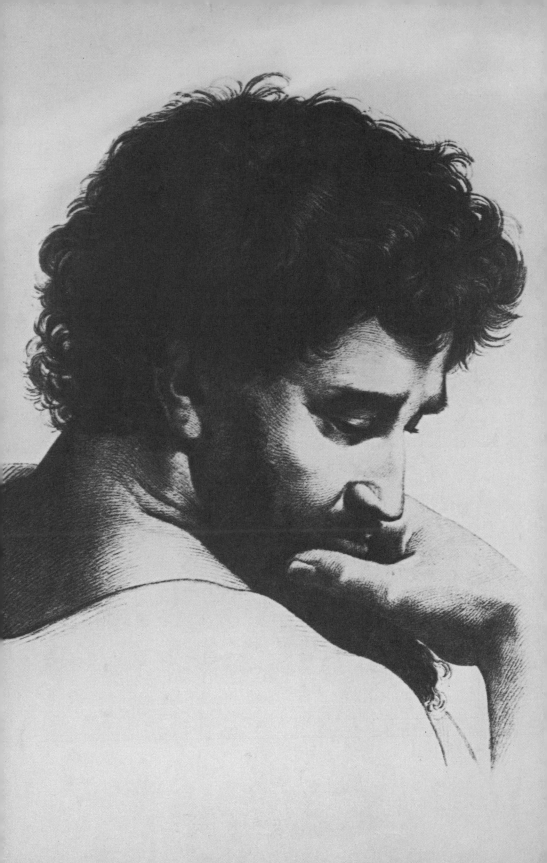

Paul, the Captain of the New Faith

THE "good news" of the Gospel, the story of the life and death and resurrection of Jesus, was meant not only for the little company of the disciples, not even for the people of Palestine, but for the whole world. The disciples did not at first realize this. They had never traveled far beyond Jerusalem and their native villages. They distrusted foreigners. They thought that any new disciples must conform to all the customs and ceremonials of the Jewish people, that they must become Jews.

There was needed a great spirit, a man of broad and farseeing mind, to whom God could impart a world-wide vision of missionary service. Not only must such a man possess a devout spirit, utterly consecrated to the will and work of the Lord Jesus Christ; he must also be a man of undaunted courage, possessing the spirit of the explorer, the soldier. Such a man was Paul of Tarsus. He possessed all the characteristics necessary for his great task. He was a provincial Jew. The father of Paul was probably a merchant who lived in Tarsus, a city of Cilicia. It was a famous city, with just the atmosphere to impress a boy who was to have the career of Paul. Here was no quiet town on the hillsides of Judea, not even a provincial capital like Jerusalem. Tarsus was a free city of the empire and the tides of the commerce and power of the empire flowed through it. It was a great center of trade. Caravans were coming and going constantly from those mysterious countries beyond the Taurus Mountains. Alongside its great granite quays lay ships from all the lands of the Mediterranean. All this must have appealed with great force to a boy of Paul's disposition. Who can doubt that he talked with the merchants of the caravans and the sailors of the ships? Later he was to be almost a sailor himself. He knew a Roman ship and how to sail her as well as the master himself. The Roman soldier was a familiar sight to him and his pulses must have thrilled to the sound of the bugles and the tramp of the legionaries on the streets of the city. This training was of inestimable value to him in his later life. He was no countryman, shy and awkward, when he visited the great capitals of the world. He knew intimately the ways of cities. It was never hard for him to get acquainted. He met on equal terms the king in his palace, the centurion of the Roman legion, the tentmaker, and the stevedore.

Paul was a singularly modern man, a man

of force and action. He was always seeking results,—definite, positive results. His missionary journeys were great campaigns. The modern word "power" was a favorite of his: "This one thing I do"; "Forgetting the things that are behind"; "All things to all men to gain some." These are the watchwords of modern business. Paul would have been at home in modern life, on the deck of a great ocean liner as well as on a Roman galley. He would be a welcome guest in modern business circles, at the meetings of great organizations, such as the Rotary or Kiwanis Clubs, as well as in the churches. He was always a gentleman. He was never fearful, at all times bold as a lion, ready to meet opposition if it came, but always courteous. He was courteous to the people of Athens, he apologized for speaking out hastily to the high priest at Jerusalem, he was even respectful in his address to the hardened reprobate.

Tarsus was not only a commercial city, but also a great center of learning. Its university ranked with those of Athens and Alexandria. There was an atmosphere of culture as well as of trade. While there is no evidence that Paul actually attended the University of Tarsus, he seems to have possessed some knowledge of Greek literature, and he may very well have had friends among the students from all over the world. This was another important formative element in that cosmopolitan atmosphere in which Paul's boyhood was spent.

We do not know exactly when Paul was born, but it was probably about the time the shepherds announced the birth of the Master whom he was to follow. While Jesus was spending the early years of his life in the quiet carpenter's shop in Nazareth, Paul was growing up in this bustling atmosphere of a great commercial city. We see the difference in the teaching. The figures which Jesus used were of the country, of his trade, of lilies and birds, of ox-yokes and candles. Paul's figures are of the roaring city, the camp, the stadium, the temple.

The early religious training of these Jewish boys must have been identical: the school, the synagogue, the simple and austere life of the home. Every Jew of the Dispersion went up to Jerusalem once a year to keep the Passover if it was possible to do so. Paul's father was probably wealthy, and doubtless when the boy was twelve years old, he went for the first time, not as Jesus went, over the hills of Samaria, but by sea and land to the holy city.

The time came when Paul's career must be decided upon. His father may have wished him to become a merchant like himself; but the boy's fine qualities of mind and his serious disposition naturally pointed to the career of Rabbi. The college where Jewish boys were trained for the office of Rabbi, for the

ministry, as we should say, was at Jerusalem.
Before Paul left home, it was required, as it
was of all Jewish boys, that he should learn
a trade. The principal business of Tarsus
was the making of tent cloth of the long fine
hair of the goats which were kept in great
numbers on the mountains surrounding
Tarsus. This was another element in Paul's
training which was destined to be of great
importance in his after life. Everywhere he
went he could, if necessary, earn a living at
his trade and come in close contact with the
people he most cared to meet.

Paul went up to Jerusalem and was entered as a student in the theological college.
The president or chief teacher was at this
time, fortunately for Paul, one of the most
enlightened scholars whom the Jewish people
have ever possessed. Gamaliel was called
the "Beauty of the Law," and the "Great
Rabbi." Paul was fortunate in coming under
the personal training of such a man. Those
must have been wonderful years which
Paul spent in Jerusalem. He loved his own
home city, he boasted of it,—"a citizen of no
mean city"; but Jerusalem was the beloved
city of every Jew, full of wonderful memories, gathering up within itself all the faith
and sacred stories of a great people.

It was at Jerusalem that Paul first came
into contact with the strange new sect of
Christians, and it is at this point that the
Book of the Acts begins the story of his

persecutions of the people of the new faith, his conversion, and his heroic service for the Master. He ceases to be Saul, the Jewish Rabbi, a member of the Sanhedrin, destined for high honors; and he becomes Paul the Apostle, the chief figure in the early years of Christianity—one of the greatest souls of all time.

To emphasize the human side of Paul's personality and message is not in any way to minimize his unique position as a "chosen vessel of God." He wrote his epistles by inspiration. As the channel of a great river is used to pour its flood from the mountain to the sea, so the Holy Spirit used the channel of this great soul to pour the divine message from the mountains of God to the sea of human life and need.

ON WAY TO DERBE AND LYSTRA

Two little Americans in eager delight have passed through the Cilician Gates. They are gazing at the Taurus Mountains in Cappadocia, Asia Minor.

St. Paul, after passing through the Cilician Gates, must have come this way in going to the Churches of Derbe and Lystra. There he found young Timothy, who became his missionary helper.

"To Timothy, my dearly beloved son, Grace, mercy, and peace from God the Father and Christ Jesus our Lord," St. Paul writes. And again, "I call to remembrance the unfeigned faith that is in thee, which dwelt first in thy grandmother Lois, and thy mother Eunice; and I am persuaded that in thee also."

Read Acts 16:1-5, page 50; II Timothy 1, pages 366-7.

THE ROMAN EMPIRE

Paul,
The Great Captain of
The New Faith

Paul did nothing by halves. He convinced himself that the followers of Jesus were in the wrong, and then he proceeded to bend all his energies to the task of destroying them. The Sanhedrin was doubtless very glad to enlist such an ardent and powerful champion. He pursued them with relentless vigor, from house to house, from village to village. Even to distant cities, armed with the authority of the law, he tracked his victims. He became the terror and the scourge of the Christian Church.

He heard that some of the hated people had taken refuge in Damascus, the capital of Syria. He secured the necessary authority and started in pursuit. It was a journey of 160 miles by a difficult road, part of it across the desert, but Paul pushed on in a blind fury. He raged, "he breathed out threatening and slaughter."

Suddenly at midday in the heat of the burning sun, Paul fell to the earth. Amid a brightness greater than the sun, there appeared the august figure of Jesus. He spoke in terms of rebuke and warning. When Paul's escort recovered, they found that the leader was blind. No longer raging and threatening, he went quietly to his lodging.

For three days he sat in darkness, and then he knew that his whole life was changed. Henceforth, he was to be, heart and soul, as he sometimes expressed it, the "bond servant of Jesus Christ." This mission was announced to him by Ananias. His sight came back. He was a new man.

Persons of the Story

Paul.
Peter.
James.
Ananias, a disciple.
Sergius Paulus, a Roman governor.
Elymas, a sorcerer.
Barnabas,
Mark,
Timothy, } *Companions of Paul.*
Silas,
Gallio, a Roman governor.
Priscilla and Aquila.
Demetrius, a silversmith.
Claudius Lysias, a Roman officer.
Felix, a Roman governor.
Drusilla, wife of Felix.
Festus, a Roman governor.
King Agrippa.
Queen Bernice, sister of Drusilla.
Publius, a Roman officer.
Paul's nephew.

The people of many towns and cities, Roman officials, soldiers, sailors, Christian disciples, mob at Jerusalem.

Places of the Story

Many cities and towns in all parts of the Roman Empire.

Paul

The Great Captain of the New Faith

The Conversion of Paul

AND Saul, yet breathing out threatenings and slaughter against the disciples of the Lord, went unto the high priest, and desired of him letters to Damascus to the synagogues, that if he found any of this way, whether they were men or women, he might bring them bound unto Jerusalem.

And as he journeyed, he came near Damascus: and suddenly there shined round about him a light from heaven: and he fell to the earth, and heard a voice saying unto him, "Saul, Saul, why persecutest thou me?"

And he said, "Who art thou, Lord?"

And the Lord said, "I am Jesus whom thou persecutest: it is hard for thee to kick against the pricks."

And he, trembling and astonished, said, "Lord, what wilt thou have me to do?"

And the Lord said unto him, "Arise, and go into the city, and it shall be told thee what thou must do."

And the men which journeyed with him stood speechless, hearing a voice, but seeing no man. And Saul arose from the earth; and when his eyes were opened, he saw no man: but they led him by the hand, and brought him into Damascus. And he was three days without sight, and neither did eat nor drink.

And there was a certain disciple at Damascus, named Ananias; and to him said the Lord in a vision, "Ananias."

And he said, "Behold, I am here, Lord."

And the Lord said unto him, "Arise, and go into the street which is called Straight, and enquire in the house of Judas for one called Saul, of Tarsus: for, behold, he prayeth, and hath seen in a vision a man named Ananias coming in, and putting his hand on him, that he might receive his sight."

Then Ananias answered, "Lord, I have heard by many of this man, how much evil he hath done to thy saints at Jerusalem: and here he hath authority from the chief priests to bind all that call on thy name."

But the Lord said unto him, "Go thy way: for he is a chosen vessel unto me, to bear my name before the Gentiles, and kings, and the children of Israel: for I will show him how great things he must suffer for my name's sake."

And Ananias went his way, and entered into the house; and putting his hands on him said, "Brother Saul, the Lord, even Jesus, that appeared unto thee in the way as thou camest, hath sent me, that thou mightest receive thy sight, and be filled with the Holy Ghost."

And immediately there fell from his eyes as it had been scales: and he received sight forthwith, and arose, and was baptized. And when he had received meat, he was strengthened. Then was Saul certain days with the disciples which were at Damascus. And straightway he preached Christ in the synagogues, that he is the Son of God. But all that heard him were amazed, and said: "Is not this he that destroyed them which called on this name in Jerusalem, and came hither for that intent, that he might bring them bound unto the chief priests?" But Saul increased the more in strength, and confounded the Jews which dwelt at Damascus, proving that this is very Christ.

SAUL ON THE ROAD TO DAMASCUS
A molding by D. Mastroianni

TRADITIONAL WINDOW

Traditional Window in the wall of Damascus, where Paul was let down in a basket and thus escaped.
Read pages 23-27

And after that many days were fulfilled, the Jews took counsel to kill him: but their laying wait was known of Saul. And they watched the gates day and night to kill him. Then the disciples took him by night, and let him down by the wall in a basket.

And when Saul was come to Jerusalem, he assayed to join himself to the disciples: but they were all afraid of him, and believed not that he was a disciple. But Barnabas took him, and brought him to the apostles, and declared unto them how he had seen the Lord in the way, and that he had spoken to him, and how he had preached boldly at Damascus in the name of Jesus. And he was with them coming in and going out at Jerusalem. And he spake boldly in the name of the Lord Jesus, and disputed against the Grecians: but they went about to slay him. Which when the brethren knew, they brought him down to Cæsarea, and sent him forth to Tarsus.   — Acts 9:1–30

THE RIVER ABANA, DAMASCUS

DAMASCUS—"A WELL CALLED DEEP"

Paul

The Great Captain of the New Faith

Years of Inactivity

AFTER his conversion, Paul needed time to adjust his life to the new conditions. He was a student and a thinker. All his life he had been accustomed to Judaism. He could not change the habits of thought of a lifetime in a moment. He must think it out and think it through. For this purpose he went away for a period to be alone with nature and with God.

He went to the desert of Arabia. This was perhaps the Sinaitic peninsula where Moses in the far-off days had talked with God. Here Paul remained for three years. We learn of this sojourn in the wilderness only through an incidental allusion in the Epistle to the Galatians, but it was one of the most important periods of Paul's life. So Jesus himself and John the Baptist and many others have gone away from the haunts of men for a time to think out the great problems of life.

When Paul, the "new man in Christ," emerged from the desert, he proceeded at once to carry out his great commission to preach the gospel of salvation, through faith in Jesus, "not only for the Jew but for the Gentiles," to the widest boundaries of the earth.

Immediately after his conversion, Paul began to preach first in Damascus and later in Jerusalem. Opposition quickly arose. From Damascus he barely escaped with his life, his new friends letting him down from the wall in a basket. It was not likely that the Jews would

29

permit a man of such prominence, whom they considered a renegade and a traitor, to work unmolested.

The hostility of the Jews at Jerusalem was bitter and implacable and it followed him all his life. It would be natural also that even the Christians of Jerusalem would have some suspicion of this man who had been so active in persecution.

Most of this time of inactivity seems to have been spent at Tarsus, his native city. We may be sure that they were not wasted years. This environment, which was so stimulating to his boyhood, must have been much more so to his early manhood. Here was a wonderful opportunity to make that contact with the outer world which was so necessary to the great apostle to the Gentiles. "I am all things to all men," he wrote. It would be possible to acquire under these conditions that universal friendliness, that broad tolerance, that wide knowledge of the world, which so distinguished Paul in later days. He would, without any doubt, make friends with the university students, with the caravan masters, with the ship captains at the docks. It was perhaps in these years that he acquired that knowledge of Greek literature which enabled him at Athens to quote from the Greek poets. He came to know the geography of the Mediterranean, and something of the sea routes to those capitals which he was later to visit.

At last, the call came and he was ready. It was a task which suited admirably his bold and adventurous spirit. The great campaign for the conquest of the world for Christ began.

HOUSES ON THE WALL—DAMASCUS

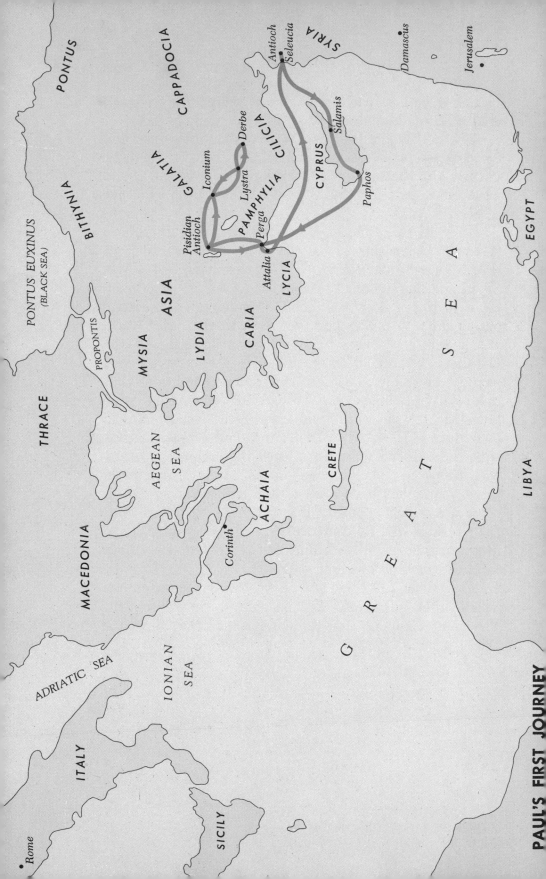

PAUL'S FIRST JOURNEY

Paul

The Great Captain of the New Faith

The First Missionary Journey

Paul had gone quietly to Antioch to work with the brethren, when the great call to wider service came. The church in obedience to the call sent out Barnabas and Paul, who was still called Saul, his Jewish name. Barnabas was one of the leaders of the church. A native of Cyprus, a wealthy man, he had given much money to the cause: his own life he had consecrated to service. He was a man of fine presence; his eloquence had won him the name of the "Son of Exhortation"; he was especially friendly to Paul. The two friends took with them a nephew of Barnabas, John Mark; and the three sailed for Cyprus, the former home of Barnabas. They must have sailed from Seleucia. The great masonry of that port is still in such good condition that it would require a comparatively small sum to make the port available for modern commerce. It is only a few hours' sail with a good wind to Salamis.

From Salamis they went to Paphos, the seat of the ancient worship of Aphrodite. Here they met a soothsayer, a worker of magic. In a vigorous controversy with Paul, he was conquered, and Sergius Paulus, the Roman proconsul, was converted. Here too the narrator of the Acts speaks abruptly of "Saul who is also called Paul." As the name of Abram was changed to Abraham, as Simon became Peter, at the great decisive moment of their lives, so Saul, the Jewish Rabbi, became now Paul, the great missionary captain of the new faith.

Henceforth, Paul is in command. Barnabas occupies a subordinate position. It is the decisive hour of Christian history. The great campaign has begun.

NOW there were in the church that was at Antioch certain prophets and teachers; as Barnabas, and Simeon that was called Niger, and Lucius of Cyrene, and Manaen, which had been brought up with Herod the tetrarch, and Saul. As they ministered to the Lord, and fasted, the Holy Ghost said, "Separate me Barnabas and Saul for the work whereunto I have called them." And when they had fasted and prayed, and laid their hands on them, they sent them away.

So they, being sent forth by the Holy Ghost, departed unto Seleucia; and from thence they sailed to Cyprus. And when they were at Salamis, they preached the word of God in the synagogues of the Jews: and they had also John to their minister. And when they had gone through the isle unto Paphos, they found a certain sorcerer, a false prophet, a Jew, whose name was Bar-jesus: which was with the deputy of the country, Sergius Paulus, a prudent man; who called for Barnabas and Saul, and desired to hear the word of God. But Elymas, the sorcerer (for so is his name by interpretation) withstood them, seeking to turn away the deputy from the faith. Then Saul (who also is called Paul) filled with the Holy Ghost, set his eyes on him, and said, "O full of all subtilty and all mischief, thou child of the devil, thou enemy of all righteousness, wilt thou not cease to pervert the right ways of the Lord? And now, behold, the hand of the Lord is upon thee, and thou shalt be blind, not seeing the sun for a season." And immediately there fell on him a mist and a darkness; and he went about seeking some to lead him by the hand. Then the deputy, when he saw what was done, believed, being astonished at the doctrine of the Lord. — Acts 13:1–12.

Campaigning in the Mountains of Asia Minor

The visit to Cyprus was not of long duration. The great spaces of the continent called to the responsive spirit of Paul. They took ship and crossed the bay of Attalia, scene of historic naval combats, to the town of Perga, once a populous city, at the present time deserted. Here an important event took place. The young companion of the two older men deserted, if that is not too harsh a word. An old writer says, "Either he did not like the work or he wanted to see his mother." Fearful of the dangers of the mountains, and they were very real, or homesick, the young man went back to Jerusalem.

Paul and Barnabas, sad, no doubt, because of the defection, went on up the wild mountain gorges of the rushing rivers, where they would encounter "perils of rivers and perils of robbers," up to the great table-land, 6,000 feet above the sea. Here were populous towns and villages.

Four stopping places are noted: Antioch in Pisidia, Iconium, Lystra, Derbe. Exciting days they were for these soldiers of the cross. At Antioch, Paul made a great address in the synagogue, which is reported nearly, if not quite, in full. Everywhere intense interest was stirred up. At Lystra the country people were filled with awe, and felt that the high gods had come to earth. They called Barnabas, Jupiter; and Paul, Mercury; and attempted to offer sacrifices to them. Then the fickle temper of the people changed. Already the hostility of the Jews was aroused. In a riot which ensued the missionaries were stoned. Paul barely escaped with his life. "Once was I stoned," he says in the great catalogue of his adventures. The mob dragged him out of the gates and left him dead, as they supposed. A sorrowful little company of disciples gathered around. One young man who looked upon the white face of the fallen hero was to be in future his beloved friend and lieutenant. Timothy was his name, and he lived with his mother, Eunice, and grandmother, Lois, devout Hebrews, up here in this remote town of the mountains. It was worth the suffering which Paul endured to find such a son.

Paul was not dead. He soon revived and dauntlessly continued his work. The next day he was able to go on to Derbe. This was the limit of their advance. They went back, boldly entering the hostile towns, Lystra, Iconium, Antioch, down through the river

ELYMAS STRICKEN BLIND
A painting by John Bianchi

gorges to Perga, where they stayed a while, and then sailed from Attalia for Antioch. The first great missionary campaign was completed.

Now when Paul and his company loosed from Paphos, they came to Perga in Pamphylia: and John departing from them returned to Jerusalem.

PAUL'S ADDRESS IN THE SYNAGOGUE AT ANTIOCH IN PISIDIA

But when they departed from Perga, they came to Antioch in Pisidia, and went into the synagogue on the sabbath day, and sat down. And after the reading of the law and the prophets, the rulers of the synagogue sent unto them, saying, "Ye men and brethren, if ye have any word of exhortation for the people, say on."

GALATIAN REGION OF PAUL'S FIRST JOURNEY

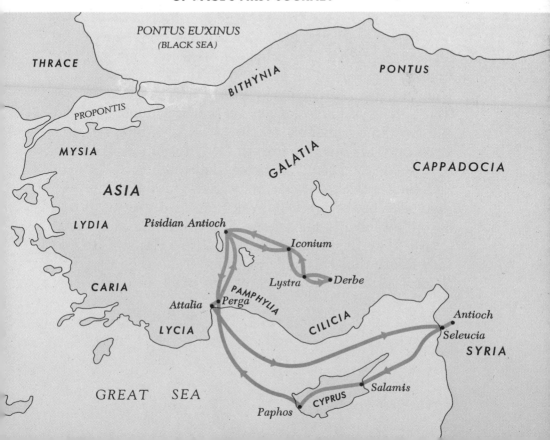

Then Paul stood up, and beckoning with his hand said, "Men of Israel, and ye that fear God, give audience. The God of this people of Israel chose our fathers, and exalted the people when they dwelt as strangers in the land of Egypt, and with an high arm brought he them out of it. And about the time of forty years suffered he their manners in the wilderness. And when he had destroyed seven nations in the land of Canaan, he divided their land to them by lot. And after that he gave unto them judges about the space of four hundred and fifty years, until Samuel, the prophet. And afterward they desired a king: and God gave unto them Saul, the son of Kish, a man of the tribe of Benjamin, by the space of forty years. And when he had removed him, he raised up unto them David to be their king; to whom also he gave testimony, and said, 'I have found David, the son of Jesse, a man after mine own heart, which shall fulfil all my will.'

"Of this man's seed hath God according to his promise raised unto Israel a Saviour, Jesus: when John had first preached before his coming the baptism of repentance to all the people of Israel. And as John fulfilled his course, he said, 'Who think ye that I am? I am not he. But, behold, there cometh one after me, whose shoes of his feet I am not worthy to loose.' Men and brethren, children of the stock of Abraham, and whosoever among you feareth God, to you is the word of this salvation sent. For they that dwell at Jerusalem, and their rulers, because they knew him not, nor yet the voices of the prophets which are read every sabbath day, they have fulfilled them in condemning him. And though they found no cause of death in him, yet desired they Pilate that he should be slain. And when they had fulfilled all that was written of him, they took him down

from the tree, and laid him in a sepulcher. But God
raised him from the dead: and he was seen many days
of them which came up with him from Galilee to Jerusalem, who are his witnesses unto the people. And we
declare unto you glad tidings, how that the promise
which was made unto the fathers, God hath fulfilled
the same unto us their children, in that he hath raised
up Jesus again; as it is also written in the second psalm,
'Thou art my Son, this day have I begotten thee.'
And as concerning that he raised him up from the dead,
now no more to return to corruption, he said on this
wise, 'I will give you the sure mercies of David.' Wherefore he saith also in another psalm, 'Thou shalt not
suffer thine Holy One to see corruption.' For David,
after he had served his own generation by the will of
God, fell on sleep, and was laid unto his fathers, and
saw corruption: but he, whom God raised again, saw no
corruption.

"Be it known unto you therefore, men and brethren,
that through this man is preached unto you the forgiveness of sins: and by him all that believe are justified
from all things, from which ye could not be justified
by the law of Moses. Beware therefore, lest that come
upon you, which is spoken of in the prophets:

'Behold, ye despisers, and wonder, and perish:
    For I work a work in your days,
A work which ye shall in no wise believe,
    Though a man declare it unto you.'"

And when the Jews were gone out of the synagogue, the Gentiles besought that these words might
be preached to them the next sabbath. Now when the
congregation was broken up, many of the Jews and

religious proselytes followed Paul and Barnabas: who, speaking to them, persuaded them to continue in the grace of God.

And the next sabbath day came almost the whole city together to hear the word of God. But when the Jews saw the multitudes, they were filled with envy, and spake against those things which were spoken by Paul, contradicting and blaspheming. Then Paul and Barnabas waxed bold, and said, "It was necessary that the word of God should first have been spoken to you: but seeing ye put it from you, and judge yourselves unworthy of everlasting life, lo, we turn to the Gentiles. For so hath the Lord commanded us, saying, 'I have set thee to be a light of the Gentiles, that thou shouldest be for salvation unto the ends of the earth.'"

And when the Gentiles heard this, they were glad, and glorified the word of the Lord: and as many as were ordained to eternal life believed. And the word of the Lord was published throughout all the region. But the Jews stirred up the devout and honourable women, and the chief men of the city, and raised persecution against Paul and Barnabas, and expelled them out of their coasts. But they shook off the dust of their feet against them, and came unto Iconium. And the disciples were filled with joy, and with the Holy Ghost.

— Acts 13:13-52.

AT ICONIUM

And it came to pass in Iconium, that they went both together into the synagogue of the Jews, and so spake, that a great multitude both of the Jews and also of the Greeks believed. But the unbelieving Jews stirred up the Gentiles, and made their minds evil affected against the brethren. Long time therefore abode they speaking boldly in the Lord, which gave testimony unto the word

PAUL AND BARNABAS WORSHIPED AT LYSTRA
A painting by Raphael Sanzio

of his grace, and granted signs and wonders to be done by their hands. But the multitude of the city was divided: and part held with the Jews, and part with the apostles.

AT LYSTRA AND DERBE

And when there was an assault made both of the Gentiles and also of the Jews with their rulers, to use them despitefully, and to stone them, they were ware of it, and fled unto Lystra and Derbe, cities of Lycaonia, and unto the region that lieth round about: and there they preached the gospel.

And there sat a certain man at Lystra, impotent in his feet, being a cripple from birth, who never had walked: the same heard Paul speak: who stedfastly beholding him, and perceiving that he had faith to be healed, said with a loud voice, "Stand upright on thy feet." And he leaped and walked.

And when the people saw what Paul had done, they lifted up their voices, saying in the speech of Lycaonia, "The gods are come down to us in the likeness of men." And they called Barnabas, "Jupiter"; and Paul, "Mercurius," because he was the chief speaker. Then the priest of Jupiter, which was before their city, brought oxen and garlands unto the gates, and would have done sacrifice with the people.

Which when the apostles, Barnabas and Paul, heard of, they rent their clothes, and ran in among the people, crying out, and saying, "Sirs, why do ye these things? We also are men of like passions with you, and preach unto you that ye should turn from these vanities unto the living God, which made heaven, and earth, and the sea, and all things that are therein: who in times past suffered all nations to walk in their own ways. Nevertheless he left not himself without witness, in that he did good, and gave us rain from heaven, and fruitful seasons, filling our hearts with food and gladness." And with these sayings scarce restrained they the people, that they had not done sacrifice unto them.

And there came thither certain Jews from Antioch and Iconium, who persuaded the people, and, having stoned Paul, drew him out of the city, supposing he had been dead. Howbeit, as the disciples stood round about him, he rose up, and came into the city: and the next day he departed with Barnabas to Derbe. And when they had preached the gospel to that city, and had taught many, they returned again to Lystra, and to Iconium, and Antioch, confirming the souls of the disciples, and exhorting them to continue in the faith, and that we must through much tribulation enter into the kingdom of God. And when they had ordained them elders in every church, and had prayed with fasting, they commended them to the Lord, on whom they believed. And after they had passed throughout Pisidia, they came to Pamphylia. And when they had preached the word in Perga, they went down into Attalia: and thence sailed to Antioch, from whence they had been recommended to the grace of God for the work which they fulfilled. And when they were come, and had gathered the church together, they rehearsed all that God had done with them, and how he had opened the door of faith unto the Gentiles. And there they abode long time with the disciples.　　　— Acts 14:1-28.

Paul

The Great Captain of the New Faith

A Division in the Council of the Church

It was great news which the two travelers, Paul and Barnabas, brought back to Antioch, "that God had opened a door of faith to the Gentiles." But there were among the Christians a good many who were strongly of the opinion that if the Gentiles were received into the church at all, they must submit to all the forms and ceremonies of the Jews. It was evident that this was a matter of very serious moment, a question of liberty or of bondage for future generations. It was too big a matter to decide at Antioch; so it was taken up to Jerusalem for discussion and action. Paul made a private report to the apostles, James, Peter, and John, and other leaders of the church, going over the matter with them carefully. Then there was called the first great council of the church.

Peter made a great speech favoring Paul. James, "the brother of Jesus," a man of austere and blameless life, possessing very great influence in the councils of the church, confirmed the opinion of Peter. Paul and Barnabas told the thrilling story of the campaign in Cyprus and Pamphilia. The case was won. It was agreed that Gentile converts need not submit to all the forms and ceremonies of Judaism. The Christian church as distinct from Judaism might almost be said to have been born at this hour. This was the "liberty" of which Paul wrote to the Galatians, wherewith Christ has made us free, "a liberty in which there is neither Jew nor Greek, circumcision or uncircumcision, barbarian or Scythian, bond or free." One condition was imposed which Paul was always scrupulous to carry out, that all gentile Christians should carefully refrain from participating in the worship of idols and from all practices associated with such worship.

AND certain men which came down from Judæa taught the brethren, and said, "Except ye be circumcised after the manner of Moses, ye cannot be saved." When therefore Paul and Barnabas had no small dissension and disputation with them, they determined that Paul and Barnabas, and certain other of them, should go up to Jerusalem unto the apostles and elders about this question. And being brought on their way by the church, they passed through Phœnicia and Samaria, declaring the conversion of the Gentiles: and they caused great joy unto all the brethren. And when they were come to Jerusalem, they were received of the church, and of the apostles and elders, and they declared all things that God had done with them. But there rose up certain of the sect of the Pharisees which believed, saying that it was needful to circumcise them, and to command them to keep the law of Moses. And the apostles and elders came together for to consider of this matter. And when there had been much disputing, Peter rose up, and said unto them, "Men and brethren, ye know how that a good while ago God made choice among us, that the Gentiles by my mouth should hear the word of the gospel, and believe. And God, which knoweth the hearts, bare them witness, giving them the Holy Ghost, even as he did unto us; and put no difference between us and them, purifying their hearts by faith. Now therefore why tempt ye God, to put a yoke upon the neck of the disciples, which neither our fathers nor we were able to bear? But we believe that through the grace of the Lord Jesus Christ we shall be saved, even as they."

Then all the multitude kept silence, and gave audience to Barnabas and Paul, declaring what miracles and wonders God had wrought among the Gentiles by them.

And after they had held their peace, James answered, saying, "Men and brethren, hearken unto me: Simeon hath declared how God at the first did visit the Gentiles, to take out of them a people for his name. And to this agree the words of the prophets; as it is written,

' "After this I will return,
    And will build again the tabernacle of David, which
        is fallen down;
    And I will build again the ruins thereof,
    And I will set it up: that the residue of men might
        seek after the LORD,
    And all the Gentiles, upon whom my name is called."
    Saith the LORD, who doeth all these things.
    Known unto God are all his works from the begin-
        ning of the world.'

"Wherefore my sentence is, that we trouble not them, which from among the Gentiles are turned to God: but that we write unto them, that they abstain from pollutions of idols, and from fornication, and from things strangled, and from blood. For Moses of old time hath in every city them that preach him, being read in the synagogues every sabbath day."

Then pleased it the apostles and elders, with the whole church, to send chosen men of their own company to Antioch with Paul and Barnabas; namely, Judas surnamed Barsabas, and Silas, chief men among the brethren: and they wrote letters by them after this manner: "The apostles and elders and brethren send greeting unto the brethren which are of the Gentiles in Antioch and Syria and Cilicia. Forasmuch as we have heard, that certain which went out from us have troubled you with words, subverting your souls, saying, 'Ye must be circumcised, and keep the law': to whom we gave no such commandment: it seemed good unto us, being assembled with one accord, to send chosen men unto you with our beloved Barnabas and Paul, men that have hazarded their lives for the name of our Lord Jesus Christ. We have sent therefore Judas and Silas, who shall also tell you the same things by mouth. For it seemed good to the Holy Ghost, and to us, to lay upon you no greater burden than these necessary things: that ye abstain from meats offered to idols, and from blood, and from things strangled, and from fornication: from which if ye keep yourselves, ye shall do well. Fare ye well."

So when they were dismissed, they came to Antioch: and when they had gathered the multitude together, they delivered the epistle: which when they had read, they rejoiced for the consolation. And Judas and Silas, being prophets also themselves, exhorted the brethren with many words, and confirmed them. And after they had tarried there a space, they were let go in peace from the brethren unto the apostles. Notwithstanding it pleased Silas to abide there still. Paul also and Barnabas continued in Antioch, teaching and preaching the word of the Lord, with many others also.

— Acts 15:1–35.

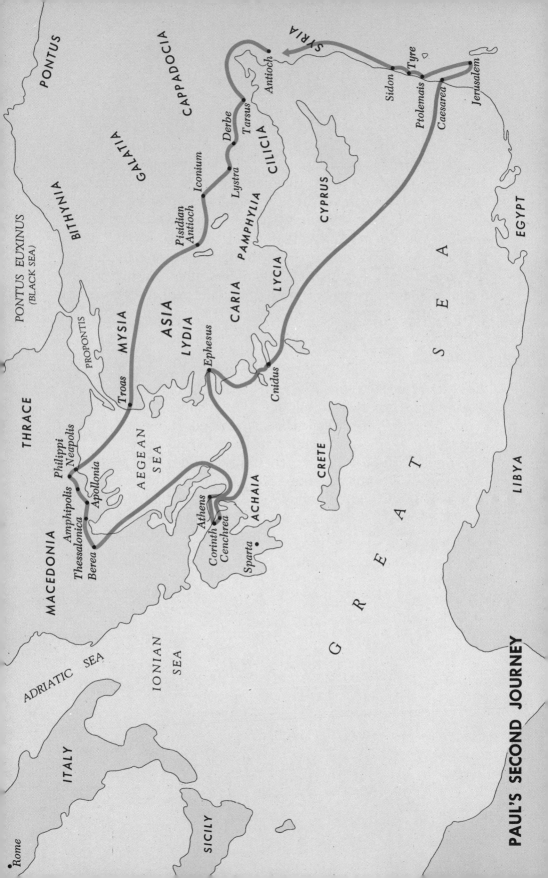

PAUL'S SECOND JOURNEY

Paul

The Great Captain of the New Faith

The Second Missionary Journey

NEW COMRADES FOR THE WAY

The great question of the relation of the Gentile converts settled, Paul was eager to be on the march. His consecrated spirit was always looking forward to new fields of conquest. The departure for the second great missionary journey was marred by differences between Paul and his friends. Paul was very zealous for the faith. We learn from Galatians that Peter had come down to Antioch at this time and had taken a less outspoken stand upon the question of the Gentiles and the Jewish law. Paul tells us that he "withstood him to his face."

Then, just as Paul and Barnabas were ready to start, Barnabas suggested that John Mark, the young man who had left them on the previous journey, be taken this time. Paul, however, positively refused. He would have no laggards or deserters in his company. This caused the separation of the two leaders. Barnabas took John Mark and went to Cyprus: Paul chose a new comrade, Silas, and departed for the old field in the north. This difference caused no permanent estrangement; Paul probably never saw Barnabas again, but he mentions him in the most friendly way in his epistles, and John Mark was one of those who ministered to the aged apostle's last days in Rome. Paul and Silas first visited the cities of the first journey.

AND some days after, Paul said unto Barnabas, "Let us go again and visit our brethren in every city where we have preached the word of the Lord, and see how they do." And Barnabas determined to take with them John, whose surname was Mark. But Paul thought not good to

49

take him with them, who departed from them from Pamphylia, and went not with them to the work. And the contention was so sharp between them, that they departed asunder one from the other: and so Barnabas took Mark, and sailed unto Cyprus; and Paul chose Silas, and departed, being recommended by the brethren unto the grace of God. And he went through Syria and Cilicia, confirming the churches.

TIMOTHY JOINS PAUL

Then came he to Derbe and Lystra: and, behold, a certain disciple was there, named Timotheus, the son of a certain woman, which was a Jewess, and believed; but his father was a Greek: which was well reported of by the brethren that were at Lystra and Iconium. Him would Paul have to go forth with him; and took and circumcised him because of the Jews which were in those quarters: for they knew all that his father was a Greek. And as they went through the cities, they delivered them the decrees for to keep, that were ordained of the apostles and elders which were at Jerusalem. And so were the churches established in the faith, and increased in number daily. Now when they had gone throughout Phrygia and the region of Galatia, and were forbidden of the Holy Ghost to preach the word in Asia, after they were come to Mysia, they assayed to go into Bithynia: but the Spirit suffered them not. And they passing by Mysia came down to Troas. — Acts 15:36–16:8.

VICTORIES IN THE CITIES OF MACEDONIA

The narrative gives no details of the early part of the second journey, which was destined to become one of the most famous and momentous in the world's history.

Onward they went, following the Roman roads from city to city, encouraging the churches, delivering the messages of the council at

CYPRUS, VISITED BY BARNABAS AND MARK

GALLIPOLI PENINSULA

Jerusalem   They went through the region which has been for so many centuries under Turkish rule. Perhaps they visited Angora, which the Turks made, in 1921, the capital of the "Turkish National Government."   In Galatia, Paul was ill (some think that this illness was at the time of the first visit), and the people were most kind to him. "If possible you would have plucked out your eyes and given them to me," he says. But it was shown to Paul that he was not to linger in Asia. A greater destiny called to him. He went on by a route which we do not exactly know until he came to Troas on the shores of the Hellespont.

Up to this time Paul had moved wholly within the sphere of Asiatic influence. Asia had been conquered by Rome, but it was simply a conquest, not an interpenetration of Roman civilization. The East was still the East. Paul stood on the shore of the Ægean; he was only four miles from the Plain of Troy, the scene of "deep-browed" Homer's immortal tale. Near by, Xerxes had watched his three million troops cross the narrow straits on a bridge of boats, marching to the conquest of Europe. He could see the high promontory of Gallipoli, where nineteen centuries later the East and the West would meet again in bloody conflict. Farther still across the misty sea, he could just discern the mountains of Europe, the Kingdom of Greece. The sea before him had been furrowed by the keels of the ships of Ulysses and the Argonauts. For an unknown Jew to preach the Gospel in Europe in the great cities of Greece and Rome would be a spiritual adventure equal to those struggles

MACEDONIAN REGION OF
PAUL'S MISSIONARY ACTIVITIES

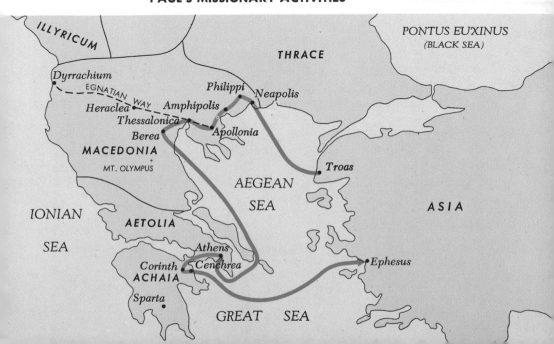

and combats of the heroes of old romance. Paul lay down to sleep
with the soft murmur of the Ægean in his ears and as he slept, he
saw a vision. A man from that far-off shore was standing by him, a
man of Macedonia, who stretched out his hand beseechingly and
cried, "Come over into Macedonia and help us."

Paul did not hesitate in making his momentous decision. He
had the soldier's instinct for obedience. The very next day he took
passage in a ship crossing the Ægean from Troas to Samothrace.
At this point the personal pronoun used in the narrative changes
abruptly. In the seventh verse of the sixteenth chapter, the narrative says that they went through the region of Phrygia and Galatia.
In the tenth verse it says, "Straightway WE sought to go forth into
Macedonia." The use of "we" continues only through the visit to
Philippi, where the style changes again to indirect narrative in
Chapter 17. In the twentieth chapter, the fifth verse, it changes
again to the direct "we," and continues to the fifteenth. There are
similar passages in the twenty-first chapter, verses 1–18, and again
from the first verse of the twenty-seventh chapter to the sixteenth
verse of the twenty-eighth chapter. The generally accepted view is that
Luke, the author of the Gospel of Luke, wrote The Acts, that when he
uses the pronoun, "we," he was actually a member of the party and
describes the events as he saw them with his own eyes. In these
passages the narrative is very vivid and dramatic.

We may suppose that Luke joined Paul and his companions,
Silas and Timothy, at Troas. Their first important city was Philippi.
Little remains of the old city now, but it is famous in history, for it
was on the plains near here that the great battle was fought in
which Brutus and Cassius, the leaders of the revolt against the
empire, were slain and the republican cause was lost.

Luke tells in his vivid and picturesque language how they went
out of the city gate to a quiet spot by the River Gaggitas where a few
devout Jewish women met for prayer. One of these women was not
Jewish by birth, but a convert. Her name was Lydia; she was a
business woman, engaged in the selling of the purple cloth in such
high favor in those days. She has the honor of being the first convert to Christianity on European soil, though she herself was not a
Greek, but a native of Thyatira in Asia. She and her whole household were baptized, and by her urgent invitation Paul and his
friends became her guests.

Another significant event took place here, the healing of a demon-possessed slave-girl. But this brought down the anger of her masters. The disciples were dragged into the market-place, beaten with rods, and thrown into prison. Then came that great scene at night: the earthquake, the dramatic conversion of the jailer, the appeal of Paul and Silas to their Roman citizenship, the humble apology of the magistrates, the joyful return to the house of Lydia.

Here Luke apparently leaves the company; perhaps Philippi was his home or perhaps he stayed behind to help establish the new church, and gives the narrative from other sources. Paul and Silas went on their conquering way through the cities of Macedonia. It has been said that the "Acts of the Apostles have made Macedonia a kind of Holy Land." It was a very important part of the Roman Empire in Paul's day. From it had come the great conqueror, Alexander, and when his empire broke up, Rome had realized its importance. While it had been conquered, many of its cities were made free. Across it ran the great Roman road, the "Via Egnatia," on which Paul walked between Thessalonica and Philippi.

At Thessalonica, Paul established one of his great churches. This city was the metropolis of Roman Macedonia. It had a distinguished Christian history for many centuries. The modern city is of great importance. During World War I it was occupied by the Allied armies. It was swept by fire and its people suffered very severely.

Paul was received with especial kindness at Berea. Here there was a friendly Jewish synagogue, which was most unusual, and here the people "searched the Scriptures daily" to confirm the teaching of Jesus.

Everywhere, however, the work of the apostle was hindered by the hostility of the Jews. From one city to another his foes followed him, inciting riots and opposition, making his work difficult, endangering his life. It was decided that the work in Macedonia must be left to other hands. Paul must not sacrifice his own life. He must go on to new fields.

And a vision appeared to Paul in the night. There stood a man of Macedonia, and prayed him, saying, "Come over into Macedonia, and help us." And after he had seen the vision, immediately we endeavoured to go into Macedonia, assuredly gathering that the Lord had called us for to preach the gospel unto them. Therefore loosing from Troas, we came with a straight course to Samothracia, and the next day to Neapolis; and from thence to Philippi, which is the chief city of that part of Macedonia, and a colony: and we were in that city abiding certain days. And on the sabbath we went out of the city by a river side, where prayer was wont to be made; and we sat down, and spake unto the women which resorted thither.

THE BAPTISM OF LYDIA

And a certain woman named Lydia, a seller of purple, of the city of Thyatira, which worshiped God, heard us: whose heart the Lord opened, that she attended unto the things which were spoken of Paul. And when she was baptized, and her household, she besought us, saying, "If ye have judged me to be faithful to the Lord, come into my house, and abide there." And she constrained us.

THE MISSIONARIES SUFFER FOR THEIR GOODNESS TO A SLAVE-GIRL

And it came to pass, as we went to prayer, a certain damsel possessed with a spirit of divination met us, which brought her masters much gain by soothsaying: the same followed Paul and us, and cried, saying, "These men are the servants of the most high God, which show unto us the way of salvation." And this did she many days.

But Paul, being grieved, turned and said to the spirit, "I command thee in the name of Jesus Christ to come out of her." And he came out the same hour.

And when her masters saw that the hope of their gains was gone, they caught Paul and Silas, and drew

THE ACROPOLIS, WITH THE TEMPLE OF ZEUS
IN THE FOREGROUND

them into the market-place unto the rulers, and brought them to the magistrates, saying, "These men, being Jews, do exceedingly trouble our city, and teach customs, which are not lawful for us to receive, neither to observe, being Romans."

And the multitude rose up together against them: and the magistrates rent off their clothes, and commanded to beat them. And when they had laid many stripes upon them, they cast them into prison, charging the jailer to keep them safely: who, having received such a charge, thrust them into the inner prison, and made their feet fast in the stocks.

THE DELIVERANCE FROM PRISON: THE EARTHQUAKE, AND A CONVERSION

And at midnight Paul and Silas prayed, and sang praises unto God: and the prisoners heard them. And suddenly there was a great earthquake, so that the foundations of the prison were shaken: and immediately all the doors were opened, and every one's bands were loosed. And the keeper of the prison awaking out of his sleep, and seeing the prison doors open, he drew out his sword, and would have killed himself, supposing that the prisoners had been fled. But Paul cried with a loud voice, saying, "Do thyself no harm: for we are all here."

Then he called for a light, and sprang in, and came trembling, and fell down before Paul and Silas, and brought them out, and said, "Sirs, what must I do to be saved?"

And they said, "Believe on the Lord Jesus Christ, and thou shalt be saved, and thy house."

And they spake unto him the word of the Lord, and to all that were in his house. And he took them

The Parthenon, Athens

THE PARTHENON, even in its ruined state, is one of the most beautiful buildings in the world. It was begun in the year 447 B.C. and finished 438 B.C. It is hard to realize that this glorious work of genius required only ten years to achieve.

A study of the Parthenon ought to destroy some of our self-complacency with respect to modern achievement. To quarry the great blocks of marble out of the heart of Pentelicon, transport them to the city and lift them to the summit of the Acropolis, without our modern mechanical contrivances, that was a great accomplishment in itself. But those old craftsmen did more than pile the stones up in an enormous heap after the manner of the Egyptian pyramids. They took those blocks of marble, gleaming white, in which the sunshine seemed to be imprisoned, coming out in exquisite tones of gold after weathering; they took this marble and fashioned it into this supremely beautiful building. By using a combination of straight lines they produced a building so marvelous in its proportions, in such perfect harmony that you lose the sense of rigidity, of severity, altogether.

Somehow, the builders added beauty to strength; to severity grace and charm. A close examination reveals the fact that while the lines seem straight, they are not really so; they are curves, imperceptible except to very close scrutiny. The floor of the temple is built on a curve, said to come within one inch of being the same as the curve of the earth's surface. The lines of the columns taper to the top and are slightly convex in the middle.

the same hour of the night, and washed their stripes; and was baptized, he and all his, straightway. And when he had brought them into his house, he set meat before them, and rejoiced, believing in God with all his house. And when it was day, the magistrates sent the serjeants, saying, "Let those men go."

And the keeper of the prison told this saying to Paul, "The magistrates have sent to let you go: now therefore depart, and go in peace."

But Paul said unto them, "They have beaten us openly uncondemned, being Romans, and have cast us into prison; and now do they thrust us out privily? Nay verily; but let them come themselves and fetch us out."

And the serjeants told these words unto the magistrates: and they feared, when they heard that they were Romans. And they came and besought them, and brought them out, and desired them to depart out of the city. And they went out of the prison, and entered into the house of Lydia: and when they had seen the brethren, they comforted them, and departed.

—Acts 16:9–40.

AT THESSALONICA

Now when they had passed through Amphipolis and Apollonia, they came to Thessalonica, where was a synagogue of the Jews: and Paul, as his manner was, went in unto them, and three sabbath days reasoned with them out of the Scriptures, opening and alleging that Christ must needs have suffered, and risen again from the dead; and that this Jesus, whom I preach unto you, is Christ. And some of them believed, and consorted with Paul and Silas; and of the devout Greeks a great multitude, and of the chief women not a few.

But the Jews which believed not, moved with envy, took unto them certain lewd fellows of the baser sort, and gathered a company, and set all the city on an uproar, and assaulted the house of Jason, and sought to bring them out to the people. And when they found them not, they drew Jason and certain brethren unto the rulers of the city, crying, "These that have turned the world upside down are come hither also; whom Jason hath received: and these all do contrary to the decrees of Cæsar, saying that there is another king, one Jesus." And they troubled the people and the rulers of the city, when they heard these things. And when they had taken security of Jason, and of the others, they let them go.

THE "MORE NOBLE" JEWS OF BEREA

And the brethren immediately sent away Paul and Silas by night unto Berea: who coming thither went into the synagogue of the Jews. These were more noble than those in Thessalonica, in that they received the word with all readiness of mind, and searched the Scriptures daily, whether those things were so. Therefore many of them believed; also of honourable women which were Greeks, and of men, not a few. But when the Jews of Thessalonica had knowledge that the word of God was preached of Paul at Berea, they came thither also, and stirred up the people. And then immediately the brethren sent away Paul to go as it were to the sea: but Silas and Timotheus abode there still. And they that conducted Paul brought him unto Athens: and receiving a commandment unto Silas and Timotheus for to come to him with all speed, they departed.

—Acts 17:1–15.

PAUL AT ATHENS

Paul went alone to Athens. Some ship, trading down the coast, took him from a Macedonian port, through those waters crowded with historic memories. He saw Olympus, home of the classic gods, lift its snowy summit to the sky. Thermopylae was not far away. He passed in sight of Marathon, where the Athenians won immortal glory; doubled Cape Sunium, its white temple of Neptune gleaming against the blue of the Ægean; and soon the Acropolis, with the Parthenon, the most beautiful temple in the world, like an exquisite cameo, backed by the wall of Mt. Pentelicon, was in sight.

Paul probably entered Athens by the Dipylon Gate, which was the principal entrance in classic times. It is called the "double gate," because, unlike the other gates, it had two entrances separated by a central pier. To-day one can trace out the foundations of this gateway, which was flanked by towers and heavily fortified.   Near by is one of the most interesting cemeteries of the ancient world. Some of the sculptured monuments, dating back to 400 B.C., are exquisitely beautiful. One would like to know where Paul found a lodging. Probably some humble family of his own race took him in, little knowing how distinguished was this insignificant traveler.

When Paul walked about the city the next day, he saw it, not indeed at the height of its fame, but still marvelously beautiful. We see to-day only the fragments of that beauty, mutilated by war and the selfishness of men. We can hardly imagine what the Acropolis was like when Paul saw it, the adornments of the age of Pericles undimmed in their glory: the Parthenon, the lovely temple of Athena Apteros, the Erectheum, the gigantic statue of Athena, made of the bronze spoils of the battle of Marathon, votive statues,

"A hundred shapes of lucid stone."

The place which interests us most in Athens, in connection with the life of Paul, is the Areopagus, "Mars' Hill," as it is translated in the English version of the New Testament. This is now a perfectly bare rock rising at some little distance from the Acropolis on its seaward side.   The ground rises between the Acropolis and the Areopagus, and you reach the rock by the road which passes over this saddle. Fifteen steps cut in the rock lead to the top of the hill. On the other sides the rock falls away steeply. At the base of the hill you find the very interesting ruins of the ancient city of Athens. Across the ravine, on the other side from the Acropolis, rises another elevation, the hill of the Pnyx, with its Bema, where public assemblies were held. At the base of the hill, amid a débris of great broken

rocks, there is the cleft in which was the shrine of the Erinyes, "the Furies," the scene of Æschylus's great tragedy, "The Eumenides."

On the summit of the rock sat the ancient court of the Areopagus, consisting of the most eminent and venerable citizens, hearing cases of supreme importance, having the power of life and death. There are traces of the foundations of altars, but we can see little of the seats of this ancient court. Here Paul was at the very heart and center of the classic world. The utmost that culture could do was within sight. The noblest works of the age of Pericles shone before him. Only a few minutes away was the theater of Dionysius, in which the greatest plays of Greek literature were produced, tragedies which rise at times very nearly to the lofty heights of Christian ethics, and yet not quite. The old culture had reached its climax and it was even then on the verge of collapse. Paul, the ambassador of the Galilean, and the old gods were face to face.

There are some authorities who hold that Paul's address to the Athenians was not delivered on the bare summit of this rock, but in the King's Stoa, where the members of the Court of the Areopagites

TEMPLE OF JUPITER AND THE ACROPOLIS, ATHENS

THE AREOPAGUS, ATHENS

THE ACROPOLIS FROM THE AREOPAGUS
This view shows the Acropolis just as Paul must have seen it. Mount Lycabettus rises in the background.

did their official business. The main reason for such a supposition would be the restricted area of the hill-top and the question whether it was or could be used for any purpose except the sitting of the court. This does not seem to be an insuperable objection and it is preferable to think of the address as being spoken on this classic hill, with the sea in sight, the Acropolis in all its glory just across the valley, and beyond, the great circle of mountains.

This address is one of the classics of literature. It is like Lincoln's Gettysburg address in its breadth and its restraint, its perfect phrasing. In addition it is a model of good taste and courtesy. Contrast it with some of the vituperative polemics of later Christian literature and it shines like a jewel. Paul was a perfect gentleman. He spoke with absolute fearlessness, with an utter disregard of consequences to himself, but he never, in speech or action, needlessly outraged the sensibilities of his hearers.

It is one of the great scenes of history, Paul standing there and speaking by invitation, and a courteous invitation, to the representative men of Athens. Perhaps the sitting of the court was just over, and those gray and venerable judges lingered to hear what this interesting Jew might say of his strange new cult.

PAUL PREACHING AT ATHENS
A painting by Raphael Sanzio

General View of Philippi

Photographed by Three Lions, Inc.

PHILIPPI WAS NAMED after Philip of Macedon, the father of Alexander the Great, who was its conqueror. In the year 42 B.C., the armies of Octavius and Anthony defeated the armies of the Roman Republic on the plains below Philippi, and in commemoration of the victory the city was given unique citizenship privileges.

It was in almost every way a Roman colony. It was like a bit of Rome in a foreign land. Groups of army veterans settled there after completing their service. The dress, the speech, and the law was Roman in every respect. In some of these strategic outpost cities the inhabitants often had more pride of Roman citizenship than the people living in Rome itself.

This particular pride explains the background of the event which took place in Philippi. After Paul and Silas had healed a young girl possessed with a spirit of divination, the men who had used the girl for profit roused the crowd and had the disciples beaten and thrown into prison. Afterward when they were asked to leave the city, Paul said: "They have beaten us openly uncondemned, being Romans" (Acts 16:37). When the crowd learned that Paul was a Roman citizen they were afraid because they had violated Roman law in dealing with them.

The site of Philippi is now deserted. Archaeologists have uncovered many parts of the city, and especially interesting is the market place. About a mile from this ancient center is the river, where the first converts in Europe were baptized.

Road to Philippi

Photographed by Three Lions, Inc.

PHILIPPI WAS the first city on the continent of Europe to receive the gospel. It was one of the few cities in which Paul preached that did not have a synagogue. While they did not have a synagogue, they met for prayer in a quiet, open enclosure on the banks of the River Gangites.

Lydia, a businesswoman of the city, was the first convert to Christianity in Europe (Acts 16:14). She was a purple merchant. The purple dye had to be gathered from certain shell-fish and was very costly. A single pound of wool dyed with it would cost as much as fifty dollars. She was a wealthy woman. Upon her conversion she invited the believers to meet in her household (Acts 16:15).

The second convert who is singled out was a demented slave girl. By telling fortunes and giving advice about the future, she became a profitable enterprise for the men who exploited her condition. Paul healed her of the spirit and as a result was put into jail. This slave girl stood in marked contrast to the wealthy Lydia (Acts 16:16-24).

The third convert in Philippi mentioned specifically was the jailer who had attempted to keep Paul and Silas in his jail. He was probably a sturdy Roman of middle-class, civil service descent (Acts 16:25-40).

Through the years, the church at Philippi remained one of Paul's favorites. The members continued to support his work, and he had great affection for them.

Egnatian Way

Photographed by Three Lions, Inc.

ON HIS JOURNEYS, Paul enjoyed the finest roads which had ever been known. They were built primarily for maintaining the Roman Empire, but they were used by civilians such as Paul. Among their many advantages, they usually were built in the straightest line between two important objectives. This was quite important to Paul, since he traveled mostly on foot during his four missionary journeys.

The Roman roads were carefully laid on a prepared foundation. They were well drained and curbed. There was a road superintendent to keep them in repair. Wells were dug at convenient intervals. Often there would be an elevated foot path for the pedestrians.

The western travels of Paul were along the famous Egnatian Way which ran from the Adriatic on the west to the Aegean on the east. It ran through Thessalonica, Berea, Apollonia, Amphipolis, Neapolis, and Philippi. Neapolis was the seaport for Philippi. This is where Paul landed, after responding to the "Macedonian call" about which he dreamed (Acts 16:9-10).

Looking at the picture of the remains of the once great road, it is difficult to imagine the glory which was Rome. At one time, this road must have been filled with Roman soldiers marching to and from the outposts of the Empire. Thinking about the little band of disciples on their way up this very road to Philippi, we wonder if those who saw them and heard them, received with understanding the everlasting significance of the Kingdom they represented.

View of Thessalonica

Photographed by Three Lions, Inc.

THE MAIN STREET of Thessalonica was a part of the great Egnatian Way. The coming of Christianity to this place was of great importance for once it was established it could spread both east and west along the key artery.

The city was refounded in 315 B.C. and named after Thessalonica, the wife of Cassander and the sister of Alexander the Great. Under the Romans it became the leading city of Macedonia. Land and sea connections made it a commercial and strategic center, which it is to this present day. Today it is called Salonika.

During Paul's second missionary journey he founded the church in Thessalonica. He had traveled from Philippi to Amphipolis to Apollonia to Thessalonica—a distance of one hundred miles. Paul began his work in the synagogue, which was his usual custom (Acts 17:1-3). Evidently, large numbers of Jews had been drawn to the city. Also, there were a number of Greek converts to Judaism. A number of the Jews believed the Gospel and became Christians. This turned the other Jews against Paul, and they brought pressure on the city officials to put him and his party out of town (Act 17:4-9).

Paul revisited Thessalonica once (1 Cor. 16: 5). The church later suffered persecution (1 Thess. 2:14). In later years the city became a stronghold for the church and was called "the orthodox city."

Today, on the Via Egnatian, there is a street and a chapel named for Paul who first preached the gospel there.

The Areopagus in Athens

Photographed by Three Lions, Inc.

PAUL PROBABLY CAME to Athens by boat (Acts 17:14) and may have docked at the Ionian port of Pirocus. Athens, capital of modern Greece, in Paul's day was virtually a free city-state under the protection of Rome. The dominant feature in the town was a hill, five hundred feet high, called the Acropolis. In earlier days it had been a fortified settlement. Later it had been a Greek religious center, and many temples had been built there. In Paul's time the city of Athens circled the base of the Acropolis.

To the north of the Acropolis was the Market Place, or Agora. There were many different shops and shrines. The citizens of Athens loved to meet there, not only to transact business and visit, but to discuss new ideas (Acts 17:21). It was because of Paul's preaching in the market place that the philosophers invited him to address them at the Areopagus.

The Areopagus was both a place and a group. It was a ridge of rock, sometimes called Mars Hill, which was located southeast of the Acropolis. It was the place where the Areopagus, the city court of Athens, met to pass on matters of welfare, morals, and religion. Paul was called before the group to give his ideas official hearing. His sermon before them is recorded in Acts 17:22-31. His reference to the fact that God does not dwell in temples made with hands (Acts 17:24), was especially appropriate at this place which was surrounded by pagan temples.

Today the market place in which Paul preached has been completely excavated. Many of the ruins of the temples still stand.

The Tribunal in Corinth

Photographed by Three Lions, Inc.

PAUL VISITED Corinth on his second missionary journey, spent eighteen months there and established a significant work (Acts 18:1-18).

Corinth was the capital of the Roman province of Achaia, which was refounded by Julius Caesar in 46 B.C. Its very position made Corinth a key city of Greece. Greece is almost cut in two by the sea. Corinth lay on a tiny isthmus of land between the Saronic Gulf to the west and the Corinthian Gulf to the east. To avoid the long and dangerous trip around the southern tip of Greece, smaller ships were hauled across the narrow isthmus on a track. It was also common to unload cargo from large ships and carry it across the isthmus to be loaded into another ship. North and south traffic in Greece also had to pass through Corinth, which caused it to be called "The Bridge of Greece." Corinth was also the market place of Greece.

Paul arrived for his first visit about 50 A.D. He was immediately challenged by the spirit of the city. It was a cosmopolitan port-city with Greeks, Romans, Jews, and adventurers from all of the Mediterranean area, which gathered in the market place in the day-time to conduct business and at night to drink and revel. In the excavation of the market place alone, thirty-three taverns were uncovered. Corinth was so widely known in the Greek world as a wicked city that the word "Corinthian" was associated with lustful debauchery. Dominating Corinth was the hill of the Acropolis with its temple of Aphrodite.

Here, in Corinth, Paul lived and preached and had great victories.

The Bema (Courthouse) in Corinth

Photographed by Three Lions, Inc.

THE EXCITING ACCOUNT of the ministry of Paul in Corinth is given in Acts 18. Modern day archaeology sheds light on, and reawakens interest in, several of Paul's experiences.

During Paul's stay in the city he joined with Priscilla and Aquilla in the trade of tent-making. They probably lived in the craftsmen's zone—west of the brilliant city.

Paul preached first in the synagogue, but was soon rebuffed. However, Crispus, the chief ruler of the synagogue, became a believer. After the Jews rejected him, Paul spent the balance of his eighteen months in Corinth preaching to the Gentiles. In excavating Corinth, the lintel of a Jewish synagogue has been found. Some have speculated as to whether this might have been part of the structure where Titus Justus and Crispus worshipped (Acts 18:4, 7-8).

The Bema, where Paul stood trial (Acts 18: 12-17), has been excavated and identified. It was the central building in a row of buildings which separated the lower Agora (market place) from the upper. It was a richly ornamented tribunal which was the seat of the Roman government. The excavations also revealed a church of the medieval period had been built upon the site of the Bema. It was probably erected here to commemorate where Paul gave his defense of himself and the Christian way.

Modern Corinth is a small town adjacent to the ruins of its predecessor. Here Greek Christians live a simple life in contrast to the so-called glamorous life of the first century.

Ruins at Ephesus

Photographed by Three Lions, Inc.

PAUL HAD A MOST significant ministry at Ephesus, the events of which are recorded in Acts 19. Later in his ministry, one of the books of the New Testament was addressed to the church in this community. One of the letters in the book of Revelation (2:1-7) is addressed to Ephesus.

Ephesus was the marketing center for Asia Minor. Then, as now, trade often followed the rivers. Ephesus stood at the mouth of the Cayster River with a commanding position for trade with the inland communities. She has been referred to as "The Treasure House of Asia."

Ephesus was the town to which the Roman governor came at certain specified times to try all the important cases of justice. On these occasions the town would experience all of the pomp and pageantry which accompanied Roman power.

The greatest glory of Ephesus was the Temple of Artemis. Artemis and Diana are the same deity. Diana is the Latin word and Artemis the Greek. The Temple was four hundred and twenty-five feet long, two hundred and twenty feet wide, and sixty feet high—one of the Seven Wonders of the World. Each of its one hundred and twenty-seven pillars of Parian marble was the gift of a king.

So effective was Paul's preaching in Ephesus that the local silversmiths, whose principal trade was in images of Diana, began to lose business (Acts 19:24-26). On the western slope of the city stand the ruins of the Great Theater where the mass meeting was held to protest Paul's preaching. The building was four hundred and ninety-five feet in diameter and seated twenty-five thousand people.

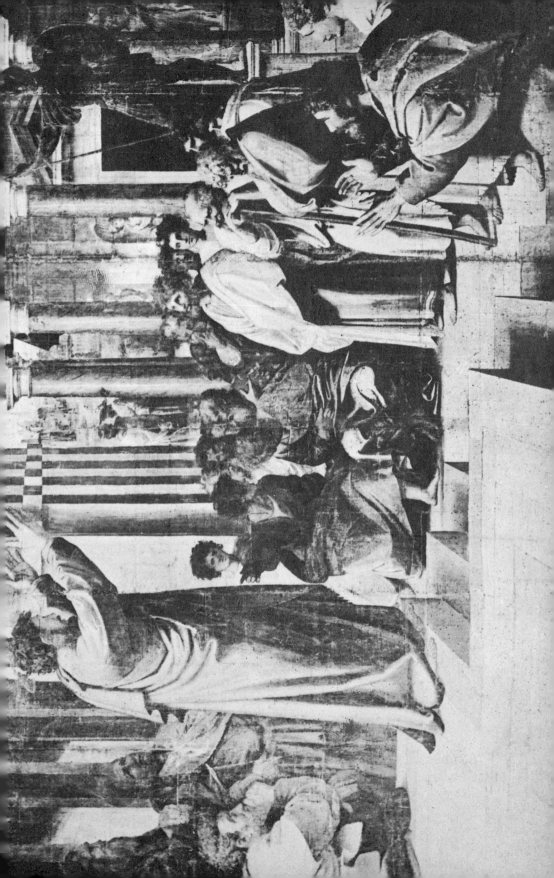

ERECHTEUM TEMPLE, ATHENS

Now while Paul waited for them at Athens, his spirit was stirred in him, when he saw the city wholly given to idolatry. Therefore disputed he in the synagogue with the Jews, and with the devout persons, and in the market daily with them that met with him. Then certain philosophers of the Epicureans, and of the Stoics, encountered him. And some said, "What will this babbler say?" other some, "He seemeth to be a setter forth of strange gods": because he preached unto them Jesus, and the resurrection. And they took him, and brought him unto Areopagus, saying, "May we know what this new doctrine, whereof thou speakest, is? For thou bringest certain strange things to our ears:

PAUL PREACHING ON MARS HILL
A molding by D. Mastroianni

we would know therefore what these things mean."
(For all the Athenians and strangers which were there
spent their time in nothing else, but either to tell, or
to hear some new thing.)   —Acts 17:16–21.

THE ADDRESS TO THE ATHENIANS

The address contains two hundred and nine words in the terse
Greek, something more in the translation. It requires two minutes to
speak it; yet it is a model of rhetoric and eloquence. It is almost exactly the same length as the Gettysburg oration. To condense into a
period of two minutes such sublime thoughts and to express them in
perfect language is to exhibit the art of the orator in its highest and
noblest manifestation.

The account in the Book of Acts says that Paul spoke in the
Jewish synagogue and reasoned in the market-place every day.
Of the Jewish synagogue there is of course nothing left.

Paul made very little impression upon Athens. There were a
few individuals converted, not enough to form into a church. That
was the price which the city and the world, too, paid for its indiffer-
ence. Would that we had letters to an Athenian church comparable
to those to the churches at Corinth and Rome, to place in our
treasure house of literature for the guidance and blessing of all
generations!

Paul's visit at Athens was, as he very well knew, a failure so
far as any large results were concerned. But his visit to the city of
philosophy and culture was not a failure; it was of the very highest
value to the world. We may think that under the divine leading,
Paul made the visit not for Athens, but for humanity. Never yet
has the world attained to the height of that proclamation, "All
nations of men . . . should seek the Lord, if haply they might feel
after him, and find him, though he be not far from any one of us."
The Revised Version translates instead of "too superstitious," "very
religious."

Then Paul stood in the midst of Mars' hill, and said,
"Ye men of Athens, I perceive that in all things ye
are too superstitious. For as I passed by, and beheld

your devotions, I found an altar with this inscription, 'TO THE UNKNOWN GOD.' Whom therefore ye ignorantly worship, him declare I unto you.

"God that made the world and all things therein, seeing that he is Lord of heaven and earth, dwelleth not in temples made with hands; neither is worshiped with men's hands, as though he needed any thing, seeing he giveth to all life, and breath, and all things; and hath made of one blood all nations of men for to dwell on all the face of the earth, and hath determined the times before appointed, and the bounds of their habitation; that they should seek the Lord, if haply they might feel after him, and find him, though he be not far from every one of us: for in him we live, and move, and have our being; as certain also of your own poets have said, 'For we are also his offspring.' Forasmuch then as we are the offspring of God, we ought not to think that the Godhead is like unto gold, or silver, or stone, graven by art and man's device. And the times of this ignorance God winked at, but now commandeth all men every-

PROPYLÆA—ATHENS

The Propylæa was the splendid entrance to the Acropolis. Through this gateway came the Pan-Athenaic processions at the annual festival which is pictured in the famous sculptures of the Parthenon. This magnificent entrance was hardly less beautiful than the Parthenon itself. The central doorway frames a magnificent view across land and sea to the island of Salamis.

PAUL IN GREECE
A painting by John Bianchi

where to repent: because he hath appointed a day, in
the which he will judge the world in righteousness by
that man whom he hath ordained; whereof he hath given
assurance unto all men, in that he hath raised him from
the dead."

And when they heard of the resurrection of the dead,
some mocked: and others said, "We will hear thee again
of this matter."

So Paul departed from among them. Howbeit
certain men clave unto him, and believed: among the
which was Dionysius, the Areopagite, and a woman
named Damaris, and others with them. — Acts 17:22–34.

PAUL AT CORINTH

It is only forty-five miles from Athens to Corinth. Paul without
his companions, Timothy and Silas, who had not yet come from
Macedonia to meet him, went down to the crowded port of Piraeus
and took one of the many ships sailing for the Isthmus of Corinth.

From the earliest years Corinth had been a great and proud
city, "The City of the Two Seas." Corinth was the seat of a great
business in ship building, metal work, pottery, and dyestuffs. Her
colonies, notably Syracuse in Sicily, became as great as the mother-
city. From every sea commerce came to her doors. She was the
center of the great trade route by sea between the East and West.
Cargoes were trans-shipped at the isthmus and smaller vessels were
dragged across. Already a ship canal was projected and actually
begun by Nero a few years later, only to be abandoned for nineteen centuries. In 1881 the canal, four miles long, was actually
completed.

In Paul's time the city, entirely destroyed at the time of the
downfall of the Greek republic, and desolate for many years, had
been rebuilt under Julius Cæsar, and had rapidly attained to something of its old importance and splendor. It was one of the largest,
wealthiest, and wickedest cities in the empire. Its streets were
thronged with merchants from the East and the West, sailors,
stevedores, Roman soldiers. Its splendid temples were filled with
worshipers.

COLUMNS OF THE TEMPLE OF
APOLLO AT CORINTH

This temple of Apollo was in the
heart of the old city of Corinth in the
days of Paul's visit. The Acro-Corinth
which rises above the plain is nearly
2,000 feet high. On the summit is a
very interesting medieval fortress with
battlements and arched gateways.
All is now silent and in ruins. The
fragments of broken gates hang upon
their hinges as they were blown to
pieces in the last siege centuries ago.

Today the site is again desolate, but it is easy to imagine what the city must have been like when it spread over the wide plain to the foot of the wonderful rock, the Acro-Corinth, which rises two thousand feet above the sea.

When Paul arrived and left the ship at the eastern port of the isthmus, Cenchrea, and came up to the great city of the plain, he would be unnoticed in the throngs. He would first seek out a suitable lodging. This he found in the house of the Jews, Aquila and Priscilla, who were among those banished from Rome by the edict of the Emperor Claudius. Like Paul they were tent-makers; very likely they lived in some obscure street called, perhaps, "The Street of the Tent-Makers." Here Paul lived for a year and a half certainly, perhaps for two years, and worked at his trade.

Although Paul was thus quietly occupied daily at his work, he could not be hidden. The synagogue began to be crowded every Sabbath to hear the wonderful tent-maker from Tarsus. The usual hostility of the Jews followed, and Paul was driven from the synagogue. This was a momentous crisis in Paul's history. No longer were the Jews his first concern. "Henceforth," he said, "I go to the Gentiles." He even changed his lodgings, it seems, and went to the house of Titus Justus, near the synagogue. But conversions among the Jews did not cease;

even Crispus, the ruler of the synagogue, became a follower of "The Way" This enraged the Jews so much that they dragged Paul before Gallio, proconsul of Achaia, who had recently come to the province. Gallio was indifferent. He refused to have anything to do with the religious quarrels of the Jews, and swept them all from his judgment seat. The tide of popular sentiment turned in favor of Paul; even Sosthenes, the new ruler of the synagogue, had a rough experience at the hands of the mob before he escaped from the judgment seat of the Roman governor who looked down in cold disdain, for "Gallio cared for none of these things." So Paul labored on, for God had "much people" in the great sinful city of Corinth; but his restless, mighty spirit was yearning for larger service across the seas. One day he said farewell and taking Priscilla and Aquila with him, sailed across the Ægean Sea to another great pagan city, Ephesus.

There would be no difficulty in finding a ship, for there was a constant flow of commerce between the two great capitals of the western and the eastern Greek provinces. The two cities have been compared with New York and Liverpool. The journey among the

THRESHING BARLEY ON CYPRUS

islands of the Ægean would require from three or four to fifteen days. Paul made a stop of a few days only at Ephesus, while the vessel was in port. The great metropolis of Asia appealed to him, however, and he promised to come back. "I will return to you if God wills," he cried to the friends who came down to the dock to say farewell. Then he continued to Jerusalem by way of Cæsarea. His stay at the capital was very short. "He saluted the church," and started afresh on his great mission, the breadth and significance of which he saw with ever clearer vision.

After these things Paul departed from Athens, and came to Corinth; and found a certain Jew named Aquila, born in Pontus, lately come from Italy, with his wife Priscilla; (because that Claudius had commanded

GATEWAY TO THE ANCIENT FORTRESS ACRO-CORINTH

This old fortress on the summit of the wonderful hill which rises 2000 feet above the plains at Corinth, was built by the Venetians in the 15th century.

all Jews to depart from Rome:) and came unto them. And because he was of the same craft, he abode with them, and wrought: for by their occupation they were tent-makers. And he reasoned in the synagogue every Sabbath, and persuaded the Jews and the Greeks. And when Silas and Timotheus were come from Macedonia, Paul was pressed in the spirit, and testified to the Jews that Jesus was Christ. And when they opposed themselves, and blasphemed, he shook his raiment, and said unto them, "Your blood be upon your own heads; I am clean: from henceforth I will go unto the Gentiles."

And he departed thence, and entered into a certain man's house, named Justus, one that worshiped God, whose house joined hard to the synagogue. And Crispus, the chief ruler of the synagogue, believed on the Lord with all his house; and many of the Corinthians hearing believed, and were baptized. Then spake the Lord to Paul in the night by a vision, "Be not afraid, but speak, and hold not thy peace: for I am with thee, and no man shall set on thee to hurt thee: for I have much people in this city." And he continued there a year and six months, teaching the word of God among them.

BEFORE GALLIO, WHO "CARED FOR NONE OF THOSE THINGS"

And when Gallio was the deputy of Achaia, the Jews made insurrection with one accord against Paul, and brought him to the judgment seat, saying, "This fellow persuadeth men to worship God contrary to the law."

And when Paul was now about to open his mouth, Gallio said unto the Jews, "If it were a matter of wrong or wicked lewdness, O ye Jews, reason would that I should bear with you: but if it be a question of words and names, and of your law, look ye to it; for I will be no judge of such matters." And he drave them from the judgment seat. Then all the Greeks took Sosthenes, the chief ruler of the synagogue, and beat him before the judgment seat. And Gallio cared for none of those things.   — Acts 18:1-17.

BACK TO JERUSALEM AND ANTIOCH

And Paul after this tarried there yet a good while, and then took his leave of the brethren, and sailed thence into Syria, and with him Priscilla and Aquila; having shorn his head in Cenchrea: for he had a vow. And he came to Ephesus, and left them there: but he himself entered into the synagogue, and reasoned with the Jews. When they desired him to tarry longer time with them, he consented not; but bade them farewell, saying, "I must by all means keep this feast that cometh in Jerusalem: but I will return again unto you, if God will." And he sailed from Ephesus. And when he had landed at Cæsarea, and gone up, and saluted the church, he went down to Antioch.   — Acts 18:18–22.

THE CILICIAN GATES

Two little Americans walk along this famous pass in Turkey, Asia Minor. A long, long highway through the Taurus Mountains, between towering rocky sides.

In ancient days, two gates across this pass kept back the enemy, unless overwhelmingly strong. The pass here is called The Cilician Gates. It leads down through Syria and Palestine to Egypt. And through this pass have marched many a fierce army with bloody weapons.

But one great and brave warrior is said to have come through here armed only with "The Shield of Faith" and the "Helmet of Salvation," and carrying "The Sword of the Spirit"—St. Paul on his way to visit the Churches of Asia which he had founded.

Read Acts 15 and 16, pages 49-59.

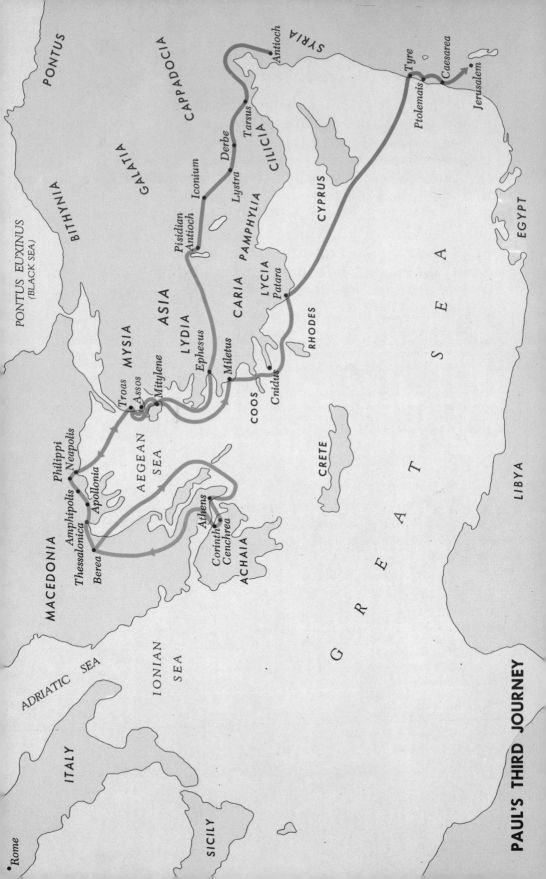

PAUL'S THIRD JOURNEY

Paul

The Great Captain of the New Faith

The Third Missionary Journey

REVISITING THE CHURCHES

Paul probably took only Timothy with him on this journey. The plan of the great apostle comprehended, first of all, a journey to the cities of Phrygia, Pamphilia, and Galatia, all of them once, and some of them twice, before visited. Very little is said of this journey, which led Paul in a wide circle back to Ephesus.

AND after he had spent some time there, he departed, and went over all the country of Galatia and Phrygia in order, strengthening all the disciples.

APOLLOS, "AN ELOQUENT MAN," SPEAKS AND TEACHES

And a certain Jew named Apollos, born at Alexandria, an eloquent man, and mighty in the Scriptures, came to Ephesus. This man was instructed in the way of the Lord; and being fervent in the spirit, he spake and taught diligently the things of the Lord, knowing only the baptism of John. And he began to speak boldly in the synagogue: whom when Aquila and Priscilla had heard, they took him unto them, and expounded unto him the way of God more perfectly. And when he was disposed to pass into Achaia, the brethren wrote, exhorting the disciples to receive him: who, when he was come, helped them much which had believed through grace: for he mightily convinced the Jews, and that publicly, showing by the Scriptures that Jesus was Christ.

— Acts 18:23-28.

81

In the City of the Great Diana

Here Paul found a great city, its roaring streets, its vast wealth, its temple of Diana, one of the wonders of the world. This magnificent temple is said to have surpassed the Parthenon even, in its dignity and splendor. It was 425 feet long and 220 feet wide. It had 127 columns, each of them the gift of a king. Within was the image of Diana, said to have fallen from heaven, not gem-encrusted, lovely in exquisitely carved marble, but an almost shapeless wooden figure. Throngs of pilgrims came to this temple and the silversmiths enjoyed a flourishing trade in little images of the figure of Diana and models of the temple. The images, eagerly bought by the pilgrims, were made of wood, silver or gold. This trade mysteriously fell off.

Paul was at work; and his converts, carrying the image of Christ in their hearts, no longer patronized the makers of the little silver images of Diana. A demonstration against the Christians was stirred up by Demetrius, a master workman. Like a flame, the spirit of hatred ran through the city. Workmen left the shops, the crowd streamed to the theater, where they shouted continually for two hours, "Great is Diana of the Ephesians." Paul was with difficulty restrained by the authorities and his friends from appearing before the mob. Fortunately there was present a cool-headed official, "The Town Clerk," who in a masterly speech calmed the wrath of the mob. After this, Paul did not remain much longer at Ephesus. He did not go before Christianity was firmly established in Asia, not only at Ephesus, but at the great apostolic churches mentioned in the Book of Revelation: Smyrna, Pergamos, Thyatira, Sardis, Philadelphia, and Laodicea.

And it came to pass, that, while Apollos was at Corinth, Paul having passed through the upper coasts came to Ephesus: and finding certain disciples, he said unto them, "Have ye received the Holy Ghost since ye believed?"

And they said unto him, "We have not so much as heard whether there be any Holy Ghost."

And he said unto them, "Unto what then were ye baptized?"

And they said, "Unto John's baptism."

Then said Paul, "John verily baptized with the baptism of repentance, saying unto the people, that they should believe on him which should come after him, that is, on Christ Jesus."

"SO MIGHTILY GREW THE WORD OF GOD"

When they heard this, they were baptized in the name of the Lord Jesus. And when Paul had laid his hands upon them, the Holy Ghost came on them; and they spake with tongues, and prophesied. And all the men were about twelve. And he went into the synagogue, and spake boldly for the space of three months, disputing and persuading the things concerning the kingdom of God.

But when divers were hardened, and believed not, but spake evil of that way before the multitude, he departed from them, and separated the disciples, disputing daily in the school of one Tyrannus. And this continued by the space of two years; so that all they which dwelt in Asia heard the word of the Lord Jesus, both Jews and Greeks. And God wrought special miracles by the hands of Paul: so that from his body were brought unto the sick handkerchiefs or aprons, and the diseases departed from them, and the evil spirits went out of them.

Then certain of the vagabond Jews, exorcists, took upon them to call over them which had evil spirits the name of the Lord Jesus, saying, "We adjure you by Jesus whom Paul preacheth." And there were seven sons of one Sceva, a Jew, and chief of the priests, which did so. And the evil spirit answered and said, "Jesus I know, and Paul I know; but who are ye?" And the man in whom the evil spirit was leaped on them, and

BURNING OF BOOKS AT EPHESUS
A painting by Eustache L. LeSueur

overcame them, and prevailed against them, so that they fled out of that house naked and wounded.

And this was known to all the Jews and Greeks also dwelling at Ephesus; and fear fell on them all, and the name of the Lord Jesus was magnified. And many that believed came, and confessed, and showed their deeds. Many of them also which used curious arts brought their books together, and burned them before all men: and they counted the price of them, and found it fifty thousand pieces of silver. So mightily grew the word of God and prevailed.

After these things were ended, Paul purposed in the spirit, when he had passed through Macedonia and Achaia, to go to Jerusalem, saying, "After I have been there, I must also see Rome." So he sent into Macedonia two of them that ministered unto him, Timotheus and Erastus; but he himself stayed in Asia for a season.

"GREAT IS DIANA OF THE EPHESIANS!"
PAUL'S MISSION HINDERS MONEY-MAKING

And the same time there arose no small stir about that way. For a certain man named Demetrius, a silversmith, which made silver shrines for Diana, brought no small gain unto the craftsmen; whom he called together with the workmen of like occupation, and said, "Sirs, ye know that by this craft we have our wealth. Moreover ye see and hear, that not alone at Ephesus, but almost throughout all Asia, this Paul hath persuaded and turned away much people, saying that they be no gods, which are made with hands: so that not only this our craft is in danger to be set at naught; but also that the temple of the great goddess Diana should be despised, and her magnificence should be destroyed, whom all Asia and the world worshipeth."

And when they heard these sayings, they were full of wrath, and cried out, saying, "Great is Diana of the Ephesians!"

And the whole city was filled with confusion: and having caught Gaius and Aristarchus, men of Macedonia, Paul's companions in travel, they rushed with one accord into the theater. And when Paul would have entered in unto the people, the disciples suffered him not. And certain of the chief of Asia, which were his friends, sent unto him, desiring him that he would not adventure himself into the theater. Some therefore cried one thing, and some another: for the assembly was confused; and the more part knew not wherefore they were come together. And they drew Alexander out of the multitude, the Jews putting him forward. And Alexander beckoned with the hand, and would have made his defence unto the people. But when they knew that he was a Jew, all with one voice about the space of two hours cried out, "Great is Diana of the Ephesians!"

And when the townclerk had appeased the people, he said, "Ye men of Ephesus, what man is there that knoweth not how that the city of the Ephesians is a worshiper of the great goddess Diana, and of the image which fell down from Jupiter? Seeing then that these things cannot be spoken against, ye ought to be quiet, and to do nothing rashly. For ye have brought hither these men, which are neither robbers of churches, nor yet blasphemers of your goddess. Wherefore if Demetrius, and the craftsmen which are with him, have a matter against any man, the law is open, and there are deputies: let them implead one another. But if ye enquire any thing concerning other matters, it shall be determined in a lawful assembly. For we are in danger to be called in question for this day's uproar, there being no cause whereby we may give an account of this concourse." And when he had thus spoken, he dismissed the assembly. — Acts 19.

ANXIETY AND TOIL

Now follows more than a year of constant activity. "Without were fightings, within were fears." Paul must have been nearly sixty years old. He was beset always by some malady, "the thorn in the flesh," of which he speaks. The care of the churches was becoming an almost overwhelming burden. Questions were constantly arising about many things: morals, church procedure, interpretation of the Gospel. Paul was constantly writing to the churches, visiting them when he could. This whole year was taken with such visits in Macedonia, and three months in Corinth. He was much upon the sea, "in labors oft," planning and directing his campaign with the skill of a great military commander and the zeal of an athlete.

He must go up to Jerusalem "for the feast," and to deliver to the authorities the collection which he had been gathering. Then "he must see Rome." He must "go to Spain." His mission was to the world. His restless heart could not be satisfied until he had visited the capital of the world, until he had reached the widest boundaries of civilization.

The journey to Jerusalem was full of danger. The churches which he visited felt that peril and tried to dissuade him from going. Paul had the same forebodings. "Ye shall see my face no more," he said. The journey up to Jerusalem from Philippi to Cæsarea is told with minute care in The Acts. Each day's sail is noted, even the state of the weather and the direction of the wind. In every city he received fresh warning of the coming trial, but still he went on, under sealed orders; if it was to die, that was no matter. "He would not be persuaded." His friends were "breaking his heart with their tears," but he was "ready not to be bound only but also to die at Jerusalem for the name of the Lord Jesus."

And after the uproar was ceased, Paul called unto him the disciples, and embraced them, and departed for to go into Macedonia. And when he had gone over those parts, and had given them much exhortation, he

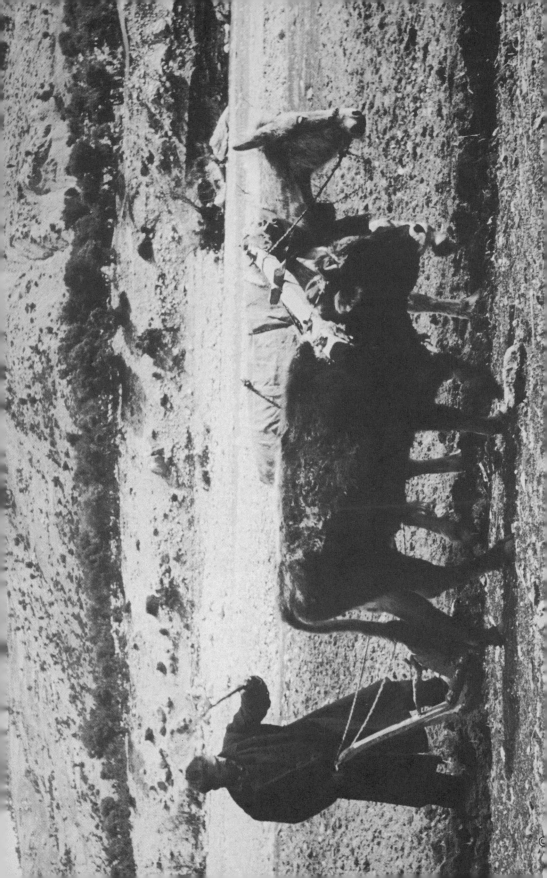

came into Greece, and there abode three months. And when the Jews laid wait for him, as he was about to sail into Syria, he purposed to return through Macedonia. And there accompanied him into Asia Sopater of Berea; and of the Thessalonians, Aristarchus and Secundus; and Gaius of Derbe, and Timotheus; and of Asia, Tychicus and Trophimus. These going before tarried for us at Troas.

THE YOUNG MAN WHO FELL ASLEEP DURING PAUL'S SERMON

And we sailed away from Philippi after the days of unleavened bread, and came unto them to Troas in five days; where we abode seven days. And upon the first day of the week, when the disciples came together to break bread, Paul preached unto them, ready to depart on the morrow; and continued his speech until midnight. And there were many lights in the upper chamber, where they were gathered together. And there sat in a window a certain young man named Eutychus, being fallen into a deep sleep: and as Paul was long preaching, he sunk down with sleep, and fell down from the third loft, and was taken up dead. And Paul went down, and fell on him, and embracing him said, "Trouble not yourselves; for his life is in him." When he therefore was come up again, and had broken bread, and eaten, and talked a long while, even till break of day, so he departed. And they brought the young man alive, and were not a little comforted.

PAUL HASTES TO BE AT JERUSALEM FOR THE PENTECOST

And we went before to ship, and sailed unto Assos, there intending to take in Paul: for so had he appointed, minding himself to go afoot. And when he met with us

PLOWING IN GREECE

at Assos, we took him in, and came to Mitylene. And we sailed thence, and came the next day over against Chios; and the next day we arrived at Samos, and tarried at Trogyllium; and the next day we came to Miletus. For Paul had determined to sail by Ephesus, because he would not spend the time in Asia: for he hasted, if it were possible for him, to be at Jerusalem the day of Pentecost.

PAUL'S SPEECH TO THE EPHESIANS: "I HAVE BEEN WITH YOU AT ALL SEASONS"

And from Miletus he sent to Ephesus, and called the elders of the church. And when they were come to him, he said unto them, "Ye know, from the first day that I came into Asia, after what manner I have been with you at all seasons, serving the Lord with all humility of mind, and with many tears, and temptations, which befell me by the lying in wait of the Jews: and how I kept back nothing that was profitable unto you, but have showed you, and have taught you publicly, and from house to house, testifying both to the Jews, and also to the Greeks, repentance toward God, and faith toward our Lord Jesus Christ. And now, behold, I go bound in the spirit unto Jerusalem, not knowing the things that shall befall me there: save that the Holy Ghost witnesseth in every city, saying that bonds and afflictions abide me. But none of these things move me, neither count I my life dear unto myself, so that I might finish my course with joy, and the ministry, which I have received of the Lord Jesus, to testify the gospel of the grace of God. And now, behold, I know that ye all, among whom I have gone preaching the kingdom of God, shall see my face no more. Wherefore I take you to record this day, that I am pure from the blood of all men. For I have not shunned to declare unto you all the counsel of God.

"Take heed therefore unto yourselves, and to all the flock, over the which the Holy Ghost hath made you overseers, to feed the church of God, which he hath purchased with his own blood. For I know this, that after my departing shall grievous wolves enter in among you, not sparing the flock. Also of your own selves shall men arise, speaking perverse things, to draw away disciples after them. Therefore watch, and remember, that by the space of three years I ceased not to warn every one night and day with tears. And now, brethren, I commend you to God, and to the word of his grace, which is able to build you up, and to give you an inheritance among all them which are sanctified. I have coveted no man's silver, or gold, or apparel. Yea, ye yourselves know that these hands have ministered unto my necessities, and to them that were with me. I have showed you all things, how that so labouring ye ought to support the weak, and to remember the words of the Lord Jesus, how he said, 'It is more blessed to give than to receive.'"

"THEY ALL WEPT SORE, SORROWING THAT THEY SHOULD SEE HIS FACE NO MORE"

And when he had thus spoken, he kneeled down, and prayed with them all. And they all wept sore, and fell on Paul's neck, and kissed him, sorrowing most of all for the words which he spake, that they should see his face no more. And they accompanied him unto the ship.

—Acts 20.

THE VOYAGE HOMEWARD

And it came to pass, that after we were gotten from them, and had launched, we came with a straight course

unto Coos, and the day following unto Rhodes, and
from thence unto Patara: and finding a ship sailing over
unto Phœnicia, we went aboard, and set forth. Now
when we had discovered Cyprus, we left it on the left
hand, and sailed into Syria, and landed at Tyre: for
there the ship was to unlade her burden. And finding
disciples, we tarried there seven days: who said to Paul
through the Spirit, that he should not go up to Jerusalem. And when we had accomplished those days,
we departed and went our way; and they all brought
us on our way, with wives and children, till we were
out of the city: and we kneeled down on the shore, and
prayed. And when we had taken our leave one of another, we took ship; and they returned home again.
And when we had finished our course from Tyre, we
came to Ptolemais, and saluted the brethren, and abode
with them one day.

PAUL IS WARNED BY AGABUS OF FUTURE IMPRISONMENT

And the next day we that were of Paul's company
departed, and came unto Cæsarea: and we entered into
the house of Philip, the evangelist, which was one of
the seven; and abode with him. And the same man
had four daughters, virgins, which did prophesy. And
as we tarried there many days, there came down from
Judæa a certain prophet, named Agabus. And when
he was come unto us, he took Paul's girdle, and bound
his own hands and feet, and said, "Thus saith the Holy
Ghost, 'So shall the Jews at Jerusalem bind the man
that owneth this girdle, and shall deliver him into the
hands of the Gentiles.'" And when we heard these
things, both we, and they of that place, besought him
not to go up to Jerusalem.

PAUL WITH EUTYCHUS
A painting by John Bianchi

"I AM READY NOT TO BE BOUND ONLY, BUT ALSO TO DIE FOR THE NAME OF THE LORD JESUS"

Then Paul answered, "What mean ye to weep and to break mine heart? For I am ready not to be bound only, but also to die at Jerusalem for the name of the Lord Jesus."

And when he would not be persuaded, we ceased, saying, "The will of the Lord be done."

And after those days we took up our carriages, and went up to Jerusalem. There went with us also certain of the disciples of Cæsarea, and brought with them one Mnason of Cyprus, an old disciple, with whom we should lodge. —Acts 21:1–16.

ISLAND OF RHODES

This island, 120 miles long by 36 miles in width, has a most interesting historic background. Its population is mostly Greek. During the Middle Ages it was the residence of the Knights of St. John.

City of Rhodes (built 482 B.C.) erected over the entrance to its harbor a brass statue to Apollo, 105 feet high. This statue was built in 290 B.C. and thrown down by an earthquake 224 B.C.

During World War II the British took over the Island of Rhodes and in March, 1947, with impressive ceremonies, returned the Island along with other Dodecanese Islands to Greek control. The climate here is delightful. The Apostle Paul visited Rhodes on his way to Jerusalem.

Read pages 91-93.

Paul Rescued From the Multitude

(Paul on the Steps of the Castle)

By Gustave Doré (1833-1883)
From Doré's Illustrations of the Bible

THIS picture deals with the first incident in the imprisonment of the Apostle Paul, which trouble eventually led him from Jerusalem, never to return, and brought him before Emperor Nero at Rome. We may read a summary of this incident on page 95 and the Biblical account in Acts on pages 98-105.

Doré, with characteristic exuberance, has depicted the whole mob of turbulent Jews milling in the square near their Temple and sweeping up the steps of the castle where they are stopped only by the long Roman spears. Paul has been addressing the people, but when he speaks of his mission to preach the Gospel to the Gentiles (page 102), the crowd once more breaks into a wild clamor and shouts, "Away with him." In order to save Paul's life, the Roman Captain has no choice but to put Paul under protective arrest. We see Paul, with a gesture of despairing disappointment, yielding himself to the guards.

Born in Strasbourg, Gustave Doré grew up amidst the wild scenery of the Vosges Mountains. His impressionable mind early became filled with the folklore of the storied Rhine which he expressed in vividly imaginative drawings. When fifteen, while visiting Paris with his father and brother, he was hired by a magazine publisher to do illustrations. Lauded as an "artistic prodigy," Gustave was soon so busy drawing that he had no time for school, not even to study art as his mother wished and as he himself planned to do.

When twenty-two, Doré was decorated with the Cross of the Legion of Honor for his illustrations of Dante's *Inferno*, probably his masterpiece. Orders poured in, and with tireless application, he set his brilliant imagination and remarkable talent to illustrating an unending succession of the world's classics—Rabelais, Balzac, Dante, Milton, Tennyson, LaFontaine, Cervantes, Hugo, Shakespeare, the Bible—producing in the thirty-five years of his meteorlike career some 100,000 drawings!

Another of his Biblical illustrations is on page 298.

Paul

The Great Captain of the New Faith

Paul in the Hands of His Foes

Paul was well received by the leaders of the church at Jerusalem on his arrival, but the storm which had been gathering quickly broke. It was suggested that he assist four Nazarites to complete their vow, and thus show that he was not hostile to Jewish customs and ceremonies. Paul readily complied, but the generous act had precisely the opposite effect. It was rumored that he had introduced Greeks to the inner court of the temple. A vast crowd of the most zealous Hebrews filled the temple enclosure. A cry went up that this was the man who taught against the People and the Law. Paul was seized, beaten, in danger of being torn to pieces by the mob. Close by the temple, the fortress Antonia raised its frowning ramparts and towers. Here always the sentries of the imperial guard kept vigilant watch over the turbulent people of Jerusalem. Claudius Lysias, commander of the fortress, was promptly notified of this disturbance. Rushing down the steps from the tower, he met Paul borne by the mob like a bit of drift-wood on the crest of a wave. "Away with him! Away with him!" shouted the rabble, just as thirty years previous the mob had shouted when Jesus was brought before Pilate. Making himself heard above the tumult, Paul asked the privilege of addressing the crowd. The surprised commander granted the request. Paul's eloquent defense was never finished. When he spoke at last of his mission to the Gentiles, the yells of the mob drowned his words. Impatient, Claudius Lysias ordered him taken to the barracks and scourged. Before the order could be carried out, the prisoner told the centurion in charge that he was a Roman citizen, free born, while the commander himself had purchased the precious privilege "with a great price "

The Storm Gathers

AND when we were come to Jerusalem, the brethren received us gladly. And the day following Paul went in with us unto James; and all the elders were present. And when he had saluted them, he declared particularly what things God had wrought among the Gentiles by his ministry. And when they heard it, they glorified the Lord, and said unto him, "Thou seest, brother, how many thousands of Jews there are which believe; and they are all zealous of the law: and they are informed of thee, that thou teachest all the Jews which are among the Gentiles to forsake Moses, saying that they ought not to circumcise their children, neither to walk after the customs. What is it therefore? The multitude must needs come together: for they will hear that thou art come. Do therefore this that we say to thee: we have four men which have a vow on them; them take, and purify thyself with them, and be at charges with them, that they may shave their heads: and all may know that those things, whereof they were informed concerning thee, are nothing; but that thou thyself also walkest orderly, and keepest the law. As touching the Gentiles which believe, we have written and concluded that they observe no such thing, save only that they keep themselves from things offered to idols, and from blood, and from strangled, and from fornication."

"THIS IS THE MAN THAT BROUGHT GREEKS ALSO INTO THE TEMPLE!"

Then Paul took the men, and the next day purifying himself with them entered into the temple, to signify the accomplishment of the days of purification, until that an offering should be offered for every one of them. And when the seven days were almost ended, the Jews which

were of Asia, when they saw him in the temple, stirred
up all the people, and laid hands on him, crying out,
"Men of Israel, help: This is the man, that teacheth
all men every where against the people, and the law,
and this place: and further brought Greeks also into
the temple, and hath polluted this holy place." (For
they had seen before with him in the city Trophimus,
an Ephesian, whom they supposed that Paul had brought
into the temple.) — Acts 21:17-29.

The Mob: "Away with Him!"

And all the city was moved, and the people ran
together: and they took Paul, and drew him out of
the temple: and forthwith the doors were shut. And
as they went about to kill him, tidings came unto the
chief captain of the band, that all Jerusalem was in an
uproar, who immediately took soldiers and centurions,
and ran down unto them: and when they saw the chief
captain and the soldiers, they left beating of Paul.
Then the chief captain came near, and took him, and
commanded him to be bound with two chains; and
demanded who he was, and what he had done. And
some cried one thing, some another, among the multitude: and when he could not know the certainty for
the tumult, he commanded him to be carried into the
castle. And when he came upon the stairs, so it was,
that he was borne of the soldiers for the violence of the
people. For the multitude of the people followed after,
crying, "Away with him." — Acts 21:30-36.

Paul's Great Defense

And as Paul was to be led into the castle, he said
unto the chief captain, "May I speak unto thee?"
Who said, "Canst thou speak Greek? Art thou not that

PAUL IN CHAINS

A painting by John Bianchi

Egyptian, which before these days madest an uproar, and leddest out into the wilderness four thousand men that were murderers?"

But Paul said, "I am a man which am a Jew of Tarsus, a city in Cilicia, a citizen of no mean city: and, I beseech thee, suffer me to speak unto the people."

And when he had given him licence, Paul stood on the stairs, and beckoned with the hand unto the people. And when there was made a great silence, he spake unto them in the Hebrew tongue, saying, "Men, brethren, and fathers, hear ye my defense which I make now unto you." And when they heard that he spake in the Hebrew tongue to them, they kept the more silence: and he saith, "I am verily a man which am a Jew, born in Tarsus, a city in Cilicia, yet brought up in this city at the feet of Gamaliel, and taught according to the perfect manner of the law of the fathers, and was zealous toward God, as ye all are this day. And I persecuted this way unto the death, binding and de-

JERUSALEM IN ROMAN TIMES

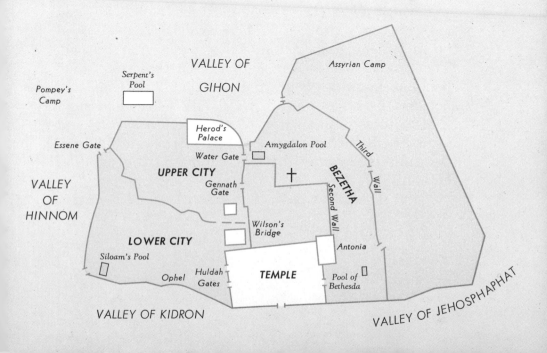

livering into prisons both men and women. As also
the high priest doth bear me witness, and all the estate
of the elders: from whom also I received letters unto
the brethren, and went to Damascus, to bring them
which were there bound unto Jerusalem, for to be
punished. And it came to pass, that, as I made my
journey, and was come nigh unto Damascus about noon,
suddenly there shone from heaven a great light round
about me. And I fell unto the ground, and heard a voice
saying unto me, 'Saul, Saul, why persecutest thou me?'

"And I answered, 'Who art thou, Lord?'

"And he said unto me, 'I am Jesus of Nazareth,
whom thou persecutest.' And they that were with me
saw indeed the light, and were afraid; but they heard
not the voice of him that spake to me.

"And I said, 'What shall I do, Lord?'

"And the Lord said unto me, 'Arise, and **go into**
Damascus; and there it shall be told thee of all **things**
which are appointed for thee to do.'

"And when I could not see for the glory of that light,
being led by the hand of them that were with me, I
came into Damascus. And one Ananias, a devout man
according to the law, having a good report of all the
Jews which dwelt there, came unto me, and stood, and
said unto me, 'Brother Saul, receive thy sight.' And
the same hour I looked up upon him. And he said,
'The God of our fathers hath chosen thee, that thou
shouldest know his will, and see that Just One, and
shouldest hear the voice of his mouth. For thou shalt
be his witness unto all men of what thou hast seen and
heard. And now why tarriest thou? Arise, and be baptized, and wash away thy sins, calling on the name of
the Lord.'

"And it came to pass, that, when I was come again

to Jerusalem, even while I prayed in the temple, I was in a trance; and saw him saying unto me, 'Make haste, and get thee quickly out of Jerusalem: for they will not receive thy testimony concerning me.'

"And I said, 'Lord, they know that I imprisoned and beat in every synagogue them that believed on thee: and when the blood of thy martyr Stephen was shed, I also was standing by, and consenting unto his death, and kept the raiment of them that slew him.'

"And he said unto me, 'Depart: for I will send thee far hence unto the Gentiles.'"

And they gave him audience unto this word, and then lifted up their voices, and said, "Away with such a fellow from the earth: for it is not fit that he should live."

And as they cried out, and cast off their clothes, and threw dust into the air, the chief captain commanded him to be brought into the castle, and bade that he should be examined by scourging; that he might know wherefore they cried so against him. And as they bound him with thongs, Paul said unto the centurion that stood by, "Is it lawful for you to scourge a man that is a Roman, and uncondemned?"

When the centurion heard that, he went and told the chief captain, saying, "Take heed what thou doest: for this man is a Roman."

Then the chief captain came, and said unto him, "Tell me, art thou a Roman?"

He said, "Yea."

And the chief captain answered, "With a great sum obtained I this freedom."

And Paul said, "But I was free born."

Then straightway they departed from him which should have examined him: and the chief captain also

PAUL, ROMAN CITIZEN
A painting by John Bianchi

was afraid, after he knew that he was a Roman, and because he had bound him.   — Acts 21:37–22:29.

Before the Sanhedrin

The Roman officials were always anxious to avoid assuming responsibility. It occurred to Claudius Lysias to turn Paul over to the Sanhedrin for examination. A tumultuous scene resulted, in which Paul, after an encounter with the high priest, skilfully arrayed the two factions, Pharisees and Sadducees, against each other. The session ended in an uproar and Claudius Lysias was again obliged to interfere, and take his prisoner for safe-keeping back to the fortress. Here Paul was for a time safe from his foes, who sullenly retired to plot against him.

"I wist not, brethren, that he was the high priest"

On the morrow, because he would have known the certainty wherefore he was accused of the Jews, he loosed him from his bands, and commanded the chief priests and all their council to appear, and brought Paul down, and set him before them.

And Paul, earnestly beholding the council, said, "Men and brethren, I have lived in all good conscience before God until this day."

And the high priest Ananias commanded them that stood by him to smite him on the mouth.

Then said Paul unto him, "God shall smite thee, thou whited wall: for sittest thou to judge me after the law, and commandest me to be smitten contrary to the law?"

And they that stood by said, "Revilest thou God's high priest?"

Then said Paul, "I wist not, brethren, that he was the high priest: for it is written, 'Thou shalt not speak evil of the ruler of thy people.'"

THE MULTITUDE IS DIVIDED

But when Paul perceived that the one part were Sadducees, and the other Pharisees, he cried out in the council, "Men and brethren, I am a Pharisee, the son of a Pharisee: of the hope and resurrection of the dead I am called in question."

And when he had so said, there arose a dissension between the Pharisees and the Sadducees: and the multitude was divided. For the Sadducees say that there is no resurrection, neither angel, nor spirit: but the Pharisees confess both. And there arose a great cry: and the scribes that were of the Pharisees' part arose, and strove, saying, "We find no evil in this man: but if a spirit or an angel hath spoken to him, let us not fight against God."

PAUL A PRISONER IN THE CASTLE: "BE OF GOOD CHEER, PAUL"

And when there arose a great dissension, the chief captain, fearing lest Paul should have been pulled in pieces of them, commanded the soldiers to go down, and to take him by force from among them, and to bring him into the castle.

And the night following the Lord stood by him, and said, "Be of good cheer, Paul: for as thou hast testified of me in Jerusalem, so must thou bear witness also at Rome."   — Acts 22:30; 23:1-11.

CONSPIRACY

Deep must have been the depression of Paul at the close of that day. The daring soul seemed at last to have been caught in a trap from which there was no escape, but there came to him, as the hours wore on, a message of divine assurance: "Be of good cheer; for as thou hast testified concerning me at Jerusalem, so must thou bear witness also at Rome."

In the morning conspiracy walked the streets of Jerusalem.
Forty men bound themselves by an oath not to eat nor drink until
Paul was slain. A clever plot was formed. Another hearing was to
be arranged before the Sanhedrin, and the assassins were to do away
with Paul as he was on the way from the fortress to the meeting of
the Sanhedrin. Very likely the plan would have succeeded, had not
the commander been warned. Paul had a nephew, a sister's son,
who was living in Jerusalem. In some manner the plot became
known to him. He hastened to the commander, who heard him with
attention and concern. The captain realized that Paul was not safe in
Jerusalem even under the protection of Rome. He was responsible
for this troublesome Roman citizen and he acted with decision. At
nine o'clock that evening Paul was on his way to the coast with a
strong escort of two hundred legionaries, seventy cavalry and two
hundred spearmen,—a large force, but Claudius Lysias was taking
no chances. Two days later, the centurion delivered his prisoner
with a letter from Claudius Lysias to Felix, the Governor.

And when it was day, certain of the Jews banded
together, and bound themselves under a curse, saying
that they would neither eat nor drink till they had killed
Paul. And they were more than forty which had made
this conspiracy. And they came to the chief priests
and elders, and said, "We have bound ourselves under
a great curse, that we will eat nothing until we have
slain Paul. Now therefore ye with the council signify
to the chief captain that he bring him down unto you
to-morrow, as though ye would enquire something more
perfectly concerning him: and we, or ever he come near,
are ready to kill him."

PAUL'S NEPHEW SAVES THE APOSTLE'S LIFE

And when Paul's sister's son heard of their lying in
wait, he went and entered into the castle, and told Paul.
Then Paul called one of the centurions unto him, and
said, "Bring this young man unto the chief captain:
for he hath a certain thing to tell him."

So he took him, and brought him to the chief captain, and said, "Paul, the prisoner, called me unto him, and prayed me to bring this young man unto thee, who hath something to say unto thee."

Then the chief captain took him by the hand, and went with him aside privately, and asked him, "What is that thou hast to tell me?"

And he said, "The Jews have agreed to desire thee that thou wouldest bring down Paul to-morrow into the council, as though they would enquire somewhat of him more perfectly. But do not thou yield unto them: for there lie in wait for him of them more than forty men, which have bound themselves with an oath, that they will neither eat nor drink till they have killed him: and now are they ready, looking for a promise from thee."

So the chief captain then let the young man depart, and charged him, "See thou tell no man that thou hast showed these things to me."

And he called unto him two centurions, saying, "Make ready two hundred soldiers to go to Cæsarea, and horsemen threescore and ten, and spearmen two hundred, at the third hour of the night; and provide them beasts, that they may set Paul on, and bring him safe unto Felix, the governor."

THE LETTER OF CLAUDIUS LYSIAS TO FELIX, THE GOVERNOR

And he wrote a letter after this manner: Claudius Lysias unto the most excellent governor Felix sendeth greeting. This man was taken of the Jews, and should have been killed of them: then came I with an army, and rescued him, having understood that he was a Roman. And when I would have known the cause wherefore they accused him, I brought him forth into

Paul Going to Cæsarea Under Escort of Roman Cavalry

From an oil painting by Edwin John Prittie, painted
expressly for The Book of Life

Paul is shown on his night journey from
Jerusalem to Cæsarea escorted by two Roman centurions and a detachment of infan-
try and cavalry. Paul is riding beside one
of the centurions. The lights of the city are
already in sight.

"And he called unto him two centurions,
saying, 'Make ready two hundred soldiers to
get to Cæsarea, the horsemen threescore and
ten, the spearmen two hundred, at the third
hour of the night. And provide them beasts,
that they may set Paul on, and bring him
safe unto Felix the governor.' " Acts 23:23, 24.

EDWIN JOHN PRITT
1912

their council: whom I perceived to be accused of questions of their law, but to have nothing laid to his charge worthy of death or of bonds. And when it was told me how that the Jews laid wait for the man, I sent straightway to thee, and gave commandment to his accusers also to say before thee what they had against him. Farewell."

A NIGHT JOURNEY UNDER ROMAN GUARD

Then the soldiers, as it was commanded them, took Paul, and brought him by night to Antipatris. On the morrow they left the horsemen to go with him, and returned to the castle: who, when they came to Cæsarea, and delivered the epistle to the governor, presented Paul also before him. And when the governor had read the letter, he asked of what province he was. And when he understood that he was of Cilicia; "I will hear thee," said he, "when thine accusers are also come." And he commanded him to be kept in Herod's judgment hall. — Acts 23:12–35.

ANANIAS PURSUES PAUL TO CÆSAREA

And after five days Ananias, the high priest, descended with the elders, and with a certain orator named Tertullus, who informed the governor against Paul. And when he was called forth, Tertullus began to accuse him, saying, "Seeing that by thee we enjoy great quietness, and that very worthy deeds are done unto this nation by thy providence, we accept it always, and in all places, most noble Felix, with all thankfulness. Notwithstanding, that I be not further tedious unto thee, I pray thee that thou wouldest hear us of thy clemency a few words. For we have found this man a pestilent fellow, and a mover of sedition among all the

Jews throughout the world, and a ringleader of the
sect of the Nazarenes: who also hath gone about to profane the temple: whom we took, and would have judged
according to our law. But the chief captain Lysias
came upon us, and with great violence took him away
out of our hands, commanding his accusers to come
unto thee: by examining of whom thyself mayest take
knowledge of all these things, whereof we accuse him."

And the Jews also assented, saying that these things
were so.   —Acts 24:1-9.

Paul, the Courteous: "I Do the More Cheerfully Answer for Myself"

Then Paul, after that the governor had beckoned
unto him to speak, answered, "Forasmuch as I know
that thou hast been of many years a judge unto this
nation, I do the more cheerfully answer for myself:
because that thou mayest understand, that there are
yet but twelve days since I went up to Jerusalem for to
worship. And they neither found me in the temple
disputing with any man, neither raising up the people,
neither in the synagogues, nor in the city: neither can
they prove the things whereof they now accuse me.
But this I confess unto thee, that after the way which
they call heresy, so worship I the God of my fathers,
believing all things which are written in the law and
in the prophets: and have hope toward God, which
they themselves also allow, that there shall be a resurrection of the dead, both of the just and unjust. And
herein do I exercise myself, to have always a conscience
void of offence toward God, and toward men.

"Now after many years I came to bring alms to my
nation, and offerings. Whereupon certain Jews from
Asia found me purified in the temple, neither with multi-

tude, nor with tumult. Who ought to have been here before thee, and object, if they had aught against me. Or else let these same here say, if they have found any evil doing in me, while I stood before the council, except it be for this one voice, that I cried standing among them, 'Touching the resurrection of the dead I am called in question by you this day.'"

And when Felix heard these things, having more perfect knowledge of that Way, he deferred them, and said, "When Lysias, the chief captain, shall come down, I will know the uttermost of your matter."

And he commanded a centurion to keep Paul, and to let him have liberty, and that he should forbid none of his acquaintance to minister or come unto him.

— Acts 24:10–23.

Paul Before Felix

Felix, the governor of the province, was not a man to inspire confidence. Tacitus, in his "Annals," says of him, "In the practice of all kinds of lust and cruelty he exercised the power of a king with the temper of a slave." But he was a Roman; the Roman law, the Roman justice, insured fair play for every citizen within the wide bounds of the empire. During this trying period, as at all times, Paul's Roman citizenship was of inestimable value to him.

Cæsarea, really the Roman capital of Judea, was a magnificent city with a fine harbor, artificially made by constructing breakwaters of huge stones, forming a complete protection for shipping on the dangerous coast. It was the residence of the Roman procurator. It contained a turbulent population of Jews and foreigners.

In five days down came Paul's enemies hot upon his trail. The high priest himself was present with a Roman lawyer to conduct the case. The prosecution completely broke down after Paul, conducting his own defence, made his simple statement of facts. Felix could not turn his prisoner over to the high priest, but he was unwilling to release him. The wife of Felix was Drusilla, a Jewess. She was curious to see the famous apostle, and Felix summoned him before them. Felix was terrified by Paul's setting forth of "righteousness and self-control and judgment." Yet his avarice overcame his sense of justice. He "hoped for a bribe."

So Paul, alternating between hope and fear, was kept in Cæsarea for two years. He who longed for action, the call to service sounding in his ears, must stay here within sight of the sea, for two years of inactivity. He was in "military custody." That is, he was chained to a soldier who was responsible with his own life for his prisoner's safe-keeping. The prisoner's right hand was chained to the soldier's left, day and night, the soldiers relieving one another on duty. There were certain mitigations of this régime. More favored prisoners were not confined in the terrible jails of the empire, but were allowed to live, chained to the guard, "in their own hired house." This was the nature of Paul's first imprisonment at Rome and probably also at Cæsarea. Paul's friends might visit him freely, and other indulgences may have been permitted.

And after certain days, when Felix came with his wife Drusilla, which was a Jewess, he sent for Paul, and heard him concerning the faith in Christ. And as he reasoned of righteousness, temperance, and judgment to come, Felix trembled, and answered, "Go thy way for this time; when I have a convenient season, I will call for thee." He hoped also that money should have been given him of Paul, that he might loose him: wherefore he sent for him the oftener, and communed with him. But after two years Porcius Festus came into Felix' room: and Felix, willing to show the Jews a pleasure, left Paul bound. — Acts 24:24–27.

"I Appeal unto Cæsar"

Matters were going very badly in the province of Judea. Felix was a corrupt and inefficient governor. The Jewish people were growing more and more restless, the spirit of insurrection which later called down upon them a terrible vengeance under Titus was seething beneath the surface. The imperial government, always sensitive to colonial conditions, removed Felix and appointed Porcius Festus in his place.

When Festus made his official visit to Jerusalem on his accession to office, he was met with an insistent demand for the person of Paul and a new trial before the Sanhedrin. Festus denied the request. Paul was a Roman citizen in his custody. He would shortly return to Cæsarea and he would see that justice was done. They could come down and present their case.

Later, the enemies of Paul came to Cæsarea, and Festus heard the case. He saw at once that a matter of religion was involved, not a political movement, as he had thought likely. He was a just man; he was favorably disposed to Paul. In perplexity, he suggested to Paul that he return to Jerusalem under his protection and appear again before the Sanhedrin. Paul knew what this would mean, death by assassination on the way. He was conscious of the justice of his cause. He stood then upon his rights as a Roman citizen and said, "I appeal unto Cæsar."

He had uttered those magic words which automatically and instantly removed his case from the provincial courts to the supreme court of the empire at Rome. The humblest citizen might make this appeal. The only exceptions were in the case of a pirate or a bandit. Paul being neither, there remained no alternative for Festus, who turned to his council, and after a moment's conference, passed formal judgment: "Thou hast appealed unto Cæsar; unto Cæsar thou shalt go."

Now when Festus was come into the province, after three days he ascended from Cæsarea to Jerusalem. Then the high priest and the chief of the Jews informed him against Paul, and besought him, and desired favour against him, that he would send for him to Jerusalem, laying wait in the way to kill him. But Festus answered, that Paul should be kept at Cæsarea, and that he himself would depart shortly thither. "Let them therefore," said he, "which among you are able, go down with me, and accuse this man, if there be any wickedness in him." And when he had tarried among them more than ten days, he went down unto Cæsarea; and the next day sitting on the judgment seat commanded

Paul to be brought.   And when he was come, the Jews
which came down from Jerusalem stood round about,
and laid many and grievous complaints against Paul,
which they could not prove; while he answered for
himself, "Neither against the law of the Jews, neither
against the temple, nor yet against Cæsar, have I offended
anything at all."

But Festus, willing to do the Jews a pleasure, answered Paul, and said, "Wilt thou go up to Jerusalem,
and there be judged of these things before me?"

Then said Paul, "I stand at Cæsar's judgment seat,
where I ought to be judged: to the Jews have I done
no wrong, as thou very well knowest.   For if I be an
offender, or have committed anything worthy of death,
I refuse not to die: but if there be none of these things
whereof these accuse me, no man may deliver me unto
them.   I appeal unto Cæsar."

Then Festus, when he had conferred with the council, answered, "Hast thou appealed unto Cæsar? Unto
Cæsar shalt thou go."   — Acts 25:1–12.

"Thou Shalt Stand Before Kings"

Just at this time, Herod Agrippa II, King of Chalcis, and his
beautiful sister, Bernice, a most fascinating woman, came to spend
"some days" on a complimentary visit to the new governor. Festus
was still in some perplexity about his prisoner. It seemed foolish to
send a man to Rome against whom no definite charge could be
formulated. He would consult his distinguished guest. He was no
expert upon the Jewish religion; he would at once compliment
Agrippa, and perhaps get some real light upon the case.

Agrippa was immediately interested. He had heard of Paul and
of the new faith which was spreading like fire through the empire.
He would be glad to grant a hearing.

With pomp and ceremony, announced by the trumpets of the
legion, surrounded by a brilliant suite, Agrippa and the beautiful
Bernice entered the audience room. Festus made a speech, explaining

the circumstances of Paul's detention. The apostle, a little elderly man, his hair whitening now, appeared, chained to a legionary. "Thou art permitted to speak for thyself," said the king. Then Paul "stretched forth his hand" in his characteristic gesture and made his splendid defense. Courteous, dignified, eloquent, he carried his audience with him upon the tide of his great argument. It is a most dramatic scene throughout: the interruption of the Roman governor when Paul mentioned the resurrection, "Paul, thou art beside thyself; much learning doth make thee mad"; the courteous but most earnest reply; the appeal to the faith of the Jewish king; the reply of the king, ironical doubtless; Paul's noble answer in which he takes the words as though they were spoken in seriousness and truth.

The hearing was over. The trumpets sounded. The king and his sister, with the governor, Festus, left the room, discussing

BERNICE

This beautiful bronze bust was found buried in the ruins of Herculaneum. It is said to represent Bernice, the daughter of Agrippa I and sister of Drusilla, wife of Felix, the Roman Governor. Drusilla perished with her child at the destruction of Pompeii. It is especially interesting then that this portrait of the sister who heard Paul speak should have been discovered in the ruins of buried Herculaneum, destroyed by the eruption of Vesuvius.

as they went, the extraordinary man and his case. There was no levity nor even unfriendliness in that talk. The king gave as his opinion that Paul might have been set at liberty, if he had not appealed to Cæsar. There was now no escape. Paul had appealed to Cæsar and to Cæsar he must go.

And after certain days King Agrippa and Bernice came unto Cæsarea to salute Festus. And when they had been there many days, Festus declared Paul's cause unto the king, saying, "There is a certain man left in bonds by Felix: about whom, when I was at Jerusalem, the chief priests and the elders of the Jews informed me, desiring to have judgment against him. To whom I answered, 'It is not the manner of the Romans to deliver any man to die, before that he which is accused have the accusers face to face, and have licence to answer for himself concerning the crime laid against him.' Therefore, when they were come hither, without any delay on the morrow I sat on the judgment seat, and commanded the man to be brought forth, against whom when the accusers stood up, they brought none accusation of such things as I supposed: but had certain questions against him of their own superstition, and of one Jesus, which was dead, whom Paul affirmed to be alive. And because I doubted of such manner of questions, I asked him whether he would go to Jerusalem, and there be judged of these matters. But when Paul had appealed to be reserved unto the hearing of Augustus, I commanded him to be kept till I might send him to Cæsar."

Then Agrippa said unto Festus, "I would also hear the man myself."

"To-morrow," said he, "thou shalt hear him."

And on the morrow, when Agrippa was come, and Bernice, with great pomp, and was entered into the place of hearing, with the chief captains, and principal men of the city, at Festus' commandment Paul was brought forth. And Festus said, "King Agrippa, and all men which are here present with us, ye see this man, about whom all the multitude of the Jews have dealt with me, both at Jerusalem, and also here, crying that he ought not to live any longer. But when I found that he had committed nothing worthy of death, and that he himself hath appealed to Augustus, I have determined

ANCIENT FORTRESS ON THE ISLAND OF CRETE
This is an ancient Venetian fortification, on the island of Crete.

to send him. Of whom I have no certain thing to write unto my lord. Wherefore I have brought him forth before you, and specially before thee, O King Agrippa, that, after examination had, I might have somewhat to write. For it seemeth to me unreasonable to send a prisoner, and not withal to signify the crimes laid against him."

Then Agrippa said unto Paul, "Thou art permitted to speak for thyself."

Then Paul stretched forth the hand, and answered for himself.

"I THINK MYSELF HAPPY, KING AGRIPPA"

"I think myself happy, King Agrippa, because I shall answer for myself this day before thee touching all the things whereof I am accused of the Jews: especially because I know thee to be expert in all customs and questions which are among the Jews: wherefore I beseech thee to hear me patiently."

"MY MANNER OF LIFE KNOW ALL THE JEWS: I LIVED A PHARISEE"

"My manner of life from my youth, which was at the first among mine own nation at Jerusalem, know all the Jews; which knew me from the beginning, if they would testify, that after the most straitest sect of our religion I lived a Pharisee. And now I stand and am judged for the hope of the promise made of God unto our fathers: unto which promise our twelve tribes, instantly serving God day and night, hope to come. For which hope's sake, King Agrippa, I am accused of the Jews. Why should it be thought a thing incredible with you, that God should raise the dead?

"I THOUGHT I OUGHT TO DO MANY THINGS CONTRARY TO THE NAME OF JESUS OF NAZARETH"

"I verily thought with myself, that I ought to do many things contrary to the name of Jesus of Nazareth. Which thing I also did in Jerusalem: and many of the saints did I shut up in prison, having received authority from the chief priests; and when they were put to death, I gave my voice against them. And I punished them oft in every synagogue, and compelled them to blaspheme; and being exceedingly mad against them, I persecuted them even unto strange cities.

"AT MIDDAY, O KING, I SAW A LIGHT FROM HEAVEN"

"Whereupon as I went to Damascus with authority and commission from the chief priests, at midday, O king, I saw in the way a light from heaven, above the brightness of the sun, shining round about me and them which journeyed with me. And when we were all fallen to the earth, I heard a voice speaking unto me, and saying in the Hebrew tongue, 'Saul, Saul, why persecutest thou me? It is hard for thee to kick against the pricks.'

"And I said, 'Who art thou, Lord?'

"And he said, 'I am Jesus whom thou persecutest. But rise, and stand upon thy feet: for I have appeared unto thee for this purpose, to make thee a minister and a witness both of these things which thou hast seen, and of those things in the which I will appear unto thee; delivering thee from the people, and from the Gentiles, unto whom now I send thee, to open their eyes, and to turn them from darkness to light, and from the power of Satan unto God, that they may receive forgiveness of sins, and inheritance among them which are sanctified by faith that is in me.'

"WHEREUPON I WAS NOT DISOBEDIENT UNTO THE HEAVENLY VISION"

"Whereupon, O King Agrippa, I was not disobedient unto the heavenly vision: but showed first unto them of Damascus, and at Jerusalem, and throughout all the coasts of Judæa, and then to the Gentiles, that they should repent and turn to God, and do works meet for repentance.

"For these causes the Jews caught me in the temple, and went about to kill me. Having therefore obtained help of God, I continue unto this day, witnessing both to small and great, saying none other things than those which the prophets and Moses did say should come: that Christ should suffer, and that he should be the first that should rise from the dead, and should show light unto the people, and to the Gentiles."

And as he thus spake for himself, Festus said with a loud voice, "Paul, thou art beside thyself; much learning doth make thee mad."

PAUL BEFORE KING AGRIPPA
A molding by D. Mastroianni

But he said, "I am not mad, most noble Festus; but speak forth the words of truth and soberness. For the king knoweth of these things, before whom also I speak freely: for I am persuaded that none of these things are hidden from him; for this thing was not done in a corner. King Agrippa, believest thou the prophets? I know that thou believest."

Then Agrippa said unto Paul, "Almost thou persuadest me to be a Christian."

And Paul said, "I would to God, that not only thou, but also all that hear me this day, were both almost, and altogether such as I am, except these bonds."

And when he had thus spoken, the king rose up, and the governor, and Bernice, and they that sat with them: and when they were gone aside, they talked between themselves, saying, "This man doeth nothing worthy of death or of bonds."

Then said Agrippa unto Festus, "This man might have been set at liberty, if he had not appealed unto Cæsar."   —Acts 25:13-26:32.

On the Sea Again—The Shipwreck

Paul must have been happy when he stood once more on the deck of a ship, outward bound. He, with some other prisoners, was in the charge of Julius, a kindly Roman officer; and two companions, Luke and Aristarchus, accompanied him. They sailed on a ship of Adramyttium, a small vessel, doubtless, trading up the coast and across the Ægean. At Andriace, the port of Myra, the prisoners were trans-shipped to one of the great wheat ships bound from Alexandria to Rome. The weather was from the first unfavorable. It was late in the autumn; and the Mediterranean, which even in summer is not free from severe storms, was in a tempestuous mood.

The ship reached Cnidus on the coast of Crete, and proceeding along the south shore, anchored in the roadstead of Fair Havens. The question now arose, whether they should winter here or proceed to Rome, for navigation of the Mediterranean was not attempted in the winter. There were probably few sailors on board with a better knowledge of navigation than Paul His advice was asked and he urged the owner, who was on the ship, the shipmaster, and the centurion to remain at the port for the winter. His wise counsel did not prevail. The same desire which makes the owner of vessels on the Great Lakes take long chances in rushing the grain and ore to port before the ice closes navigation in the fall, influenced the master of the Egyptian ship to risk the voyage to Puteoli, the port of Rome, or at least as far as Phœnix, a more sheltered port than Fair Havens.

There was a sudden change to better weather, a light wind sprang up from the south, and they were sailing along the coast under the lee of the Cretan shore, when suddenly the wind veered, and swept down with the force of a hurricane from the ravines of Mount Ida. The master of the ship was unprepared; he even had the ship's boat towing astern. There was nothing to do but run before the gale. The island of Clauda was about twenty miles to the southwest.   Under the lee of this island where there was calmer water they did the best they could under the perilous circumstances. They got the boat aboard with difficulty; then they "undergirded" the ship. The seams of ancient ships were always in danger of opening during a gale. Accordingly, they passed heavy cables under the vessel and fastened them taut on the deck. Then they shortened sail, reefing the great mainsail. The only thing which could be done in addition was to "lie to," bring the vessel up into the wind on the starboard tack in order not to be blown upon the African coast. A small sail was set to keep from falling off into the trough of the sea. This done, they could only wait for fair weather. But no fair weather came.

Day after day the storm roared on. The ship began to leak. Some of the cargo and her "spare gear" were thrown into the sea, the passengers helping the crew. Provisions ran short. Despair was on every face. Then Paul stood up and told them of a vision which had come to him in the night. An angel stood beside him, saying "Fear not, Paul; thou must be brought before Cæsar: and, lo, God hath given thee all them that sail with thee." There was no immediate lessening of the peril. For fourteen days they drifted up the Mediterranean, until the roar of breakers was heard.

By sounding their depth they found twenty fathoms and then fifteen. They put out four anchors from the stern to prevent the ship from going ashore and anxiously waited for the day. Some of

Latomia at Syracuse, Sicily

Paul's ship, the "Twin Brethren," put in
at the port of Syracuse and remained there
three days. There is a tradition that the
apostle preached in the extensive catacombs of the city. This illustration shows
the famous "latomia" or quarries in which
the Athenian prisoners were confined when
Syracuse broke the imperial power of Athens
in the famous siege of the city. The choicest
young men of Athens miserably perished in
these quarries.

the sailors, on the pretext of carrying out anchors from the bow, attempted to escape. Paul warned the centurion that for the safety of all, no one must leave the ship. The centurion ordered the soldiers to cut the rope, and the boat drifted away. The faint light of dawn revealed the terrible danger of their position The ship was settling fast. Two hundred and seventy-six people were gathered on deck waiting for the end. Paul bade them to be of good cheer, and to eat something. He himself took bread and gave thanks to God and began to eat. New courage came to them all. The ports were opened and the cargo of grain was allowed to run into the sea, which helped to give the sinking ship some buoyancy. Day broke, a wild stormy morning. Through the spray they saw the coast of the island of Malta, with a little bay and a sandy beach. They cast off the anchors, hoisted the foresail, and drove the ship upon the beach, where the bow remained fast though the stern began at once to break up. The ungrateful soldiers wished to kill the prisoners lest they escape. The centurion, out of regard for Paul, prevented this act of cruelty, which ordinarily would not be repugnant to a Roman, and ordered every man to save himself. Some swam ashore; others, on planks and wreckage, came safely to the beach. The entire ship's company was saved. Such was the fortunate ending of one of the most dramatic stories of shipwreck in literature.

And when it was determined that we should sail into Italy, they delivered Paul and certain other prisoners unto one named Julius, a centurion of Augustus' band. And entering into a ship of Adramyttium, we launched, meaning to sail by the coasts of Asia; one Aristarchus, a Macedonian of Thessalonica, being with us. And the next day we touched at Sidon. And Julius courteously entreated Paul, and gave him liberty to go unto his friends to refresh himself. And when we had launched from thence, we sailed under Cyprus, because the winds were contrary. And when we had sailed over the sea of Cilicia and Pamphylia, we came to Myra, a city of Lycia. And there the centurion found a ship of Alexandria sailing into Italy; and he put us therein.

THE ISLAND OF CRETE

The Island of Crete was visited by Paul on his voyage to Rome.

PAUL'S ADVICE AT FAIR HAVENS IS NOT FOLLOWED

And when we had sailed slowly many days, and scarce were come over against Cnidus, the wind not suffering us, we sailed under Crete, over against Salmone, and, hardly passing it, came unto a place which is called "The Fair Havens"; nigh whereunto was the city of Lasea.

Now when much time was spent, and when sailing was now dangerous, because the fast was now already past, Paul admonished them, and said unto them, "Sirs, I perceive that this voyage will be with hurt and much damage, not only of the lading and ship, but also of our lives."

THE STORM

Nevertheless the centurion believed the master and the owner of the ship, more than those things which were spoken by Paul. And because the haven was not commodious to winter in, the more part advised to depart thence also, if by any means they might attain to

MOROSINI FOUNTAIN, CRETE

Phenice, and there to winter; which is an haven of
Crete, and lieth toward the southwest and northwest.
And when the south wind blew softly, supposing that
they had obtained their purpose, loosing thence, they
sailed close by Crete. But not long after there arose
against it a tempestuous wind, called Euroclydon. And
when the ship was caught, and could not bear up into
the wind, we let her drive. And running under a certain island which is called Clauda, we had much work
to come by the boat: which when they had taken up,
they used helps, undergirding the ship; and, fearing lest
they should fall into the quicksands, struck sail, and so
were driven. And we being exceedingly tossed with a
tempest, the next day they lightened the ship; and the
third day we cast out with our own hands the tackling
of the ship. And when neither sun nor stars in many
days appeared, and no small tempest lay on us, all
hope that we should be saved was then taken away.

PAUL ENCOURAGES HIS FELLOW-SAILORS

But after long abstinence Paul stood forth in the midst of them, and said, "Sirs, ye should have hearkened unto me, and not have loosed from Crete, and to have gained this harm and loss. And now I exhort you to be of good cheer: for there shall be no loss of any man's life among you, but of the ship. For there stood by me this night the angel of God, whose I am, and whom I serve, saying, 'Fear not, Paul; thou must be brought before Cæsar: and, lo, God hath given thee all them that sail with thee.' Wherefore, sirs, be of good cheer: for I believe God, that it shall be even as it was told me. Howbeit we must be cast upon a certain island."

—Acts 27:1-26.

THE ESCAPE TO LAND

But when the fourteenth night was come, as we were driven up and down in Adria, about midnight the ship-

ISLAND OF MALTA

THE BAY OF NAPLES

ST. PAUL AT PUTEOLI

Over this pretty port off the Gulf of Naples, Italian boatmen row and ships with spread sails move against the picturesque background of Italian buildings along the shore.

Over these same waters, nearly two thousand years ago, in a ship of Alexandria, "Whose sign was Castor and Pollux," came sailing St. Paul, Apostle to the Gentiles, on his way to Rome.

"And we came the next day to Puteoli," wrote St. Luke in the Book of Acts, "where we found brethren, and were desired to tarry with them seven days; and so we went toward Rome." (Acts 28:11; page 139, and map on page 138)

Today, Roman Puteoli is Italian Pozzuoli.

men deemed that they drew near to some country; and sounded, and found it twenty fathoms: and when they had gone a little further, they sounded again, and found it fifteen fathoms.

Then fearing lest we should have fallen upon rocks, they cast four anchors out of the stern, and wished for the day. And as the shipmen were about to flee out of the ship, when they had let down the boat into the sea, under colour as though they would have cast anchors out of the foreship, Paul said to the centurion and to the soldiers, "Except these abide in the ship, ye cannot be saved." Then the soldiers cut off the ropes of the boat, and let her fall off.

And while the day was coming on, Paul besought them all to take meat, saying, "This day is the fourteenth day that ye have tarried and continued fasting, having taken nothing. Wherefore I pray you to take some meat: for this is for your health: for there shall not an hair fall from the head of any of you." And when he had thus spoken, he took bread, and gave thanks to God in presence of them all: and when he had broken it, he began to eat. Then were they all of good cheer, and they also took some meat. And we were in all in the ship two hundred threescore and sixteen souls. And when they had eaten enough, they lightened the ship, and cast out the wheat into the sea. And when it was day, they knew not the land: but they discovered a certain creek with a shore, into the which they were minded, if it were possible, to thrust in the ship. And when they had taken up the anchors, they committed themselves unto the sea, and loosed the rudder bands, and hoisted up the mainsail to the wind, and made toward shore. And falling into a place where two seas met, they ran the ship aground; and the forepart stuck fast, and remained unmovable, but the hinder part was broken with the violence of the waves. And the soldiers' counsel was to kill the prisoners, lest any of them should swim out, and escape. But the centurion, willing to save Paul, kept them from their purpose; and commanded that they which could swim should cast themselves first into the sea, and get to land: and the rest, some on boards, and some on broken pieces of the ship. And so it came to pass, that they escaped all safe to land.

On the Island of Malta

And when they were escaped, then they knew that the island was called Melita. And the barbarous people shewed us no little kindness: for they kindled a fire, and received us every one, because of the present rain, and because of the cold. And when Paul had gathered a bundle of sticks, and laid them on the fire, there came a viper out of the heat, and fastened on his hand. And when the barbarians saw the venomous beast hang on his hand, they said among themselves, "No doubt this man is a murderer, whom, though he hath escaped the sea, yet vengeance suffereth not to live." And he shook off the beast into the fire, and felt no harm. Howbeit they looked when he should have swollen, or fallen down dead suddenly: but after they had looked a great while, and saw no harm come to him, they changed their minds, and said that he was a god.

In the same quarters were possessions of the chief man of the island, whose name was Publius; who received us, and lodged us three days courteously. And it came to pass, that the father of Publius lay sick of a fever and of a bloody flux: to whom Paul entered in, and prayed, and laid his hands on him, and healed him. So when this was done, others also, which had diseases in the island,

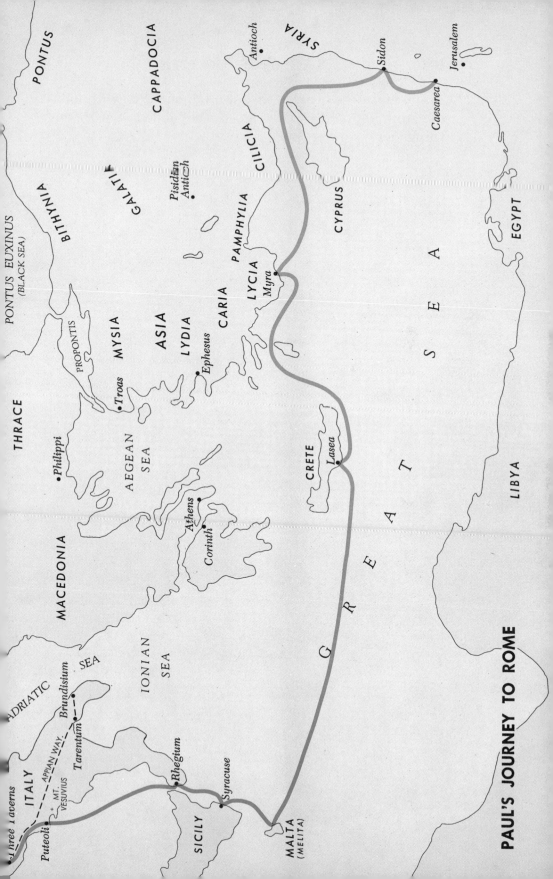

PAUL'S JOURNEY TO ROME

came, and were healed: who also honoured us with many honours; and when we departed, they laded us with such things as were necessary.

—Acts 27: 27–28: 10.

ISLAND OF MALTA

Paul

The Great Captain of the New Faith

Onward to Rome

It was necessary to remain three months on the island of Malta, until navigation opened in the spring. Another Alexandrian grain ship, the "Castor and Pollux," had wintered in the island and on this ship Julius, the Centurion, and his prisoner proceeded to Rome. They put in for three days at the famous city of Syracuse, on the south shore of Sicily. There is a tradition that Paul was permitted to go ashore here, and that he preached in the catacombs of the Church of San Giovanni.

Another stop was made at Rhegium, waiting for a fair wind to take them through the straits of Messina. The wind sprang up and held until they entered the bay of Naples. No smoke-plume by day, no pillar of fire by night arose from the cone of Vesuvius. The giant was slumbering, but it would be only a few years before the fair cities which Paul saw as the "Castor and Pollux" sailed past Capri and up the bay to Puteoli would be in ruins.

Landing at Puteoli, Paul proceeded along the famous Appian Way, the "Queen of Roads." At the Appii Forum a little party of Christians from Rome had come to meet and cheer the apostle on his journey. At the "Three Taverns" another group extended a welcome. So Paul did not come unfriended and alone to the metropolis of the world. "When he saw the brethren, he thanked God and took courage." Paul was permitted to lodge by himself, always chained to the soldier, who was his guard. To this house his friends thronged. Here in the great corrupt city his influence spread. For two years, in his "own hired dwelling," he lived, and thus the Book of the Acts comes suddenly to an end.

But Christianity did not come to an end and it is believed that for some time Paul continued his active career. The early church believed that Paul was liberated after his imprisonment; that he visited again the churches of Macedonia and Asia Minor, that he even took the

137

long meditated journey to Spain, and remained there for two years, that he was again imprisoned at Rome, where he met a martyr's death in the last year of Nero's reign.

"As the martyr and his executioners passed on (from the Ostian gate), their way was crowded with a motley multitude of goers and comers between the metropolis and its harbour—merchants hastening to superintend the unloading of their cargoes—sailors eager to squander the profits of their last voyage in the dissipations of the capital—officials of the government charged with the administration of the provinces, or the command of the legions on the Euphrates or the Rhine—Chaldean astrologers—Phrygian eunuchs—dancing-girls from Syria, with their painted turbans—mendicant priests from Egypt, howling for Osiris—Greek adventurers, eager to coin their national cunning into Roman gold—representatives of the avarice and ambition, the fraud and lust, the superstition and intelligence, of the Imperial world. Through the dust and tumult of that busy throng, the small troop of soldiers threaded their way silently, under the bright sky of an Italian midsummer. They were marching, though they knew it not, in a procession more really

ROMAN REGION
DURING PAUL'S JOURNEY

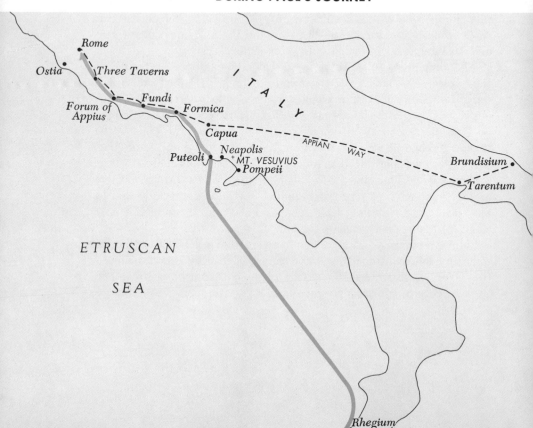

triumphal than any they had ever followed, in the train of general or emperor, along the Sacred Way. Their prisoner, now at last and for ever delivered from captivity, rejoiced to follow his Lord "without the gate." The place of execution was not far distant, and there the sword of the headsman ended his long course of sufferings, and released that heroic soul from that feeble body. Weeping friends took up his corpse, and carried it for burial to those subterranean labyrinths, where, through many ages of oppression, the persecuted Church found refuge for the living, and sepulchers for the dead.

"Thus dies the apostle, the prophet, and the martyr, bequeathing to the Church, in her government and her discipline, the legacy of his apostolic labours; leaving his prophetic words to be her living oracles; pouring forth his blood to be the seed of a thousand martyrdoms. Thenceforth, among the glorious company of the apostles, among the goodly fellowship of the prophets, among the noble army of martyrs, his name has stood pre-eminent. And wherever the church throughout all the world acknowledges God and his Christ, there Paul of Tarsus is revered as the great teacher of a redemption freely offered to all men."—*Conybeare and Howson.*

AND after three months we departed in a ship of Alexandria, which had wintered in the isle, whose sign was Castor and Pollux. And landing at Syracuse, we tarried there three days. And from thence we fetched a compass, and came to Rhegium: and after one day the south wind blew, and we came the next day to Puteoli: where we found brethren, and were desired to tarry with them seven days: and so we went toward Rome. And from thence, when the brethren heard of us, they came to meet us as far as Appii forum, and "The Three Taverns": whom when Paul saw, he thanked God, and took courage.

PAUL, A PRISONER IN HIS OWN HOUSE, SPEAKS TO HIS BRETHREN OF ROME

And when we came to Rome, the centurion delivered the prisoners to the captain of the guard: but Paul was suffered to dwell by himself with a soldier that kept him. And it came to pass, that after three days Paul called the chief of the Jews together: and when they were come together, he said unto them, "Men and brethren, though I have committed nothing against the people, or customs of our fathers, yet was I delivered prisoner from Jerusalem into the hands of the Romans, who, when they had examined me, would have let me go, because there was no cause of death in me. But when the Jews spake against it, I was constrained to appeal unto Cæsar; not that I had aught to accuse my nation of. For this cause therefore have I called for you, to see you, and to speak with you: because that for the hope of Israel I am bound with this chain."

And they said unto him, "We neither received letters out of Judæa concerning thee, neither any of the brethren that came showed or spake any harm of thee. But we desire to hear of thee what thou thinkest: for as concerning this sect, we know that everywhere it is spoken against." And when they had appointed him a day, there came many to him into his lodging; to whom he expounded and testified the Kingdom of God, persuading them concerning Jesus, both out of the law of Moses, and out of the prophets, from morning till evening. And some believed the things which were spoken, and some believed not.

And when they agreed not among themselves, they departed, after that Paul had spoken one word, "Well spake the Holy Ghost by Esaias, the prophet, unto our fathers, saying,

'Go unto this people, and say,
"Hearing ye shall hear, and shall not understand,
And seeing ye shall see, and not perceive:

For the heart of this people is waxed gross,
And their ears are dull of hearing,
And their eyes have they closed;
Lest they should see with their eyes,
And hear with their ears, and understand with
    their heart,
And should be converted,
And I should heal them.''

Be it known therefore unto you, that the salvation of God is sent unto the Gentiles, and that they will hear it."

And when he had said these words, the Jews departed, and had great reasoning among themselves.

"PAUL DWELT TWO YEARS PREACHING THE KINGDOM OF GOD"

And Paul dwelt two whole years in his own hired house, and received all that came in unto him, preaching the kingdom of God, and teaching those things which concern the Lord Jesus Christ, with all confidence, no man forbidding him.   — Acts 28:11-31.

ANCIENT TYRE

Once stood here the great port city of Tyre, but today it lies under the sea except for a few stones on this beach. But it was still standing the day that St. Paul bade the little group of sorrowing Christians there good-bye. He was sailing for Acre in Palestine on his way up to Jerusalem.

"We departed and went our way," writes St. Luke who was with him, "and they all brought us on our way, with wives and children, till we were out of the city; and we kneeled down on the shore, and prayed. And when we had taken our leave one of another, we took ship; and they returned home again."

Read Ezekiel 27 and Volume 5:380-5.

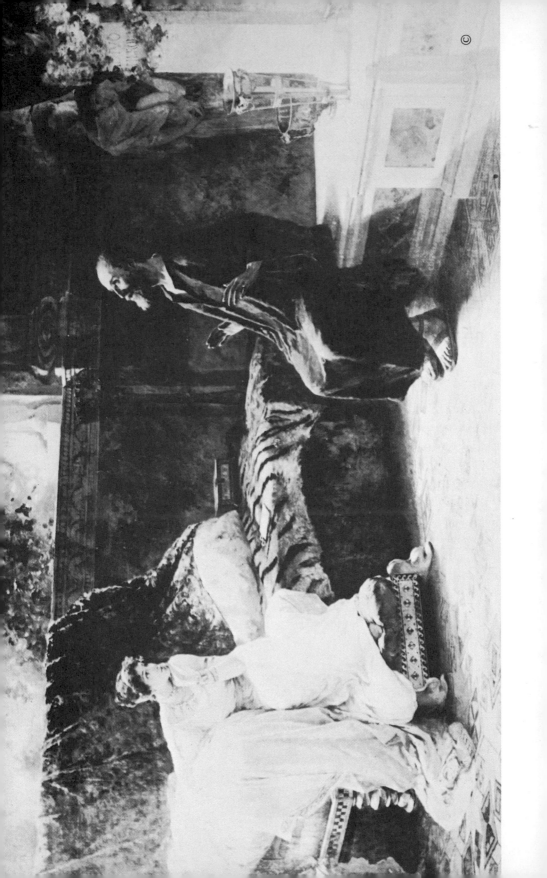

QUESTIONS

Give an outline of Paul's first missionary journey. What places did he visit? What events happened? Who were his companions? Who was Bar-Jesus? Sergius Paulus? Elymas? What people thought Paul and his companions gods?

Where did Paul go after his first journey? What discussion arose in the church? Who took part in the council? What was the decision? Describe Paul's second missionary journey. What places did he visit? What happened? What difference did he have with Barnabas before starting? Who were his companions? What new friend and companion did Paul find at Derbe? What are the "we" portions of The Acts? What vision did Paul have near Troas? What historical event happened at Philippi, not related to the Acts of the Apostles? Who was Lydia? What happened to Paul at Philippi? Who was Jason? For what were the Jews at Berea noted? Give an outline of Paul's sermon at Athens. Where was it preached? Was St. Paul's work at Athens a failure? Who was Dionysius? Damaris? Where did Paul lodge at Corinth? Who came to him at Corinth? Who was Priscilla? Aquila? Gallio? Crispus? How long did Paul live at Corinth? Where did Paul go after leaving Corinth?

Give an account of the third missionary journey. Name the companions of Paul, the places visited, the events. Who was Diana of the Ephesians? What was the principal business of the Ephesians? Who was Sceva? Demetrius? Eutychus? Sopater? Aristarchus? What places did Paul visit on his way to Jerusalem? What occurred when Paul reached Jerusalem?

What caused the riot? Who rescued Paul? What was the value of Roman citizenship? How did Paul attain it? How did the centurion? What happened at the meeting of the Sanhedrin? What conspiracy was formed against Paul? How was it forestalled? What was Paul's escort to Cæsarea? Before what authorities did he appear? Who might appeal to Cæsar? Outline Paul's defense before Agrippa. Describe Paul's voyage to Rome. How many times had Paul been shipwrecked before? What advice did Paul give the centurion and the shipmaster? How many days did the storm last? Where did the wreck occur? How long before Paul could sail again for Rome? What was the sign of the ship on which he sailed? At what port did they touch? Who met Paul in Italy? How long did Paul live at Rome? How did he probably meet his death?

PAUL IN THE PALACE OF NERO
A painting by DeMartini

NOTES

Letters to Damascus. This shows two things: that the followers of Jesus had already gone far afield, for Damascus was outside of Palestine, away to the northeast; and, that Saul was a man of vigor who intended to root out this pestilent sect from all its hiding places.

Kick against the pricks. The figure is that of an ox kicking against the goad, only to be hurt the more. Saul may have been already fighting off a growing conviction — after all, the teaching of Jesus was right, and he was the Son of God.

The Grecians, the very people who had brought about the death of Stephen.

Cæsarea. The seaport for most of the northern travel on the Mediterranean.

Tarsus. Saul's native place, on the southern shore of Asia Minor.

Barnabas. A man of Cyprus, a friend of Paul. It was he who guaranteed Paul to the church at Jerusalem, who brought him to Antioch, and who was his companion on his first missionary journey.

King Herod. Agrippa I, son of Aristobulus and grandson of Herod the Great, who was king when Jesus was born. Herod was given the title of King by the Romans, but he was subordinate to the emperor at Rome.

Days of unleavened bread. This phrase simply refers to the passover. Peter must have recalled that it was at the passover his Lord was arrested and crucified.

Quaternion. Group of four.

John whose surname was Mark. This was the man who later wrote the gospel of Mark. His mother was sister of Barnabas, and he went with Paul and Barnabas on their first missionary journey, but left when the travelers started for the long trip over the mountains to the interior of Asia Minor (Acts 13:17). Paul was displeased, and later, when Barnabas proposed to take him on a second trip, refused. The result was a separation between Paul and Barnabas. The latter took Mark and went to Cyprus (Acts 15:36–41), and never traveled with Paul again. Many years later, after Mark had proved himself, Paul speaks kindly of him (Col. 4:10). It is said that Mark was with Peter, from whom he obtained much of the material for his Gospel.

Seleucia. The seaport of Antioch, at the mouth of the Orontes

TRADITIONAL HOUSE OF SAINT PAUL, ROME

CAMEL CARAVAN IN PERGA, A CITY VISITED BY PAUL

Salamis. The nearest port of Cyprus, on a bay at the eastern end.

Paphos. The capital of Cyprus, the residence of the Roman governor.

Deputy. Literally, "proconsul," as in the Revised Version. The head of the province.

Also called Paul. From this time on, the writer of Acts uses "Paul" exclusively. We do not know the history of the change of name. Paulus (Paul) was a Latin name. Possibly Paul, who was a Roman citizen, already had a Roman name; possibly he adopted it because, going into the Roman world, a Roman name would be convenient, and this was akin in sound to his Jewish name Saul; as in our day foreigners sometimes adopt English names of kindred sound. Such changes of names were common in the ancient world. It has been suggested that he who calls himself "the least of the apostles" chose a name meaning "little" out of modesty.

Perga in Pamphilia. A city on the south shore of Asia Minor, directly across from Cyprus.

Antioch in Pisidia. Over the Taurus range from Perga, a journey of hardship and danger. Paul is now fairly launched on his missionary life work.

Men of Israel. The writer perhaps gives this address at Antioch as an example of Paul's missionary preaching.

In the speech of Lycaonia. Like the people in many parts of the Roman Empire, the natives of Lystra understood two languages: Greek, in which Paul could speak to them, and the old native speech of the country, which they still spoke in their homes. Compare this situation with that in Wales, where English and Welsh are used.

Attalia. As they found no convenient ship at Perga they went to another port, where they found a vessel sailing probably to Seleucia, the port of Antioch.

Came together to consider this matter. The question was, "Must Gentiles become Jews in order to be Christians? Must they keep the Jewish law?" It was an important problem, for if the answer was "Yes," then Christianity was simply a sect in Judaism, not an independent religion. The answer of the council at Jerusalem, themselves all Jews, was "No"; Gentile converts need not keep Jewish law. Paul saw the great importance of this position for Christian progress, and urged it vigorously in his letter to the Galatians.

Syria and Cilicia. The regions nearest Antioch on the north and west. Perhaps Paul visited his old home, Tarsus in Cilicia.

Timotheus. The Timothy of Paul's epistles, a much loved companion of Paul for many years.

Phrygia and the region of Galatia. Or, "the Phrygian region of Galatia." There is much discussion as to the Galatia of Acts and Paul's letters. The word was used in two senses: the old native kingdom in the interior of Asia Minor, or the new, larger Roman province reaching almost from the Black Sea to the Mediterranean. Many think that Acts and Paul use it to mean the Roman province of Galatia. If so, the churches of Derbe, Lystra, and the other cities of Paul's first missionary journey were the churches of Galatia. If not, Paul now made a great detour to the northeast and founded a new group of churches before he went on to Europe. There is a growing tendency to regard the Galatia of Paul's journeys as the Roman province, not the old kingdom.

Asia. The Roman province of Asia, in the western part of Asia Minor.

Troas. A seaport opposite Philippi.

Macedonia was in Europe, and now comes the story of how Christianity passed from Asia to Europe.

A colony. A body of Roman citizens, officially sent to settle at some important point, there to represent the power and the authority of Rome. The colonists were still citizens of the city of Rome, and were proud to make their colony a little Rome.

Where prayer was wont to be made. Perhaps the Jews were so few that there was no synagogue, only a gathering place for prayer on the Sabbath.

Uncondemned, being Romans. Paul was a Roman citizen, and penalties for violating the rights of a citizen were severe. If public apology were made, the position of the new Christians would be more secure.

Thessalonica. An ancient city of Macedonia and an important seaport at the head of the Gulf of Thessalonica. It is still an important city of nearly three hundred thousand people. Called Salonica at the time of World War I.

Epicureans and stoics. Two of the parties of philosophers who made Athens famous. They thought Paul was another philosopher of a new school, and wanted to hear what his philosophy was.

Mars' Hill. "The Areopagus," as in the Revised Version. It had long been the meeting place of the Athenian council, and made a convenient gathering place to hear this new philosopher Paul.

Ye are too superstitious. That would be a tactless way to begin. The Revised Version gives a much better translation, "I perceive that you are very religious," and Paul proceeds to mention the altar "to the unknown god" as an example. He compliments them, not condemns them.

We are also his offspring is found in two Greek poets, Aratus and Cleanthes.

The Areopagite. A member of the great Athenian council meeting on the Areopagus. No one could be a member unless he had held some high office and passed the age of sixty.

Aquila and Priscilla became staunch Christians and energetic workers for the church. They later lived in Ephesus (I Cor. 16:19), where their house was a meeting place for the church.

Unto John's baptism. This shows that the hope of the Messiah which John preached had gone out even farther than the teaching of Jesus.

Brought their books together. Books of magic, charms, and incantations.

Fifty thousand pieces of silver. More than ten thousand dollars.

Silver shrines for Diana. Better, "shrines of Diana." One of the famous things in Ephesus was the temple of Diana, containing an image which tradition said came down from Jupiter. Many pilgrims visited the temple, and silversmiths made models of the temple and the image for sale to them. Demetrius is afraid that Paul will spoil this trade, and raises a mob against him. The story which follows is a fine example of the hopeless confusion of mob rule.

Town clerk. A high officer, through whom communications passed between the city and the government of the empire. If inquiry about this mob were made from Rome, he would have to answer.

Tarried for us. Once before in this book the first person has been used, in the account of the journey of Paul from Troas to Philippi; then it is dropped when Paul went on from Philippi. After many years Paul again comes to Philippi, and when he leaves, the narrative again uses "we," which continues to Jerusalem. Evidently some one who later wrote out the story joined Paul's party at Troas and went to Philippi, then dropped out and now joined Paul's party again and went with them to Jerusalem. It is usually thought that this unknown companion of Paul was Luke, the writer of Acts and the Gospel of Luke, and that on these travels he gained in part his knowledge of Paul's missionary journeys. The "we passages," as they are called, are also found in the account of Paul's voyage to Rome, Acts 27; 28. The writer was of Paul's party on that eventful journey.

Sailed to Assos. What follows gives a list of the ports of call of ancient shipping down the Ægean; a route full of historic memories of the great days of Greece.

Finished our course. Revised Version, "our voyage." They landed finally at Ptolemais, the ancient Accho, the modern Acre, a little north of Mount Carmel.

Took up our carriages. Modern English, "baggage," as in the Revised Version. When the Authorized Version was made, "carriages" were things carried.

An old disciple. A convert in the early days of Christianity.

Be at charges. Pay the costs of the sacrifices at the close of the period of the vow.

The chief captain of the band. The officer commanding the Roman garrison in the Castle of Antonia, overlooking the temple from the north.

In the Hebrew tongue. The language of the Hebrew people, which was not the ancient Hebrew of the Old Testament, but Aramaic, a related language.

Contrary to the law. Because Paul had not as yet been condemned of crime.

Felix. The Roman governor of Judea.

Having understood that he was a Roman. Lysias twists the facts a little in his own favor.

The chief captain Lysias . . . with great violence. The council for the plaintiff twists the facts a little against Lysias.

Drusilla. Of the family of Herod, sister of Herod Agrippa II and of Bernice, mentioned later.

Festus, a Roman who was sent to succeed Felix. He was a better man, but died after two years.

I appeal unto Cæsar. Paul had been kept in prison for two years without being brought to trial. Further delay was useless,

ST. PAUL AT WRITING DESK
A painting by Rembrandt van Rijn

and he exercised the right of a Roman citizen to demand trial before the emperor. There was nothing else to do but to send him to Rome.

Agrippa. Herod Agrippa II, the ruler of a section of country northeast of Palestine.

Almost thou persuadest me to be a Christian. Revised Version, "With but little persuasion thou wouldst fain make me a Christian." These words may be a sneer at Paul and the Christians.

Myra. Here, about three centuries later, lived Bishop Nicholas, famed for generosity, who became St. Nicholas, the Santa Claus of Christmas.

The fast. The Jewish day of Atonement. This marks the voyage as being in September or early October, when the period of storms was near.

To come by the boat. Modern English, "to secure the boat," as in Revised Version. The boat, usually towed, was hauled on board, though with difficulty.

The quicksands. The Syrtis, a dangerous sand-bank on the African shore.

In Adria. That part of the Mediterranean between Greece, Italy and Africa; not the present Adriatic Sea.

Melita. Malta.

Barbarous. Not "savage" or "uncivilized," but, "not speaking either Greek or Latin."

Fetched a compass. "Made a circuit," the wind not allowing direct sailing.

Rhegium. The modern Reggio, on the Italian side of the Straits of Messina.

Puteoli. In the Bay of Naples, at that time the chief port of Rome for vessels from the south.

Two whole years. During these years Paul probably wrote Colossians, Ephesians, Philemon, and Philippians. He received messages from his churches and aid from friends and made some converts even among the Roman soldiers. What happened at the end of the two years we do not know. Tradition said that he was freed in 66 A.D., traveled in the east again, was once more arrested and was martyred in Rome in 68 A.D. Whatever his end, he was one of the world's greatest heroes.

The Letters of Paul, the Great Captain of the New Faith

THE letters of the apostle came into being for much the same reason which caused the writing of the Gospels. Paul was primarily a man of action. He was never so happy as when he was on the sea, on the great military roads of the empire, bringing the good news of salvation through Jesus and the resurrection from the dead to new people, in far-away lands. He went about like a conqueror, establishing new posts far in the enemies' country, preaching Christ in remote cities and provinces.

He was the apostle to the Gentiles, and this very fact made his work perplexing and difficult. The Gentiles who became his converts were the products of paganism. They had been brought up in the atmosphere of paganism. They had been worshipers at the temples of the gods; their standard of morals was different from that of the new faith. These people knew nothing about the Old Testament and the long history of faith which preceded the coming of Jesus. We can hardly imagine how great was the gulf between the pagan faith and the Christian faith. The position of the woman and the slave was pitiful in the extreme. "In the temple of Aphrodite at Corinth, there were a thousand women slaves dedicated to the goddess. The priests of the goddess owned them, and received the wages of their shame." There were fine souls like Socrates and Plato, but they were few and far between. It was the task of Paul, and it was the greatest task a soul ever undertook, to bring these Gentile Christians into the knowledge and practice of faith in Jesus Christ, to break down the "middle wall of partition," as he calls it, between Jew and Gentile. Another great task was to reconcile the Jewish convert to the Gentile, to teach to the world the great Christian doctrine of complete equality and freedom, that there can be in Christ "neither Jew nor Greek, neither bond nor free, neither male nor female."

Paul founded a church at some point, filled its members with his own great enthusiasm, and went on to a new field. He found, to his distress, that after he had gone, the enthusiasm waned; the Gentiles, to some extent, resumed their old pagan customs; strife broke out between factions. To correct these abuses, to impart instruction, to rebuke sternly the evildoers, to give a new vision of love and devotion to Jesus,—this was his purpose in writing the

series of letters which are included in the
New Testament.

There are two elements in these letters;
one is concerned with disputes and abuses
which may not now even exist. It is difficult for us to understand and appreciate these
passages. But after Paul has rebuked his
converts, he often breaks out into a strain
of impassioned and splendid eloquence, rising to flights of poetic fervor which are for all
time. We may find them, perhaps, even
more inspiring than did the members of the
churches of Corinth and Galatia.

Like the Gospels, these epistles were
written on papyrus. It is believed that most
of Paul's letters were dictated. It is thought
that the "infirmity of the flesh," from which
Paul always suffered, was perhaps a defect
in eye-sight. It would be natural, then, for
some friend who was a good penman and
perhaps a stenographer, for good short-
hand systems were in vogue then, to act
as secretary. He would take down Paul's
words, we will say, in short-hand, then make
a fair copy or several copies, and bring them
back for Paul to sign, and add his personal
greeting. The Epistle to the Romans was
written evidently by Tertius, who sends his
own personal salutation: "I, Tertius, who
wrote this epistle, salute you in the Lord."
—Romans 16:22; 7:178.

Then the epistle would be sent by some
traveler to its destination. It would be a

great day for the church at Philippi, at Thessalonica, at Ephesus, when a letter came from Paul! It would be eagerly read and discussed. Copies would be made for individuals and for other churches, and so the New Testament would gradually come into being. It is supposed that Paul wrote other letters, perhaps many others, which have not been preserved. The papyrus on which they were written was very frail and easily destroyed. Even the more enduring parchment of later days was only less fragile. Fire, weather, confiscation by enemies, all conspired against any possibility of our recovering the original documents. The same is true of the classics. Many of the most valuable works of the Greek dramatists have actually perished; not a fragment remains; or in some cases only a few verses. It is a fact, however, that we possess manuscripts of the New Testament which are older, nearer the source, than those of any of the classics.

It is of the utmost importance to keep one thing constantly in view in studying the Epistles. Paul was intensely practical. He was writing for the needs of his time, of his own people. Some of the problems of which he wrote most earnestly have disappeared, even his vocabulary sometimes seems strange to us. At first sight "meat offered to idols," may no longer be a problem, although the principles connected with such problems are the same at all times. Paul gave inspired advice as to applying ethical principles to certain conditions: as to head covering in the churches, getting married when persecution seemed certain, or when the immediate urgency of the missionary task was overwhelming. In general Paul gave to Christians this practical advice: do nothing which might in any way hinder the progress of the gospel. But Paul also laid down the great principles of absolute equality before God. There is no distinction, he said, between man and woman, Jew or Gentile, bond or free. All are one in Christ Jesus. Many of the sins which Paul denounced are sins of today: the vulgar sins of sensuality and lust, avarice, selfishness, the worship of false gods. It does not take away from the inspiration or the universality or the validity of the Epistles to remember that they were written first for the little churches of Galatia and Thessalonica and Corinth and then for humanity in all places and in all times.

These Pauline Epistles develop the great truths of the teachings of Christ given to us in the four Gospels. In a very real sense they are commentaries on the Saviour's personal teachings, and of redemption through His death and resurrection.

The Letters of Paul

The Great Captain of the New Faith

The Epistle to the Romans

I am not ashamed of the gospel of Christ; for it is the power of God unto salvation.

Paul had all the instincts of a great statesman and a great military commander. He chose with unerring judgment the strategic points, the centers from which Christianity would quickly spread to the surrounding country. Rome was the greatest of all these centers: "All roads lead to Rome." The eagles of her imperial legions flew to the outermost bounds of civilization. A church at Rome must necessarily possess a commanding influence. The little churches, far away in remote lands, on the shores of alien seas, would look up to the church in the imperial capital for guidance and direction. It was of supreme importance then that Paul, the apostle to the Gentiles, should visit Rome, should have a great concern for the proper instruction and guidance of the metropolitan church.

No one knows who founded the church at Rome. However, it is more important to learn how the church of Rome grew. Like seeds blown upon the wind the followers of "The Way" were scattered over all the empire. The same roads which were built for the movements of the legions and the caravans of commerce helped the pioneers of Jesus on their journeys. There were many Jews in Rome. Very early, perhaps, the seed took root and became speedily a flowering vine. Many of the Roman Christians were known to Paul. He wrote this great epistle to the church to prepare the way for his coming. It is naturally not so personal and intimate and affectionate as the letters to the churches which he had himself visited. It is more like a state document. "It is a grand summary of the doctrine and practise of Christianity."

On the argumentative and doctrinal side it reaches the highest point of Paul's inspired teaching. It is courteous, tactful, but none

159

the less authoritative. At first reading we may not always understand the arguments of Paul, which occasionally seem long and involved. For the persistent and faithful student, however, the study of this epistle brings its own rich and abundant reward.

His style has been compared to that of Oliver Cromwell. "Nowhere perhaps will there be found so exact a parallel to the style of Paul as in the Letters and Speeches of Oliver Cromwell. In the Protector's brain there lay the best and truest thoughts about England and her complicated affairs which existed at the time in these islands; but, when he tried to express them in speech or letter, there issued from his mind the most extraordinary mixture of exclamations, questions, arguments soon losing themselves in the sands of words, unwieldy parentheses, and morsels of beautiful pathos or subduing eloquence. Yet, as you read these amazing utterances, you come by degrees to feel that you are getting to see the very heart and soul of the Puritan Era, and that you would rather be beside this man than any other representative of the period."—*James Stalker*.

The style is only occasionally involved. In many places it is clear as crystal, as exquisite as a product of the goldsmith's art. When we remember the many responsibilities and burdens of the apostle to the Gentiles; when we realize that these letters were dictated extemporaneously to an amanuensis, the wonder of the lucid and beautiful periods grows. Like the other epistles, the letter to the Romans is full of sublime passages. There is no more noble utterance even in Corinthians than that great eighth chapter from beginning to end like organ music, opening with the words, "There is therefore now no condemnation to them which are in Christ Jesus," and closing with that magnificent finale, "For I am persuaded, that neither death, nor life, nor angels, nor principalities, nor powers, nor things present, nor things to come, nor height, nor depth, nor any other creature, shall be able to separate us from the love of God, which is in Christ Jesus our Lord."

The main epistle closes with the fifteenth chapter. The sixteenth is very interesting indeed. It is a little letter of recommendation to Phebe. It has been inferred that she was a wealthy widow of Cenchrea, who was going to Rome on business. It is interesting to conjecture how it all came about. Cenchrea is the eastern port of Corinth. Phebe was a member of the church there, a church which Paul must have visited often, of which he was, doubtless, the founder.

He had been entertained at her house. She told him of her intended journey to the great capital. "Well, Phebe," he would say, "I will give you a letter of recommendation to the friends at Rome; and perhaps you will take a letter which I am writing now to the church at Rome." So this letter with its many salutations came to be joined to the great epistle which Phebe brought to Rome. This is characteristic of the Christian church, of the life of Jesus, and the life of Paul. The most sublime moments are closely joined to the every-day life and business of humanity.

Paul, a servant of Jesus Christ, called to be an apostle, separated unto the gospel of God, (which he had promised afore by his prophets in the Holy Scriptures,) concerning his Son Jesus Christ our Lord, which was made of the seed of David according to the flesh; and declared to be the Son of God with power, according to the spirit of holiness, by the resurrection from the dead: by whom we have received grace and apostleship, for obedience to the faith among all nations, for his name: among whom are ye also the called of Jesus Christ:

To all that be in Rome, beloved of God, called to be saints: Grace to you and peace from God our Father, and the Lord Jesus Christ.

"As Much as in Me Is, I Am Ready to Preach the Gospel to You That Are at Rome Also"

FIRST, I thank my God through Jesus Christ for you all, that your faith is spoken of throughout the whole world. For God is my witness, whom I serve with my spirit in the gospel of his Son, that without ceasing I make mention of you always in my prayers; making request, if by any means now at length I might have a prosperous journey by the will of God to come unto you. For I long to see you,

that I may impart unto you some spiritual gift, to the end ye may be established; that is, that I may be comforted together with you by the mutual faith both of you and me. Now I would not have you ignorant, brethren, that oftentimes I purposed to come unto you, (but was let hitherto,) that I might have some fruit among you also, even as among other Gentiles.

I am debtor both to the Greeks, and to the Barbarians; both to the wise, and to the unwise. So, as much as in me is, I am ready to preach the gospel to you that are at Rome also. — Romans 1:1-15.

SALVATION THROUGH THE GOSPEL OF CHRIST

For I am not ashamed of the gospel of Christ: for it is the power of God unto salvation to every one that believeth; to the Jew first, and also to the Greek. For therein is the righteousness of God revealed from faith to faith: as it is written, "The just shall live by faith." — Romans 1:16, 17.

"UNGODLINESS OF MEN"

For the wrath of God is revealed from heaven against all ungodliness and unrighteousness of men, who hold the truth in unrighteousness; because that which may be known of God is manifest in them; for God hath showed it unto them. For the invisible things of him from the creation of the world are clearly seen, being understood by the things that are made, even his eternal power and Godhead; so that they are without excuse: because that, when they knew God, they glorified him not as God, neither were thankful; but became vain in their imaginations, and their foolish heart was darkened. Professing themselves to be wise, they became fools, and changed the glory of the uncorruptible God into an image

INTERIOR OF THE COLISEUM

made like to corruptible man, and to birds, and fourfooted beasts, and creeping things. Wherefore God also gave them up to uncleanness through the lusts of their own hearts, to dishonour their own bodies between themselves: who changed the truth of God into a lie, and worshiped and served the creature more than the Creator, who is blessed forever. Amen.

For this cause God gave them up unto vile affections: for even their women did change the natural use into that which is against nature: and likewise also the men, leaving the natural use of the woman, burned in their lust one toward another; men with men working that which is unseemly, and receiving in themselves that recompence of their error which was meet. And even as they did not like to retain God in their knowledge, God gave them over to a reprobate mind, to do those things which are not convenient; being filled with all unrighteousness, fornication, wickedness, covetousness, maliciousness; full of envy, murder, debate, deceit, malignity; whisperers, backbiters, haters of God, despiteful, proud, boasters, inventors of evil things, disobedient to parents, without understanding, covenantbreakers, without natural affection, implacable, unmerciful: who knowing the judgment of God, that they which commit such things are worthy of death, not only do the same, but have pleasure in them that do them. — Romans 1:18–32.

"THE JUDGMENT OF GOD IS ACCORDING TO TRUTH"

Therefore thou art inexcusable, O man, whosoever thou are that judgest: for wherein thou judgest another, thou condemnest thyself; for thou that judgest doest the same things. But we are sure that the judgment of God is according to truth against them which commit such things. And thinkest thou this, O man, that judgest them

which do such things, and doest the same, that thou shalt
escape the judgment of God?   Or despisest thou the
riches of his goodness and forbearance and longsuffering;
not knowing that the goodness of God leadeth thee to
repentance?   But after thy hardness and impenitent
heart treasurest up unto thyself wrath against the day of
wrath and revelation of the righteous judgment of God;
who will render to every man according to his deeds: to
them who by patient continuance in well doing seek for
glory and honour and immortality, eternal life: but unto
them that are contentious, and do not obey the truth,
but obey unrighteousness, indignation, and wrath, tribulation and anguish, upon every soul of man that doeth evil,
of the Jew first, and also of the Gentile; but glory, honour,
and peace, to every man that worketh good, to the Jew
first, and also to the Gentile.   — Romans 2:1-10.

"THERE IS NO RESPECT OF PERSONS WITH GOD"

For there is no respect of persons with God. For as many
as have sinned without law shall also perish without law:
and as many as have sinned in the law shall be judged
by the law; (for not the hearers of the law are just before
God, but the doers of the law shall be justified.   For
when the Gentiles, which have not the law, do by nature
the things contained in the law, these, having not the
law, are a law unto themselves: which show the work of
the law written in their hearts, their conscience also bearing witness, and their thoughts the meanwhile accusing
or else excusing one another;) in the day when God shall
judge the secrets of men by Jesus Christ according to
my gospel.

Behold, thou art called a Jew, and restest in the law,
and makest thy boast of God, and knowest his will, and
approvest the things that are more excellent, being

instructed out of the law; and art confident that thou thyself art a guide of the blind, a light of them which are in darkness, and instructor of the foolish, a teacher of babes, which hast the form of knowledge and of the truth in the law. Thou therefore which teachest another, teachest thou not thyself? Thou that preachest a man should not steal, dost thou steal? Thou that sayest a man should not commit adultery, dost thou commit adultery? Thou that abhorrest idols, dost thou commit sacrilege? Thou that makest thy boast of the law, through breaking the law dishonourest thou God? For the name of God is blasphemed among the Gentiles through you, as it is written. For circumcision verily profiteth, if thou keep the law: but if thou be a breaker of the law, thy circumcision is made uncircumcision. Therefore if the uncircumcision keep the righteousness of the law, shall not his uncircumcision be counted for circumcision? And shall not uncircumcision which is by nature, if it fulfil the law, judge thee, who by the letter and circumcision dost transgress the law? For he is not a Jew, which is one outwardly; neither is that circumcision, which is outward in the flesh: but he is a Jew, which is one inwardly; and circumcision is that of the heart, in the spirit, and not in the letter; whose praise is not of men, but of God. — Romans 2:11–29.

THE ADVANTAGE OF THE JEW: IS HE THE GOD OF THE JEWS ONLY?

What advantage then hath the Jew? or what profit is there of circumcision? Much every way: chiefly, because that unto them were committed the oracles of God. For what if some did not believe? Shall their unbelief make the faith of God without effect? God forbid: yea, let God be true, but every man a liar; as it is written,

THE APPIAN WAY LEADING INTO ROME

"That thou mightest be justified in thy sayings,
    And mightest overcome when thou art judged."

But if our unrighteousness commend the righteousness
of God, what shall we say? Is God unrighteous who
taketh vengeance? (I speak as a man.) God forbid: for
then how shall God judge the world? For if the truth
of God hath more abounded through my lie unto his
glory; why yet am I also judged as a sinner? And not
rather, (as we be slanderously reported, and as some
affirm that we say,) let us do evil, that good may come?
whose damnation is just.

What then? Are we better than they? No, in no
wise: for we have before proved both Jews and Gentiles, that they are all under sin; as it is written,

"There is none righteous, no, not one:
    There is none that understandeth,
    There is none that seeketh after God.
    They are all gone out of the way, they are together
        become unprofitable;
    There is none that doeth good, no, not one.
    Their throat is an open sepulcher;
    With their tongues they have used deceit;
    The poison of asps is under their lips:
    Whose mouth is full of cursing and bitterness:
    Their feet are swift to shed blood:
    Destruction and misery are in their ways:
    And the way of peace have they not known:
    There is no fear of God before their eyes."

Now we know that what things soever the law saith,
it saith to them who are under the law: that every
mouth may be stopped, and all the world may become
guilty before God. Therefore by the deeds of the law

there shall no flesh be justified in his sight: for by the law is the knowledge of sin. — Romans 3:1-20.

"ALL HAVE SINNED AND COME SHORT OF THE GLORY OF GOD"

But now the righteousness of God without the law is manifested, being witnessed by the law and the prophets; even the righteousness of God which is by faith of Jesus Christ unto all and upon all them that believe: for there is no difference: for all have sinned, and come short of the glory of God; being justified freely by his grace through the redemption that is in Christ Jesus: whom God hath set forth to be a propitiation through faith in his blood, to declare his righteousness for the remission of sins that are past, through the forbearance of God; to declare, I say, at this time his righteousness: that he might be just, and the justifier of him which believeth in Jesus. Where is boasting then? It is excluded. By what law? Of works? Nay: but by the law of faith. Therefore we conclude that a man is justified by faith without the deeds of the law. Is he the God of the Jews only? Is he not also of the Gentiles? Yes, of the Gentiles also: seeing it is one God, which shall justify the circumcision by faith, and uncircumcision through faith. Do we then make void the law through faith? God forbid: yea, we establish the law. — Romans 3:21-31.

"ABRAHAM BELIEVED GOD, AND IT WAS COUNTED UNTO HIM FOR RIGHTEOUSNESS"

What shall we say then that Abraham, our father, as pertaining to the flesh, hath found? For if Abraham were justified by works, he hath whereof to glory; but not before God. For what saith the Scripture? Abraham

believed God, and it was counted unto him for righteousness. Now to him that worketh is the reward not reckoned of grace, but of debt. But to him that worketh not, but believeth on him that justifieth the ungodly, his faith is counted for righteousness. Even as David also describeth the blessedness of the man, unto whom God imputeth righteousness without works, saying,

"Blessed are they whose iniquities are forgiven,
And whose sins are covered.
Blessed is the man to whom the LORD will not impute
sin."

Cometh this blessedness then upon the circumcision only, or upon the uncircumcision also? For we say that faith was reckoned to Abraham for righteousness. How was it then reckoned? When he was in circumcision, or in uncircumcision? Not in circumcision, but in uncircumcision. And he received the sign of circumcision, a seal of the righteousness of the faith which he had yet being uncircumcised: that he might be the father of all them that believe, though they be not circumcised: that righteousness might be imputed unto them also: and the father of circumcision to them who are not of the circumcision only, but who also walk in the steps of that faith of our father Abraham, which he had being yet uncircumcised. For the promise, that he should be the heir of the world, was not to Abraham, or to his seed, through the law, but through the righteousness of faith. For if they which are of the law be heirs, faith is made void, and the promise made of none effect: because the law worketh wrath: for where no law is, there is no transgression. Therefore it is of faith, that it might be by grace; to the end the promise might be sure to all the seed; not to that only which is of the law, but to that also which is of the faith of Abraham; who is the father of us all, (as it is written, "I have made thee a father of many nations,") before him whom he believed, even God, who quickeneth the dead, and calleth those things which be not as though they were; who against hope believed in hope, that he might become the father of many nations, according to that which was spoken, "So shall thy seed be." And being not weak in faith, he considered not his own body now dead, when he was about an hundred years old, neither yet the deadness of Sarah's womb; he staggered not at the promise of God through unbelief; but was strong in faith, giving glory to God; and being fully persuaded that, what he had promised, he was able also to perform. And therefore it was imputed to him for righteousness. Now it was not written for his sake alone, that it was imputed to him; but also for us, to whom it shall be imputed, if we believe on him that raised up Jesus our Lord from the dead; who was delivered for our offences, and was raised again for our justification.

— Romans 4.

"BEING JUSTIFIED BY FAITH, WE HAVE PEACE WITH GOD THROUGH OUR LORD JESUS CHRIST"

Therefore being justified by faith, we have peace with God through our Lord Jesus Christ: by whom also we have access by faith into this grace wherein we stand, and rejoice in hope of the glory of God. And not only so, but we glory in tribulations also: knowing that tribulation worketh patience; and patience, experience; and experience, hope: and hope maketh not ashamed; because the love of God is shed abroad in our hearts by the Holy Ghost which is given unto us. For when we were yet without strength, in due time Christ died for the ungodly. For scarcely for a righteous man will one die: yet peradventure for a good man some one would even dare to die. But God commendeth his love toward us, in that, while we were yet sinners, Christ died for us. Much more then, being now justified by his blood, we shall be saved from wrath through him. For if, when we were enemies, we were reconciled to God by the death of his Son, much more, being reconciled, we shall be saved by his life. And not only so, but we also joy in God through our Lord Jesus Christ, by whom we have now received the atonement.

Wherefore, as by one man sin entered into the world, and death by sin; and so death passed upon all men, for that all have sinned: (for until the law sin was in the world: but sin is not imputed when there is no law. Nevertheless death reigned from Adam to Moses, even over them that had not sinned after the similitude of Adam's transgression, who is the figure of him that was to come. But not as the offence, so also is the free gift. For if through the offence of one many be dead, much more the grace of God, and the gift by grace, which is by one man, Jesus Christ, hath abounded unto many. And not as it was by one that sinned, so is the gift: for the judgment was by one to condemnation, but the free gift is of many offences unto justification. For if by one man's offence death reigned by one; much more they which receive abundance of grace and of the gift of righteousness shall reign in life by one, Jesus Christ.) Therefore as by the offence of one, judgment came upon all men to condemnation; even so by the righteousness of one, the free gift came upon all men unto justification of life. For as by one man's disobedience many were made sinners, so by the obedience of one shall many be made righteous. Moreover the law entered, that the offence might abound. But where sin abounded,

grace did much more abound: that as sin hath reigned unto death, even so might grace reign through righteousness unto eternal life by Jesus Christ our Lord.

— Romans 5.

"IF WE ARE DEAD WITH CHRIST WE SHALL ALSO LIVE WITH HIM"

What shall we say then? Shall we continue in sin, that grace may abound? God forbid. How shall we, that are dead to sin, live any longer therein? Know ye not, that so many of us as were baptized into Jesus Christ were baptized into his death? Therefore we are buried with him by baptism into death: that like as Christ was raised up from the dead by the glory of the Father, even so we also should walk in newness of life. For if we have been planted together in the likeness of his death, we shall be also in the likeness of his resurrection: knowing this, that our old man is crucified with him, that the body of sin might be destroyed, that henceforth we should not serve sin. For he that is dead is freed from sin. Now if we be dead with Christ, we believe that we shall also live with him: knowing that Christ being raised from the dead dieth no more; death hath no more dominion over him. For in that he died, he died unto sin once: but in that he liveth, he liveth unto God. Likewise reckon ye also yourselves to be dead indeed unto sin, but alive unto God through Jesus Christ our Lord. Let not sin therefore reign in your mortal body, that ye should obey it in the lusts thereof. Neither yield ye your members as instruments of unrighteousness unto sin: but yield yourselves unto God, as those that are alive from the dead, and your members as instruments of righteousness unto God. For sin shall not have dominion over you: for ye are not under the law, but under grace.

THE ARCH OF DRUSUS, ROME

What then? Shall we sin, because we are not under the law, but under grace? God forbid. Know ye not, that to whom ye yield yourselves servants to obey, his servants ye are to whom ye obey; whether of sin unto death, or of obedience unto righteousness? But God be thanked, that ye were the servants of sin, but ye have obeyed from the heart that form of doctrine which was delivered you. Being then made free from sin, ye became the servants of righteousness. I speak after the manner of men because of the infirmity of your flesh: for as ye have yielded your members servants to uncleanness and to iniquity unto iniquity; even so now yield your members servants to righteousness unto holiness. For when ye were the servants of sin, ye were free from righteousness. What fruit had ye then in those things whereof ye are now ashamed? For the end of those things is death. But now being made free from sin, and become servants to God, ye have your fruit unto holiness, and the end everlasting life. For the wages of sin is death; but the gift of God is eternal life through Jesus Christ our Lord. — Romans 6.

"SERVE IN NEWNESS OF SPIRIT, NOT IN THE OLDNESS OF LETTER"

Know ye not, brethren, (for I speak to them that know the law,) how that the law hath dominion over a man as long as he liveth? For the woman which hath an husband is bound by the law to her husband so long as he liveth; but if the husband be dead, she is loosed from the law of her husband. So then if, while her husband liveth, she be married to another man, she shall be called an adulteress: but if her husband be dead, she is free from that law; so that she is no adulteress, though she be married to another man. Wherefore, my brethren, ye also are become dead to the law by the body of Christ; that ye should be married to another, even to him who is raised from the dead, that we should bring forth fruit unto God. For when we were in the flesh, the motions of sins, which were by the law, did work in our members to bring forth fruit unto death. But now we are delivered from the law, that being dead wherein we were held; that we should serve in newness of spirit, and not in the oldness of the letter.

What shall we say then? Is the law sin? God forbid. Nay, I had not known sin, but by the law: for I had not known lust, except the law had said, "Thou shalt not covet." But sin, taking occasion by the commandment, wrought in me all manner of concupiscence. For without the law sin was dead. For I was alive without the law once: but when the commandment came, sin revived, and I died. And the commandment, which was ordained to life, I found to be unto death. For sin, taking occasion by the commandment, deceived me, and by it slew me. Wherefore the law is holy, and the commandment holy, and just, and good. Was then that which is good made death unto me? God forbid. But sin, that it might appear sin, working death in me by that which is good; that sin by the commandment might become exceeding sinful. — Romans 7:1–13.

THE STRUGGLE OF THE TWO FORCES, GOOD AND EVIL, FOR THE POSSESSION OF THE SOUL

For we know that the law is spiritual: but I am carnal, sold under sin. For that which I do I allow not: for that I would, that do I not; but what I hate, that do I. If then I do that which I would not, I consent unto the law that it is good. Now then it is no more I that do it, but sin that dwelleth in me. For I know that in me (that is,

in my flesh,) dwelleth no good thing: for to will is present with me; but how to perform that which is good I find not. For the good that I would I do not: but the evil which I would not, that I do. Now if I do that I would not, it is no more I that do it, but sin that dwelleth in me. I find then a law, that, when I would do good, evil is present with me. For I delight in the law of God after the inward man: but I see another law in my members, warring against the law of my mind, and bringing me into captivity to the law of sin which is in my members. O wretched man that I am! Who shall deliver me from the body of this death? I thank God through Jesus Christ our Lord. So then with the mind I myself serve the law of God; but with the flesh the law of sin.

—Romans 7:14–25.

"THERE IS NO CONDEMNATION TO THOSE WHO WALK AFTER THE SPIRIT"

There is therefore now no condemnation to them which are in Christ Jesus, who walk not after the flesh but after the Spirit. For the law of the Spirit of life in Christ Jesus hath made me free from the law of sin and death. For what the law could not do, in that it was weak through the flesh, God sending his own Son in the likeness of sinful flesh, and for sin, condemned sin in the flesh: that the righteousness of the law might be fulfilled in us, who walk not after the flesh, but after the Spirit. For they that are after the flesh do mind the things of the flesh; but they that are after the Spirit the things of the Spirit. For to be carnally minded is death; but to be spiritually minded is life and peace. Because the carnal mind is enmity against God: for it is not subject to the law of God, neither indeed can be. So then they that are in the flesh cannot please God. But

ROMAN CHARIOT
An engraving by Gustaf Zerner

ye are not in the flesh, but in the Spirit, if so be that the Spirit of God dwell in you. Now if any man have not the Spirit of Christ, he is none of his. And if Christ be in you, the body is dead because of sin; but the Spirit is life because of righteousness. But if the Spirit of him that raised up Jesus from the dead dwell in you, he that raised up Christ from the dead shall also quicken your mortal bodies by his Spirit that dwelleth in you.

Therefore, brethren, we are debtors, not to the flesh, to live after the flesh. For if ye live after the flesh, ye shall die: but if ye through the Spirit do mortify the deeds of the body, ye shall live. For as many as are led by the Spirit of God, they are the sons of God. For ye have not received the spirit of bondage again to fear; but ye have received the Spirit of adoption, whereby we cry, "Abba, Father."   — Romans 8:1-15.

WE ARE SONS OF GOD AND JOINT-HEIRS WITH CHRIST

The Spirit itself beareth witness with our spirit, that we are the children of God: and if children, then heirs; heirs of God, and joint-heirs with Christ; if so be that we suffer with him, that we may be also glorified together.

For I reckon that the sufferings of this present time are not worthy to be compared with the glory which shall be revealed in us. For the earnest expectation of the creature waiteth for the manifestation of the sons of God. For the creature was made subject to vanity, not willingly, but by reason of him who hath subjected the same in hope, because the creature itself also shall be delivered from the bondage of corruption into the glorious liberty of the children of God. For we know that the whole creation groaneth and travaileth in pain together until now. And not only they, but ourselves also, which have the firstfruits of the Spirit, even we ourselves groan within

CONVERSION OF PAUL
A painting by Peter Paul Rubens

ourselves, waiting for the adoption, to wit, the redemption of our body. For we are saved by hope: but hope that is seen, is not hope: for what a man seeth, why doth he yet hope for? But if we hope for that we see not, then do we with patience wait for it.

Likewise the Spirit also helpeth our infirmities: for we know not what we should pray for as we ought: but the Spirit itself maketh intercession for us with groanings which cannot be uttered. And he that searcheth the hearts knoweth what is the mind of the Spirit, because he maketh intercession for the saints according to the will of God. And we know that all things work together for good to them that love God, to them who are the called according to his purpose. For whom he did foreknow, he also did predestinate to be conformed to the image of his Son, that he might be the firstborn among many brethren. Moreover whom he did predestinate, them he also called: and whom he called, them he also justified: and whom he justified, them he also glorified.

What shall we then say to these things? If God be for us, who can be against us? He that spared not his own Son, but delivered him up for us all, how shall he not with him also freely give us all things? Who shall lay any thing to the charge of God's elect? It is God that justifieth. Who is he that condemneth? It is Christ that died, yea rather, that is risen again, who is even at the right hand of God, who also maketh intercession for us.
— Romans 8:16–34.

"WHO SHALL SEPARATE US FROM THE LOVE OF CHRIST?"

Who shall separate us from the love of Christ? Shall tribulation, or distress, or persecution, or famine, or nakedness, or peril, or sword? As it is written,

"For thy sake we are killed all the day long;
We are accounted as sheep for the slaughter."

Nay in all these things we are more than conquerors through him that loved us. For I am persuaded, that neither death, nor life, nor angels, nor principalities, nor powers, nor things present, nor things to come, nor height, nor depth, nor any other creature, shall be able to separate us from the love of God, which is in Christ Jesus our Lord.   —Romans 8:35–39.

God's Relations with the Jews
"I could wish myself accursed for my brethren"

I say the truth in Christ, I lie not, my conscience also bearing me witness in the Holy Ghost, that I have great heaviness and continual sorrow in my heart. For I could wish that myself were accursed from Christ for my brethren, my kinsmen according to the flesh: who are Israelites; to whom pertaineth the adoption, and the glory, and the covenants, and the giving of the law, and the service of God, and the promises; whose are the fathers, and of whom as concerning the flesh Christ came, who is over all, God blessed forever.   Amen.   —Romans 9:1-5.

"Is there unrighteousness with God? God forbid"

Not as though the word of God hath taken none effect. For they are not all Israel, which are of Israel: neither, because they are the seed of Abraham, are they all children: but "In Isaac shall thy seed be called." That is, they which are the children of the flesh, these are not the children of God: but the children of the promise are counted for the seed. For this is the word of promise, "At this time will I come, and Sarah shall have a son." And not only this; but when Rebecca also had conceived by one, even by our father Isaac; (for the children being not yet born, neither having done any good or evil, that the purpose of God, according to election might stand,

Head of Hermes

Photograph by Alinari Brothers, Florence, Italy

THIS statue, which is called by some "probably the most beautiful statue in the world," was discovered on the Esquiline Hill in Rome. It was formerly called the "Belvedere Antinous." It is probably a copy of a Greek original by Praxiteles of the 4th Century. It has not been injured by restoration, but was broken across the ankles when found and has been unskillfully put together. A French critic has called this the most perfectly proportioned statue of the human body in the world.

not of works, but of him that calleth;) it was said unto her, "The elder shall serve the younger." As it is written, "Jacob have I loved, but Esau have I hated."

What shall we say then? Is there unrighteousness with God? God forbid. For he saith to Moses, "I will have mercy on whom I will have mercy, and I will have compassion on whom I will have compassion." So then it is not of him that willeth, nor of him that runneth, but of God that showeth mercy. For the Scripture saith unto Pharaoh, "Even for this same purpose have I raised thee up, that I might show my power in thee, and that my name might be declared throughout all the earth." Therefore hath he mercy on whom he will have mercy, and whom he will he hardeneth.

Thou wilt say then unto me, "Why doth he yet find fault? For who hath resisted his will?"

Nay but, O man, who art thou that repliest against God? Shall the thing formed say to him that formed it, "Why hast thou made me thus?" Hath not the potter power over the clay, of the same lump to make one vessel unto honour, and another unto dishonour? What if God, willing to shew his wrath, and to make his power known, endured with much longsuffering the vessels of wrath fitted to destruction: and that he might make known the riches of his glory on the vessels of mercy, which he had afore prepared unto glory, even us, whom he hath called, not of the Jews only, but also of the Gentiles? As he saith also in Hosea,

"I will call them my people, which were not my people;
And her beloved, which was not beloved.
And it shall come to pass, that in the place where it
    was said unto them, 'Ye are not my people';
There shall they be called the children of the living
    God."

Esaias also crieth concerning Israel, "Though the number of the children of Israel be as the sand of the sea, a remnant shall be saved: for he will finish the work, and cut it short in righteousness: because a short work will the Lord make upon the earth."

And as Esaias said before,

"Except the Lord of Sabaoth had left us a seed,
We had been as Sodoma, and been made like unto Gomorrha."

What shall we say then? That the Gentiles, which followed not after righteousness, have attained to righteousness, even the righteousness which is of faith. But Israel, which followed after the law of righteousness, hath not attained to the law of righteousness. Wherefore? Because they sought it not by faith, but as it were by the works of the law. For they stumbled at that stumbling-stone; as it is written,

"Behold, I lay in Sion a stumblingstone and rock of offence:
And whosoever believeth on him shall not be ashamed."
— Romans 9:6-33.

"CHRIST IS THE END OF THE LAW"

Brethren, my heart's desire and prayer to God for Israel is, that they might be saved. For I bear them record that they have a zeal of God, but not according to knowledge. For they being ignorant of God's righteousness, and going about to establish their own righteousness, have not submitted themselves unto the righteousness of God. For Christ is the end of the law for righteousness to every one that believeth. For Moses describeth the righteousness which is of the law, that the man which doeth those things shall live by them. But the righteousness which is of faith speaketh on this wise, "Say not in thine heart, 'Who shall ascend into heaven?' (that is, to bring Christ down from above:) or, 'Who shall descend into the deep?' (that is, to bring up Christ again from the dead.)" But what saith it? The word is nigh thee, even in thy mouth, and in thy heart: that is, the word of faith, which we preach; that if thou shalt confess with thy mouth the Lord Jesus, and shalt believe in thine heart that God hath raised him from the dead, thou shalt be saved. For with the heart man believeth unto righteousness; and with the mouth confession is made unto salvation. For the Scripture saith, "Whosoever believeth on him shall not be ashamed." For there is no difference between the Jew and the Greek: for the same Lord over all is rich unto all that call upon him. For whosoever shall call upon the name of the Lord shall be saved. How then shall they call on him in whom they have not believed? And how shall they believe in him of whom they have not heard? And how shall they hear without a preacher? And how shall they preach, except they be sent? as it is written, "How beautiful are the feet of them that preach the gospel of peace, and bring glad tidings of good things!"

But they have not all obeyed the gospel. For Esaias saith, "Lord, who hath believed our report?" So then faith cometh by hearing, and hearing by the word of God. But I say, have they not heard? Yes verily,

"Their sound went into all the earth,
And their words unto the ends of the world."

But I say, Did not Israel know? First Moses saith,

"I will provoke you to jealousy by them
that are no people,
And by a foolish nation I will anger you."

But Esaias is very bold, and saith,

"I was found of them that sought me not;
I was made manifest unto them that asked
not after me."

But to Israel he saith, "All day long I have stretched
forth my hands unto a disobedient and gainsaying
people."

— Romans 10.

GOD HATH NOT CAST AWAY HIS PEOPLE

I say then, hath God cast away his people? God forbid. For I also am an Israelite, of the seed of Abraham, of the tribe of Benjamin. God hath not cast away his people which he foreknew. Wot ye not what the Scripture saith of Elias—how he maketh intercession to God against Israel, saying, "Lord, they have killed thy prophets, and they digged down thine altars; and I am left alone, and they seek my life."

But what saith the answer of God unto him? "I have reserved to myself seven thousand men who have not bowed the knee to the image of Baal." Even so then at this present time also there is a remnant according to the election of grace. And if by grace, then is it no more of works: otherwise grace is no more grace. But if it be of works, then is it no more grace: otherwise work is no more work. What then? Israel hath not obtained that which he seeketh for; but the election hath obtained it, and the rest were blinded (according as it is written, God hath given them the spirit of slumber, eyes that they should not see, and ears that they should not hear;) unto this day. And David saith,

"Let their table be made a snare, and a trap,
And a stumblingblock, and a recompence unto them:

Let their eyes be darkened, that they may not see,
And bow down their back alway."

I say then, have they stumbled that they should fall?
God forbid: but rather through their fall salvation is
come unto the Gentiles, for to provoke them to jealousy.
Now if the fall of them be the riches of the world, and
the diminishing of the riches of the Gentiles; how much
more their fulness?

For I speak to you Gentiles, inasmuch as I am the
apostle of the Gentiles, I magnify mine office: if by any
means I may provoke to emulation them which are my
flesh, and might save some of them. For if the casting
away of them be the reconciling of the world, what shall
the receiving of them be, but life from the dead? For if
the firstfruit be holy, the lump is also holy: and if the
root be holy, so are the branches. And if some of the
branches be broken off, and thou, being a wild olive-tree,
wert grafted in among them, and with them partakest of
the root and fatness of the olive-tree; boast not against
the branches. But if thou boast, thou bearest not the
root, but the root thee. Thou wilt say then, "The branches
were broken off, that I might be grafted in." Well; because of unbelief they were broken off, and thou standest
by faith. Be not highminded, but fear: for if God spared
not the natural branches, take heed lest he also spare not
thee. Behold therefore the goodness and severity of God:
on them which fell, severity; but toward thee, goodness,
if thou continue in his goodness; otherwise thou also shalt
be cut off. And they also, if they abide not still in unbelief, shall be grafted in: for God is able to graft them
in again. For if thou wert cut out of the olive-tree which
is wild by nature, and wert grafted contrary to nature
into a good olive-tree: how much more shall these, which

be the natural branches, be grafted into their own olive-tree?

For I would not, brethren, that ye should be ignorant of this mystery, lest ye should be wise in your own conceits; that blindness in part is happened to Israel, until the fulness of the Gentiles be come in. — Romans 11:1-25.

"ALL ISRAEL SHALL BE SAVED"

And so all Israel shall be saved: as it is written,

"There shall come out of Sion the Deliverer,
And shall turn away ungodliness from Jacob:
For this is my covenant unto them,
When I shall take away their sins."

As concerning the gospel, they are enemies for your sakes: but as touching the election, they are beloved for the fathers' sakes. For the gifts and calling of God are without repentance. For as ye in times past have not believed God, yet have now obtained mercy through their unbelief: even so have these also now not believed, that through your mercy they also may obtain mercy. For God hath concluded them all in unbelief, that he might have mercy upon all.

O the depth of the riches both of the wisdom and knowledge of God! How unsearchable are his judgments, and his ways past finding out! For who hath known the mind of the Lord? Or who hath been his counsellor? Or who hath first given to him, and it shall be recompensed unto him again? For of him, and through him, and to him, are all things: to whom be glory forever. Amen.

— Romans 11:26-36.

Paul Sets Forth the Principles of Human Conduct in the Light of Our Relations to God

"present your bodies a living sacrifice to god"

I beseech you therefore, brethren, by the mercies of God, that ye present your bodies a living sacrifice, holy, acceptable unto God, which is your reasonable service. And be not conformed to this world: but be ye transformed by the renewing of your mind, that ye may prove what is that good, and acceptable, and perfect will of God.   — Romans 12:1, 2.

"we, being many, are one body in christ"

For I say, through the grace given unto me, to every man that is among you, not to think of himself more highly than he ought to think; but to think soberly, according as God hath dealt to every man the measure of faith. For as we have many members in one body, and all members have not the same office: so we, being many, are one body in Christ, and every one members one of another. Having then gifts differing according to the grace that is given to us, whether prophecy, let us prophesy according to the proportion of faith; or ministry, let us wait on our ministering: or he that teacheth, on teaching; or he that exhorteth, on exhortation: he that giveth, let him do it with simplicity; he that ruleth, with diligence; he that showeth mercy, with cheerfulness.
— Romans 12:3–8.

"be kindly affectioned one to another"

Let love be without dissimulation. Abhor that which is evil; cleave to that which is good. Be kindly affectioned one to another with brotherly love; in honour preferring one another; not slothful in business; fervent

in spirit; serving the Lord; rejoicing in hope; patient in tribulation; continuing instant in prayer; distributing to the necessity of saints; given to hospitality. Bless them which persecute you; bless, and curse not. Rejoice with them that do rejoice, and weep with them that weep. Be of the same mind one toward another. Mind not high things, but condescend to men of low estate. Be not wise in your own conceits. Recompense to no man evil for evil. Provide things honest in the sight of all men. If it be possible, as much as lieth in you, live peaceably with all men. Dearly beloved, avenge not yourselves, but rather give place unto wrath: for it is written, "'Vengeance is mine; I will repay,' saith the Lord." Therefore if thine enemy hunger, feed him; if he thirst, give him drink: for in so doing thou shalt heap coals of fire·on his head. Be not overcome of evil, but overcome evil with good.

— Romans 12:9–21.

BE YE SUBJECT TO THE HIGHER POWERS

Let every soul be subject unto the higher powers. For there is no power but of God: the powers that be are ordained of God. Whosoever therefore resisteth the power, resisteth the ordinance of God: and they that resist shall receive to themselves damnation. For rulers are not a terror to good works, but to the evil. Wilt thou then not be afraid of the power? Do that which is good, and thou shalt have praise of the same: for he is the minister of God to thee for good. But if thou do that which is evil, be afraid; for he beareth not the sword in vain: for he is the minister of God, a revenger to execute wrath upon him that doeth evil. Wherefore ye must needs be subject, not only for wrath, but also for conscience' sake. For for this cause pay ye tribute also: for they are God's ministers, attending continually upon this

THE APPIAN WAY
An engraving by Gustaf Zerner

very thing. Render therefore to all their dues: tribute to whom tribute is due; custom to whom custom; fear to whom fear; honour to whom honour. Owe no man any thing, but to love one another: for he that loveth another hath fulfilled the law. For this, "Thou shalt not commit adultery, Thou shalt not steal, Thou shalt not kill, Thou shalt not bear false witness, Thou shalt not covet," and if there be any other commandment, it is briefly comprehended in this saying, namely, "Thou shalt love thy neighbour as thyself."
—Romans 13:1–9.

"LOVE IS THE FULFILLING OF THE LAW"

Love worketh no ill to his neighbour; therefore love is the fulfilling of the law.

And that, knowing the time, that now it is high time to awake out of sleep: for now is our salvation nearer than when we believed. The night is far spent, the day is at hand: let us therefore cast off the works of darkness, and let us put on the armour of light. Let us walk honestly, as in the day; not in rioting and drunkenness, not in chambering and wantonness, not in strife and envying. But put ye on the Lord Jesus Christ, and make not provision for the flesh, to fulfil the lusts thereof.
—Romans 13:10–14.

"WHO ART THOU THAT JUDGEST?"

Him that is weak in the faith receive ye, but not to doubtful disputations. For one believeth that he may eat all things: another, who is weak, eateth herbs. Let not him that eateth despise him that eateth not; and let not him which eateth not judge him that eateth: for God hath received him. Who art thou that judgest another man's servant? To his own master he standeth or falleth. Yea, he shall be holden up: for God is able to make him stand. One man esteemeth one day above another: another esteemeth every day alike. Let every man be fully persuaded in his own mind. He that regardeth the day, regardeth it unto the Lord; and he that regardeth not the day, to the Lord he doth not regard it. He that eateth, eateth to the Lord, for he giveth God thanks; and he that eateth not, to the Lord he eateth not, and giveth God thanks. For none of us liveth to himself, and no man dieth to himself. For whether we live, we live unto the Lord; and whether we die, we die unto the Lord: whether we live therefore, or die, we are the Lord's. For to this end Christ both died, and rose, and revived, that he might be Lord both of the dead and living. But why dost thou judge thy brother? Or why dost thou set at naught thy brother? For we shall all stand before the judgment seat of Christ. For it is written,

"As I live, saith the Lord, every knee shall bow to me,
And every tongue shall confess to God."

So then every one of us shall give account of himself to God.

Let us not therefore judge one another any more: but judge this rather, that no man put a stumblingblock or an occasion to fall in his brother's way. I know, and am persuaded by the Lord Jesus, that there is nothing unclean of itself: but to him that esteemeth anything to be unclean, to him it is unclean. But if thy brother be grieved with thy meat, now walkest thou not charitably. Destroy not him with thy meat, for whom Christ died. Let not then your good be evil spoken of: for the Kingdom of God is not meat and drink; but righteousness, and peace, and joy in the Holy Ghost. For he that in these things serveth Christ is acceptable to God, and approved of men. Let us therefore follow after the things which make for peace, and things wherewith one may edify

another. For meat destroy not the work of **God.** **All**
things indeed are pure; but it is evil for that man who
eateth with offence. It is good neither to eat flesh, nor
to drink wine, nor anything whereby thy brother stum-
bleth, or is offended, or is made weak. Hast thou faith?
Have it to thyself before God. Happy is he that condemneth not himself in that thing which he alloweth. And he
that doubteth is damned if he eat, because he eateth not
of faith: for whatsoever is not of faith is sin. — Romans 14.

"WE OUGHT TO BEAR THE INFIRMITIES OF THE WEAK"

We then that are strong ought to bear the infirmities
of the weak, and not to please ourselves. Let every one
of us please his neighbour for his good to edification. For
even Christ pleased not himself; but, as it is written,
"The reproaches of them that reproached thee fell on
me." For whatsoever things were written aforetime were
written for our learning, that we through patience and
comfort of the Scriptures might have hope. Now the God
of patience and consolation grant you to be likeminded
one toward another according to Christ Jesus: that ye
may with one mind and one mouth glorify God, even the
Father of our Lord Jesus Christ. Wherefore receive ye
one another, as Christ also received us to the glory of
God. Now I say that Jesus Christ was a minister of the
circumcision for the truth of God, to confirm the promises made unto the fathers: and that the Gentiles might
glorify God for his mercy; as it is written,

> "For this cause I will confess to thee
> among the Gentiles,
> And sing unto thy name."

And again he saith,

> "Rejoice, ye Gentiles, with his people."

And again,

"Praise the Lord, all ye Gentiles;
And laud him, all ye people."

"TRE FONTANE"—THE THREE FOUNTAINS

And again, Esaias saith,

"There shall be a root of Jesse,
And he that shall rise to reign over the Gentiles;
In him shall the Gentiles trust."

Now the God of hope fill you with all joy and peace in believing, that ye may abound in hope, through the power of the Holy Ghost. — Romans 15:1–13.

Paul's Personal Messages to the Church He Hopes Some Day to See

And I myself also am persuaded of you, my brethren, that ye also are full of goodness, filled with all knowledge, able also to admonish one another. Nevertheless, brethren, I have written the more boldly unto you in some sort, as putting you in mind, because of the grace that is given to me of God, that I should be the minister of Jesus Christ to the Gentiles, ministering the gospel of God, that the offering up of the Gentiles might be acceptable, being sanctified by the Holy Ghost. I have therefore whereof I may glory through Jesus Christ in those things which pertain to God. For I will not dare to speak of any of those things which Christ hath not wrought by me, to make the Gentiles obedient, by word and deed, through mighty signs and wonders, by the power of the Spirit of God; so that from Jerusalem, and round about unto Illyricum, I have fully preached the gospel of Christ. Yea, so have I strived to preach the gospel, not where Christ was named, lest I should build upon another man's foundation: but as it is written,

"To whom he was not spoken of, they shall see:
And they that have not heard shall understand."

For which cause also I have been much hindered from coming to you. But now having no more place in these parts, and having a great desire these many years to come unto you; whensoever I take my journey into Spain, I will come to you: for I trust to see you in my journey, and to be brought on my way thitherward by you, if first I be somewhat filled with your company. But now I go unto Jerusalem to minister unto the saints. For it hath pleased them of Macedonia and Achaia to make a certain contribution for the poor saints which are at Jerusalem. It hath pleased them verily; and their debtors they are. For if the Gentiles have been made partakers of their spiritual things, their duty is also to minister unto them in carnal things. When therefore I have performed this, and have sealed to them this fruit, I will come by you into Spain. And I am sure that, when I come unto you, I shall come in the fulness of the blessing of the gospel of Christ. Now I beseech you, brethren, for the Lord Jesus Christ's sake, and for the love of the Spirit, that ye strive together with me in your prayers to God for me; that I may be delivered from them that do not believe in Judæa; and that my service which I have for Jerusalem may be accepted of the saints; that I may come unto you with joy by the will of God, and may with you be refreshed. Now the God of peace be with you all. Amen. — Romans 15:14–33.

The Letter of Recommendation for Phebe

I commend unto you Phebe, our sister, which is a servant of the church which is at Cenchrea: that ye receive her in the Lord, as becometh saints, and that ye assist her in whatsoever business she hath need of you: for she hath been a succourer of many, and of myself also. Greet Priscilla and Aquila, my helpers in

Christ Jesus: who have for my life laid down their own necks: unto whom not only I give thanks, but also all the churches of the Gentiles. Likewise greet the church that is in their house. Salute my well-beloved Epænetus, who is the firstfruits of Achaia unto Christ. Greet Mary, who bestowed much labour on us. Salute Andronicus and Junia, my kinsmen, and my fellowprisoners, who are of note among the apostles, who also were in Christ before me. Greet Amplias, my beloved, in the Lord. Salute Urbane, our helper in Christ, and Stachys, my beloved. Salute Apelles, approved in Christ. Salute them which are of Aristobulus' household. Salute Herodion, my kinsman. Greet them that be of the household of Narcissus, which are in the LORD. Salute Tryphena and Tryphosa, who labour in the Lord. Salute the beloved Persis, which laboured much in the Lord. Salute Rufus chosen in the Lord, and his mother and mine. Salute Asyncritus, Phlegon, Hermas, Patrobas, Hermes, and the brethren which are with them. Salute Philologus, and Julia, Nereus, and his sister, and Olympas, and all the saints which are with them. Salute one another with an holy kiss. The churches of Christ salute you.

Now I beseech you, brethren, mark them which cause divisions and offences contrary to the doctrine which ye have learned; and avoid them. For they that are such serve not our Lord Jesus Christ, but their own belly; and by good words and fair speeches deceive the hearts of the simple. For your obedience is come abroad unto all men. I am glad therefore on your behalf: but yet I would have you wise unto that which is good, and simple concerning evil. And the God of peace shall bruise Satan under your feet shortly. The grace of our Lord Jesus Christ be with you. Amen.

— Romans 16:1–20.

CASTLE OF SAINT ANGELO, ROME

TERTIUS, TO WHOM PAUL HAS DICTATED THE
LETTER, SENDS HIS GREETING

Timotheus, my workfellow, and Lucius, and Jason, and Sosipater, my kinsmen, salute you.

I, Tertius, who wrote this epistle, salute you in the

INTERIOR OF THE MAMERTINE PRISON, ROME

Lord. Gaius, mine host, and of the whole church,
saluteth you. Erastus, the chamberlain of the city,
saluteth you, and Quartus, a brother. The grace of our
Lord Jesus Christ be with you all. Amen. Now to
him that is of power to stablish you according to my
gospel, and the preaching of Jesus Christ, according
to the revelation of the mystery, which was kept secret
since the world began, but now is made manifest, and
by the Scriptures of the prophets, according to the
commandment of the everlasting God, made known to
all nations for the obedience of faith: to God only wise,
be glory through Jesus Christ forever. Amen.

— Romans 16:21–27.

THE MAMERTINE PRISON

PAUL BEFORE THE COURT
A painting by John Bianchi

The Letters of Paul

The Great Captain of the New Faith

The First Epistle to the Corinthians

But thanks be to God, which giveth us the victory through our Lord Jesus Christ.

We may say that Paul had two methods of preaching to the Gentile world. One was through his presence, the words which he spoke in the synagogue, on the streets of the city, in the homes of his friends. Nearly all these sermons have perished. The other method, which may have seemed, at first, incidental, was through his letters to the churches. While some of these letters have been lost, many have come down to us providentially preserved by the Holy Spirit, who directed their writing. They reveal to us the methods and the teaching, indeed, the very soul of the great apostle.

The supreme expression of Paul's ministry through the epistles is found in the letters to the Corinthians. If the Epistle to the Galatians has in it the spirit of the sea, the Epistles to the Corinthians are the majestic mountains of faith, their summits seen afar, now clear in the light of dawn, now misty and cloud-capped, now glorious in the sunset. Like all the epistles, they are the children of controversy. In the providence of God these old conflicts and unseemly disputes in the early church became the starting-point for this glorious setting forth of eternal and imperishable truths.

Some time after Paul left Corinth, the brilliant and beautiful "city of the two seas," the usual reports of trouble began to reach him at Ephesus. While Paul was on the ground, his commanding personality kept the contentious and unruly spirits in check. It was a bold man who opposed Paul to his face! The conditions at Corinth were especially serious, as they might naturally be in a city with such marked pagan characteristics. Gross immorality among church-members was reported; there was a relapse into heathen observances; and worst of all, the spirit of schism had lifted its head. Four distinct

207

parties had been formed; the members of one calling themselves for Paul himself, "The Paulists"; one for Apollos, a very able man, who had come to Corinth from Ephesus, "The Apollonians"; one for Peter or Cephas, "The Cephians"; one for Christ, "The Christians." Against all this folly and discord and immorality Paul shot his burning arrows, his winged words of sharp rebuke, of stern command.

The first chapter of First Corinthians is one of the most splendid appeals for the unity of the faith ever written: "Now I beseech you, brethren, by the name of our Lord Jesus Christ, that ye all speak the same thing, and that there be no divisions among you"; "Is Christ divided? Was Paul crucified for you?"

He strikes at the prevalent immoralities straight from the shoulder without mincing words. The rebuke went home.

He speaks of the gifts of the church. Some of these gifts may be unfamiliar today, like the speaking in tongues. There is a delightfully human passage in which he emphasizes the unity of the church, and asks: What if the body were one enormous eye or ear? This passage culminates in that exquisite poem, famous for all ages: "Though I speak with the tongues of men and of angels, and have not charity . . . " ("Love" is a better translation of the Greek than "charity.")

Then there is the loftiest mountain peak of all, that sublime chapter on the resurrection, which has been the comfort of the living, which has been read at the service for the dead through the centuries as the uncounted hosts of the redeemed have "put on immortality." The very loftiest height of Christian eloquence is found in those words beginning "So also is the resurrection of the dead." Upon a little church in a great pagan city, a church contentious, ungrateful, immoral, the wealth of a mighty soul, the greatest interpreter of the Christian faith in all time, was thus lavished.

The epistles abound in splendid imagery; inspired passage follows inspired passage as God through Paul is speaking to the Corinthian Church—"Know ye not that ye are the temple of God?" "I am made all things to all men, that I might by all means save some"; "I determined not to know anything among you save Jesus Christ and him crucified."

He enunciates in these epistles the spiritual doctrine of personal accountability. One of the most serious questions which had arisen in the Corinthian church related to the eating of "meat offered to

Temple of Apollo and the Acro-Corinth

This wide plain with its scattered farms, this lonely spot with its fragments of a temple, was once the site of one of the most famous cities of antiquity, roaring with trade, glittering with wealth. It was to this very spot that the Apostle to the Gentiles came from Athens. Here he lived for two years and a half working at his trade but preaching those doctrines which would one day go to the ends of the earth and revolutionize human society.

idols." Animals were sacrificed in the heathen temples and the carcasses were offered for sale in the public markets. Some of the members of the church were greatly shocked because other members made a practice of eating this meat. It seems strange that this should have been such a burning question. Paul's decision is a statement of the great universal principle of Christian obligation and courtesy. There is no reason, he says, why a Christian should not eat meat offered to idols, but, and here is the magnificent principle which has universal application: "Wherefore, if meat make my brother to offend, I will eat no flesh while the world standeth, lest I make my brother to offend."

These epistles afford an intimate picture of an apostolic church and the life of a pagan city, in the first century. It is a satisfaction to know that the admonitions and appeals of Paul were effectual. Later writers speak of the conduct of the members of the Corinthian church as exemplary. Clement, a contemporary of Paul, speaks in a letter, evidently out of his own personal experience, of the impression produced upon every stranger who visited the church of Corinth by the exemplary conduct of its members and specifies particularly the possession of virtues, the opposites of their former faults.

Paul, called to be an apostle of Jesus Christ through the will of God, and Sosthenes, our brother, unto the church of God which is at Corinth, to them that are sanctified in Christ Jesus, called to be saints, with all that in every place call upon the name of Jesus Christ our Lord, both theirs and ours:

Grace be unto you, and peace, from God our Father, and from the Lord Jesus Christ.

I THANK my God always on your behalf, for the grace of God which is given you by Jesus Christ; that in every thing ye are enriched by him, in all utterance, and in all knowledge; even as the testimony of Christ was confirmed in you: so that ye come behind in no gift; waiting for the coming of our Lord Jesus Christ: who shall also confirm you unto the end, that ye may be blameless in the day of our Lord Jesus Christ.   God is faithful, by whom ye were called unto the fellowship of his Son, Jesus Christ our Lord.

—I Corinthians 1:1–9.

LET THERE BE NO DIVISIONS IN THE CHURCH. "IS CHRIST DIVIDED?"

Now I beseech you, brethren, by the name of our Lord Jesus Christ, that ye all speak the same thing, and that there be no divisions among you; but that ye be perfectly joined together in the same mind and in the same judgment. For it hath been declared unto me of you, my brethren, by them which are of the house of Chloe, that there are contentions among you. Now this I say, that every one of you saith, "I am of Paul"; "and I of Apollos"; "and I of Cephas"; "and I of Christ." Is Christ divided? Was Paul crucified for you? Or were ye

RUINS OF ANCIENT CORINTH

baptized in the name of Paul? I thank God that I baptized none of you, but Crispus and Gaius; lest any should say that I had baptized in mine own name. And I baptized also the household of Stephanas: besides, I know not whether I baptized any other. For Christ sent me not to baptize, but to preach the gospel: not with wisdom of words, lest the cross of Christ should be made of none effect.

For the preaching of the cross is to them that perish foolishness; but unto us which are saved it is the power of God. For it is written,

"I will destroy the wisdom of the wise,
And will bring to nothing the understanding of the prudent."

Where is the wise? Where is the scribe? Where is the disputer of this world? Hath not God made foolish the wisdom of this world? For after that in the wisdom of God the world by wisdom knew not God, it pleased God by the foolishness of preaching to save them that believe. For the Jews require a sign, and the Greeks seek after wisdom: but we preach Christ crucified, unto the Jews a stumblingblock, and unto the Greeks foolishness; but unto them which are called, both Jews and Greeks, Christ the power of God, and the wisdom of God. Because the foolishness of God is wiser than men; and the weakness of God is stronger than men.

For ye see your calling, brethren, how that not many wise men after the flesh, not many mighty, not many noble, are called: but God hath chosen the foolish things of the world to confound the wise; and God hath chosen the weak things of the world to confound the things which are mighty; and base things of the world, and things which are despised, hath God chosen, yea, and

APOSTLE PHILIP
A painting by Anthony Gruerio

things which are not, to bring to naught things that are: that no flesh should glory in his presence. But of him are ye in Christ Jesus, who of God is made unto us wisdom, and righteousness, and sanctification, and redemption: that, according as it is written, "He that glorieth, let him glory in the LORD." — I Corinthians 1:10–31.

"I DETERMINED NOT TO KNOW ANYTHING AMONG YOU, SAVE JESUS CHRIST, AND HIM CRUCIFIED"

And I, brethren, when I came to you, came not with excellency of speech or of wisdom, declaring unto you the testimony of God. For I determined not to know anything among you, save Jesus Christ, and him crucified. And I was with you in weakness, and in fear, and in much trembling. And my speech and my preaching was not with enticing words of man's wisdom, but in demonstration of the Spirit and of power: that your faith should not stand in the wisdom of men, but in the power of God.

Howbeit we speak wisdom among them that are perfect: yet not the wisdom of this world, nor of the princes of this world, that come to naught: but we speak the wisdom of God in a mystery, even the hidden wisdom, which God ordained before the world unto our glory: which none of the princes of this world knew: for had they known it, they would not have crucified the Lord of glory. But as it is written,

"Eye hath not seen, nor ear heard,
    Neither have entered into the heart of man,
    The things which God hath prepared for them that
        love him."

But God hath revealed them unto us by his Spirit; for the Spirit searcheth all things, yea, the deep things of God. For what man knoweth the things of a man, save

the spirit of man which is in him? Even so the things of
God knoweth no man, but the Spirit of God. Now we
have received, not the spirit of the world, but the spirit
which is of God; that we might know the things that are
freely given to us of God. Which things also we speak,
not in the words which man's wisdom teacheth, but which
the Holy Ghost teacheth; comparing spiritual things with
spiritual. But the natural man receiveth not the things
of the Spirit of God: for they are foolishness unto him;
neither can he know them, because they are spiritually
discerned. But he that is spiritual judgeth all things,
yet he himself is judged of no man. For who hath known
the mind of the Lord, that he may instruct him? But
we have the mind of Christ.   — I Corinthians 2.

"I HAVE PLANTED; APOLLOS WATERED; BUT GOD GAVE THE INCREASE"

And I, brethren, could not speak unto you as unto
spiritual, but as unto carnal, even as unto babes in Christ.
I have fed you with milk, and not with meat: for hitherto
ye were not able to bear it, neither yet now are ye able.
For ye are yet carnal: for whereas there is among you
envying, and strife, and divisions, are ye not carnal, and
walk as men? For while one saith, "I am of Paul"; and
another, "I am of Apollos"; are ye not carnal? Who then
is Paul, and who is Apollos, but ministers by whom ye
believed, even as the Lord gave to every man? I have
planted, Apollos watered; but God gave the increase. So
then neither is he that planteth anything, neither he
that watereth; but God that giveth the increase. Now
he that planteth and he that watereth are one: and every
man shall receive his own reward according to his own
labour. For we are labourers together with God: ye are
God's husbandry, ye are God's building.

According to the grace of God which is given unto me, as a wise masterbuilder, I have laid the foundation, and another buildeth thereon. But let every man take heed how he buildeth thereupon. For other foundation can no man lay than that is laid, which is Jesus Christ. Now if any man build upon this foundation gold, silver, precious stones, wood, hay, stubble; every man's work shall be made manifest: for the day shall declare it, because it shall be revealed by fire; and the fire shall try every man's work of what sort it is. If any man's work abide which he hath built thereupon, he shall receive a reward.   If any man's work shall be burned, he shall suffer loss: but he himself shall be saved; yet so as by fire.

Know ye not that ye are the temple of God, and that the Spirit of God dwelleth in you? If any man defile the temple of God, him shall God destroy; for the temple of God is holy, which temple ye are. Let no man deceive himself. If any man among you seemeth to be wise in this world, let him become a fool, that he may be wise.

— I Corinthians 3:1–18.

"THE WISDOM OF THIS WORLD IS FOOLISHNESS WITH GOD"

For the wisdom of this world is foolishness with God. For it is written, "He taketh the wise in their own craftiness."   And again, "The Lord knoweth the thoughts of the wise, that they are vain." Therefore let no man glory in men. For all things are yours; whether Paul, or Apollos, or Cephas, or the world, or life, or death, or things present, or things to come; all are yours; and ye are Christ's; and Christ is God's.   — I Corinthians 3:19–23.

STEWARDSHIP

Let a man so account of us, as of the ministers of Christ, and stewards of the mysteries of God. Moreover it is required in stewards, that a man be found faithful. But with me it is a very small thing that I should be judged of you, or of man's judgment: yea, I judge not mine own self. For I know nothing by myself; yet am I not hereby justified: but he that judgeth me is the Lord. Therefore judge nothing before the time, until the Lord come, who both will bring to light the hidden things of darkness, and will make manifest the counsels of the hearts: and then shall every man have praise of God.

And these things, brethren, I have in a figure transferred to myself and to Apollos for your sakes; that ye might learn in us not to think of men above that which is written, that no one of you be puffed up for one against another. For who maketh thee to differ from another? And what hast thou that thou didst not receive? Now if thou didst receive it, why dost thou glory, as if thou hadst not received it? Now ye are full, now ye are rich, ye have reigned as kings without us: and I would to God ye did reign, that we also might reign with you. For I think that God hath set forth us, the apostles, last, as it were appointed to death: for we are made a spectacle unto the world, and to angels, and to men. We are fools for Christ's sake, but ye are wise in Christ; we are weak, but ye are strong; ye are honourable, but we are despised. — I Corinthians 4:1–10.

THE SUFFERINGS OF PAUL FOR THE CHURCH

Even unto this present hour we both hunger, and thirst, and are naked, and are buffeted, and have no certain dwelling-place, and labour, working with our own hands: being reviled, we bless; being persecuted, we suffer it: being defamed, we intreat: we are made as filth of the world, and are the offscouring of all things unto this day.

I write not these things to shame you, but as my

ST. PAUL'S CHURCH AT CORINTH

beloved sons I warn you. For though ye have ten thousand instructors in Christ, yet have ye not many fathers: for in Christ Jesus I have begotten you through the gospel. Wherefore I beseech you, be ye followers of me. For this cause have I sent unto you Timotheus, who is my beloved son, and faithful in the Lord, who shall bring you into remembrance of my ways which be in Christ, as I teach everywhere in every church. Now some are puffed up, as though I would not come to you. But I will come to you shortly, if the Lord will, and will know, not the speech of them which are puffed up, but the power.

— I Corinthians 4:11–19.

"THE KINGDOM OF GOD IS IN POWER"

For the kingdom of God is not in word, but in power. What will ye? Shall I come unto you with a rod, or in love, and in the spirit of meekness? — I Corinthians 4:20, 21.

ON THE SINS OF THE FLESH

It is reported commonly that there is fornication among you, and such fornication as is not so much as named among the Gentiles, that one should have his father's wife. And ye are puffed up, and have not rather mourned, that he that hath done this deed might be taken away from among you. For I verily, as absent in body, but present in spirit, have judged already, as though I were present, concerning him that hath so done this deed, in the name of our Lord Jesus Christ, when ye are gathered together, and my spirit, with the power of our Lord Jesus Christ, to deliver such an one unto Satan for the destruction of the flesh, that the spirit may be saved in the day of the Lord Jesus. Your glorying is not good. Know ye not that a little leaven leaveneth the whole lump? —I Corinthians 5:1–6.

CLEANSE THE CHURCH OF THE OLD EVIL

Purge out therefore the old leaven, that ye may be a new lump, as ye are unleavened. For even Christ our passover is sacrificed for us: therefore let us keep the feast, not with old leaven, neither with the leaven of malice and wickedness; but with the unleavened bread of sincerity and truth.

I wrote unto you in an epistle not to company with fornicators: yet not altogether with the fornicators of this world, or with the covetous, or extortioners, or with idolaters; for then must ye needs go out of the world. But now I have written unto you not to keep company, if any man that is called a brother be a fornicator, or covetous, or an idolater, or a railer, or a drunkard, or an extortioner; with such an one, no, not to eat. For what have I to do to judge them also that are without? Do not ye judge them that are within? But them that are without God judgeth. Therefore put away from among yourselves that wicked person. — I Corinthians 5:7–13.

On Lawsuits Between Christians

Dare any of you, having a matter against another, go to law before the unjust, and not before the saints? Do ye not know that the saints shall judge the world? and if the world shall be judged by you, are ye unworthy to judge the smallest matters? Know ye not that we shall judge angels? How much more things that pertain to this life? If then ye have judgments of things pertaining to this life, set them to judge who are least esteemed in the church. I speak to your shame. Is it so, that there is not a wise man among you, no, not one that shall be able to judge between his brethren? But brother goeth to law with brother, and that before the unbelievers. Now therefore there is utterly a fault among you, because ye go to law one with another. Why do ye not rather take wrong? Why do ye not rather suffer yourselves to be defrauded? Nay, ye do wrong, and defraud, and that your brethren. Know ye not that the unrighteous shall not inherit the kingdom of God? Be not deceived: neither fornicators, nor idolaters, nor adulterers, nor effeminate, nor abusers of themselves with mankind, nor thieves, nor covetous, nor drunkards, nor revilers, nor extortioners, shall inherit the kingdom of God. And such were some of you: but ye are washed, but ye are sanctified, but ye are justified in the name of the Lord Jesus, and by the Spirit of our God. —I Corinthians 6:1-11.

"ALL THINGS ARE LAWFUL, BUT ALL THINGS ARE NOT EXPEDIENT"

All things are lawful unto me, but all things are not expedient: all things are lawful for me, but I will not be brought under the power of any. Meats for the belly, and the belly for meats: but God shall destroy both it and them. Now the body is not for fornication, but for the Lord; and the Lord for the body. And God hath both raised up the Lord, and will also raise up us by his own power.

Know ye not that your bodies are the members of Christ? Shall I then take the members of Christ, and make them the members of an harlot? God forbid. What? Know ye not that he which is joined to an harlot is one body? For two, saith he, shall be one flesh. But he that is joined unto the Lord is one spirit. Flee fornication. Every sin that a man doeth is without the body; but he that committeth fornication sinneth against his own body. What? Know ye not that your body is the temple of the Holy Ghost which is in you, which ye have of God, and ye are not your own? For ye are bought with a price:

APOSTLE ANDREW
A painting by Anthony Gruerio

therefore glorify God in your body, and in your spirit, which are God's. — I Corinthians 6:12–20.

PAUL ANSWERS VEXED QUESTIONS OF THE CHURCH

CONCERNING MARRIAGE

Now concerning the things whereof ye wrote unto me: it is good for a man not to touch a woman. Nevertheless, to avoid fornication, let every man have his own wife, and let every woman have her own husband. Let the husband render unto the wife due benevolence: and likewise also the wife unto the husband. The wife hath not power of her own body, but the husband: and likewise also hath the husband not power of his own body, but the wife. Defraud ye not one the other, except it be with consent for a time, that ye may give yourselves to fasting and prayer; and come together again, that Satan tempt you not for your incontinency. But I speak this by permission, and not of commandment. For I would that all men were even as I myself. But every man hath his proper gift of God, one after this manner, and another after that.

I say therefore to the unmarried and widows, it is good for them if they abide even as I. But if they cannot contain, let them marry: for it is better to marry than to burn. And unto the married I command, yet not I, but the Lord, let not the wife depart from her husband: but and if she depart, let her remain unmarried, or be reconciled to her husband: and let not the husband put away his wife. But to the rest speak I, not the Lord: if any brother hath a wife that believeth not, and she be pleased to dwell with him, let him not put her away. And the woman which hath an husband that believeth not, and if he be pleased to dwell with her, let her not leave him. For the unbelieving husband is sanctified by the wife, and the unbelieving wife is sanctified by the husband: else were your children unclean; but now are they holy. But if the unbelieving depart, let him depart. A brother or a sister is not under bondage in such cases: but God hath called us to peace. For what knowest thou, O wife, whether thou shalt save thy husband? Or how knowest thou, O man, whether thou shalt save thy wife? But as God hath distributed to every man, as the Lord hath called every one, so let him walk. And so ordain I in all churches. Is any man called being circumcised? Let him not become uncircumcised. Is any called in uncircumcision? Let him not be circumcised. Circumcision is nothing, and uncircumcision is nothing, but the keeping of the commandments of God. Let every man abide in the same calling wherein he was called. Art thou called being a servant? Care not for it: but if thou mayest be made free, use it rather. For he that is called in the Lord, being a servant, is the Lord's freeman: likewise also he that is called, being free, is Christ's servant. Ye are bought with a price; be not ye the servants of men. Brethren, let every man, wherein he is called, therein abide with God.

Now concerning virgins I have no commandment of the Lord: yet I give my judgment, as one that hath obtained mercy of the Lord to be faithful. I suppose therefore that this is good for the present distress, I say, that it is good for a man so to be. Art thou bound unto a wife? Seek not to be loosed. Art thou loosed from a wife? Seek not a wife. But and if thou marry, thou hast not sinned; and if a virgin marry, she hath not sinned. Nevertheless such shall have trouble in the flesh: but I spare you. But this I say, brethren, the time is short: it remaineth, that both they that have wives be as though they had none;

and they that weep, as though they wept not; and they that rejoice, as though they rejoiced not; and they that buy as though they possessed not; and they that use this world, as not abusing it: for the fashion of this world passeth away. But I would have you without carefulness. He that is unmarried careth for the things that belong to the Lord, how he may please the Lord: but he that is married careth for the things that are of the world, how he may please his wife. There is difference also between a wife and a virgin. The unmarried woman careth for the things of the Lord, that she may be holy both in body and in spirit; but she that is married careth for the things of the world, how she may please her husband. And this I speak for your own profit; not that I may cast a snare upon you, but for that which is comely, and that ye may attend upon the Lord without distraction. But if any man think that he behaveth himself uncomely toward his virgin, if she pass the flower of her age, and need so require, let him do what he will, he sinneth not: let them marry. Nevertheless he that standeth steadfast in his heart, having no necessity, but hath power over his own will, and hath so decreed in his heart that he will keep his virgin, doeth well. So then he that giveth her in marriage doeth well; but he that giveth her not in marriage doeth better. The wife is bound by the law as long as her husband liveth; but if her husband be dead, she is at liberty to be married to whom she will; only in the Lord. But she is happier if she so abide, after my judgment: and I think also that I have the Spirit of God. — I Corinthians 7.

"Concerning Things Offered Unto Idols"

Now as touching things offered unto idols, we know that we all have knowledge. Knowledge puffeth up, but charity edifieth. And if any man think that he knoweth anything, he knoweth nothing yet as he ought to know. But if any man love God, the same is known of him. As concerning therefore the eating of those things that are offered in sacrifice unto idols, we know that an idol is nothing in the world, and that there is none other God but one. For though there be that are called gods, whether in heaven or in earth, (as there be gods many, and lords many,) yet to us there is but one God, the Father, of whom are all things, and we in him; and one Lord Jesus Christ, by whom are all things, and we by him. Howbeit there is not in every man that knowledge: for some with conscience of the idol unto this hour eat it as a thing offered unto an idol; and their conscience being weak is defiled. But meat commendeth us not to God: for neither, if we eat, are we the better; neither, if we eat not, are we the worse. —I Corinthians 8:1–8.

THE LAW OF LIBERTY—OBLIGATION TO WEAKNESS

But take heed lest by any means this liberty of yours become a stumblingblock to them that are weak. For if any man see thee which hast knowledge sit at meat in the idol's temple, shall not the conscience of him which is weak be emboldened to eat those things which are offered to idols; and through thy knowledge shall the weak brother perish, for whom Christ died? But when ye sin so against the brethren, and wound their weak conscience, ye sin against Christ.

Wherefore, if meat make my brother to offend, I will eat no flesh while the world standeth, lest I make my brother to offend. —I Corinthians 8:9–13.

PAUL'S DEFENSE OF HIS MINISTRY

Am I not an apostle? Am I not free? Have I not seen Jesus Christ our Lord? Are not ye my work in the Lord?

If I be not an apostle unto others, yet doubtless I am to you: for the seal of mine apostleship are ye in the Lord. Mine answer to them that do examine me is this, have we not power to eat and to drink? Have we not power to lead about a sister, a wife, as well as other apostles, and as the brethren of the Lord, and Cephas? Or I only and Barnabas, have not we power to forbear working? Who goeth a warfare any time at his own charges? Who planteth a vineyard, and eateth not of the fruit thereof? Or who feedeth a flock, and eateth not of the milk of the flock? Say I these things as a man or saith not the law the same also? For it is written in the law of Moses, "Thou shalt not muzzle the mouth of the ox that treadeth out the corn." Doth God take care for oxen? Or saith he it altogether for our sakes? For our sakes, no doubt, this is written: that he that ploweth should plow in hope; and that he that thresheth in hope should be partaker of his hope. If we have sown unto you spiritual things, is it a great thing if we shall reap your carnal things? If others be partakers of this power over you, are not we rather? Nevertheless we have not used this power; but suffer all things, lest we should hinder the gospel of Christ. Do ye not know that they which minister about holy things live of the things of the temple? And they which wait at the altar are partakers with the altar? Even so hath the Lord ordained that they which preach the gospel should live of the gospel. But I have used none of these things: neither have I written these things, that it should be so done unto me: for it were better for me to die, than that any man should make my glorying void.

For though I preach the gospel, I have nothing to glory of: for necessity is laid upon me; yea, woe is unto me, if I preach not the gospel! For if I do this thing willingly, I have a reward: but if against my will, a dispensation of the gospel is committed unto me. —I Corinthians 9:1–17.

"ALL THINGS TO ALL MEN"

What is my reward then? Verily that, when I preach the gospel, I may make the gospel of Christ without charge, that I abuse not my power in the gospel. For though I be free from all men, yet have I made myself servant unto all, that I might gain the more. And unto the Jews I became as a Jew, that I might gain the Jews; to them that are under the law, as under the law, that I might gain them that are under the law; to them that are without law, as without law, (being not without law to God, but under the law to Christ,) that I might gain them that are without law. To the weak became I as weak, that I might gain the weak: I am made all things to all men, that I might by all means save some. And this I do for the gospel's sake, that I might be partaker thereof with you.

Know ye not that they which run in a race run all, but one receiveth the prize? So run, that ye may obtain. —I Corinthians 9:18–24.

"TEMPERATE IN ALL THINGS"

And every man that striveth for the mastery is temperate in all things. Now they do it to obtain a corruptible crown; but we an incorruptible. I therefore so run, not as uncertainly; so fight I, not as one that beateth the air: but I keep under my body, and bring it into subjection: lest that by any means, when I have preached to others, I myself should be a castaway.

Moreover, brethren, I would not that ye should be ignorant, how that all our fathers were under the cloud, and all passed through the sea; and were all baptized

unto Moses in the cloud and in the sea; and did all eat
the same spiritual meat; and did all drink the same spiritual drink: for they drank of that spiritual Rock that
followed them: and that Rock was Christ. But with
many of them God was not well pleased: for they were
overthrown in the wilderness.

Now these things were our examples, to the intent
we should not lust after evil things, as they also lusted.
Neither be ye idolaters, as were some of them; as it is
written, "The people sat down to eat and drink, and rose
up to play." Neither let us commit fornication, as
some of them committed, and fell in one day three and
twenty thousand. Neither let us tempt Christ, as some
of them also tempted, and were destroyed of serpents.
Neither murmur ye, as some of them also murmured, and
were destroyed of the destroyer. Now all these things
happened unto them for ensamples: and they are written
for our admonition, upon whom the ends of the world
are come. — I Corinthians 9:25–10:11.

"LET HIM THAT THINKETH HE STANDETH TAKE HEED LEST HE FALL"

Wherefore let him that thinketh he standeth take
heed lest he fall. There hath no temptation taken you
but such as is common to man: but God is faithful, who
will not suffer you to be tempted above that ye are able;
but will with the temptation also make a way to escape,
that ye may be able to bear it.

Wherefore, my dearly beloved, flee from idolatry.
I speak as to wise men; judge ye what I say. The cup
of blessing which we bless, is it not the communion of
the blood of Christ? The bread which we break, is it
not the communion of the body of Christ? For we being
many are one bread, and one body: for we are all par-

takers of that one bread. Behold Israel after the flesh: are not they which eat of the sacrifices partakers of the altar? What say I then, that the idol is anything, or that which is offered in sacrifice to idols is anything? But I say, that the things which the Gentiles sacrifice, they sacrifice to devils, and not to God: and I would not that ye should have fellowship with devils. Ye cannot drink the cup of the Lord, and the cup of devils: ye cannot be partakers of the Lord's table, and of the table of devils. Do we provoke the Lord to jealousy? are we stronger than he? —I Corinthians 10:12-22.

"Do All to the Glory of God"

All things are lawful for me, but all things are not expedient: all things are lawful for me, but all things edify not. Let no man seek his own, but every man another's wealth. Whatsoever is sold in the shambles, that eat, asking no question for conscience' sake: for the earth is the Lord's, and the fulness thereof. If any of them that believe not bid you to a feast, and ye be disposed to go; whatsoever is set before you, eat, asking no question for conscience' sake. But if any man say unto you, "This is offered in sacrifice unto idols," eat not for his sake that showed it, and for conscience' sake: for the earth is the Lord's, and the fulness thereof: conscience, I say, not thine own, but of the other: for why is my liberty judged of another man's conscience? For if I by grace be a partaker, why am I evil spoken of for that for which I give thanks?

Whether therefore ye eat, or drink, or whatsoever ye do, do all to the glory of God. Give none offence, neither to the Jews, nor to the Gentiles, nor to the church of God: even as I please all men in all things, not seeking mine own profit, but the profit of many, that they may be saved.

Be ye followers of me, even as I also am of Christ. Now I praise you, brethren, that ye remember me in all things, and keep the ordinances, as I delivered them to you. But I would have you know, that the head of every man is Christ; and the head of the woman is the man; and the head of Christ is God. Every man praying or prophesying, having his head covered, dishonoureth his head. But every woman that prayeth or prophesieth with her head uncovered dishonoureth her head: for that is even all one as if she were shaven. For if the woman be not covered, let her also be shorn: but if it be a shame for a woman to be shorn or shaven, let her be covered. For a man indeed ought not to cover his head, forasmuch as he is the image and glory of God: but the woman is the glory of the man. For the man is not of the woman; but the woman of the man. Neither was the man created for the woman; but the woman for the man. For this cause ought the woman to have power on her head because of the angels. Nevertheless neither is the man without the woman, neither the woman without the man, in the Lord. For as the woman is of the man, even so is the man also by the woman; but all things of God. Judge in yourselves: is it comely that a woman pray unto God uncovered? Doth not even nature itself teach you, that, if a man have long hair, it is a shame unto him? But if a woman have long hair, it is a glory to her: for her hair is given her for a covering. But if any man seem to be contentious, we have no such custom, neither the churches of God. Now in this that I declare unto you I praise you not, that ye come together not for the better, but for the worse. For first of all, when ye come together in the church, I hear that there be divisions among you; and I partly believe it. For there must be also heresies among you, that they which are approved may be made manifest among you.　　—I Corinthians 10:23-11:19.

THE LORD'S SUPPER

When ye come together therefore into one place, this is not to eat the Lord's supper. For in eating every one taketh before other his own supper: and one is hungry, and another is drunken. What? Have ye not houses to eat and to drink in? Or despise ye the church of God, and shame them that have not? What shall I say to you? Shall I praise you in this? I praise you not. For I have received of the Lord that which also I delivered unto you, that the Lord Jesus the same night in which he was betrayed took bread: and when he had given thanks, he brake it, and said, "Take, eat: this is my body, which is broken for you: this do in remembrance of me." After the same manner also he took the cup, when he had supped, saying, "This cup is the new testament in my blood: this do ye, as oft as ye drink it, in remembrance of me. For as often as ye eat this bread, and drink this cup, ye do shew the Lord's death till he come." Wherefore whosoever shall eat this bread, and drink this cup of the Lord, unworthily, shall be guilty of the body and blood of the Lord. But let a man examine himself, and so let him eat of that bread, and drink of that cup. For he that eateth and drinketh unworthily, eateth and drinketh damnation to himself, not discerning the Lord's body. For this cause many are weak and sickly among you, and many sleep. For if we would judge ourselves, we should not be judged. But when we are judged, we are chastened of the Lord, that we should not be condemned with the world. Wherefore, my brethren, when ye come together to eat, tarry one for another. And if any man hunger, let him eat at home; that ye come not together unto condemnation. And the rest will I set in order when I come.

— I Corinthians 11:20-34.

THE LAST SUPPER
A molding by D. Mastroianni

"There Are Diversities of Gifts, But the Same Spirit"

Now concerning spiritual gifts, brethren, I would not have you ignorant. Ye know that ye were Gentiles, carried away unto these dumb idols, even as ye were led. Wherefore I give you to understand, that no man speaking by the Spirit of God calleth Jesus accursed: and that no man can say that Jesus is the Lord, but by the Holy Ghost.

Now there are diversities of gifts, but the same Spirit. And there are differences of administrations, but the same Lord. And there are diversities of operations, but it is the same God which worketh all in all. But the manifestation of the Spirit is given to every man to profit withal. For to one is given by the Spirit the word of wisdom; to another the word of knowledge by the same Spirit; to another faith by the same Spirit; to another the gifts of healing by the same Spirit; to another the working of miracles; to another prophecy; to another discerning of spirits; to another divers kinds of tongues; to another the interpretation of tongues: but all these worketh that one and the selfsame Spirit, dividing to every man severally as he will.

For as the body is one, and hath many members, and all the members of that one body, being many, are one body: so also is Christ. For by one Spirit are we all baptized into one body, whether we be Jews or Gentiles, whether we be bond or free; and have been all made to drink into one Spirit. For the body is not one member, but many.

If the foot shall say, "Because I am not the hand, I am not of the body"; is it therefore not of the body?

And if the ear shall say, "Because I am not the eye, I am not of the body"; is it therefore not of the body?

If the whole body were an eye, where were the hearing? If the whole were hearing, where were the smelling? But now hath God set the members every one of them in the body, as it hath pleased him. And if they were all one member, where were the body? But now are they many members, yet but one body. And the eye cannot say unto the hand, "I have no need of thee": nor again the head to the feet, "I have no need of you." Nay, much more those members of the body, which seem to be more feeble, are necessary: and those members of the body, which we think to be less honourable, upon these we bestow more abundant honour; and our uncomely parts have more abundant comeliness. For our comely parts have no need: but God hath tempered the body together, having given more abundant honour to that part which lacked: that there should be no schism in the body; but that the members should have the same care one for another. And whether one member suffer, all the members suffer with it; or one member be honoured, all the members rejoice with it. Now ye are the body of Christ, and members in particular. And God hath set some in the church, first apostles, secondarily prophets, thirdly teachers, after that miracles, then gifts of healings, helps, governments, diversities of tongues. Are all apostles? Are all prophets? Are all teachers? Are all workers of miracles? Have all the gifts of healing? Do all speak with tongues? Do all interpret?

But covet earnestly the best gifts: and yet show I unto you a more excellent way. —I Corinthians 12.

The Spirit Which Animates All Is Love

Though I speak with the tongues of men and of angels, and have not charity, I am become as sounding brass, or a tinkling cymbal. And though I have the gift

THE RETURN OF THE PRODIGAL SON
A painting by Charles Gleyre

of prophecy, and understand all mysteries, and all knowledge; and though I have all faith, so that I could remove mountains, and have not charity, I am nothing. And though I bestow all my goods to feed the poor, and though I give my body to be burned, and have not charity, it profiteth me nothing. Charity suffereth long, and is kind; charity envieth not; charity vaunteth not itself, is not puffed up, doth not behave itself unseemly, seeketh not her own, is not easily provoked, thinketh no evil; rejoiceth not in iniquity, but rejoiceth in the truth; beareth all things, believeth all things, hopeth all things, endureth all things. Charity never faileth: but whether there be prophecies, they shall fail; whether there be tongues, they shall cease; whether there be knowledge, it shall vanish away. For we know in part, and we prophesy in part. But when that which is perfect is come, then that which is in part shall be done away. When I was a child, I spake as a child, I understood as a child, I thought as a child: but when I became a man, I put away childish things. For now we see through a glass, darkly; but then face to face: now I know in part; but then shall I know even as also I am known. And now abideth faith, hope, charity, these three; but the greatest of these is charity.   — I Corinthians 13.

The Best of Spiritual Gifts Is the Most Useful

Follow after charity, and desire spiritual gifts, but rather that ye may prophesy. For he that speaketh in an unknown tongue speaketh not unto men, but unto God: for no man understandeth him; howbeit in the spirit he speaketh mysteries. But he that prophesieth speaketh unto men to edification, and exhortation, and comfort. He that speaketh in an unknown tongue edifieth himself; but he that prophesieth edifieth the church. I would that ye all spake with tongues, but rather that ye prophesied: for greater is he that prophesieth than he that speaketh with tongues, except he interpret, that the church may receive edifying.

Now, brethren, if I come unto you speaking with tongues, what shall I profit you, except I shall speak to you either by revelation, or by knowledge, or by prophesying, or by doctrine? And even things without life giving sound, whether pipe or harp, except they give a distinction in the sounds, how shall it be known what is piped or harped? For if the trumpet give an uncertain sound, who shall prepare himself to the battle?

So likewise ye, except ye utter by the tongue words easy to be understood, how shall it be known what is spoken? For ye shall speak into the air. There are, it may be, so many kinds of voices in the world, and none of them is without signification. Therefore if I know not the meaning of the voice, I shall be unto him that speaketh a barbarian, and he that speaketh shall be a barbarian unto me. Even so ye, forasmuch as ye are zealous of spiritual gifts, seek that ye may excel to the edifying of the church. Wherefore let him that speaketh in an unknown tongue pray that he may interpret. For if I pray in an unknown tongue, my spirit prayeth, but my understanding is unfruitful.

What is it then? I will pray with the spirit, and I will pray with the understanding also: I will sing with the spirit, and I will sing with the understanding also. Else when thou shalt bless with the spirit, how shall he that occupieth the room of the unlearned say "Amen" at thy giving of thanks, seeing he understandeth not what thou sayest? For thou verily givest thanks well, but the other is not edified. I thank my God, I speak with tongues more than ye all: yet in the church I had rather speak five words with my understanding, that by my voice I might teach others also, than ten thousand words in an unknown tongue.

Brethren, be not children in understanding: howbeit in malice be ye children, but in understanding be men. In the law it is written, "'With men of other tongues and other lips will I speak unto this people; and yet for all that will they not hear me,' saith the Lord." Wherefore tongues are for a sign, not to them that believe, but to them that believe not: but prophesying serveth not for them that believe not, but for them which believe. If therefore the whole church be come together into one place, and all speak with tongues, and there come in those that are unlearned, or unbelievers, will they not say that ye are mad? But if all prophesy, and there come in one that believeth not, or one unlearned, he is convinced of all, he is judged of all: and thus are the secrets of his heart made manifest; and so falling down on his face he will worship God, and report that God is in you of a truth.

How is it then, brethren? When ye come together, every one of you hath a Psalm, hath a doctrine, hath a tongue, hath a revelation, hath an interpretation. Let all things be done unto edifying. If any man speak in an unknown tongue, let it be by two, or at the most by three, and that by course; and let one interpret. But if there be no interpreter, let him keep silence in the church; and let him speak to himself, and to God. Let the prophets speak two or three, and let the other judge. If anything be revealed to another that sitteth by, let the first hold his peace. For ye may all prophesy one by one, that all may learn, and all may be comforted. And the spirits of the prophets are subject to the prophets. For God is not the author of confusion, but of peace, as in all churches of the saints.

Let your women keep silence in the churches: for it is not permitted unto them to speak; but they are commanded to be under obedience, as also saith the law. And if they will learn anything, let them ask their husbands at home: for it is a shame for women to speak in the church.

What? Came the word of God out from you? Or came it unto you only? If any man think himself to be a prophet, or spiritual, let him acknowledge that the things that I write unto you are the commandments of the Lord. But if any man be ignorant, let him be ignorant. Wherefore, brethren, covet to prophesy, and forbid not to speak with tongues. Let all things be done decently and in order. — I Corinthians 14.

On the Resurrection of the Dead and the Appearances of Christ After the Resurrection

Moreover, brethren, I declare unto you the gospel which I preached unto you, which also ye have received, and wherein ye stand; by which also ye are saved, if ye keep in memory what I preached unto you, unless ye have believed in vain. For I delivered unto you first of all that which I also received, how that Christ died for our sins according to the Scriptures; and that he was buried, and that he rose again the third day according to the Scriptures: and that he was seen of Cephas, then of the twelve: after that, he was seen of above five hundred brethren at once; of whom the greater part remain unto this present, but some are fallen asleep. After that, he was seen of James; then of all the apostles. And last of all he was seen of me also, as of one born out of due time.

For I am the least of the apostles, that am not meet to be called an apostle, because I persecuted the church of God. But by the grace of God I am what I am: and his grace which was bestowed upon me was not in vain; but I laboured more abundantly than they all: yet not I, but the grace of God which was with me. Therefore whether it were I or they, so we preach, and so ye believed.

Now if Christ be preached that he rose from the dead, how say some among you that there is no resurrection of the dead? But if there be no resurrection of the dead, then is Christ not risen: And if Christ be not risen, then is our preaching vain, and your faith is also vain. Yea, and we are found false witnesses of God; because we have testified of God that he raised up Christ: whom he raised not up, if so be that the dead rise not. For if the dead rise not, then is not Christ raised: and if Christ be not raised, your faith is vain; ye are yet in your sins. Then they also which are fallen asleep in Christ are perished. If in this life only we have hope in Christ, we are of all men most miserable.

— I Corinthians 15:1–19.

"NOW IS CHRIST RISEN FROM THE DEAD"

But now is Christ risen from the dead, and become the firstfruits of them that slept. For since by man came death, by man came also the resurrection of the dead.

For as in Adam all die, even so in Christ shall all be made alive. But every man in his own order: Christ the firstfruits; afterward they that are Christ's at his coming. Then cometh the end, when he shall have delivered up the kingdom to God, even the Father; when he shall have put down all rule and all authority and power. For he must reign, till he hath put all enemies under his feet. The last enemy that shall be destroyed is death. For he hath put all things under his feet. But when he saith all things are put under him, it is manifest that he is excepted, which did put all things under him.

And when all things shall be subdued unto him, then shall the Son also himself be subject unto him that put all things under him, that God may be all in all. Else what shall they do which are baptized for the dead, if the dead rise not at all? Why are they then baptized for the dead?

And why stand we in jeopardy every hour? I protest by your rejoicing which I have in Christ Jesus our Lord, I die daily. If after the manner of men I have fought with beasts at Ephesus, what advantageth it me, if the dead rise not? Let us eat and drink; for to-morrow we die. Be not deceived: evil communications corrupt good manners. Awake to righteousness, and sin not; for some have not the knowledge of God: I speak this to your shame.

But some man will say, "How are the dead raised up and with what body do they come?" Thou fool, that which thou sowest is not quickened, except it die: and that which thou sowest, thou sowest not that body that shall be, but bare grain, it may chance of wheat, or of some other grain: but God giveth it a body as it hath pleased him, and to every seed his own body. All flesh is not the same flesh: but there is one kind of flesh of men, another flesh of beasts, another of fishes, and another of birds. There are also celestial bodies, and bodies terrestrial: but the glory of the celestial is one, and the glory of the terrestrial is another. There is one glory of the sun, and another glory of the moon.

and another glory of the stars: for one star differeth
from another star in glory.   — I Corinthians 15:20–41.

"SO ALSO IS THE RESURRECTION FROM THE DEAD. IT IS SOWN IN WEAKNESS; IT IS RAISED IN POWER"

So also is the resurrection of the dead. It is sown
in corruption; it is raised in incorruption: it is sown in
dishonour; it is raised in glory: it is sown in weakness;
it is raised in power: it is sown a natural body; it is
raised a spiritual body. There is a natural body, and
there is a spiritual body. And so it is written, The
first man Adam was made a living soul; the last Adam
was made a quickening spirit. Howbeit that was not
first which is spiritual, but that which is natural; and
afterward that which is spiritual. The first man is of
the earth, earthy: the second man is the Lord from
heaven. As is the earthy, such are they also that are
earthy: and as is the heavenly, such are they also that
are heavenly. And as we have borne the image of the
earthy, we shall also bear the image of the heavenly.

Now this I say, brethren, that flesh and blood cannot
inherit the Kingdom of God; neither doth corruption
inherit incorruption. Behold, I show you a mystery;
We shall not all sleep, but we shall all be changed, in
a moment, in the twinkling of an eye, at the last trump:
for the trumpet shall sound, and the dead shall be raised
incorruptible, and we shall be changed. For this corruptible must put on incorruption, and this mortal
must put on immortality. So when this corruptible
shall have put on incorruption, and this mortal shall
have put on immortality, then shall be brought to pass
the saying that is written, "Death is swallowed up in
victory."   — I Corinthians 15:42–54

PRISCILLA, A LEADER IN THE NEW CHURCH
A painting by Horatio van Velt

"O DEATH, WHERE IS THY STING? O GRAVE, WHERE IS THY VICTORY?"

O death, where is thy sting? O grave, where is thy victory? The sting of death is sin; and the strength of sin is the law. But thanks be to God, which giveth us the victory through our Lord Jesus Christ. Therefore, my beloved brethren, be ye steadfast, unmovable, always abounding in the work of the LORD, forasmuch as ye know that your labour is not in vain in the LORD.

— I Corinthians 15:55–58.

THE COLLECTION FOR THE POOR: PAUL'S CLOSING MESSAGES

Now concerning the collection for the saints, as I have given order to the churches of Galatia, even so do ye. Upon the first day of the week let every one of you lay by him in store, as God hath prospered him, that there be no gatherings when I come. And when I come, whomsoever ye shall approve by your letters, them will I send to bring your liberality unto Jerusalem. And if it be meet that I go also, they shall go with me.

Now I will come unto you, when I shall pass through Macedonia: for I do pass through Macedonia. And it may be that I will abide, yea, and winter with you, that ye may bring me on my journey whithersoever I go. For I will not see you now by the way; but I trust to tarry a while with you, if the Lord permit. But I will tarry at Ephesus until Pentecost. For a great door and effectual is opened unto me, and there are many adversaries.

Now if Timotheus come, see that he may be with you without fear: for he worketh the work of the Lord, as I also do. Let no man therefore despise him: but conduct him forth in peace, that he may come unto me: for I look for him with the brethren.

As touching our brother Apollos, I greatly desired him to come unto you with the brethren: but his will was not at all to come at this time; but he will come when he shall have convenient time. —I Corinthians 16:1-12.

"WATCH YE, STAND FAST IN THE FAITH"

Watch ye, stand fast in the faith, quit you like men, be strong. Let all your things be done with charity.

I beseech you, brethren, (ye know the house of Stephanas, that it is the firstfruits of Achaia, and that they have addicted themselves to the ministry of the saints,) that ye submit yourselves unto such, and to every one that helpeth with us, and laboureth. I am glad of the coming of Stephanas and Fortunatus and Achaicus: for that which was lacking on your part they have supplied. For they have refreshed my spirit and yours: therefore acknowledge ye them that are such.

The churches of Asia salute you. Aquila and Priscilla salute you much in the Lord, with the church that is in their house. All the brethren greet you. Greet ye one another with an holy kiss.

The salutation of me, Paul, with mine own hand. If any man love not the Lord Jesus Christ, let him be Anathema Maran-atha.

The grace of our Lord Jesus Christ be with you. My love be with you all in Christ Jesus. Amen.

—I Corinthians 16:13-24.

The Letters of Paul

The Great Captain of the New Faith

The Second Epistle to the Corinthians

The things which are seen are temporal; but the things which
are not seen are eternal.

Paul undoubtedly wrote more epistles than have been preserved
in our New Testament. Of those which the Holy Spirit saw fit to
retain we have two epistles addressed to the church at Corinth. They
are direct from the burning heart of Paul to the Corinthian saints;
and for Christians of all ages they have been an unfailing source of
spiritual strength and blessing.

The Corinthians had rebelled against Paul's authority as an apostle of Christ and had turned away into sin. Just before this second
epistle was written, however, they had repented and had acknowledged again his apostleship. Paul tells the church that its members
are freely forgiven, although he sternly denounces those who still
make division and strife. The epistle contains many noble passages:
"For we know that if our earthly house of this tabernacle were dissolved, we have a building of God, an house not made with hands,
eternal in the heavens"; "Where the Spirit of the LORD is, there
is liberty."

Paul, an apostle of Jesus Christ by the will of
God, and Timothy, our brother, unto the church of
God which is at Corinth, with all the saints which are
in all Achaia:

Grace be to you and peace from God our Father,
and from the Lord Jesus Christ.

Thankfulness for the Pleasant Relations with the Corinthian Church

BLESSED be God, even the Father of our Lord Jesus Christ, the Father of mercies, and the God of all comfort; who comforteth us in all our tribulation, that we may be able to comfort them which are in any trouble, by the comfort wherewith we ourselves are comforted of God. For as the sufferings of Christ abound in us, so our consolation also aboundeth by Christ. And whether we be afflicted, it is for your consolation and salvation, which is effectual in the enduring of the same sufferings which we also suffer: or whether we be comforted, it is for your consolation and salvation. And our hope of you is steadfast, knowing, that as ye are partakers of the sufferings, so shall ye be also of the consolation. For we would not, brethren, have you ignorant of our trouble which came to us in Asia, that we were pressed out of measure, above strength, insomuch that we despaired even of life: but we had the sentence of death in ourselves, that we should not trust in ourselves, but in God which raiseth the dead: who delivered us from so great a death, and doth deliver: in whom we trust that he will yet deliver us; ye also helping together by prayer for us, that for the gift bestowed upon us by the means of many persons thanks may be given by many on our behalf.

For our rejoicing is this, the testimony of our conscience, that in simplicity and godly sincerity, not with fleshly wisdom, but by the grace of God, we have had our conversation in the world, and more abundantly to you-ward. For we write none other things unto you, than what ye read or acknowledge; and I trust ye shall acknowledge even to the end; as also ye have acknowledged

GREEK TEMPLE OF CONCORDIA AT GIRGENTI, SICILY

us in part, that we are your rejoicing, even as ye also are ours in the day of the Lord Jesus.

And in this confidence I was minded to come unto you before, that ye might have a second benefit; and to pass by you into Macedonia, and to come again out of Macedonia unto you, and of you to be brought on my way toward Judæa.

When I therefore was thus minded, did I use lightness? Or the things that I purpose, do I purpose according to the flesh, that with me there should be yea yea, and nay nay? But as God is true, our word toward you was not yea and nay. For the Son of God, Jesus Christ, who was preached among you by us, even by me and Silvanus and Timotheus, was not yea and nay, but in him was yea. — II Corinthians 1:1-19.

"FOR ALL THE PROMISES OF GOD ARE YEA"

For all the promises of God in him are yea, and in him Amen, unto the glory of God by us. Now he which stablisheth us with you in Christ, and hath anointed us, is God; who hath also sealed us, and given the earnest of the Spirit in our hearts.

Moreover I call God for a record upon my soul, that to spare you I came not as yet unto Corinth. Not for that we have dominion over your faith, but are helpers of your joy: for by faith ye stand. — II Corinthians 1:20-24.

"MY JOY IS THE JOY OF YOU ALL"

But I determined this with myself, that I would not come again to you in heaviness. For if I make you sorry, who is he then that maketh me glad, but the same which is made sorry by me? And I wrote this same unto you, lest, when I came, I should have sorrow from them of whom I ought to rejoice; having confidence in you all, that my joy is the joy of you all. For out of much affliction and anguish of heart I wrote unto you with many tears; not that ye should be grieved, but that ye might know the love which I have more abundantly unto you.

But if any have caused grief, he hath not grieved me, but in part: that I may not overcharge you all. Sufficient to such a man is this punishment, which was inflicted of many. So that contrariwise ye ought rather to forgive him, and comfort him, lest perhaps such a one should be swallowed up with overmuch sorrow. Wherefore I beseech you that ye would confirm your love toward him. For to this end also did I write, that I might know the proof of you, whether ye be obedient in all things. To whom ye forgive anything, I forgive also: for if I forgave anything, to whom I forgave it, for your sakes forgave I it in the person of Christ; lest Satan should get an advantage of us: for we are not ignorant of his devices.

Furthermore, when I came to Troas to preach Christ's gospel, and a door was opened unto me of the Lord, I had no rest in my spirit, because I found not Titus, my brother: but taking my leave of them, I went from thence into Macedonia. Now thanks be unto God, which always causeth us to triumph in Christ, and maketh manifest the savour of his knowledge by us in every place. For we are unto God a sweet savour of Christ, in them that are saved, and in them that perish: to the one we are the savour of death unto death; and to the other the savour of life unto life. And who is sufficient for these things? For we are not as many, which corrupt the word of God: but as of sincerity, but as of God, in the sight of God speak we in Christ. — II Corinthians 2.

"YE ARE OUR EPISTLE WRITTEN IN OUR HEARTS"

Do we begin again to commend ourselves? Or need we, as some others, epistles of commendation to you, or letters of commendation from you? Ye are our epistle written in our hearts, known and read of all men: forasmuch as ye are manifestly declared to be the epistle of Christ ministered by us, written not with ink, but with the Spirit of the living God; not in tables of stone, but in fleshy tables of the heart. And such trust have we through Christ to God-ward: not that we are sufficient of ourselves to think anything as of ourselves; but our sufficiency is of God; who also hath made us able ministers of the new testament; not of the letter, but of the spirit: for the letter killeth, but the spirit giveth life. But if the ministration of death, written and engraven in stones, was glorious, so that the children of Israel could not steadfastly behold the face of Moses for the glory of his countenance; which glory was to be done away: how shall not the ministration of the spirit be rather glorious? For if the ministration of condemnation be glory, much more doth the ministration of righteousness exceed in glory. For even that which was made glorious had no glory in this respect, by reason of the glory that excelleth. For if that which is done away was glorious, much more that which remaineth is glorious.

Seeing then that we have such hope, we use great plainness of speech: and not as Moses, which put a veil over his face, that the children of Israel could not steadfastly look to the end of that which is abolished: but their minds were blinded: for until this day remaineth the same veil untaken away in the reading of the old testament; which veil is done away in Christ. But even unto this day, when Moses is read, the veil is upon

THE TEMPLE OF JUNO, GIRGENTI, SICILY

APOSTLE JAMES, THE GREATER

A painting by Anthony Gruerio

their heart. Nevertheless when it shall turn to the Lord, the veil shall be taken away. — II Corinthians 3:1–16.

"WHERE THE SPIRIT OF THE LORD IS, THERE IS LIBERTY"

Now the Lord is that Spirit: and where the Spirit of the Lord is, there is liberty. But we all, with open face beholding as in a glass the glory of the Lord, are changed into the same image from glory to glory, even as by the Spirit of the Lord. — II Corinthians 3:17, 18.

"WE PREACH NOT OURSELVES BUT CHRIST JESUS THE LORD"

Therefore seeing we have this ministry, as we have received mercy, we faint not; but have renounced the hidden things of dishonesty, not walking in craftiness, nor handling the word of God deceitfully; but by manifestation of the truth commending ourselves to every man's conscience in the sight of God. But if our gospel be hid, it is hid to them that are lost: in whom the god of this world hath blinded the minds of them which believe not, lest the light of the glorious gospel of Christ, who is the image of God, should shine unto them. For we preach not ourselves, but Christ Jesus the Lord; and ourselves your servants for Jesus' sake. For God, who commanded the light to shine out of darkness, hath shined in our hearts, to give the light of the knowledge of the glory of God in the face of Jesus Christ.

— II Corinthians 4:1–6.

"WE ARE TROUBLED ON EVERY SIDE, YET NOT DISTRESSED"

But we have this treasure in earthen vessels, that the excellency of the power may be of God, and not of us. We are troubled on every side, yet not distressed; we

RUINS AT CORINTH

are perplexed, but not in despair; persecuted, but not forsaken; cast down, but not destroyed; always bearing about in the body the dying of the Lord Jesus, that the life also of Jesus might be made manifest in our body.

For we which live are always delivered unto death for Jesus' sake, that the life also of Jesus might be made manifest in our mortal flesh. So then death worketh in us, but life in you. We having the same spirit of faith, according as it is written, "I believed, and therefore have I spoken"; we also believe, and therefore speak; knowing that he which raised up the Lord Jesus shall raise up us also by Jesus, and shall present us with you. For all things are for your sakes, that the abundant grace might through the thanksgiving of many redound to the glory of God. — II Corinthians 4:7–15.

"THE THINGS WHICH ARE SEEN ARE TEMPORAL; THE THINGS WHICH ARE NOT SEEN ARE ETERNAL"

For which cause we faint not; but though our outward man perish, yet the inward man is renewed day by day. For our light affliction, which is but for a moment, worketh for us a far more exceeding and eternal weight of glory; while we look not at the things which are seen, but at the things which are not seen: for the things which are seen are temporal; but the things which are not seen are eternal.

For we know that if our earthly house of this tabernacle were dissolved, we have a building of God, an house not made with hands, eternal in the heavens. For in this we groan, earnestly desiring to be clothed upon with our house which is from heaven: if so be that being clothed we shall not be found naked. For we that are in this tabernacle do groan, being burdened: not for that we would be unclothed, but clothed upon, that mortality might be swallowed up of life. Now he that hath wrought us for the selfsame thing is God, who also hath given unto us the earnest of the Spirit. Therefore we are always confident, knowing that, whilst we are at home in the body, we are absent from the Lord: (for we walk by faith, not by sight:) we are confident, I say, and willing rather to be absent from the body, and to be present with the Lord. Wherefore we labour, that, whether present or absent, we may be accepted of him. For we must all appear before the judgment seat of Christ; that every one may receive the things done in his body, according to that he hath done, whether it be good or bad.

Knowing therefore the terror of the Lord, we persuade men; but we are made manifest unto God; and I trust also are made manifest in your consciences. For we commend not ourselves again unto you, but give you occasion to glory on our behalf, that ye may have somewhat to answer them which glory in appearance, and not in heart. For whether we be beside ourselves, it is to God: or whether we be sober, it is for your cause. For the love of Christ constraineth us; because we thus judge, that if one died for all, then were all dead: and that he died for all, that they which live should not henceforth live unto themselves, but unto him which died for them, and rose again. Wherefore henceforth know we no man after the flesh: yea, though we have known Christ after the flesh, yet now henceforth know we him no more. Therefore if any man be in Christ, he is a new creature: old things are passed away; behold, all things are become new. And all things are of God, who hath reconciled us to himself by Jesus Christ, and hath given to us the ministry of reconciliation; to wit, that God was in Christ, reconciling the world unto himself, not imputing their trespasses unto them; and hath committed unto us the word of reconciliation.

— II Corinthians 4:16–5:19.

"WE ARE AMBASSADORS FOR CHRIST"

Now then we are ambassadors for Christ, as though God did beseech you by us: we pray you in Christ's stead, be ye reconciled to God. For he hath made him to be sin for us, who knew no sin; that we might be made the righteousness of God in him.   — II Corinthians 5:20, 21.

"IN ALL THINGS APPROVING OURSELVES AS THE MINISTERS OF GOD"

We then, as workers together with him, beseech you also that ye receive not the grace of God in vain.

(For he saith,

"I have heard thee in a time accepted,
And in the day of salvation have I succoured thee":

behold, now is the accepted time; behold, now is the day of salvation.) Giving no offence in anything, that the ministry be not blamed: but in all things approving ourselves as the ministers of God, in much patience, in afflictions, in necessities, in distresses, in stripes, in imprisonments, in tumults, in labours, in watchings, in fastings; by pureness, by knowledge, by longsuffering, by kindness, by the Holy Ghost, by love unfeigned, by the word of truth, by the power of God, by the armour of righteousness on the right hand and on the left, by honour and dishonour, by evil report and good report: as deceivers, and yet true; as unknown, and yet well known; as dying, and, behold, we live; as chastened, and not killed; as sorrowful, yet alway rejoicing; as poor, yet making many rich; as having nothing, and yet possessing all things.

O ye Corinthians, our mouth is open unto you, our heart is enlarged. Ye are not straitened in us, but ye are straitened in your own bowels. Now for a recompence in the same, (I speak as unto my children,) be ye also enlarged.

Be ye not unequally yoked together with unbelievers: for what fellowship hath righteousness with unrighteousness? And what communion hath light with darkness? And what concord hath Christ with Belial? Or what part hath he that believeth with an infidel? And what agreement hath the temple of God with idols? For ye are the temple of the living God; as God hath said, "I will dwell in them, and walk in them; and I will be their God, and they shall be my people." Wherefore

> "'Come out from among them, and be ye separate,'
> Saith the LORD,
> 'And touch not the unclean thing;
> And I will receive you,
> And will be a Father unto you,
> And ye shall be my sons and daughters,'
> Saith the LORD Almighty."

Having therefore these promises, dearly beloved, let us cleanse ourselves from all filthiness of the flesh and spirit, perfecting holiness in the fear of God.

Receive us; we have wronged no man, we have corrupted no man, we have defrauded no man. I speak not this to condemn you: for I have said before, that ye are in our hearts to die and live with you. Great is my boldness of speech toward you, great is my glorying of you: I am filled with comfort, I am exceeding joyful in all our tribulation.   — II Corinthians 6: 7:1-4.

APOSTLE BARTHOLOMEW
A painting by Anthony Gruerio

PAUL'S REJOICING AT THE REPENTANCE OF THE
CHURCH OF CORINTH

For, when we were come into Macedonia, our flesh
had no rest, but we were troubled on every side: without
were fightings, within were fears.　Nevertheless God,
that comforteth those that are cast down, comforted us
by the coming of Titus; and not by his coming only, but
by the consolation wherewith he was comforted in you,
when he told us your earnest desire, your mourning, your
fervent mind toward me; so that I rejoiced the more.

For though I made you sorry with a letter, I do not
repent, though I did repent: for I perceive that the same
epistle hath made you sorry, though it were but for a
season.　Now I rejoice not that ye were made sorry,
but that ye sorrowed to repentance: for ye were made
sorry after a godly manner, that ye might receive damage
by us in nothing.　For godly sorrow worketh repentance
to salvation not to be repented of: but the sorrow of the
world worketh death.　For behold this selfsame thing,
that ye sorrowed after a godly sort, what carefulness it
wrought in you, yea, what clearing of yourselves, yea,
what indignation, yea, what fear, yea, what vehement
desire, yea, what zeal, yea, what revenge! In all things
ye have approved yourselves to be clear in this matter.
Wherefore, though I wrote unto you, I did it not for his
cause that had done the wrong, nor for his cause that
suffered wrong, but that our care for you in the sight
of God might appear unto you.　Therefore we were comforted in your comfort: yea, and exceedingly the more
joyed we for the joy of Titus, because his spirit was refreshed by you all.　For if I have boasted anything to
him of you, I am not ashamed; but as we spake all things
to you in truth, even so 'our boasting, which I made
before Titus, is found a truth.　And his inward affection

is more abundant toward you, whilst he remembereth the obedience of you all, how with fear and trembling ye received him. I rejoice therefore that I have confidence in you in all things.   — II Corinthians 7:5–16.

THE POVERTY AND RICHES OF THE MACEDONIAN CHURCHES

Moreover, brethren, we do you to wit of the grace of God bestowed on the churches of Macedonia; how that in a great trial of affliction the abundance of their joy and their deep poverty abounded unto the riches of their liberality. For to their power, I bear record, yea, and beyond their power they were willing of themselves; praying us with much intreaty that we would receive the gift, and take upon us the fellowship of the ministering to the saints. And this they did, not as we hoped, but first gave their own selves to the Lord, and unto us by the will of God. Insomuch that we desired Titus, that as he had begun, so he would also finish in you the same grace also.

Therefore, as ye abound in everything, in faith, and utterance, and knowledge, and in all diligence, and in your love to us, see that ye abound in this grace also. I speak not by commandment, but by occasion of the forwardness of others, and to prove the sincerity of your love. For ye know the grace of our Lord Jesus Christ, that, though he was rich, yet for your sakes he became poor, that ye through his poverty might be rich. And herein I give my advice: for this is expedient for you, who have begun before, not only to do, but also to be forward a year ago. Now therefore perform the doing of it; that as there was a readiness to will, so there may be a performance also out of that which ye have. For if there be first a willing mind, it is accepted

according to that a man hath, and not according to that he hath not. For I mean not that other men be eased, and ye burdened: but by an equality, that now at this time your abundance may be a supply for their want, that their abundance also may be a supply for your want: that there may be equality: as it is written, "He that had gathered much had nothing over; and he that had gathered little had no lack."

But thanks be to God, which put the same earnest care into the heart of Titus for you. For indeed he accepted the exhortation; but being more forward, of his own accord he went unto you. And we have sent with him the brother, whose praise is in the gospel throughout all the churches; and not that only, but who was also chosen of the churches to travel with us with this grace, which is administered by us to the glory of the same Lord, and declaration of your ready mind: avoiding this, that no man should blame us in this abundance which is administered by us: providing for honest things, not only in the sight of the Lord, but also in the sight of men. And we have sent with them our brother, whom we have oftentimes proved diligent in many things, but now much more diligent, upon the great confidence which I have in you. Whether any do enquire of Titus, he is my partner and fellow-helper concerning you: or our brethren be enquired of, they are the messengers of the churches, and the glory of Christ. Wherefore shew ye to them, and before the churches, the proof of your love, and of our boasting on your behalf. — II Corinthians 8.

PAUL EXHORTS THE CHURCH OF CORINTH TO SUSTAIN
ITS REPUTATION FOR GENEROSITY

For as touching the ministering to the saints, it is

PORTRAIT OF PAUL
A painting by John Bianchi

superfluous for me to write to you: for I know the forwardness of your mind, for which I boast of you to them
of Macedonia, that Achaia was ready a year ago; and
your zeal hath provoked very many. Yet have I sent
the brethren, lest our boasting of you should be in vain
in this behalf; that, as I said, ye may be ready: lest
haply if they of Macedonia come with me, and find you
unprepared, we (that we say not, ye) should be ashamed
in this same confident boasting. Therefore I thought
it necessary to exhort the brethren, that they would go
before unto you, and make up beforehand your bounty,
whereof ye had notice before, that the same might be
ready, as a matter of bounty, and not as of covetousness. But this I say, he which soweth sparingly shall
reap also sparingly; and he which soweth bountifully
shall reap also bountifully. Every man according as he
purposeth in his heart, so let him give; not grudgingly,
or of necessity: for God loveth a cheerful giver. And
God is able to make all grace abound toward you; that
ye, always having all sufficiency in all things, may
abound to every good work: (as it is written,

"He hath dispersed abroad; he hath given to the poor:
His righteousness remaineth forever."

Now he that ministereth seed to the sower both minister
bread for your food, and multiply your seed sown, and
increase the fruits of your righteousness;) being enriched
in every thing to all bountifulness, which causeth through
us thanksgiving to God. For the administration of this
service not only supplieth the want of the saints, but is
abundant also by many thanksgivings unto God; whiles
by the experiment of this ministration they glorify God
for your professed subjection unto the gospel of Christ,
and for your liberal distribution unto them, and unto

all men; and by their prayer for you, which long after you for the exceeding grace of God in you. Thanks be unto God for his unspeakable gift. — II Corinthians 9.

"WE WILL NOT BOAST, BUT GLORY IN THE LORD"

Now I, Paul, myself beseech you by the meekness and gentleness of Christ, who in presence am base among you, but being absent am bold toward you: but I beseech you, that I may not be bold when I am present with that confidence, wherewith I think to be bold against some, which think of us as if we walked according to the flesh. For though we walk in the flesh, we do not war after the flesh: (for the weapons of our warfare are not carnal, but mighty through God to the pulling down of strongholds;) casting down imaginations, and every high thing that exalteth itself against the knowledge of God, and bringing into captivity every thought to the obedience of Christ; and having in a readiness to revenge all disobedience, when your obedience is fulfilled.

Do ye look on things after the outward appearance? If any man trust to himself that he is Christ's, let him of himself think this again, that, as he is Christ's, even so are we Christ's. For though I should boast somewhat more of our authority, which the Lord hath given us for edification, and not for your destruction, I should not be ashamed: that I may not seem as if I would terrify you by letters. "For his letters," say they, "are weighty and powerful; but his bodily presence is weak, and his speech contemptible." Let such an one think this, that, such as we are in word by letters when we are absent, such will we be also in deed when we are present. For we dare not make ourselves of the number, or compare ourselves with some that commend themselves: but they measuring themselves by themselves, and

comparing themselves among themselves, are not wise. But we will not boast of things without our measure, but according to the measure of the rule which God hath distributed to us, a measure to reach even unto you. For we stretch not ourselves beyond our measure, as though we reached not unto you: for we are come as far as to you also in preaching the gospel of Christ: not boasting of things without our measure, that is, of other men's labours; but having hope, when your faith is increased, that we shall be enlarged by you according to our rule abundantly, to preach the gospel in the regions beyond you, and not to boast in another man's line of things made ready to our hand. But he that glorieth, let him glory in the Lord. For not he that commendeth himself is approved, but whom the Lord commendeth.

— II Corinthians 10.

The Service Record of Paul, He Is Not the Least Among the Apostles

Would to God ye could bear with me a little in my folly: and indeed bear with me. For I am jealous over you with godly jealousy: for I have espoused you to one husband, that I may present you as a chaste virgin to Christ. But I fear, lest by any means, as the serpent beguiled Eve through his subtilty, so your minds should be corrupted from the simplicity that is in Christ. For if he that cometh preacheth another Jesus, whom we have not preached, or if ye receive another spirit, which ye have not received, or another gospel, which ye have not accepted, ye might well bear with him. For I suppose I was not a whit behind the very chiefest apostles. But though I be rude in speech, yet not in knowledge; but we have been thoroughly made manifest among you in all things.

— II Corinthians 11:1-6

PAUL'S ESCAPE AT DAMASCUS
An engraving by Gustaf Zerner

"HAVE I COMMITTED AN OFFENCE IN ABASING MYSELF THAT YE MIGHT BE EXALTED?"

Have I committed an offence in abasing myself that ye might be exalted, because I have preached to you the gospel of God freely? I robbed other churches, taking wages of them, to do you service. And when I was present with you, and wanted, I was chargeable to no man: for that which was lacking to me the brethren which came from Macedonia supplied: and in all things I have kept myself from being burdensome unto you, and so will I keep myself. As the truth of Christ is in me, no man shall stop me of this boasting in the regions of Achaia. Wherefore? Because I love you not? God knoweth. But what I do, that I will do, that I may cut off occasion from them which desire occasion; that wherein they glory, they may be found even as we. For such are false apostles, deceitful workers, transforming themselves into the apostles of Christ. And no marvel; for Satan himself is transformed into an angel of light. Therefore it is no great thing if his ministers also be transformed as the ministers of righteousness; whose end shall be according to their works.   — II Corinthians 11:7-15.

"LET NO MAN THINK ME A FOOL"

I say again, let no man think me a fool; if otherwise, yet as a fool receive me, that I may boast myself a little. That which I speak, I speak it not after the Lord, but as it were foolishly, in this confidence of boasting. Seeing that many glory after the flesh I will glory also. For ye suffer fools gladly, seeing ye yourselves are wise. For ye suffer, if a man bring you into bondage, if a man devour you, if a man take of you, if a man exalt himself, if a man smite you on the face.

— II Corinthians 11:16-20.

"IF I MUST NEEDS GLORY, I WILL GLORY OF MINE INFIRMITIES"

I speak as concerning reproach, as though we had been weak. Howbeit whereinsoever any is bold, (I speak foolishly,) I am bold also. Are they Hebrews? So am I. Are they Israelites? So am I. Are they the seed of Abraham? So am I. Are they ministers of Christ? (I speak as a fool) I am more; in labours more abundant, in stripes above measure, in prisons more frequent, in deaths oft. Of the Jews five times received I forty stripes save one. Thrice was I beaten with rods, once was I stoned; thrice I suffered shipwreck, a night and a day I have been in the deep; in journeyings often, in perils of waters, in perils of robbers, in perils by mine own countrymen, in perils by the heathen, in perils in the city, in perils in the wilderness, in perils in the sea, in perils among false brethren; in weariness and painfulness, in watchings often, in hunger and thirst, in fastings often, in cold and nakedness: beside those things that are without, that which cometh upon me daily, the care of all the churches. Who is weak, and I am not weak? Who is offended, and I burn not? If I must needs glory, I will glory of the things which concern mine infirmities. The God and Father of our Lord Jesus Christ, which is blessed for evermore, knoweth that I lie not. In Damascus the governor under Aretas, the king, kept the city of the Damascenes with a garrison, desirous to apprehend me: and through a window in a basket was I let down by the wall, and escaped his hands.

— II Corinthians 11:21–33.

"IT IS NOT EXPEDIENT FOR ME DOUBTLESS TO GLORY: I WILL COME TO VISIONS OF THE LORD"

It is not expedient for me doubtless to glory. I will come to visions and revelations of the Lord. I knew

a man in Christ above fourteen years ago, (whether in
the body, I cannot tell; or whether out of the body,
I cannot tell: God knoweth;) such an one caught up
to the third heaven. And I knew such a man, (whether
in the body, or out of the body, I cannot tell: God
knoweth;) how that he was caught up into paradise,
and heard unspeakable words, which it is not lawful for
a man to utter.

Of such an one will I glory: yet of myself I will not
glory, but in mine infirmities. For though I would desire to glory, I shall not be a fool; for I will say the truth:
but now I forbear, lest any man should think of me
above that which he seeth me to be, or that he heareth
of me.   — II Corinthians 12:1–6.

"THE THORN IN THE FLESH"

"MY GRACE IS SUFFICIENT FOR THEE"

And lest I should be exalted above measure through
the abundance of the revelations, there was given to me
a thorn in the flesh, the messenger of Satan to buffet
me, lest I should be exalted above measure. For this
thing I besought the LORD thrice, that it might depart
from me. And he said unto me, "My grace is sufficient
for thee: for my strength is made perfect in weakness."
Most gladly therefore will I rather glory in my infirmities, that the power of Christ may rest upon me.
Therefore I take pleasure in infirmities, in reproaches,
in necessities, in persecutions, in distresses for Christ's
sake: for when I am weak, then am I strong.

I am become a fool in glorying; ye have compelled
me: for I ought to have been commended of you: for
in nothing am I behind the very chiefest apostles, though
I be nothing. Truly the signs of an apostle were wrought
among you in all patience, in signs, and wonders, and

ST. PAUL LANDING AT MALTA
An engraving by Gustave Doré

mighty deeds. For what is it wherein ye were inferior to other churches, except it be that I myself was not burdensome to you? Forgive me this wrong.

— II Corinthians 12:7–13.

"THE THIRD TIME I AM READY TO COME TO YOU"
"I SEEK NOT YOURS, BUT YOU"

Behold, the third time I am ready to come to you; and I will not be burdensome to you: for I seek not yours, but you: for the children ought not to lay up for the parents, but the parents for the children. And I will very gladly spend and be spent for you; though the more abundantly I love you, the less I be loved.

But be it so, I did not burden you: nevertheless, being crafty, I caught you with guile. Did I make a gain of you by any of them whom I sent unto you? I desired Titus, and with him I sent a brother. Did Titus make a gain of you? Walked we not in the same spirit? Walked we not in the same steps?

Again, think ye that we excuse ourselves unto you? We speak before God in Christ: but we do all things, dearly beloved, for your edifying. For I fear, lest, when I come, I shall not find you such as I would, and that I shall be found unto you such as ye would not: lest there be debates, envyings, wraths, strifes, backbitings, whisperings, swellings, tumults: and lest, when I come again, my God will humble me among you, and that I shall bewail many which have sinned already, and have not repented of the uncleanness and fornication and lasciviousness which they have committed.

This is the third time I am coming to you. In the mouth of two or three witnesses shall every word be established. I told you before, and foretell you, as if I were present, the second time: and being absent now I write to them which heretofore have sinned, and to all other, that, if I come again, I will not spare: since ye seek a proof of Christ speaking in me, which to you-ward is not weak, but is mighty in you. For though he was crucified through weakness, yet he liveth by the power of God. For we also are weak in him, but we shall live with him by the power of God toward you.

Examine yourselves, whether ye be in the faith; prove your own selves. Know ye not your own selves, how that Jesus Christ is in you, except ye be reprobates? But I trust that ye shall know that we are not reprobates. Now I pray to God that ye do no evil; not that we should appear approved, but that ye should do that which is honest, though we be as reprobates. For we can do nothing against the truth, but for the truth. For we are glad, when we are weak, and ye are strong: and this also we wish, even your perfection. — II Corinthians 12:14–13:9.

Farewell

Therefore I write these things being absent, lest being present I should use sharpness, according to the power which the LORD hath given me to edification, and not to destruction.

Finally, brethren, farewell. Be perfect, be of good comfort, be of one mind, live in peace; and the God of love and peace shall be with you.

Greet one another with an holy kiss.

All the saints salute you.

The grace of the Lord Jesus Christ, and the love of God, and the communion of the Holy Ghost, be with you all. Amen. — II Corinthians 13:10–14.

The Letters of Paul

The Great Captain of the New Faith

The Epistle to the Galatians

Stand fast in the liberty wherewith Christ hath made us free.

This is the most impetuous of Paul's letters. It was written in hot haste. Paul had heard that his converts in Galatia were in danger of being turned from what he had taught as the essence of the gospel. Jewish Christians had come to them and urged that if they wished to be Christians they must first become Jews and keep the Jewish law; and these Gentile Christians were almost persuaded to yield. The arguments used we can in part gather from Paul's letter. "Paul," they said, "was not an original apostle. What authority had he? No such interpretation had been given by the apostles at Jerusalem." They doubtless urged also that the Messianic hope was a Jewish hope; did the Gentiles expect to come into the Jewish Messianic Kingdom without keeping the Jewish laws? Paul knew this position to be a denial of the Gospel of Christ. He was the more distressed because of the warm affection between himself and the Galatians.

On the occasion of Paul's first visit, he says in this letter, he had been received by them with hospitality and kindness, which touched him deeply. He was detained in Galatia by illness; he was the "evangelist to the Galatians against his will." These warm-hearted people treated him as an "angel of God, even as Christ Jesus himself." They would have "plucked out their own eyes" to give him. He hears now with the most profound regret that they have turned from the liberty of the gospel which he taught to the old bondage of custom and tradition.

This splendid epistle was written, perhaps, on the march. There are no salutations from any church where he is temporarily staying. We may imagine even that it was written on ship-board, some glorious morning on the Ægean, its waves flashing in the sun, the

278

white temple of Cape Sunion in sight against the blue of the sky; for it is a sea-epistle; the strength, the vigor, the boundless spaces of the sea seem to be in it. It is the great proclamation of the liberty of the gospel. "Stand fast in the liberty wherewith Christ hath made you free" is its key-note. It is an impetuous flow of rebuke changing into the tenderest pleading. "O foolish Galatians; who hath bewitched you?" "Ye did run well; who did hinder you that ye should not obey the truth?" It is full of those inspired passages, characteristic of Paul, in which a profound spiritual truth is set forth in language which is at once simple and sublime, wholly worthy of the truth which it illumines. Paul makes also a magnificent defense of his own apostleship, in which he gives us incidentally certain data regarding his life which we should not otherwise possess. We must remember always that these letters were not written to satisfy our own curiosity with respect to events and dates. They were not primarily written for us at all. They came out of the burning heart of Paul to meet the needs of his own churches, his own children. They are written for them, for their times, and we may be thankful that they are also so perfectly suited to the needs of Christians in all times. If certain passages are not easily understood or are difficult to apply, still the lesson is there.

There has been much discussion as to the location of the Galatian churches. In the third century B.C. a band of Celts or Gauls turned for some reason from the western migration of the rest of the Celtic tribes, crossed the Hellespont, and fought their way into the north central part of Asia Minor. Here they made their homes and founded a kingdom called Galatia. Their capital was Ancyra, the modern Angora, or Ankara, famous as the capital of Turkey since World War I. In 25 A.D. the name, "Galatia," was given to a new Roman province, extending from the old kingdom almost to the Taurus Mountains in southern Asia Minor. The province of Galatia included the cities in which Paul preached on his first missionary journey.

The problem is: How do Paul and the author of Acts use the name, "Galatia"? Do they mean the old, northern kingdom of Galatia or the new Roman province of Galatia? If they mean the old kingdom, then the Galatian churches were among the Celts, and were not founded till Paul's second journey. If they mean the Roman province, then the churches were those in Antioch, Iconium,

Derbe, and Lystra, and were founded on the first journey. There is a strong tendency to regard these churches of South Galatia as those to which Paul sent his letter. See also the note on Phrygia and the region of Galatia. (See 8:35, 37.)

Paul, an apostle, (not of men, neither by man, but by Jesus Christ, and God the Father, who raised him from the dead;) and all the brethren which are with me, unto the churches of Galatia:

Grace be to you and peace from God the Father, and from our Lord Jesus Christ, who gave himself for our sins, that he might deliver us from this present evil world, according to the will of God and our Father: to whom be glory forever and ever. Amen.

"The Gospel of the Revelation of Christ"

I MARVEL that ye are so soon removed from him that called you into the grace of Christ unto another gospel: which is not another; but there be some that trouble you, and would pervert the gospel of Christ. But though we, or an angel from heaven, preach any other gospel unto you than that which we have preached unto you, let him be accursed. As we said before, so say I now again, if any man preach any other gospel unto you than that ye have received, let him be accursed. For do I now persuade men, or God? Or do I seek to please men? For if I yet pleased men, I should not be the servant of Christ.

But I certify you, brethren, that the gospel which was preached of me is not after man. For I neither received it of man, neither was I taught it, but by the revelation of Jesus Christ. For ye have heard of my conversation in time past in the Jews' religion, how that beyond measure I persecuted the church of God, and wasted it: and profited in the Jews' religion above many my equals in mine own nation, being more exceedingly zealous of the traditions of my fathers.

But when it pleased God, who separated me from my mother's womb, and called me by his grace, to reveal his Son in me, that I might preach him among the heathen; immediately I conferred not with flesh and blood: neither went I up to Jerusalem to them which were apostles before me; but I went into Arabia, and returned again unto Damascus.

Then after three years I went up to Jerusalem to see Peter, and abode with him fifteen days. But other of the apostles saw I none, save James, the Lord's brother. Now the things which I write unto you, behold, before God, I lie not. Afterwards I came into the regions of Syria and Cilicia; and was unknown by face unto the churches of Judæa which were in Christ: but they had heard only, that "he which persecuted us in times past now preacheth the faith which once he destroyed." And they glorified God in me.   — Galatians 1.

The Freedom of the Gospel

Then fourteen years after I went up again to Jerusalem with Barnabas, and took Titus with me also. And I went up by revelation, and communicated unto them that gospel which I preach among the Gentiles, but privately to them which were of reputation, lest by any means I should run, or had run, in vain. But neither Titus, who was with me, being a Greek, was compelled to be circumcised: and that because of false brethren unawares brought in, who came in privily to spy out our liberty which we have in Christ Jesus, that they might bring us into bondage: to whom we gave place by subjection, no, not for an hour; that the truth

RUINS OF TEMPLE OF APOLLO, DELPHI, GREECE

of the gospel might continue with you. But of these who seemed to be somewhat, (whatsoever they were, it maketh no matter to me: God accepteth no man's person:) for they who seemed to be somewhat in conference added nothing to me: but contrariwise, when they saw that the gospel of the uncircumcision was committed unto me, as the gospel of the circumcision was unto Peter; (for he that wrought effectually in Peter to the apostleship of the circumcision, the same was mighty in me toward the Gentiles:) and when James, Cephas, and John, who seemed to be pillars, perceived the grace that was given unto me, they gave to me and Barnabas the right hands of fellowship; that we should go unto the heathen, and they unto the circumcision. Only they would that we should remember the poor; the same which I also was forward to do.

But when Peter was come to Antioch, I withstood him to the face, because he was to be blamed. For before that certain came from James, he did eat with the Gentiles: but when they were come, he withdrew and separated himself, fearing them which were of the circumcision. And the other Jews dissembled likewise with him; insomuch that Barnabas also was carried away with their dissimulation. But when I saw that they walked not uprightly according to the truth of the gospel, I said unto Peter before them all, "If thou, being a Jew, livest after the manner of Gentiles, and not as do the Jews, why compellest thou the Gentiles to live as do the Jews? We who are Jews by nature, and not sinners of the Gentiles, knowing that a man is not justified by the works of the law, but by the faith of Jesus Christ, even we have believed in Jesus Christ, that we might be justified by the faith of Christ, and not by the works of the law: for by the works of the law shall no flesh be justified. But if, while we seek to be justified by Christ, we ourselves also are found sinners, is therefore Christ the minister of sin? God forbid.''

For if I build again the things which I destroyed, I make myself a transgressor. For I through the law am dead to the law, that I might live unto God. I am crucified with Christ: nevertheless I live; yet not I, but Christ liveth in me: and the life which I now live in the flesh I live by the faith of the Son of God, who loved me, and gave himself for me. I do not frustrate the grace of God: for if righteousness come by the law, then Christ is dead in vain.   — Galatians 2.

"O FOOLISH GALATIANS, WHO HATH BEWITCHED YOU, THAT YE SHOULD NOT OBEY THE TRUTH?"

O foolish Galatians, who hath bewitched you, that ye should not obey the truth, before whose eyes Jesus Christ hath been evidently set forth, crucified among you? This only would I learn of you: received ye the Spirit by the works of the law, or by the hearing of faith? Are ye so foolish? Having begun in the Spirit, are ye now made perfect by the flesh? Have ye suffered so many things in vain, if it be yet in vain? He therefore that ministereth to you the Spirit, and worketh miracles among you, doeth he it by the works of the law, or by the hearing of faith? Even as Abraham believed God, and it was accounted to him for righteousness. Know ye therefore that they which are of faith, the same are the children of Abraham.   And the Scripture, foreseeing that God would justify the heathen through faith, preached before the gospel unto Abraham, saying, "In thee shall all nations be blessed." So then they which be of faith are blessed with faithful Abraham.   For as many as are of the works of the law are under the curse:

for it is written, "Cursed is every one that continueth not in all things which are written in the book of the law to do them." But that no man is justified by the law in the sight of God, it is evident: for, "The just shall live by faith." And the law is not of faith: but, "The man that doeth them shall live in them." Christ hath redeemed us from the curse of the law, being made a curse for us: for it is written, "Cursed is every one that hangeth on a tree": that the blessing of Abraham might come on the Gentiles through Jesus Christ; that we might receive the promise of the Spirit through faith.

Brethren, I speak after the manner of men; though it be but a man's covenant, yet if it be confirmed, no man disannulleth, or addeth thereto. Now to Abraham and his seed were the promises made. He saith not, "And to seeds," as of many; but as of one, "And to thy seed," which is Christ. And this I say, that the covenant, that was confirmed before of God in Christ, the law, which was four hundred and thirty years after, cannot disannul, that it should make the promise of none effect. For if the inheritance be of the law, it is no more of promise: but God gave it to Abraham by promise. Wherefore then serveth the law? It was added because of transgressions, till the seed should come to whom the promise was made; and it was ordained by angels in the hand of a mediator. Now a mediator is not a mediator of one, but God is one. Is the law then against the promises of God? God forbid: for if there had been a law given which could have given life, verily righteousness should have been by the law. But the Scripture hath concluded all under sin, that the promise by faith of Jesus Christ might be given to them that believe. — Galatians 3:1–22.

THE ERECHTHEION

"THE LAW OUR SCHOOLMASTER"

But before faith came, we were kept under the law, shut up unto the faith which should afterwards be revealed. Wherefore the law was our schoolmaster to bring us unto Christ, that we might be justified by faith. But after that faith is come, we are no longer under a schoolmaster. For ye are all the children of God by faith in Christ Jesus. For as many of you as have been baptized into Christ have put on Christ.

— Galatians 3:23–27.

"THERE IS NEITHER BOND NOR FREE: FOR YE ARE ALL ONE IN CHRIST JESUS"

There is neither Jew nor Greek, there is neither bond nor free, there is neither male nor female: for ye are all one in Christ Jesus. And if ye be Christ's, then are ye Abraham's seed, and heirs according to the promise.

Now I say, that the heir, as long as he is a child, differeth nothing from a servant, though he be lord of all; but is under tutors and governors until the time appointed of the father. Even so we, when we were children, were in bondage under the elements of the world: but when the fulness of the time was come, God sent forth his Son, made of a woman, made under the law, to redeem them that were under the law, that we might receive the adoption of sons.   — Galatians 3:28–4:5.

SONS OF GOD

And because ye are sons, God hath sent forth the Spirit of his Son into your hearts, crying, "Abba, Father." Wherefore thou art no more a servant, but a son; and if a son, then an heir of God through Christ.

Howbeit then, when ye knew not God, ye did service unto them which by nature are no gods. But now,

after that ye have known God, or rather are known of
God, how turn ye again to the weak and beggarly
elements, whereunto ye desire again to be in bondage?
Ye observe days, and months, and times, and years. I am
afraid of you, lest I have bestowed upon you labour in vain.

Brethren, I beseech you, be as I am; for I am as ye
are: ye have not injured me at all. Ye know how
through infirmity of the flesh I preached the gospel
unto you at the first. And my temptation which was
in my flesh ye despised not, nor rejected; but received
me as an angel of God, even as Christ Jesus. Where is
then the blessedness ye spake of? For I bear you record,
that, if it had been possible, ye would have plucked out
your own eyes, and have given them to me. Am I
therefore become your enemy, because I tell you the truth?
They zealously affect you, but not well; yea, they would
exclude you, that ye might affect them. But it is good
to be zealously affected always in a good thing, and not
only when I am present with you. My little children,
of whom I travail in birth again until Christ be formed
in you, I desire to be present with you now, and to
change my voice; for I stand in doubt of you.

Tell me, ye that desire to be under the law, do ye
not hear the law? For it is written, that Abraham had
two sons, the one by a bondmaid, the other by a free-
woman. But he who was of the bondwoman was born
after the flesh; but he of the freewoman was by promise. Which things are an allegory: for these are the two
covenants; the one from the Mount Sinai, which gender-
eth to bondage, which is Agar. For this Agar is Mount
Sinai in Arabia, and answereth to Jerusalem which
now is, and is in bondage with her children. But Jerusalem which is above is free, which is the mother of us
all. For it is written.

APOSTLE THOMAS
A painting by Anthony Gruerio

"Rejoice, thou barren that beareth not;
Break forth and cry, thou that travailest not:
For the desolate hath many more children than she
 which hath an husband."

Now we, brethren, as Isaac was, are the children of promise. But as then he that was born after the flesh persecuted him that was born after the Spirit, even so it is now. Nevertheless what saith the Scripture? Cast out the bondwoman and her son: for the son of the bondwoman shall not be heir with the son of the free-woman. So then, brethren, we are not children of the bondwoman, but of the free. — Galatians 4:6–31.

"STAND FAST IN THE LIBERTY WHEREWITH CHRIST HATH MADE US FREE"

Stand fast therefore in the liberty wherewith Christ hath made us free, and be not entangled again with the yoke of bondage. Behold, I, Paul, say unto you, that if ye be circumcised, Christ shall profit you nothing. For I testify again to every man that is circumcised, that he is a debtor to do the whole law. Christ is become of no effect unto you, whosoever of you are justified by the law; ye are fallen from grace. For we through the Spirit wait for the hope of righteousness by faith. For in Jesus Christ neither circumcision availeth any thing, nor uncircumcision; but faith which worketh by love. Ye did run well; who did hinder you that ye should not obey the truth? This persuasion cometh not of him that calleth you. A little leaven leaveneth the whole lump. I have confidence in you through the Lord, that ye will be none otherwise minded: but he that troubleth you shall bear his judgment, whosoever he be. And I, brethren, if I yet preach circumcision, why do I yet suffer persecution? Then is the offence of the cross ceased. I would they were even cut off which trouble you.

For, brethren, ye have been called unto liberty; only use not liberty for an occasion to the flesh, but by love serve one another. For all the law is fulfilled in one word, even in this; "Thou shalt love thy neighbour as thyself." But if ye bite and devour one another. take heed that ye be not consumed one of another.

— Galatians 5:1-15

"WALK IN THE SPIRIT, AND YE SHALL NOT FULFIL THE LUST OF THE FLESH'

This I say then, walk in the Spirit, and ye shall not fulfil the lust of the flesh. For the flesh lusteth against the Spirit, and the Spirit against the flesh: and these are contrary the one to the other: so that ye cannot do the things that ye would. But if ye be led of the Spirit, ye are not under the law. Now the works of the flesh are manifest, which are these: adultery, fornication, uncleanness, lasciviousness, idolatry, witchcraft, hatred, variance, emulations, wrath, strife, seditions, heresies, envyings, murders, drunkenness, revellings, and such like: of the which I tell you before, as I have also told you in time past, that they which do such things shall not inherit the kingdom of God. But the fruit of the Spirit is love, joy, peace, longsuffering, gentleness, goodness, faith, meekness, temperance: against such there is no law. And they that are Christ's have crucified the flesh with the affections and lusts. If we live in the Spirit, let us also walk in the Spirit. Let us not be desirous of vain glory, provoking one another, envying one another. — Galatians 5:16-26.

The Site of Ephesus

THIS photograph shows us what remains today of the once proud city of Ephesus, where Paul spent about three years (53-57 A.D.) on his third missionary journey (see pages 80-87) and to the churches of which region he addressed his majestic Epistle to the Ephesians (see pages 299-314).

The Ephesus which Paul knew was a city of wealth and splendor, with broad avenues, imposing temples, and extensive bazaars (see page 82). Its artificial harbor and location on the connecting highways of Asia Minor made it the most easily accessible city in Asia. As the known history of Ephesus began over six hundred years before Paul's time, its culture was a mixture of the Oriental and Grecian civilizations which had alternately dominated that region. In 190 B.C. the city was incorporated into the Roman province of Asia.

From its prehistoric beginnings Ephesus was famed for being the center of worship of the mother goddess of the earth, who, legend says, was born in the woods near Ephesus where her temple was built when her image fell from the sky. Under Greek rule, the Asiatic goddess of the temple assumed more or less the character of the Greek goddess Artemis and, under Roman rule, became identified with Diana. As she was believed to be the mother of all living things, Diana's worship was widespread and vast wealth poured into her temple which was so beautiful, it was said, that the sun saw nothing in its course more magnificent. In time, as Christianity spread throughout Asia Minor, the pilgrims came in fewer numbers, and finally in 262 A.D., when the temple was burned, its influence had so far diminished that it was never rebuilt. Diana was dead.

The city itself soon lost its importance and the sculptured stones of its great buildings were carried away to Italy and Constantinople. In 1308 the Turks took possession of what little remained of the city and destroyed it. Today, thanks to excavations by Mr. J. T. Wood of the British Museum, who worked from 1863-74 by permission of the Turkish government, we know once more where the harbor, streets, and buildings of Ephesus were located in the days when Paul preached there.

"Bear Ye One Another's Burdens"

Brethren, if a man be overtaken in a fault, ye which are spiritual, restore such an one in the spirit of meekness; considering thyself, lest thou also be tempted. Bear ye one another's burdens, and so fulfil the law of Christ. For if a man think himself to be something, when he is nothing, he deceiveth himself. But let every man prove his own work, and then shall he have rejoicing in himself alone, and not in another. For every man shall bear his own burden.

Let him that is taught in the word communicate unto him that teacheth in all good things. Be not deceived; God is not mocked: for whatsoever a man soweth, that shall he also reap. For he that soweth to his flesh shall of the flesh reap corruption; but he that soweth to the Spirit shall of the Spirit reap life everlasting. And let us not be weary in well doing: for in due season we shall reap, if we faint not. As we have therefore opportunity, let us do good unto all men, especially unto them who are of the household of faith.

Galatians 6:1–10.

Paul's Postscript

Ye see how large a letter I have written unto you with mine own hand.

As many as desire to make a fair show in the flesh, they constrain you to be circumcised; only lest they should suffer persecution for the cross of Christ. For neither they themselves who are circumcised keep the law; but desire to have you circumcised, that they may glory in your flesh. But God forbid that I should glory, save in the cross of our Lord Jesus Christ, by whom the world is crucified unto me, and I unto the world. For in Christ Jesus neither circumcision availeth anything, nor uncircumcision, but a new creature. And as many as walk according to this rule, peace be on them, and mercy, and upon the Israel of God.

From henceforth let no man trouble me: for I bear in my body the marks of the Lord Jesus.

Brethren, the grace of our Lord Jesus Christ be with your spirit. Amen.   — Galatians 6:11–18.

GOLDEN GATE

We are on the site of Solomon's Temple, looking at the back of the Golden Gate in the wall.

It is fast shut up, and has been so for generations. Native tradition is that the Messiah will ride through it some day. It is closed till he comes.

In the background, the Mount of Olives.

Paul at Ephesus

By Gustave Doré (1833-1883)

From Doré's Illustrations of the Bible

THIS picture illustrates the dramatic incident of the burning of the books of magic which occurred during Paul's stay at Ephesus. The Bible story is given on page 85. Dore, well-known French illustrator of the world's literary masterpieces, has given us this vivid picture of the scene. In the right background is the famous temple to Diana, popular native goddess of pagan Asia Minor, described on pages 82 and 293. In the foreground, on the porch of another great building, Paul stands in flowing robes. An excited crowd, bearing huge, bound volumes, is seen pressing forward to fling the books into the fire.

The Bible tells us that the value of these books on the "curious arts" was "fifty thousand pieces of silver," or about $10,000. This information helps us to understand how widespread in those credulous times was the practice of the false and deceitful arts of magic and sorcery, and how effective was Paul's "reasoning and persuading as to the things concerning the kingdom of God." When we read of the impressive victory of "the Word of God" over the Jewish exorcists (page 83) which in turn led to this spectacular public renouncement of customary beliefs in magic, and when we read of the great public demonstration stirred up against Paul by Demetrius and the shrine-makers of Diana's temple (see pages 85-7 and Volume 2, pages 333-6), we realize something of the nature and magnitude of the missionary task which faced Paul and the early Christians. But so great was the force of Paul's teachings that pilgrims and converts, traveling from Ephesus to their distant homes, helped extend the Gospel to every part of Asia Minor.

Dore, another of whose Bible pictures is given on page 97, illustrated the entire Bible, this tremendous task occupying him for four years. His superb imagination and unique gift of drawing created the best known modern picturization of the Holy Scriptures which we have.

The Letters of Paul

The Great Captain of the New Faith

The Epistle to the Ephesians

*Put on the whole armour of God, that ye may be able to stand
against the wiles of the devil.*

This epistle might perhaps be better called the "Epistle to the
Ephesian Churches." There are no salutations to individual members, and the lofty, sustained tone of the epistle seems fitted for a
larger audience than the membership of a single church. It was
written probably during Paul's first imprisonment at Rome. We
may perhaps see the effect of Paul's residence in the imperial city.
Up to this time he has been deeply concerned with the life of the
individual, provincial churches. He is beginning now to see Christianity as a mighty whole. The Kingdom of God in its splendor
rises before him. Did he foresee that one day it would conquer
Rome, that it would itself become a great world-wide empire of
faith?

He speaks of himself as an "ambassador in chains." He may
be in chains but he is none the less the ambassador of the King of
Kings. The high destiny of the redeemed, the continuity of faith,
the democracy of the church, the validity and sacredness of family
and social relations,—these are the great themes of which he treats.
From beginning to end the epistle marches upon the heights. It
contains the great devotional passages in the third chapter—"For
this cause I bow my knees unto the Father of our Lord Jesus Christ";
"Now unto him that is able to do exceeding abundantly above all
that we ask or think, according to the power that worketh in us,
unto him be glory in the church by Christ Jesus throughout all ages,
world without end"; and on to that last splendid call to the Christian warfare—"Finally be strong in the Lord, and in the power of
his might,' which has roused all the generations of Christian war-
riors and martyrs, which inspired the great warrior passages in the

Pilgrim's Progress, such hymns as "Onward, Christian Soldiers," and such poems as Blake's "Jerusalem" . . .

"I will not cease from mental fight
Nor shall my sword sleep in my hand . . ."

Paul chained to a Roman legionary had ample opportunity to study his armor and nobly he transmutes this familiarity which was supposed to be a degradation into spiritual power.

"The close of the Epistle to the Ephesians contains a remarkable example of the forcible imagery of St. Paul. Considered simply in itself, the description of the Christian's armor is one of the most striking passages in the sacred volume. But if we view it in connection with the circumstances with which the Apostle was surrounded, we find a new and living emphasis in his enumeration of all the parts of the heavenly panoply,—the belt of sincerity and truth, with which the loins are girded for the spiritual war,—the breastplate of that righteousness the inseparable links whereof are faith and love,— the strong sandals, with which the feet of Christ's soldiers are made ready, not for such errands of death and despair as those on which the Prætorian soldiers were daily sent, but for the universal message of the gospel of peace,— the large shield of confident trust, wherewith the whole man is protected, and whereon the fiery arrows of the Wicked One fall harmless and dead,— the close-fitting helmet, with which the hope of salvation invests the head of the believer,— and finally, the sword of the Spirit, the Word of God, which, when wielded by the Great Captain of our Salvation, turned the tempter in the wilderness to flight, while in the hands of His chosen Apostle (with whose memory the sword seems inseparably associated), it became the means of establishing Christianity on the earth."—*Conybeare and Howson.*

Paul, an apostle of Jesus Christ by the will of God, to the saints which are at Ephesus, and to the faithful in Christ Jesus:

Grace be to you, and peace, from God our Father, and from the Lord Jesus Christ.

"HE HATH PUT ALL THINGS UNDER HIS FEET"

BLESSED be the God and Father of our Lord Jesus Christ, who hath blessed us with all spiritual blessings in heavenly places in Christ: according as he hath chosen us in him before the foundation of the world, that we should be holy and without blame before him in love: having predestinated us unto the adoption of children by Jesus Christ to himself, according to the good pleasure of his will, to the praise of the glory of his grace, wherein he hath made us accepted in the beloved. In whom we have redemption through his blood, the forgiveness of sins, according to the riches of his grace; wherein he hath abounded toward us in all wisdom and prudence; having made known unto us the mystery of his will, according to his good pleasure which he hath purposed in himself: that in the dispensation of the fulness of times he might gather together in one all things in Christ, both which are in heaven, and which are on earth; even in him: in whom also we have obtained an inheritance, being predestinated according to the purpose of him who worketh all things after the counsel of his own will: that we should be to the praise of his glory, who first trusted in Christ. In whom ye also trusted, after that ye heard the word of truth, the gospel of your salvation: in whom also after that ye believed, ye were sealed with that holy Spirit of promise, which is the earnest of our inheritance until the redemption of the purchased possession, unto the praise of his glory.

Wherefore I also, after I heard of your faith in the Lord Jesus, and love unto all the saints, cease not to give thanks for you, making mention of you in my prayers; that the God of our Lord Jesus Christ, the Father of glory, may give unto you the spirit of wisdom and revelation in the knowledge of him: the eyes of your understanding being enlightened; that ye may know what is the hope of his calling, and what the riches of the glory of his inheritance in the saints, and what is the exceeding greatness of his power to us-ward who believe, according to the working of his mighty power, which he wrought in Christ, when he raised him from the dead, and set him at his own right hand in the heavenly places, far above all principality, and power, and might, and dominion, and every name that is named, not only in this world, but also in that which is to come: and hath put all things under his feet, and gave him to be the head over all things to the church, which is his body, the fulness of him that filleth all in all. — Ephesians 1.

"YOU HATH HE QUICKENED"

And you hath he quickened, who were dead in trespasses and sins; wherein in time past ye walked according to the course of this world, according to the prince of the power of the air, the spirit that now worketh in the children of disobedience: among whom also we all had our conversation in times past in the lusts of our flesh, fulfilling the desires of the flesh and of the mind; and were by nature the children of wrath, even as others. But God, who is rich in mercy, for his great love wherewith he loved us, even when we were dead in sins, hath quickened us together with Christ, (by grace ye are saved;) and hath raised us up together, and made us sit together in heavenly places in Christ Jesus: that

A PALESTINIAN RIDES HIS DONKEY DOWN THE NARROW, STEEP ROAD OF THE MOUNT OF OLIVES

in the ages to come he might show the exceeding riches of his grace in his kindness toward us through Christ Jesus. For by grace are ye saved through faith; and that not of yourselves: it is the gift of God: not of works, lest any man should boast.

For we are his workmanship, created in Christ Jesus unto good works, which God hath before ordained that we should walk in them. — Ephesians 2:1–10.

"FOR HE IS OUR PEACE"

Wherefore remember, that ye being in time past Gentiles in the flesh, who are called Uncircumcision by that which is called the Circumcision in the flesh made by hands; that at that time ye were without Christ, being aliens from the commonwealth of Israel, and strangers from the covenants of promise, having no hope, and without God in the world: but now in Christ Jesus ye who sometimes were far off are made nigh by the blood of Christ. For he is our peace, who hath made both one, and hath broken down the middle wall of partition between us; having abolished in his flesh the enmity, even the law of commandments contained in ordinances; for to make in himself of twain one new man, so making peace; and that he might reconcile both unto God in one body by the cross, having slain the enmity thereby: and came and preached peace to you which were afar off, and to them that were nigh. For through him we both have access by one Spirit unto the Father. Now therefore ye are no more strangers and foreigners, but fellow-citizens with the saints, and of the household of God; and are built upon the foundation of the apostles and prophets, Jesus Christ himself being the chief corner stone; in whom all the building fitly framed together groweth unto an holy temple in the Lord: in whom ye also are builded together for an habitation of God through the Spirit.

For this cause I, Paul, the prisoner of Jesus Christ for you Gentiles, if ye have heard of the dispensation of the grace of God which is given me to you-ward: how that by revelation he made known unto me the mystery; (as I wrote afore in few words, whereby, when ye read, ye may understand my knowledge in the mystery of Christ) which in other ages was not made known unto the sons of men, as it is now revealed unto his holy apostles and prophets by the Spirit; that the Gentiles should be fellowheirs, and of the same body, and partakers of his promise in Christ by the gospel: whereof I was made a minister, according to the gift of the grace of God given unto me by the effectual working of his power.   — Ephesians 2:11-3:7.

THE UNSEARCHABLE RICHES OF CHRIST

Unto me, who am less than the least of all saints, is this grace given, that I should preach among the Gentiles the unsearchable riches of Christ; and to make all men see what is the fellowship of the mystery, which from the beginning of the world hath been hid in God, who created all things by Jesus Christ: to the intent that now unto the principalities and powers in heavenly places might be known by the church the manifold wisdom of God, according to the eternal purpose which he purposed in Christ Jesus our Lord: in whom we have boldness and access with confidence by the faith of him. Wherefore I desire that ye faint not at my tribulations for you, which is your glory.

For this cause I bow my knees unto the Father of our Lord Jesus Christ, of whom the whole family in heaven and earth is named, that he would grant you,

PTOLEMAIS ON THE MEDITERRANEAN

Very ancient is this port city, the Accho of the Old Testament when Israel came into the Holy Land. The Tribe of Asher inherited it, but did not drive out the inhabitants as Moses commanded. The Asherites settled down to live with its pagan inhabitants.

But when St. Paul landed there on his way to Jerusalem, its Roman name was Ptolemais. St. Luke who traveled with St. Paul writes, "When we had finished our course from Tyre, we came to Ptolemais, and saluted the brethren, and abode with them one day." There was, you see, a young Christian Church already there.

Today Ptolemais is called Acre.

Read pages 87-94.

RUINS OF ROMAN AQUEDUCT ALONG THE APPIAN WAY

according to the riches of his glory, to be strengthened
with might by his Spirit in the inner man; that Christ
may dwell in your hearts by faith; that ye, being rooted
and grounded in love, may be able to comprehend
with all saints what is the breadth, and length, and
depth and height; and to know the love of Christ,
which passeth knowledge, that ye might be filled with
all the fulness of God.

Now unto him that is able to do exceeding abundantly above all that we ask or think, according to the
power that worketh in us, unto him be glory in the
church by Christ Jesus throughout all ages, world without end. Amen.   — Ephesians 3:8–21.

"ONE LORD, ONE FAITH, ONE BAPTISM"

I therefore, the prisoner of the LORD, beseech you
that ye walk worthy of the vocation wherewith ye are
called, with all lowliness and meekness, with longsuffering, forbearing one another in love; endeavouring
to keep the unity of the Spirit in the bond of peace.
There is one body, and one Spirit, even as ye are called
in one hope of your calling; one Lord, one faith, one
baptism, one God and Father of all, who is above all,
and through all, and in you all. But unto every one of
us is given grace according to the measure of the gift of
Christ. Wherefore he saith,

> "When he ascended up on high,
> He led captivity captive,
> And gave gifts unto men."

(Now that he ascended, what is it but that he also
descended first into the lower parts of the earth? He
that descended is the same also that ascended up far
above all heavens, that he might fill all things.) And

he gave some, apostles; and some, prophets; and some, evangelists; and some, pastors and teachers; for the perfecting of the saints, for the work of the ministry, for the edifying of the body of Christ: till we all come in the unity of the faith, and of the knowledge of the Son of God, unto a perfect man, unto the measure of the stature of the fulness of Christ: that we henceforth be no more children, tossed to and fro, and carried about with every wind of doctrine, by the sleight of men, and cunning craftiness, whereby they lie in wait to deceive; but speaking the truth in love, may grow up into him in all things, which is the head, even Christ: from whom the whole body fitly joined together and compacted by that which every joint supplieth, according to the effectual working in the measure of every part, maketh increase of the body unto the edifying of itself in love.   — Ephesians 4:1–16.

"PUT OFF THE OLD MAN"

This I say therefore, and testify in the LORD, that ye henceforth walk not as other Gentiles walk, in the vanity of their mind, having the understanding darkened, being alienated from the life of God through the ignorance that is in them, because of the blindness of their heart: who being past feeling have given themselves over unto lasciviousness, to work all uncleanness with greediness. But ye have not so learned Christ; if so be that ye have heard him, and have been taught by him, as the truth is in Jesus: that ye put off concerning the former conversation the old man, which is corrupt according to the deceitful lusts; and be renewed in the spirit of your mind; and that ye put on the new man, which after God is created in righteousness and true holiness.

Wherefore putting away lying, speak every man truth with his neighbour: for we are members one of another. Be ye angry, and sin not: let not the sun go down upon your wrath: neither give place to the devil. Let him that stole steal no more: but rather let him labour, working with his hands the thing which is good, that he may have to give to him that needeth. Let no corrupt communication proceed out of your mouth, but that which is good to the use of edifying, that it may minister grace unto the hearers. And grieve not the holy Spirit of God, whereby ye are sealed unto the day of redemption.   —Ephesians 4:17–30.

"BE KIND ONE TO ANOTHER"

Let all bitterness, and wrath, and anger, and clamour, and evil speaking, be put away from you, with all malice: and be ye kind one to another, tenderhearted, forgiving one another, even as God for Christ's sake hath forgiven you.   —Ephesians 4:31, 32.

"BE YE FOLLOWERS OF GOD AS DEAR CHILDREN"

Be ye therefore followers of God, as dear children; and walk in love, as Christ also hath loved us, and hath given himself for us an offering and a sacrifice to God for a sweetsmelling savour. But fornication, and all uncleanness, or covetousness, let it not be once named among you, as becometh saints; neither filthiness, nor foolish talking, nor jesting, which are not convenient: but rather giving of thanks. For this ye know, that no whoremonger, nor unclean person, nor covetous man, who is an idolater, hath any inheritance in the kingdom of Christ and of God. Let no man deceive you with vain words: for because of these things cometh the wrath of God upon the children of disobedience. Be not ye therefore partakers with them.   — Ephesians 5:1-7.

APOSTLE MATTHEW
A painting by Anthony Gruerio

"WALK AS CHILDREN OF LIGHT"

For ye were sometimes darkness, but now are ye light in the Lord: walk as children of light: (for the fruit of the Spirit is in all goodness and righteousness and truth;) proving what is acceptable unto the Lord. And have no fellowship with the unfruitful works of darkness, but rather reprove them. For it is a shame even to speak of those things which are done of them in secret. But all things that are reproved are made manifest by the light: for whatsoever doth make manifest is light. Wherefore he saith, "Awake thou that sleepest, and arise from the dead, and Christ shall give thee light."

See then that ye walk circumspectly, not as fools, but as wise, redeeming the time, because the days are evil. Wherefore be ye not unwise, but understanding what the will of the Lord is.

And be not drunk with wine, wherein is excess; but be filled with the Spirit; speaking to yourselves in psalms and hymns and spiritual songs, singing and making melody in your heart to the Lord; giving thanks always for all things unto God and the Father in the name of our Lord Jesus Christ; submitting yourselves one to another in the fear of God.

Wives, submit yourselves unto your own husbands, as unto the Lord. For the husband is the head of the wife, even as Christ is the head of the church: and he is the saviour of the body. Therefore as the church is subject unto Christ, so let the wives be to their own husbands in everything. Husbands, love your wives, even as Christ also loved the church, and gave himself for it; that he might sanctify and cleanse it with the washing of water by the word, that he might present it to himself a glorious church, not having spot, or wrinkle, or any such thing; but that it should be holy and without blemish. So ought men to love their wives as their own bodies. He that loveth his wife loveth himself. For no man ever yet hated his own flesh; but nourisheth and cherisheth it, even as the Lord the church: for we are members of his body, of his flesh, and of his bones. For this cause shall a man leave his father and mother, and shall be joined unto his wife, and they two shall be one flesh. This is a great mystery: but I speak concerning Christ and the church. Nevertheless let every one of you in particular so love his wife even as himself; and the wife see that she reverence her husband.

Children, obey your parents in the Lord: for this is right. Honour thy father and mother; which is the first commandment with promise; that it may be well with thee, and thou mayest live long on the earth. And, ye fathers, provoke not your children to wrath: but bring them up in the nurture and admonition of the Lord. Servants, be obedient to them that are your masters according to the flesh, with fear and trembling, in singleness of your heart, as unto Christ; not with eyeservice, as menpleasers; but as the servants of Christ, doing the will of God from the heart; with good will doing service, as to the Lord, and not to men: knowing that whatsoever good thing any man doeth, the same shall he receive of the Lord, whether he be bond or free. And, ye masters, do the same things unto them, forbearing threatening: knowing that your Master also is in heaven; neither is there respect of persons with him.

— Ephesians 5:8–6:9.

"PUT ON THE WHOLE ARMOUR OF GOD"

Finally, my brethren, be strong in the Lord, and in the power of his might. Put on the whole armour of God, that ye may be able to stand against the wiles of the devil. For we wrestle not against flesh and blood, but against principalities, against powers, against the rulers of the darkness of this world, against spiritual wickedness in high places. Wherefore take unto you the whole armour of God, that ye may be able to withstand in the evil day, and having done all, to stand. Stand therefore, having your loins girt about with truth, and having on the breastplate of righteousness; and your feet shod with the preparation of the gospel of peace; above all, taking the shield of faith, wherewith ye shall be able to quench all the fiery darts of the wicked. And take the helmet of salvation, and the sword of the Spirit, which is the word of God: praying always with all prayer and supplication in the Spirit, and watching thereunto with all perseverance and supplication for all saints; and for me, that utterance may be given unto me, that I may open my mouth boldly, to make known the mystery of the gospel, for which I am an ambassador in bonds: that therein I may speak boldly, as I ought to speak.   — Ephesians 6:10–20.

PAUL SENDS HIS MESSENGER, TYCHICUS

But that ye also may know my affairs, and how I do, Tychicus, a beloved brother and faithful minister in the Lord, shall make known to you all things: whom I have sent unto you for the same purpose, that ye might know our affairs, and that he might comfort your hearts.

Peace be to the brethren, and love with faith, from God the Father and the Lord Jesus Christ. Grace be with all them that love our Lord Jesus Christ in sincerity. Amen.   — Ephesians 6:21–24.

APOSTLE JAMES THE LESS
A painting by Anthony Gruerio

The Letters of Paul

The Great Captain of the New Faith

The Epistle to the Philippians

I can do all things through Christ which strengtheneth me.

The church at Philippi was one of Paul's favorite churches. He had been cruelly treated at Philippi on his first visit, but the church had long ago made up for that first indignity by its affection and constant ministry to Paul's temporal needs.

The immediate occasion of writing seems to have been the arrival at Rome of Epaphroditus with a generous gift. Paul must have stood in need of such assistance. The weary months were passing on, and he was obliged to rent a house of his own, and provide his own supplies, for the Roman government did not pay the expenses of its prisoners. In spite of the circumstances in which it is written, this epistle is full of light and the spirit of rejoicing: "Rejoice in the Lord, and again I say 'Rejoice.'" Again he says, "... whatsoever things are true, whatsoever things are honest, whatsoever things are just, whatsoever things are pure, whatsoever things are lovely, whatsoever things are of good report; if there be any virtue, and if there be any praise, think on these things," and adds that splendid passage, revealing perhaps as nothing else does, the dauntless spirit of the man—"Brethren, I count not myself to have apprehended: but this one thing I do, forgetting those things which are behind, and reaching forth unto those things which are before, I press toward the mark for the prize of the high calling of God in Christ Jesus."

"St. Paul tells us in the Epistle to the Philippians that throughout the Praetorian quarter he was well known as a prisoner for the cause of Christ, and he sends special salutations to the Philippian Church from the Christians of the imperial household. These notices bring before us very vividly the moral contrasts by which the Apostle was surrounded. The soldier to whom he was chained to-day might have been in Nero's bodyguard yesterday; his comrade who next relieved guard might have been one of the executioners of Octavia, and might have carried her head to Poppaea a few weeks before.

"History has few stronger contrasts than when it shows us Paul preaching Christ under the walls of Nero's palace. Thenceforward there were but two religions in the Roman world: the worship of the emperor, and the worship of the Saviour. The old superstitions had long been worn out; they had lost all hold on educated minds . . . Over against the altars of Nero and Poppaea, the voice of a prisoner was daily heard. Men listened, and knew that self-sacrifice was better than ease, humiliation more exalted than pride, to suffer nobler than to reign."—*Conybeare and Howson.*

In this epistle the glorious truth is presented that "our conversation (daily walk of life) is in heaven; from whence also we look for the Saviour, the Lord Jesus Christ." "Therefore, my brethren," Paul cried, "stand fast in the Lord."

Paul and Timotheus, the servants of Jesus Christ, to all the saints in Christ Jesus which are at Philippi, with the bishops and deacons: Grace be unto you, and peace, from God our Father, and from the Lord Jesus Christ.

"I THANK MY GOD UPON EVERY REMEMBRANCE OF YOU"

I THANK my God upon every remembrance of you, always in every prayer of mine for you all making request with joy, for your fellowship in the gospel from the first day until now; being confident of this very thing, that he which hath begun a good work in you will perform it until the day of Jesus Christ: even as it is meet for me to think this of you all, because I have you in my heart; inasmuch as both in my bonds, and in the defence and confirmation of the gospel, ye all are partakers of my grace. For God is my record, how greatly I long after you all in the bowels of Jesus Christ. And this I pray, that your love may abound yet more and more in knowledge and in all judgment; that ye may approve things that are excellent; that ye may be sincere and without offence till the day of Christ; being filled with the fruits of righteousness, which are by Jesus Christ, unto the glory and praise of God.

But I would ye should understand, brethren, that the things which happened unto me have fallen out rather unto the furtherance of the gospel; so that my bonds in Christ are manifest in all the palace, and in all other places; and many of the brethren in the Lord, waxing confident by my bonds, are much more bold to speak the word without fear. — Philippians 1:1-14.

PAUL REJOICES IN WHATEVER WAY CHRIST IS PREACHED

Some indeed preach Christ even of envy and strife; and some also of good will: the one preach Christ of contention, not sincerely, supposing to add affliction to my bonds: but the other of love, knowing that I am set for the defence of the gospel.

What then? Notwithstanding, every way, whether in pretence, or in truth, Christ is preached; and I therein do rejoice, yea, and will rejoice. For I know that this shall turn to my salvation through your prayer, and the supply of the Spirit of Jesus Christ, according to my earnest expectation and my hope, that in nothing I shall be ashamed, but that with all boldness, as always, so now also Christ shall be magnified in my body, whether it be by life, or by death. For to me to live is Christ, and to die is gain. But if I live in the flesh, this is the fruit of my labour: yet what I shall choose I wot not. For I am in a strait betwixt two, having a desire to depart, and to be with Christ; which is far better: nevertheless to abide in the flesh is more needful for you.

APOSTLE SIMON
A painting by Anthony Gurerio

And having this confidence, I know that I shall abide and continue with you all for your furtherance and joy of faith; that your rejoicing may be more abundant in Jesus Christ for me by my coming to you again. Only let your conversation be as it becometh the gospel of Christ: that whether I come and see you, or else be absent, I may hear of your affairs, that ye stand fast in one spirit, with one mind striving together for the faith of the gospel; and in nothing terrified by your adversaries: which is to them an evident token of perdition, but to you of salvation, and that of God. For unto you it is given in the behalf of Christ, not only to believe on him, but also to suffer for his sake; having the same conflict which ye saw in me, and now hear to be in me. — Philippians 1:15–30.

"LET THIS MIND BE IN YOU, WHICH WAS ALSO IN CHRIST JESUS"

If there be therefore any consolation in Christ, if any comfort of love, if any fellowship of the Spirit, if any bowels and mercies, fulfil ye my joy, that ye be like-minded, having the same love, being of one accord, of one mind. Let nothing be done through strife or vainglory; but in lowliness of mind let each esteem other better than themselves. Look not every man on his own things, but every man also on the things of others. Let this mind be in you, which was also in Christ Jesus: who, being in the form of God, thought it not robbery to be equal with God: but made himself of no reputation, and took upon him the form of a servant and was made in the likeness of men: and being found in fashion as a man, he humbled himself, and became obedient unto death, even the death of the cross. — Philippians 2.1–8.

"AT THE NAME OF JESUS EVERY KNEE SHOULD BOW"

Wherefore God also hath highly exalted him, and given him a name which is above every name: that at the name of Jesus every knee should bow, of things in heaven, and things in earth, and things under the earth; and that every tongue should confess that Jesus Christ is Lord, to the glory of God the Father.　　—Philippians 2:9–11.

"WORK OUT YOUR OWN SALVATION"

Wherefore, my beloved, as ye have always obeyed, not as in my presence only, but now much more in my absence, work out your own salvation with fear and trembling. For it is God which worketh in you both to will and to do of his good pleasure. Do all things without murmurings and disputings: that ye may be blameless and harmless, the sons of God, without rebuke, in the midst of a crooked and perverse nation, among whom ye shine as lights in the world; holding forth the word of life; that I may rejoice in the day of Christ, that I have not run in vain, neither laboured in vain. Yea, and if I be offered upon the sacrifice and service of your faith, I joy, and rejoice with you all. For the same cause also do ye joy, and rejoice with me.

　　— Philippians 2:12–18.

TIMOTHY AND EPAPHRODITUS ARE TO COME TO THEM

But I trust in the Lord Jesus to send Timotheus shortly unto you, that I also may be of good comfort, when I know your state. For I have no man likeminded, who will naturally care for your state. For all seek their own, not the things which are Jesus Christ's. But ye know the proof of him, that, as a son with the father, he hath served with me in the gospel. Him therefore I hope to send presently, so soon as I shall see how it will go with me. But I trust in the Lord that I also myself shall come shortly. Yet I supposed it necessary to send to you Epaphroditus, my brother, and companion in labour, and fellowsoldier, but your messenger, and he that ministered to my wants. For he longed after you all, and was full of heaviness, because that ye had heard that he had been sick. For indeed he was sick nigh unto death: but God had mercy on him; and not on him only, but on me also, lest I should have sorrow upon sorrow. I sent him therefore the more carefully, that, when ye see him again, ye may rejoice, and that I may be the less sorrowful. Receive him therefore in the Lord with all gladness; and hold such in reputation: because for the work of Christ he was nigh unto death, not regarding his life, to supply your lack of service toward me. — Philippians 2:19–30.

"WHAT THINGS WERE GAIN TO ME, I COUNTED LOSS FOR CHRIST"

Finally, my brethren, rejoice in the Lord. To write the same things to you, to me indeed is not grievous, but for you it is safe. Beware of dogs, beware of evil workers, beware of the concision. For we are the circumcision, which worship God in the spirit, and rejoice in Christ Jesus, and have no confidence in the flesh. Though I might also have confidence in the flesh. If any other man thinketh that he hath whereof he might trust in the flesh, I more: circumcised the eighth day, of the stock of Israel, of the tribe of Benjamin, an Hebrew of the Hebrews; as touching the law, a Pharisee; concerning zeal, persecuting the church; touching the righteousness which is in the law, blameless. But what things were gain to me, those I counted loss for Christ. Yea doubtless, and I count all things but loss for the excellency of the knowledge of Christ Jesus my Lord: for whom I have suffered the loss of all things, and do count them but dung, that I may win Christ, and be found in him, not having mine own righteousness, which is of the law, but that which is through the faith of Christ, the righteousness which is of God by faith: that I may know him, and the power of his resurrection, and the fellowship of his sufferings, being made comformable unto his death; if by any means I might attain unto the resurrection of the dead. Not as though I had already attained, either were already perfect: but I follow after, if that I may apprehend that for which also I am apprehended of Christ Jesus. — Philippians 3:1-12.

"THIS ONE THING I DO"

Brethren, I count not myself to have apprehended: but this one thing I do, forgetting those things which are behind, and reaching forth unto those things which are before, I press toward the mark for the prize of the high calling of God in Christ Jesus. Let us therefore, as many as be perfect, be thus minded: and if in anything ye be otherwise minded, God shall reveal even this unto you. Nevertheless, whereto we have already attained, let us walk by the same rule, let us mind the same thing.

Brethren, be followers together of me, and mark them which walk so as ye have us for an ensample. (For many walk, of whom I have told you often, and now tell you even weeping, that they are the enemies of the cross of Christ: whose end is destruction, whose God is their belly, and whose glory is in their shame, who mind earthly things.) For our conversation is in heaven; from whence also we look for the Saviour, the Lord Jesus Christ: who shall change our vile body, that it may be fashioned like unto his glorious body, according to the working whereby he is able even to subdue all things unto himself.   — Philippians 3:13–21.

"THINK ON THESE THINGS"

Therefore, my brethren dearly beloved and longed for, my joy and crown, so stand fast in the Lord, my dearly beloved.

I beseech Euodias, and beseech Syntyche, that they be of the same mind in the Lord. And I intreat thee also, true yokefellow, help those women which laboured with me in the gospel, with Clement also, and with other my fellowlabourers, whose names are in the book of life.

Rejoice in the Lord alway: and again I say, 'Rejoice.' Let your moderation be known unto all men. The Lord is at hand. Be careful for nothing; but in every thing by prayer and supplication with thanksgiving let your requests be made known unto God. And the peace of God, which passeth all understanding, shall keep your hearts and minds through Christ Jesus.

Finally, brethren, whatsoever things are true, whatsoever things are honest, whatsoever things are just, whatsoever things are pure, whatsoever things are lovely, whatsoever things are of good report; if there be any virtue, and if there be any praise, think on these things. Those things, which ye have both learned, and received, and heard, and seen in me, do: and the God of peace shall be with you.   — Philippians 4:1–9.

"I CAN DO ALL THINGS THROUGH CHRIST WHICH STRENGTHENETH ME"

But I rejoiced in the Lord greatly, that now at the last your care of me hath flourished again; wherein ye were also careful, but ye lacked opportunity. Not that I speak in respect of want: for I have learned, in whatsoever state I am, therewith to be content. I know both how to be abased, and I know how to abound: everywhere and in all things I am instructed both to be full and to be hungry, both to abound and to suffer need. I can do all things through Christ which strengtheneth me. Notwithstanding ye have well done, that ye did communicate with my affliction.

— Philippians 4:10–14.

PAUL'S GRATITUDE TO THE CHURCH OF PHILIPPI

Now ye Philippians know also, that in the beginning of the gospel, when I departed from Macedonia, no church communicated with me as concerning giving and receiving, but ye only. For even in Thessalonica ye sent once and again unto my necessity. Not because I desire a gift: but I desire fruit that may abound to your account. But I have all, and abound: I am full, having received of Epaphroditus the things which were sent from you, an odour of a sweet smell, a sacrifice acceptable, wellpleasing to God. But my God shall supply all your need according to his riches in glory by Christ Jesus. Now unto God and our Father be glory forever and ever. Amen.

— Philippians 4:15–20.

SALUTATIONS

Salute every saint in Christ Jesus. The brethren which are with me greet you. All the saints salute you, chiefly they that are of Cæsar's household.

The grace of our Lord Jesus Christ be with you all. Amen.

— Philippians 4:21–23.

The Letters of Paul

The Great Captain of the New Faith

The Epistle to the Colossians

Let the word of Christ dwell in you richly in all wisdom.

Colossae was, in ancient times, a very important city of Phrygia. With Laodicea, which later overshadowed it, and Hierapolis, it was one of a group of cities which Paul never actually visited. Through Epaphras, who founded churches in these cities, and Timothy, who worked in them, Paul was deeply interested. He asked that the letter be read also in the church at Laodicea. Perhaps for the very reason that the apostle felt a certain restraint in writing to those with whom he had no personal acquaintance the letter seems to be less "like Paul" than the others. It is filled with good instruction and advice, but it has fewer of those lofty and sustained passages which break in upon the doctrinal portions than some of the other epistles.

Reports had come to Paul, while in prison in Rome, that a strange philosophy, of which no former letter gives any trace, was creeping into the church at Colossae. This philosophy taught that God was so far off that man could not reach him. Worship could be given only to beings who stood between God and man. Paul warned against all such false "philosophy and vain deceit after the tradition of the world and not after Christ." For Christ Jesus is the only mediator between God and man. He took up the many terms which the system of thought used, and tried to show how the simple gospel supplied all the religious value claimed for them.

Paul, an apostle of Jesus Christ by the will of God, and Timotheus, our brother, to the saints and faithful brethren in Christ which are at Colosse:

Grace be unto you, and peace, from God our Father and the Lord Jesus Christ.

326

THANKSGIVING FOR THE FAITH OF THE COLOSSIANS

WE give thanks to God and the Father of our Lord Jesus Christ, praying always for you, since we heard of your faith in Christ Jesus, and of the love which ye have to all the saints for the hope which is laid up for you in heaven, whereof ye heard before in the word of the truth of the gospel; which is come unto you, as it is in all the world; and bringeth forth fruit, as it doth also in you, since the day ye heard of it, and knew the grace of God in truth: as ye also learned of Epaphras, our dear fellowservant, who is for you a faithful minister of Christ; who also declared unto us your love in the Spirit. — Colossians 1:1-8.

"WE DO NOT CEASE TO PRAY FOR YOU"

For this cause we also, since the day we heard it, do not cease to pray for you, and to desire that ye might be filled with the knowledge of his will in all wisdom and spiritual understanding; that ye might walk worthy of the Lord unto all pleasing, being fruitful in every good work, and increasing in the knowledge of God; strengthened with all might, according to his glorious power, unto all patience and longsuffering with joyfulness; giving thanks unto the Father, which hath made us meet to be partakers of the inheritance of the saints in light: who hath delivered us from the power of darkness, and hath translated us into the kingdom of his dear Son: in whom we have redemption through his blood, even the forgiveness of sins: who is the image of the invisible God, the firstborn of every creature: for by him were all things created, that are in heaven, and that are in earth, visible and invisible, whether they be thrones, or dominions, or principalities, or powers: all things were created by him, and for him: and he is

before all things, and by him all things consist. And
he is the head of the body, the church: who is the beginning, the firstborn from the dead; that in all things
he might have the pre-eminence.

For it pleased the Father that in him should all
fulness dwell; and, having made peace through the
blood of his cross, by him to reconcile all things unto
himself; by him, I say, whether they be things in earth,
or things in heaven. — Colossians 1:9-20.

"YOU HATH HE RECONCILED"

And you, that were sometime alienated and enemies
in your mind by wicked works, yet now hath he reconciled in the body of his flesh through death, to present
you holy and unblameable and unreproveable in his
sight: if ye continue in the faith grounded and settled,
and be not moved away from the hope of the gospel,
which ye have heard, and which was preached to every
creature which is under heaven; whereof I, Paul, am
made a minister; who now rejoice in my sufferings for
you, and fill up that which is behind of the afflictions of
Christ in my flesh for his body's sake, which is the
church: whereof I am made a minister, according to
the dispensation of God which is given to me for you,
to fulfil the word of God; even the mystery which hath
been hid from ages and from generations, but now is
made manifest to his saints: to whom God would make
known what is the riches of the glory of this mystery
among the Gentiles; which is Christ in you, the hope
of glory: whom we preach, warning every man, and
teaching every man in all wisdom; that we may present
every man perfect in Christ Jesus: whereunto I also
labour, striving according to his working, which worketh
in me mightily. — Colossians 1:21-29

"I WOULD THAT YE KNEW WHAT GREAT CONFLICT I HAVE FOR YOU": "WALK YE IN CHRIST"

For I would that ye knew what great conflict I have for you, and for them at Laodicea, and for as many as have not seen my face in the flesh; that their hearts might be comforted, being knit together in love, and unto all riches of the full assurance of understanding, to the acknowledgment of the mystery of God, and of the Father, and of Christ; in whom are hid all the treasures of wisdom and knowledge. And this I say, lest any man should beguile you with enticing words. For though I be absent in the flesh, yet am I with you in the spirit, joying and beholding your order, and the steadfastness of your faith in Christ.

As ye have therefore received Christ Jesus the Lord, so walk ye in him: rooted and built up in him, and stablished in the faith, as ye have been taught, abounding therein with thanksgiving.　　　— Colossians 2:1–7.

WARNINGS

Beware lest any man spoil you through philosophy and vain deceit, after the tradition of men, after the rudiments of the world, and not after Christ. For in him dwelleth all the fulness of the Godhead bodily. And ye are complete in him, which is the head of all principality and power: in whom also ye are circumcised with the circumcision made without hands, in putting off the body of the sins of the flesh by the circumcision of Christ: buried with him in baptism, wherein also ye are risen with him through the faith of the operation of God, who hath raised him from the dead. And you, being dead in your sins and the uncircumcision of your flesh, hath he quickened together with him, having forgiven you all trespasses; blotting out the

TEMPLE OF ZEUS, ATHENS

handwriting of ordinances that was against us, which was contrary to us and took it out of the way, nailing it to his cross; and having spoiled principalities and powers, he made a show of them openly, triumphing over them in it.

Let no man therefore judge you in meat, or in drink, or in respect of an holyday, or of the new moon, or of the sabbath days: which are a shadow of things to come; but the body is of Christ. Let no man beguile you of your reward in a voluntary humility and worshiping of angels, intruding into those things which he hath not seen, vainly puffed up by his fleshly mind, and not holding the Head, from which all the body by joints and bands having nourishment ministered, and knit together, increaseth with the increase of God.

Wherefore if ye be dead with Christ from the rudiments of the world, why, as though living in the world, are ye subject to ordinances: touch not; taste not; handle not; (which all are to perish with the using;) after the commandments and doctrines of men? Which things have indeed a show of wisdom in will worship, and humility, and neglecting of the body; not in any honour to the satisfying of the flesh.   — Colossians 2:8-23.

"SEEK THOSE THINGS WHICH ARE ABOVE"

If ye then be risen with Christ, seek those things which are above, where Christ sitteth on the right hand of God. Set your affection on things above, not on things on the earth. For ye are dead, and your life is hid with Christ in God. When Christ, who is our life, shall appear, then shall ye also appear with him in glory.

Mortify therefore your members which are upon the earth: fornication, uncleanness, inordinate affection, evil concupiscence, and covetousness, which is idolatry: for which things' sake the wrath of God cometh on the children of disobedience: in the which ye also walked some time, when ye lived in them. But now ye also put off all these: anger, wrath, malice, blasphemy, filthy communication out of your mouth. — Colossians 3:1-8.

"PUT ON THE NEW MAN"

Lie not one to another, seeing that ye have put off the old man with his deeds; and have put on the new man, which is renewed in knowledge after the image of him that created him: where there is neither Greek nor Jew, circumcision nor uncircumcision, Barbarian, Scythian, bond nor free: but Christ is all, and in all.

Put on therefore, as the elect of God, holy and beloved, bowels of mercies, kindness, humbleness of mind, meekness, longsuffering; forbearing one another, and forgiving one another, if any man have a quarrel against any: even as Christ forgave you, so also do ye. And above all these things put on charity, which is the bond of perfectness. And let the peace of God rule in your hearts, to the which also ye are called in one body; and be ye thankful. Let the word of Christ dwell in you richly in all wisdom; teaching and admonishing one another in psalms and hymns and spiritual songs, singing with grace in your hearts to the Lord. And whatsoever ye do in word or deed, do all in the name of the Lord Jesus, giving thanks to God and the Father by him.

Wives, submit yourselves unto your own husbands, as it is fit in the Lord. Husbands, love your wives, and be not bitter against them. Children, obey your parents in all things: for this is well pleasing unto the Lord. Fathers, provoke not your children to anger, lest they be discouraged. Servants, obey in all things your masters according to the flesh; not with eyeservice, as menpleasers; but in singleness of heart, fearing God: and whatsoever ye do, do it heartily, as to the Lord, and not unto men; knowing that of the Lord ye shall receive the reward of the inheritance: for ye serve the Lord Christ. But he that doeth wrong shall receive for the wrong which he hath done: and there is no respect of persons.

Masters, give unto your servants that which is just and equal; knowing that ye also have a Master in heaven. Continue in prayer, and watch in the same with thanksgiving; withal praying also for us, that God would open unto us a door of utterance, to speak the mystery of Christ, for which I am also in bonds: that I may make it manifest, as I ought to speak. Walk in wisdom toward them that are without, redeeming the time. Let your speech be alway with grace, seasoned with salt, that ye may know how ye ought to answer every man. — Colossians 3:9–4:6.

"MY BROTHERS TYCHICUS AND ONESIMUS"

All my state shall Tychicus declare unto you, who is a beloved brother, and a faithful minister and fellowservant in the Lord: whom I have sent unto you for the same purpose, that he might know your estate, and comfort your hearts; with Onesimus, a faithful and beloved brother, who is one of you. They shall make known unto you all things which are done here. — Colossians 4:7–9.

MESSAGES OF FRIENDS

Aristarchus, my fellowprisoner, saluteth you, and Marcus, sister's son to Barnabas, (touching whom ye received commandments: if he come unto you, receive him;) and Jesus, which is called Justus, who are of the circumcision. These only are my fellowworkers unto the Kingdom of God, which have been a comfort unto me. Epaphras, who is one of you, a servant of Christ, saluteth you, always labouring fervently for you in prayers, that ye may stand perfect and complete in all the will of God. For I bear him record, that he hath a great zeal for you, and them that are in Laodicea, and them in Hierapolis. Luke, the beloved physician, and Demas, greet you. Salute the brethren which are in Laodicea, and Nymphas, and the church which is in his house. And when this epistle is read among you, cause that it be read also in the church of the Laodiceans; and that ye likewise read the epistle from Laodicea. And say to Archippus, "Take heed to the ministry which thou hast received in the Lord, that thou fulfil it."

The salutation by the hand of me, Paul. Remember my bonds. Grace be with you. Amen. — Colossians 4:10–18.

ANCIENT SALAMIS

The Island of Cyprus this, off the coast of Syria. When St. Paul with Barnabus landed here at the port of Salamis, it was a Roman trading center, swarming with merchants, a rich business city.

Near where this arch stands, was a great stone forum with massive pillars, and at its upper end a temple to the pagan god Zeus, whose sacrifices were human beings. Today, only poisonous vipers live among its stones. Today the fallen city of Salamis is deserted.

But what a strange adventure St. Paul had on the Island of Cyprus! Read about Sergius Paulus and Elymas the sorcerer. Acts 13:1-12, page 34.

The Letters of Paul

The Great Captain of the New Faith

The First Epistle to the Thessalonians

But let us, since we are of the day, be sober, putting on the breast-plate of faith and love; and for a helmet the hope of salvation.

The epistles of Paul to the Thessalonians are considered to be the earliest Christian literature which we possess. They were written from Corinth probably, both of them apparently in 51, only twenty years after the crucifixion of Jesus.

Unfortunately the people of those times did not attach the same importance to such details as dates and place-names as we do. Paul dated none of his epistles and the exact date of each is a matter of conjecture. We may, by the aid of certain data from the imperial records and statements in The Acts make a fairly close approximation, but we cannot be absolutely sure.

Paul who depended a great deal upon human companionship, was very much alone at Corinth. It is very delightful to find this man of supreme genius and power forming intimate friendships with the younger men of the churches. He says of his life in Corinth that he was "in weakness and fear and much trembling." It must then have been a happy day in the tent-maker's shop when Timothy and Silas, who had been left behind in Macedonia, arrived at Corinth. The reports which they gave of the conditions at Thessalonica were not reassuring, but opposition always aroused Paul to action. Since he could not at once go to his beloved church, he would write; and so the first epistle, which was destined to be treasured and loved by Christian people for nineteen hundred years and to the end of time, was written in that poor tent-maker's house at Corinth, to a poor little struggling church in Macedonia: the tent-maker of Corinth to the tent-makers of Thessalonica,—for the leading industry of the great city which was named for the sister of Alexander the Great is or was until quite recently the making of

336

coarse cloth of goat's hair. During World War I and for about fifteen years afterward the city and gulf, on the head of which the city is situated, were called Salonika. Then the old name, Thessalonica, was again restored but spelled Thessalonike, and continues to the present time. The German Army occupied it during World War II. Today it is a city of nearly 300,000 population.

Timothy told Paul, and he must have smiled when he said it, there in the work-shop where he found Paul busy sewing the coarse goat's-hair cloth, that some of the church members at Thessalonica were criticising the apostle because he "traveled about having no business." Others had themselves abandoned work because the "coming of the Lord was near." Paul made vigorous defense of his apostleship and of his own independent activity, and advised the church members to go to work regardless of the question of the coming of the Lord.

One question disturbed them. They had understood that Christ was soon coming again to set up a kingdom. Some of their number had died, and they were distressed that these should have no share in the coming kingdom. To them death seemed the end of hope, and Paul, in the letter, reminded them of the resurrection when "the Lord himself shall descend from heaven with a shout," and saints, dead as well as living, shall be caught up together "to meet the Lord in the air; and so shall we ever be with the Lord. Wherefore comfort one another with these words."

"In no epistle is the character of Paul more frankly disclosed. His affectionate and ardent disposition, his devotedness to the welfare of his fellow men, his generous recognition of the beginnings of good in his converts, his solicitude for their progress, his purity of motive, and untiring energy are clearly reflected in this letter. He felt for his converts all the love and responsibility of a parent. It was with pain he absented himself from them; with difficulty he was prevented from revisiting them; with delight he looked forward to the time when this should be possible. A great nature absorbed in great aims shines through every page of the letter."

Paul, and Silvanus, and Timotheus, unto the church of the Thessalonians which is in God the Father and in the Lord Jesus Christ:

Grace be unto you, and peace, from God our Father, and the Lord Jesus Christ.

"WE GIVE THANKS TO GOD ALWAYS FOR YOU ALL"

WE give thanks to God always for you all, making mention of you in our prayers; remembering without ceasing your work of faith, and labour of love, and patience of hope in our Lord Jesus Christ, in the sight of God and our Father; knowing, brethren beloved, your election of God. For our gospel came not unto you in word only, but also in power, and in the Holy Ghost, and in much assurance; as ye know what manner of men we were among you for your sake. And ye became followers of us, and of the Lord, having received the word in much affliction, with joy of the Holy Ghost: so that ye were ensamples to all that believe in Macedonia and Achaia. For from you sounded out the word of the Lord not only in Macedonia and Achaia, but also in every place your faith to God-ward is spread abroad; so that we need not to speak anything. For they themselves show of us what manner of entering in we had unto you, and how ye turned to God from idols to serve the living and true God; and to wait for his Son from heaven, whom he raised from the dead, even Jesus, which delivered us from the wrath to come.

— I Thessalonians 1:1-10.

"WE WERE GENTLE AMONG YOU, EVEN AS A
NURSE CHERISHETH HER CHILDREN"

For yourselves, brethren, know our entrance in unto you, that it was not in vain: but even after that we had

THEATER OF DIONYSIUS, ATHENS

suffered before, and were shamefully entreated, as ye
know, at Philippi, we were bold in our God to speak unto
you the gospel of God with much contention. For our
exhortation was not of deceit, nor of uncleanness, nor in
guile: but as we were allowed of God to be put in trust
with the gospel, even so we speak; not as pleasing men,
but God, which trieth our hearts. For neither at any
time used we flattering words, as ye know, nor a cloak
of covetousness; God is witness: nor of men sought we
glory, neither of you, nor yet of others, when we might
have been burdensome, as the apostles of Christ. But
we were gentle among you, even as a nurse cherisheth
her children: so being affectionately desirous of you,
we were willing to have imparted unto you, not the gospel
of God only, but also our own souls, because ye were
dear unto us. For ye remember, brethren, our labour
and travail: for labouring night and day, because we
would not be chargeable unto any of you, we preached
unto you the gospel of God. Ye are witnesses, and
God also, how holily and justly and unblameably we
behaved ourselves among you that believe: as ye know
how we exhorted and comforted and charged every one
of you, as a father doth his children, that ye would walk
worthy of God, who hath called you unto his kingdom
and glory.	— I Thessalonians 2:1–12.

"YE RECEIVED THE WORD OF GOD NOT AS THE WORD OF MEN"

For this cause also thank we God without ceasing,
because, when ye received the word of God which ye
heard of us, ye received it not as the word of men, but
as it is in truth, the word of God, which effectually
worketh also in you that believe.	— I Thessalonians 2:13.

"YE ALSO HAVE SUFFERED"

For ye, brethren, became followers of the churches of God which in Judæa are in Christ Jesus: for ye also have suffered like things of your own countrymen, even as they have of the Jews: who both killed the Lord Jesus, and their own prophets, and have persecuted us; and they please not God, and are contrary to all men: forbidding us to speak to the Gentiles that they might be saved, to fill up their sins alway: for the wrath is come upon them to the uttermost.   — I Thessalonians 2:14–16.

PAUL DESIRES AGAIN TO SEE HIS FRIENDS AT THESSALONICA

But we, brethren, being taken from you for a short time in presence, not in heart, endeavoured the more abundantly to see your face with great desire. Wherefore we would have come unto you, even I, Paul, once and again; but Satan hindered us. For what is our hope, or joy, or crown of rejoicing? Are not even ye in the presence of our Lord Jesus Christ at his coming? For ye are our glory and joy.   — I Thessalonians 2:17–20.

"WHEN TIMOTHY CAME FROM YOU UNTO US, WE WERE COMFORTED"

Wherefore when we could no longer forbear, we thought it good to be left at Athens alone; and sent Timotheus, our brother, and minister of God, and our fellowlabourer in the gospel of Christ, to establish you, and to comfort you concerning your faith: that no man should be moved by these afflictions: for yourselves know that we are appointed thereunto. For verily, when we were with you, we told you before that we should suffer tribulation; even as it came to pass, and

ye know. For this cause, when I could no longer forbear, I sent to know your faith, lest by some means the
tempter have tempted you, and our labour be in vain.
But now when Timotheus came from you unto us, and
brought us good tidings of your faith and charity, and
that ye have good remembrance of us always, desiring
greatly to see us, as we also to see you: therefore, brethren, we were comforted over you in all our affliction and
distress by your faith: for now we live, if ye stand fast
in the Lord. For what thanks can we render to God
again for you, for all the joy wherewith we joy for your
sakes before our God; night and day praying exceedingly that we might see your face, and might perfect
that which is lacking in your faith?

Now God himself and our Father, and our Lord
Jesus Christ, direct our way unto you. And the Lord
make you to increase and abound in love one toward
another, and toward all men, even as we do toward you:
to the end he may stablish your hearts unblameable in
holiness before God, even our Father, at the coming of
our Lord Jesus Christ with all his saints. — I Thessalonians 3.

"WE EXHORT YOU THAT AS YE HAVE RECEIVED OF US HOW YE OUGHT TO WALK, SO YE WOULD ABOUND MORE AND MORE"

Furthermore then we beseech you, brethren, and
exhort you by the Lord Jesus, that as ye have received
of us how ye ought to walk and to please God, so ye
would abound more and more. For ye know what
commandments we gave you by the Lord Jesus. For
this is the will of God, even your sanctification, that ye
should abstain from fornication: that every one of you
should know how to possess his vessel in sanctification
and honour; not in the lust of concupiscence, even as

SCENERY AT THESSALONICA

the Gentiles which know not God: that no man go beyond and defraud his brother in any matter: because that the Lord is the avenger of all such, as we also have forewarned you and testified. For God hath not called us unto uncleanness, but unto holiness. He therefore that despiseth, despiseth not man, but God, who hath also given unto us his holy Spirit.

But as touching brotherly love ye need not that I write unto you: for ye yourselves are taught of God to love one another. And indeed ye do it toward all the brethren which are in all Macedonia: but we beseech you, brethren, that ye increase more and more; and that ye study to be quiet, and to do your own business, and to work with your own hands, as we commanded you; that ye may walk honestly toward them that are without, and that ye may have lack of nothing.

— I Thessalonians 4:1–12.

"CONCERNING THEM WHICH ARE ASLEEP"

But I would not have you to be ignorant, brethren, concerning them which are asleep, that ye sorrow not, even as others which have no hope. For if we believe that Jesus died and rose again, even so them also which sleep in Jesus will God bring with him. For this we say unto you by the word of the Lord, that we which are alive and remain unto the coming of the Lord shall not prevent them which are asleep. For the Lord himself shall descend from heaven with a shout, with the voice of the archangel, and with the trump of God: and the dead in Christ shall rise first: then we which are alive and remain shall be caught up together with them in the clouds, to meet the Lord in the air: and so shall we ever be with the Lord. Wherefore comfort one another with these words.

— I Thessalonians 4:13–18.

"OF THE TIMES AND THE
SEASONS YE HAVE NO NEED
THAT I WRITE; YE ARE
ALL THE CHILDREN
OF LIGHT"

But of the times and
the seasons, brethren, ye
have no need that I write
unto you. For yourselves
know perfectly that the day
of the Lord so cometh as a
thief in the night. For
when they shall say, "Peace
and safety," then sudden
destruction cometh upon
them, as travail upon a
woman with child; and
they shall not escape. But
ye, brethren, are not in
darkness, that that day
should overtake you as a
thief. Ye are all the children of light, and the children of the day: we are not
of the night, nor of darkness. Therefore let us not
sleep, as do others; but let
us watch and be sober. For
they that sleep sleep in the
night; and they that be
drunken are drunken in
the night. But let us, who
are of the day, be sober,
putting on the breastplate

THE STATUE OF ATHENA
PARTHENOS

This statue of the goddess, who was
considered to be the protectress of
Athens and its patron divinity, is a
copy of Phidias' colossal statue of the
goddess which stood on the Acropolis.
The helmeted goddess is represented
as standing with one hand on her
shield, the other holding a small statue
of victory. The sacred snake is coiled
inside her shield. The original of ivory
and gold was forty-two and one-half
feet high. It would be in full view of
Paul, as the little unknown man from
Palestine preached to the Athenians of
the one God "who made the heavens
and earth, in whom we live and move
and have our being."

of faith and love; and for an helmet, the hope of salvation. For God hath not appointed us to wrath, but to obtain salvation by our Lord Jesus Christ, who died for us, that, whether we wake or sleep, we should live together with him. Wherefore comfort yourselves together, and edify one another, even as also ye do.

And we beseech you, brethren, to know them which labour among you, and are over you in the Lord, and admonish you; and to esteem them very highly in love for their work's sake. And be at peace among yourselves.

Now we exhort you, brethren, warn them that are unruly, comfort the feebleminded, support the weak, be patient toward all men. See that none render evil for evil unto any man; but ever follow that which is good, both among yourselves, and to all men. Rejoice evermore. Pray without ceasing. In every thing give thanks: for this is the will of God in Christ Jesus concerning you. Quench not the Spirit. Despise not prophesyings. Prove all things; hold fast that which is good. Abstain from all appearance of evil.　　　　— I Thessalonians 5:1-22.

CLOSING

And the very God of peace sanctify you wholly; and I pray God your whole spirit and soul and body be preserved blameless unto the coming of our Lord Jesus Christ. Faithful is he that calleth you, who also will do it.

Brethren, pray for us.

Greet all the brethren with an holy kiss. I charge you by the Lord that this epistle be read unto all the holy brethren.

The grace of our Lord Jesus Christ be with you. Amen.　　　　— I Thessalonians 5:23-28.

The Letters of Paul

The Great Captain of the New Faith

The Second Epistle to the Thessalonians

If any will not work neither let him eat.

It is believed that the Second Epistle to the Thessalonians was written as supplementary to, and explanatory of, the first, perhaps a few months later, while Timothy and Silas were still at Corinth. It emphasizes and enforces the teaching of the first.

Paul, and Silvanus, and Timotheus, unto the church of the Thessalonians in God our Father and the Lord Jesus Christ:

Grace unto you, and peace, from God our Father and the Lord Jesus Christ.

"WE PRAY ALWAYS FOR YOU"

WE are bound to thank God always for you, brethren, as it is meet, because that your faith groweth exceedingly, and the charity of every one of you all toward each other aboundeth; so that we ourselves glory in you in the churches of God for your patience and faith in all your persecutions and tribulations that ye endure: which is a manifest token of the righteous judgment of God, that ye may be counted worthy of the Kingdom of God, for which ye also suffer: seeing it is a righteous thing with God to recompense tribulation to them that trouble you; and to you who are troubled rest with us, when the Lord Jesus shall be revealed from heaven with his mighty

347

angels, in flaming fire taking vengeance on them that know not God, and that obey not the gospel of our Lord Jesus Christ: who shall be punished with everlasting destruction from the presence of the Lord, and from the glory of his power; when he shall come to be glorified in his saints, and to be admired in all them that believe (because our testimony among you was believed) in that day. Wherefore also we pray always for you, that our God would count you worthy of this calling, and fulfil all the good pleasure of his goodness, and the work of faith with power: that the name of our Lord Jesus Christ may be glorified in you, and ye in him, according to the grace of our God and the Lord Jesus Christ.

— II Thessalonians 1.

BE NOT TROUBLED BECAUSE OF REPORTS THAT THE DAY OF CHRIST IS AT HAND

Now we beseech you, brethren, by the coming of our Lord Jesus Christ, and by our gathering together unto him, that ye be not soon shaken in mind, or be troubled, neither by spirit, nor by word, nor by letter as from us, as that day of Christ is at hand. Let no man deceive you by any means: for that day shall not come, except there come a falling away first, and that man of sin be revealed, the son of perdition; who opposeth and exalteth himself above all that is called God, or that is worshiped; so that he as God sitteth in the temple of God, showing himself that he is God. Remember ye not, that, when I was yet with you, I told you these things? And now ye know what withholdeth that he might be revealed in his time. For the mystery of iniquity doth already work: only he who now letteth will let, until he be taken out of the way. And then shall that Wicked be revealed, whom the Lord shall consume with the spirit of his mouth, and shall destroy with the brightness of his coming: even him, whose coming is after the working of Satan with all power and signs and lying wonders, and with all deceivableness of unrighteousness in them that perish; because they received not the love of the truth, that they might be saved. And for this cause God shall send them strong delusion, that they should believe a lie: that they all might be damned who believed not the truth, but had pleasure in unrighteousness.

But we are bound to give thanks alway to God for you, brethren beloved of the Lord, because God hath from the beginning chosen you to salvation through sanctification of the Spirit and belief of the truth: whereunto he called you by our gospel, to the obtaining of the glory of our Lord Jesus Christ. Therefore, brethren, stand fast, and hold the traditions which ye have been taught, whether by word, or our epistle.

Now our Lord Jesus Christ himself, and God, even our Father, which hath loved us, and hath given us everlasting consolation and good hope through grace, comfort your hearts, and stablish you in every good word and work. — II Thessalonians 2.

"BRETHREN, PRAY FOR US"

Finally, brethren, pray for us, that the word of the Lord may have free course, and be glorified, even as it is with you: and that we may be delivered from unreasonable and wicked men: for all men have not faith. But the Lord is faithful, who shall stablish you, and keep you from evil. And we have confidence in the Lord touching you, that ye both do and will do the things which we command you. And the Lord direct your hearts into the love of God, and into the patient waiting for Christ. — II Thessalonians 3:1-5.

"YOURSELVES KNOW HOW YE OUGHT TO FOLLOW US"

Now we command you, brethren, in the name of our Lord Jesus Christ, that ye withdraw yourselves from every brother that walketh disorderly, and not after the tradition which he received of us. For yourselves know how ye ought to follow us: for we behaved not ourselves disorderly among you; neither did we eat any man's bread for naught; but wrought with labour and travail night and day, that we might not be chargeable to any of you: not because we have not power, but to make ourselves an ensample unto you to follow us. For even when we were with you, this we commanded you, that if any would not work, neither should he eat. For we hear that there are some which walk among you disorderly, working not at all, but are busybodies. Now them that are such we command and exhort by our Lord Jesus Christ, that with quietness they work, and eat their own bread. — II Thessalonians 3:6–12.

"BE NOT WEARY IN WELL DOING"

But ye, brethren, be not weary in well doing.

And if any man obey not our word by this epistle, note that man, and have no company with him, that he may be ashamed. Yet count him not as an enemy, but admonish him as a brother. — II Thessalonians 3:13–15.

CLOSING

Now the Lord of peace himself give you peace always by all means. The Lord be with you all.

The salutation of Paul with mine own hand, which is the token in every epistle: so I write. The grace of our Lord Jesus Christ be with you all. Amen.

— II Thessalonians 3:16–18.

TIMOTHY RECEIVES THE EPISTLE FROM PAUL
An engraving by Carl Niemann

The Letters of Paul

The Great Captain of the New Faith

The First Epistle to Timothy

A group of three epistles: I Timothy, II Timothy, and Titus, are called pastoral epistles because they are addressed to the two most intimate friends of Paul, as leaders and pastors of the churches. A very interesting question arises with respect to the date of these epistles. They do not fit into any period in Paul's life which is narrated in The Acts. A bold conjecture is made that this is a period of the apostle's life of which we have practically no record. There was a very widespread and clear tradition in the early church to the effect that Paul was released from prison after he was brought to trial before Cæsar. Clement of Rome says, "Paul . . . having become a herald both in the East and in the West, received the noble renown of his faith, having taught righteousness to the whole world, having come to the boundary of the West." It is thought by some that Paul proceeded to Spain and that he made another trip to the East: Troas, Ephesus, Crete,—before he was arrested at Rome or elsewhere. This time there was no escape, for the tide of persecution was rising, a tide which all but engulfed the church in blood. We know that even in The Acts there are gaps in Paul's life which are not even touched upon; for the catalogue of his trials in II Corinthians contains many labors and perils not mentioned elsewhere. It is a fascinating theme for the imagination: those unrecorded journeys of the great commander as he visits the forces in the field for the last time.

It is supposed that the First Epistle to Timothy and the Epistle to Titus, were written after Paul's first imprisonment; and the Second Epistle to Timothy after his second arrest, shortly before his death.

There are touching personal data: Paul urges Timothy not to forget the cloak which he left with Carpus at Troas, "the books and the parchments." And then, in contrast, is that splendid confession of faith — "I charge thee, therefore, before God, and the Lord Jesus Christ, who shall judge the quick and the dead at his appearing and his kingdom: preach the word; be instant in season, out of season; reprove, rebuke, exhort with all longsuffering and doctrine. For the time will come when they will not endure sound doctrine; but after their own lusts shall they heap to themselves teachers, having itching ears; and they shall turn away their ears from the truth, and shall be turned unto fables. But watch thou in all things, endure afflictions, do the work of an evangelist, make full proof of thy ministry. For I am now ready to be offered, and the time of my departure is at hand. I have fought a good fight, I have finished my course, I have kept the faith: henceforth there is laid up for me a crown of righteousness, which the Lord, the righteous judge, shall give me at that day: and not to me only, but unto all them also that love his appearing."

Paul, an apostle of Jesus Christ by the commandment of God our Saviour, and Lord Jesus Christ, which is our hope; unto Timothy, my own son in the faith:

Grace, mercy, and peace, from God our Father and Jesus Christ our Lord.

"GIVE NO HEED TO FABLES; THE END OF THE COMMANDMENT IS CHARITY"

AS I besought thee to abide still at Ephesus, when I went into Macedonia, that thou mightest charge some that they teach no other doctrine, neither give heed to fables and endless genealogies, which minister questions, rather than godly edifying which is in faith: so do. Now the end of the commandment is charity out of a pure heart, and of a good conscience, and of faith unfeigned: from which some having swerved have turned aside unto vain jangling; desiring to be teachers of the law; understanding neither what they say, nor whereof they affirm. But we know that the law is good, if a man use it lawfully; knowing this, that the law is not made for a righteous man, but for the lawless and disobedient, for the ungodly and for sinners, for unholy and profane, for murderers of fathers and murderers of mothers, for manslayers, for whoremongers, for them that defile themselves with mankind, for menstealers, for liars, for perjured persons, and if there be any other thing that is contrary to sound doctrine; according to the glorious gospel of the blessed God, which was committed to my trust. — I Timothy 1:1–11.

"CHRIST JESUS CAME INTO THE WORLD TO SAVE SINNERS; OF WHOM I AM CHIEF"

And I thank Christ Jesus our Lord, who hath enabled me, for that he counted me faithful, putting me into the ministry; who was before a blasphemer, and a persecutor, and injurious: but I obtained mercy, because I did it ignorantly in unbelief. And the grace of our Lord was exceeding abundant with faith and love which is in Christ Jesus. This is a faithful saying, and worthy of all acceptation, that Christ Jesus came into the world to save sinners; of whom I am chief. Howbeit for this cause I obtained mercy, that in me first Jesus Christ might show forth all longsuffering, for a pattern to them which should hereafter believe on him to life everlasting. Now unto the King eternal, immortal, invisible, the only wise God, be honour and glory forever and ever. Amen.

This charge I commit unto thee, son Timothy, according to the prophecies which went before on thee, that thou by them mightest war a good warfare; holding faith, and a good conscience; which some having put away concerning faith have made shipwreck: of whom is

Hymenæus and Alexander; whom I have delivered unto Satan, that they may learn not to blaspheme.

— I Timothy 1:12–20.

"PRAY FOR ALL MEN"

I exhort therefore, that, first of all, supplications, prayers, intercessions, and giving of thanks, be made for all men; for kings, and for all that are in authority; that we may lead a quiet and peaceable life in all godliness and honesty. For this is good and acceptable in the sight of God our Saviour; who will have all men to be saved, and to come unto the knowledge of the truth. For there is one God, and one mediator between God and men, the man Christ Jesus; who gave himself a ransom for all, to be testified in due time. Whereunto I am ordained a preacher, and an apostle, (I speak the truth in Christ, and lie not;) a teacher of the Gentiles in faith and verity.

— I Timothy 2:1–7.

"LET WOMEN ADORN THEMSELVES WITH GOOD WORKS"

I will therefore that men pray everywhere, lifting up holy hands, without wrath and doubting. In like manner also, that women adorn themselves in modest apparel, with shamefacedness and sobriety; not with broided hair, or gold, or pearls, or costly array; but (which becometh women professing godliness) with good works. Let the woman learn in silence with all subjection. But I suffer not a woman to teach, nor to usurp authority over the man, but to be in silence. For Adam was first formed, then Eve. And Adam was not deceived, but the woman being deceived was in the transgression. Notwithstanding she shall be saved in childbearing, if they continue in faith and charity and holiness with sobriety.

— I Timothy 2:8–15.

THE QUALITIES OF THE LEADERS OF THE CHURCH

This is a true saying, "If a man desire the office of a bishop, he desireth a good work." A bishop then must be blameless, the husband of one wife, vigilant, sober, of good behaviour, given to hospitality, apt to teach; not given to wine, no striker, not greedy of filthy lucre; but patient, not a brawler, not covetous; one that ruleth well his own house, having his children in subjection with all gravity; (for if a man know not how to rule his own house, how shall he take care of the church of God?) Not a novice, lest being lifted up with pride, he fall into the condemnation of the devil. Moreover he must have a good report of them which are without; lest he fall into reproach and the snare of the devil. Likewise must the deacons be grave, not double-tongued, not given to much wine, not greedy of filthy lucre; holding the mystery of the faith in a pure conscience. And let these also first be proved; then let them use the office of a deacon, being found blameless. Even so must their wives be grave, not slanderers, sober, faithful in all things. Let the deacons be the husbands of one wife, ruling their children and their own houses well. For they that have used the office of a deacon well purchase to themselves a good degree, and great boldness in the faith which is in Christ Jesus.

These things write I unto thee, hoping to come unto thee shortly: but if I tarry long, that thou mayest know how thou oughtest to behave thyself in the house of God, which is the church of the living God, the pillar and ground of the truth. And without controversy great is the mystery of godliness: God was manifest in the flesh, justified in the Spirit, seen of angels, preached unto the Gentiles, believed on in the world, received up into glory. — I Timothy 3.

"EVERY CREATURE OF GOD IS GOOD, AND NOTHING TO BE REFUSED IF IT BE RECEIVED WITH THANKSGIVING"

Now the Spirit speaketh expressly, that in the latter times some shall depart from the faith, giving heed to seducing spirits, and doctrines of devils; speaking lies in hypocrisy; having their conscience seared with a hot iron; forbidding to marry, and commanding to abstain from meats, which God hath created to be received with thanksgiving of them which believe and know the truth. For every creature of God is good, and nothing to be refused, if it be received with thanksgiving: for it is sanctified by the word of God and prayer.

— I Timothy 4:1–5.

"REFUSE OLD WIVES' FABLES; EXERCISE THYSELF TO GODLINESS"

If thou put the brethren in remembrance of these things, thou shalt be a good minister of Jesus Christ, nourished up in the words of faith and of good doctrine, whereunto thou hast attained. But refuse profane and old wives' fables, and exercise thyself rather unto godliness. For bodily exercise profiteth little: but godliness is profitable unto all things, having promise of the life that now is, and of that which is to come. This is a faithful saying and worthy of all acceptation. For therefore we both labour and suffer reproach, because we trust in the living God, who is the Saviour of all men, specially of those that believe. These things command and teach.

— I Timothy 4:6–11.

"LET NO MAN DESPISE THY YOUTH, BUT BE THOU AN EXAMPLE"

Let no man despise thy youth; but be thou an example of the believers, in word, in conversation, in charity,

Christian Girl of Bethlehem

(Photographed by Three Lions, Inc.)

BETHLEHEM has been a village since earliest days of Israel's history. It lies on the stony hillside of Judea about six miles south of Jerusalem. It was the home of Naomi, mother-in-law of Ruth the Moabitess, about whom one of the loveliest stories in all the Bible was written. The fields of Boaz lie eastward from Bethlehem. From them Ruth could see on the distant eastern horizon, beyond the deep valley of the Jordan River and the Dead Sea, the blue mountains of her native Moab. Because her heart was attached to the Lord God of Israel and to her mother-in-law, she resisted all temptation to homesickness and desire to return to her homeland.

The young women of Bethlehem have always been noted for their loveliness and vivacity, and for the distinctive and colorful clothing which they have worn. This Christian girl of Bethlehem wears the gown and headgear that were familiar to the Crusaders who came to Palestine in the middle ages. The dress has changed but little over the centuries.

in spirit, in faith, in purity. Till I come, give attendance
to reading, to exhortation, to doctrine. Neglect not the
gift that is in thee, which was given thee by prophecy,
with the laying on of the hands of the presbytery. Med-
itate upon these things; give thyself wholly to them;
that thy profiting may appear to all. Take heed unto
thyself, and unto the doctrine; continue in them: for
in doing this thou shalt both save thyself, and them that
hear thee.   — I Timothy 4:12–16.

CONCERNING THE BEHAVIOR OF WOMEN

Rebuke not an elder, but intreat him as a father;
and the younger men as brethren; the elder women as
mothers; the younger as sisters, with all purity. Honour
widows that are widows indeed. But if any widow have
children or nephews, let them learn first to shew piety
at home, and to requite their parents: for that is good
and acceptable before God. Now she that is a widow
indeed, and desolate, trusteth in God, and continueth
in supplications and prayers night and day. But she
that liveth in pleasure is dead while she liveth. And
these things give in charge, that they may be blameless.
But if any provide not for his own, and specially for
those of his own house, he hath denied the faith, and is
worse than an infidel. Let not a widow be taken into
the number under threescore years old, having been the
wife of one man, well reported of for good works; if she
have brought up children, if she have lodged strangers,
if she have washed the saints' feet, if she have relieved
the afflicted, if she have diligently followed every good
work. But the younger widows refuse: for when they
have begun to wax wanton against Christ, they will
marry; having damnation, because they have cast off
their first faith. And withal they learn to be idle,

wandering about from house to house; and not only idle, but tattlers also and busybodies, speaking things which they ought not. I will therefore that the younger women marry, bear children, guide the house, give none occasion to the adversary to speak reproachfully. For some are already turned aside after Satan. If any man or woman that believeth have widows, let them relieve them, and let not the church be charged; that it may relieve them that are widows indeed. — I Timothy 5:1–16.

"THE LABOURER IS WORTHY OF HIS REWARD"

Let the elders that rule well be counted worthy of double honour, especially they who labour in the word and doctrine. For the Scripture saith, "Thou shalt not muzzle the ox that treadeth out the corn" and, "The labourer is worthy of his reward." Against an elder receive not an accusation, but before two or three witnesses. Them that sin rebuke before all, that others also may fear. I charge thee before God, and the Lord Jesus Christ, and the elect angels, that thou observe these things without preferring one before another, doing nothing by partiality. Lay hands suddenly on no man, neither be partaker of other men's sins: keep thyself pure. Drink no longer water, but use a little wine for thy stomach's sake and thine often infirmities. Some men's sins are open beforehand, going before to judgment; and some men they follow after. Likewise also the good works of some are manifest beforehand; and they that are otherwise cannot be hid.

— I Timothy 5:17–25.

"GODLINESS WITH CONTENTMENT"

Let as many servants as are under the yoke count their own masters worthy of all honour, that the name of God and his doctrine be not blasphemed. And they that have believing masters, let them not despise them, because they are brethren; but rather do them service, because they are faithful and beloved, partakers of the benefit. These things teach and exhort.

If any man teach otherwise, and consent not to wholesome words, even the words of our Lord Jesus Christ, and to the doctrine which is according to godliness; he is proud, knowing nothing, but doting about questions and strifes of words, whereof cometh envy, strife, railings, evil surmisings, perverse disputings of men of corrupt minds, and destitute of the truth, supposing that gain is godliness: from such withdraw thyself. But godliness with contentment is great gain. For we brought nothing into this world, and it is certain we can carry nothing out. And having food and raiment let us be therewith content. But they that will be rich fall into temptation and a snare, and into many foolish and hurtful lusts, which drown men in destruction and perdition. — I Timothy 6:1-9.

"THE LOVE OF MONEY IS THE ROOT OF ALL EVIL; FOLLOW AFTER RIGHTEOUSNESS"

For the love of money is the root of all evil: which while some coveted after, they have erred from the faith, and pierced themselves through with many sorrows.

But thou, O man of God, flee these things; and follow after righteousness, godliness, faith, love, patience, meekness. Fight the good fight of faith, lay hold on eternal life, whereunto thou art also called, and hast professed a good profession before many witnesses. I give thee charge in the sight of God, who quickeneth all things, and before Christ Jesus, who before Pontius Pilate witnessed a good confession; that thou keep this

OLD FASHIONED TAILOR AND HARNESS MAKER

commandment without spot, unrebukeable, until the appearing of our Lord Jesus Christ: which in his times he shall show, who is the blessed and only Potentate, the King of kings, and Lord of lords; who only hath immortality, dwelling in the light which no man can approach unto; whom no man hath seen, nor can see: to whom be honour and power everlasting. Amen.

Charge them that are rich in this world, that they be not highminded, nor trust in uncertain riches, but in the living God, who giveth us richly all things to enjoy; that they do good, that they be rich in good works, ready to distribute, willing to communicate; laying up in store for themselves a good foundation against the time to come, that they may lay hold on eternal life.

O Timothy, keep that which is committed to thy trust, avoiding profane and vain babblings, and oppositions of science falsely so called: which some professing have erred concerning the faith.

Grace be with thee. Amen.

—I Timothy 6:10-21.

THE MOUNT OF OLIVES
FROM THE EAST

The Mount of Olives from the side opposite to Jerusalem. The road in the foreground is the road to Jericho.

The Letters of Paul

The Great Captain of the New Faith

The Second Epistle to Timothy

Paul, an apostle of Jesus Christ by the will of God, according to the promise of life which is in Christ Jesus, to Timothy, my dearly beloved son:

Grace, mercy, and peace, from God the Father and Christ Jesus our Lord.

"GREATLY DESIRING TO SEE THEE"

I THANK God, whom I serve from my forefathers with pure conscience, that without ceasing I have remembrance of thee in my prayers night and day; greatly desiring to see thee, being mindful of thy tears, that I may be filled with joy; when I call to remembrance the unfeigned faith that is in thee, which dwelt first in thy grandmother Lois, and thy mother Eunice; and I am persuaded that in thee also.

— II Timothy 1:1–5.

"STIR UP THE GIFT OF GOD"

Wherefore I put thee in remembrance that thou stir up the gift of God, which is in thee by the putting on of my hands. For God hath not given us the spirit of fear; but of power, and of love, and of a sound mind. Be not thou therefore ashamed of the testimony of our Lord, nor of me his prisoner: but be thou partaker of the afflictions of the gospel according to the power of God; who hath saved us, and called us with an holy calling,

366

not according to our works, but according to his own purpose and grace, which was given us in Christ Jesus before the world began, but is now made manifest by the appearing of our Saviour Jesus Christ, who hath abolished death, and hath brought life and immortality to light through the gospel: whereunto I am appointed a preacher, and an apostle, and a teacher of the Gentiles. For the which cause I also suffer these things: nevertheless I am not ashamed: for I know whom I have believed, and am persuaded that he is able to keep that which I have committed unto him against that day.

— II Timothy 1:6–12.

"HOLD FAST THE FORM OF SOUND WORDS"

Hold fast the form of sound words, which thou hast heard of me, in faith and love which is in Christ Jesus. That good thing which was committed unto thee keep by the Holy Ghost which dwelleth in us.

This thou knowest, that all they which are in Asia be turned away from me; of whom are Phygellus and Hermogenes. The Lord give mercy unto the house of Onesiphorus; for he oft refreshed me, and was not ashamed of my chain: but, when he was in Rome, he sought me out very diligently, and found me. The Lord grant unto him that he may find mercy of the Lord in that day: and in how many things he ministered unto me at Ephesus, thou knowest very well.

— II Timothy 1:13–18.

"ENDURE HARDNESS AS A GOOD SOLDIER OF JESUS CHRIST"

Thou therefore, my son, be strong in the grace that is in Christ Jesus. And the things that thou hast heard of me among many witnesses, the same commit thou to faithful men, who shall be able to teach others also.

Thou therefore endure hardness, as a good soldier of Jesus Christ. No man that warreth entangleth himself with the affairs of this life; that he may please him who hath chosen him to be a soldier. And if a man also strive for masteries, yet is he not crowned, except he strive lawfully. The husbandman that laboureth must be first partaker of the fruits. Consider what I say; and the Lord give thee understanding in all things. Remember that Jesus Christ of the seed of David was raised from the dead according to my gospel: wherein I suffer trouble, as an evildoer, even unto bonds; but the word of God is not bound. Therefore I endure all things for the elect's sakes, that they may also obtain the salvation which is in Christ Jesus with eternal glory. It is a faithful saying: "For if we be dead with him, we shall also live with him: if we suffer, we shall also reign with him: if we deny him, he also will deny us: if we believe not, yet he abideth faithful: he cannot deny himself."

— II Timothy 2:1–13.

"STUDY TO SHOW THYSELF APPROVED UNTO GOD"

Of these things put them in remembrance, charging them before the Lord that they strive not about words to no profit, but to the subverting of the hearers. Study to show thyself approved unto God, a workman that needeth not to be ashamed, rightly dividing the word of truth. But shun profane and vain babblings: for they will increase unto more ungodliness. And their word will eat as doth a canker: of whom is Hymenæus and Philetus; who concerning the truth have erred, saying that the resurrection is past already; and overthrow the faith of some.

Nevertheless the foundation of God standeth sure, having this seal, "The LORD knoweth them that are

THE THESEION, ATHENS

his"; and, "Let every one that nameth the name of Christ depart from iniquity." But in a great house there are not only vessels of gold and of silver, but also of wood and of earth; and some to honour, and some to dishonour. If a man therefore purge himself from these, he shall be a vessel unto honour, sanctified, and meet for the master's use, and prepared unto every good work.

Flee also youthful lusts: but follow righteousness, faith, charity, peace, with them that call on the Lord out of a pure heart. But foolish and unlearned questions avoid, knowing that they do gender strifes. And the servant of the Lord must not strive; but be gentle unto all men, apt to teach, patient, in meekness instructing those that oppose themselves; if God peradventure will give them repentance to the acknowledging of the truth; and that they may recover themselves out of the snare of the devil, who are taken captive by him at his will.   — II Timothy 2:14–26.

PERSECUTION MUST COME; "BUT CONTINUE THOU IN THE THINGS WHICH THOU HAST LEARNED"

This know also, that in the last days perilous times shall come. For men shall be lovers of their own selves, covetous, boasters, proud, blasphemers, disobedient to parents, unthankful, unholy, without natural affection, trucebreakers, false accusers, incontinent, fierce, despisers of those that are good, traitors, heady, highminded, lovers of pleasures more than lovers of God; having a form of godliness, but denying the power thereof: from such turn away. For this sort are they which creep into houses, and lead captive silly women laden with sins, led away with divers lusts, ever learning, and never able to come to the knowledge of the truth. Now as Jannes and Jambres withstood Moses, so do these also resist the truth: men of corrupt minds, reprobate concerning the faith. But they shall proceed no further: for their folly shall be manifest unto all men, as theirs also was.

But thou hast fully known my doctrine, manner of life, purpose, faith, longsuffering, charity, patience, persecutions, afflictions, which came unto me at Antioch, at Iconium, at Lystra; what persecutions I endured: but out of them all the Lord delivered me. Yea, and all that will live godly in Christ Jesus shall suffer persecution. But evil men and seducers shall wax worse and worse deceiving, and being deceived. But continue thou in the things which thou hast learned and hast been assured of, knowing of whom thou hast learned them; and that from a child thou hast known the Holy Scriptures, which are able to make thee wise unto salvation through faith which is in Christ Jesus. All scripture is given by inspiration of God, and is profitable for doctrine, for reproof, for correction, for instruction in righteousness: that the man of God may be perfect, thoroughly furnished unto all good works.   — II Timothy 3.

I CHARGE THEE PREACH THE WORD; MY WORK IS NEARING AN END

I charge thee therefore before God, and the Lord Jesus Christ, who shall judge the quick and the dead at his appearing and his kingdom: preach the word; be instant in season, out of season; reprove, rebuke, exhort with all longsuffering and doctrine. For the time will come when they will not endure sound doctrine; but after their own lusts shall they heap to themselves teachers, having itching ears; and they shall turn away their ears from the truth, and shall be turned unto fables. But watch thou in all things, endure afflictions,

do the work of an evangelist, make full proof of thy
ministry. — II Timothy 4:1–5.

"I HAVE FOUGHT A GOOD FIGHT; I HAVE FINISHED MY COURSE"

For I am now ready to be offered, and the time of my
departure is at hand. I have fought a good fight, I have
finished my course, I have kept the faith: henceforth
there is laid up for me a crown of righteousness, which
the Lord, the righteous judge, shall give me at that day:
and not to me only, but unto all them also that love his
appearing.

Do thy diligence to come shortly unto me: for Demas
hath forsaken me, having loved this present world, and
is departed unto Thessalonica; Crescens to Galatia,
Titus unto Dalmatia. Only Luke is with me. Take
Mark, and bring him with thee: for he is profitable to
me for the ministry. And Tychicus have I sent to
Ephesus. The cloak that I left at Troas with Carpus,
when thou comest, bring with thee, and the books, but
especially the parchments. Alexander, the coppersmith,
did me much evil: the Lord reward him according to
his works: of whom be thou ware also; for he hath
greatly withstood our words. At my first answer no
man stood with me, but all men forsook me: I pray God
that it may not be laid to their charge. Notwithstanding
the Lord stood with me, and strengthened me; that
by me the preaching might be fully known, and that all
the Gentiles might hear: and I was delivered out of the
mouth of the lion. And the Lord shall deliver me from
every evil work, and will preserve me unto his heavenly
kingdom: to whom be glory forever and ever. Amen.
— II Timothy 4:6–18.

TEMPLE OF THE WINGLESS VICTORY, ATHENS

CLOSING WORDS

Salute Prisca and Aquila, and the household of Onesiphorus. Erastus abode at Corinth: but Trophimus have I left at Miletum sick. Do thy diligence to come before winter. Eubulus greeteth thee, and Pudens, and Linus, and Claudia, and all the brethren.

The Lord Jesus Christ be with thy spirit. Grace be with you. Amen. — II Timothy 4:19–22

THE THRESHINGFLOOR

"Thou shalt not muzzle the ox when he treadeth out the corn," commands the Bible, for Israel must be just. Also "The laborer is worthy of his reward."

And today one sees threshingfloors on the countryside of Palestine and across Jordan. Wheat and barley are the main crops, and they mean life to the people. Bread is an essential food in Palestine. We see the loaves, round and flat, piled up in the markets. The Arab breaks open a loaf and wraps a flap of it around a piece of cheese or some dates, that may be his lunch. Or he uses a small flap of it as a spoon at his regular meal. Yes, the oxen on the threshingfloor supply the main food of the East.

The Letters of Paul

The Great Captain of the New Faith

The Epistle to Titus

Paul, a servant of God, and an apostle of Jesus Christ, according to the faith of God's elect, and the acknowledging of the truth which is after godliness; in hope of eternal life, which God, that cannot lie, promised before the world began; but hath in due times manifested his word through preaching, which is committed unto me according to the commandment of God our Saviour;

To Titus, mine own son after the common faith: Grace, mercy, and peace, from God the Father and the Lord Jesus Christ our Saviour.

CONCERNING THE BEHAVIOR OF THE CRETANS
"REBUKE THEM SHARPLY"

FOR this cause left I thee in Crete, that thou shouldest set in order the things that are wanting, and ordain elders in every city, as I had appointed thee: if any be blameless, the husband of one wife, having faithful children not accused of riot or unruly. For a bishop must be blameless, as the steward of God; not self-willed, not soon angry, not given to wine, no striker, not given to filthy lucre; but a lover of hospitality, a lover of good men, sober, just, holy, temperate; holding fast the faithful word as he hath been taught, that he may be able by sound doctrine both to exhort and to convince the gainsayers.

ISLE OF CRETE

For there are many unruly and vain talkers and deceivers, specially they of the circumcision: whose mouths must be stopped, who subvert whole houses, teaching things which they ought not, for filthy lucre's sake. One of themselves, even a prophet of their own, said, "The Cretans are alway liars, evil beasts, slow bellies." This witness is true. Wherefore rebuke them sharply, that they may be sound in the faith; not giving heed to Jewish fables, and commandments of men, that turn from the truth. Unto the pure all things are pure: but unto them that are defiled and unbelieving is nothing pure; but even their mind and conscience is defiled. They profess that they know God; but in works they deny him, being abominable, and disobedient, and unto every good work reprobate. — Titus 1.

"SPEAK THOU THE THINGS WHICH BECOME SOUND DOCTRINE"

But speak thou the things which become sound doctrine: that the aged men be sober, grave, temperate, sound in faith, in charity, in patience, the aged women likewise, that they be in behaviour as becometh holiness, not false accusers, not given to much wine, teachers of good things; that they may teach the young women to be sober, to love their husbands, to love their children, to be discreet, chaste, keepers at home, good, obedient to their own husbands, that the word of God be not blasphemed. Young men likewise exhort to be sober minded. In all things showing thyself a pattern of good works: in doctrine showing uncorruptness, gravity, sincerity, sound speech, that cannot be condemned; that he that is of the contrary part may be ashamed, having no evil thing to say of you. Exhort servants to be obedient unto their own masters, and to please them well in all things; not answering again; not purloining, but showing all good fidelity; that they may adorn the doctrine of God our Saviour in all things. For the grace of God that bringeth salvation hath appeared to all men, teaching us that, denying ungodliness and worldly lusts, we should live soberly, righteously, and godly, in this present world; looking for that blessed hope, and the glorious appearing of the great God and our Saviour Jesus Christ; who gave himself for us, that he might redeem us from all iniquity, and purify unto himself a peculiar people, zealous of good works.

These things speak, and exhort, and rebuke with all authority. Let no man despise thee.

Put them in mind to be subject to principalities and powers, to obey magistrates, to be ready to every good work, to speak evil of no man, to be no brawlers, but gentle, showing all meekness unto all men. For we ourselves also were sometimes foolish, disobedient, deceived, serving divers lusts and pleasures, living in malice and envy, hateful, and hating one another. But after that the kindness and love of God our Saviour toward man appeared, not by works of righteousness which we have done, but according to his mercy he saved us, by the washing of regeneration, and renewing of the Holy Ghost; which he shed on us abundantly through Jesus Christ our Saviour; that being justified by his grace, we should be made heirs according to the hope of eternal life. This is a faithful saying, and these things I will that thou affirm constantly, that they which have believed in God might be careful to maintain good works. These things are good and profitable unto men. But avoid foolish questions, and genealogies, and contentions, and strivings about the law; for they are unprofitable and vain. A man that is an heretic after the first and second admonition reject; knowing that he that is such is subverted, and sinneth, being condemned of himself.

When I shall send Artemas unto thee, or Tychicus, be diligent to come unto me to Nicopolis: for I have determined there to winter. Bring Zenas, the lawyer, and Apollos on their journey diligently, that nothing be wanting unto them. And let ours also learn to maintain good works for necessary uses, that they be not unfruitful.

All that are with me salute thee. Greet them that love us in the faith.

Grace be with you all. Amen.   —Titus 2; 3.

ROAD OVER BROOK KIDRON
He is going across the bridge over the Brook Kidron, Jerusalem, past the Garden of Gethsemane, the walled enclosure with buildings. (Middle right) Read Matthew 26:36, Volume 7:248.

The Letters of Paul

The Great Captain of the New Faith

The Epistle to Philemon

Without thy mind would I do nothing.

Paul must have written many personal letters to his intimate friends who were scattered all over the Roman Empire. Only one has been preserved; but that one is so perfect, so exquisitely beautiful in thought and structure that we are almost reconciled to the loss of others.

The circumstances were these: a Christian of the church at Colossae had a Phrygian slave named Onesimus. Slavery was one of the great curses of society in this period of the empire. The slave had absolutely no rights, no standing in any court of justice. These slaves were for the most part prisoners of war, and this was their punishment. In the year of the arrival of Paul at Rome, the prefect of the city, Pedandus Secundus, was killed by one of his slaves, whereupon the whole body of slaves belonging to Pedandus,—men, women, and children, to the number of thousands, were executed together, though they had no part whatever in the assassination.

Onesimus, the slave of Philemon, though belonging to the lowest class of slaves, was a man of unusual character and ability. He ran away, and managed somehow—it must have been by the exercise of extraordinary cunning—to reach Rome, drawn by the irresistible attraction of the imperial city. Here he might have starved or have been killed in some brawl, but for one circumstance: Paul was at Rome, living in his own hired house, a prisoner, but that house became quickly the center of an extraordinary influence. People flocked to hear him speak. It is a tradition that he converted some of the soldiers to whom he was chained.

One day, somebody brought Onesimus, to the "mission." Possibly he had seen or heard Paul at Ephesus when his master was there on a visit. The slave was converted. He became of inestimable value in his ministrations to Paul. We may imagine what it

meant to Paul to have this trained servant take care of him. But Paul felt that he could not keep Onesimus. He must go back to his master. Nothing perhaps better illustrates the character of Paul, his power over individuals. He could send the man back across the seas to far off Colossae, back to slavery, when he had tasted freedom, and expect him to get there! There would be a thousand chances for escape, but he was to go straight as an arrow to the mark.

Paul, however, would write a letter to Philemon, and it is one of the most courteous, tactful, beautiful letters ever written. He salutes, first, Philemon and his wife, Apphia, and Archippus, perhaps a son. If he was a young lad, how proud he would be to be called by Paul, "our fellowsoldier"! Then he goes on to say that Paul, the aged, Paul, the prisoner, is sending to him "his own son," Onesimus. He would gladly retain his services; but he not only returns him but if, as was extremely likely, Onesimus had stolen any property on his hasty departure, he, Paul, would repay it. Then he makes the request which is the most wonderful thing in the letter: he asks that Philemon may possess Onesimus forever, not as a slave, but as a "brother beloved." He concludes by expressing his confidence that Philemon will not only be obedient but that he will do more than Paul asks. "Without thy mind I would do nothing"— how noble the courtesy of Paul! We may be very sure that Philemon was touched by the letter and that Onesimus had a hearty welcome to his master's house.

The Epistle of Paul to Philemon is an excellent illustration of the application of the gospel to social problems. The Kingdom of God is to come not by violence but by steady development. He always counsels obedience to authorities and to established custom. All things are to be done decently and in order. He was the greatest soldier of the ages, but he never lifted a sword in battle. He proclaimed a doctrine of absolute democracy, but he lighted no fires of insurrection. He places woman on a spiritual equality with man, but he counsels her not in any way to overstep the bonds of modesty, not to shock or to violate the conventions of the society of that day. In this he follows absolutely the teaching and examples of the Lord Jesus, the Prince of Peace.

Paul, a prisoner of Jesus Christ, and Timothy, our brother, unto Philemon, our dearly beloved, and fellowlabourer, and to our beloved Apphia, and Archippus, our fellowsoldier, and to the church in thy house:

Grace to you, and peace, from God our Father and the Lord Jesus Christ.

I THANK my God, making mention of thee always in my prayers, hearing of thy love and faith which thou hast toward the Lord Jesus, and toward all saints; that the communication of thy faith may become effectual by the acknowledging of every good thing which is in you in Christ Jesus. For we have great joy and consolation in thy love, because the bowels of the saints are refreshed by thee, brother.

Wherefore, though I might be much bold in Christ to enjoin thee that which is convenient, yet for love's sake I rather beseech thee, being such an one as Paul, the aged, and now also a prisoner of Jesus Christ.

I beseech thee for my son Onesimus, whom I have begotten in my bonds: which in time past was to thee unprofitable, but now profitable to thee and to me: whom I have sent again: thou therefore receive him, that is, mine own bowels: whom I would have retained with me, that in thy stead he might have ministered unto me in the bonds of the gospel: but without thy mind would I do nothing; that thy benefit should not be as it were of necessity, but willingly. For perhaps he therefore departed for a season, that thou shouldest receive him forever; not now as a servant, but above a servant, a brother beloved, specially to me, but how much more unto thee, both in the flesh, and in the Lord? If thou count me therefore a partner, receive him as myself.

If he hath wronged thee, or oweth thee aught, put that on mine account; I, Paul, have written it with mine own hand, I will repay it: albeit I do not say to thee how thou owest unto me even thine own self besides. Yea, brother, let me have joy of thee in the Lord: refresh my bowels in the Lord. Having confidence in thy obedience I wrote unto thee, knowing that thou wilt also do more than I say. But withal prepare me also a lodging: for I trust that through your prayers I shall be given unto you.

There salute thee Epaphras, my fellowprisoner in Christ Jesus; Marcus, Aristarchus, Demas, Lucas, my fellow labourers.

The grace of our Lord Jesus Christ be with your spirit. Amen. — Philemon.

CARAVAN ON THE ROAD, NEAR SEA OF GALILEE

These camels are marching, with the driver mounted on the foremost, along the road not far from ancient Samaria. So the camels must have looked as they brought goods from all the country around to the capital of Israel.

ANCIENT DAMASCUS

Letters of Leaders of the Early Church

AUL was the great captain of the new faith, but there were many others who followed in the train of the Master, and influenced the life of the new church by example and precept. Far and wide they went over every road in the empire and upon the ships of the sea, carrying the story of the cross, the glory of the resurrection, to the people of every land. Paul was not the only writer of letters among this company. Doubtless all the leaders of "The Way" wrote letters of instruction, of rebuke, of encouragement to the churches which sprang up everywhere. Only a few of these letters have come down to us. The authorship of some of these is in doubt, but they are all the inspired word of God. All were written by men who either had been with Jesus or had been commissioned by his spirit for this task. Some of these letters were written after the fires of persecution had begun to blaze. Such letters carry exhortations to stand firm in

time of peril. And the church did stand firm
through three centuries of martyrdom until
the church was established, and the blood
of martyrs which is the seed of that church
had sprung up into its abundant harvest.

Letters of Leaders

Of the Early Church

The Epistle to the Hebrews

Looking unto Jesus the Author and Finisher of our Faith.

THE EXALTATION OF CHRIST

GOD HATH MADE HIS SON SO MUCH BETTER THAN THE ANGELS

The authorship of this great religious document, which takes its place with the Epistle to the Romans and the Epistle of James, has always been in doubt. Even the writers of the second century did not certainly know who was the author. The Churches of the West held that it was not written by Paul, but probably by Barnabas. In the East, the opinion was strongly in favor of a Pauline authorship. Origen, the great leader of the church, holds that the author was not Paul; but he adds, "If then any church receive the epistle as Paul's, let it be commended for this, for not without reason have the ancient men handed it down as the work of Paul. But who it was that really wrote the epistle, God only knows." Different writers have ascribed its authorship to Luke, Clement, Titus, Silas, Barnabas, Apollos, Mark. Erasmus favored Clement; Luther believed Apollos to have been the author. There are a few who still think that Paul wrote the epistle. One writer says, "It seems fitting that the author of an epistle which begins by virtually proclaiming God as the only speaker in Scripture, and Jesus Christ as the one speaker in the New Testament should himself retire into the background."

The epistle is addressed to no particular church, but it is quite generally agreed that it was addressed to Jewish Christians. Differences of opinion prevail as to the particular locality or residence of the Jewish people to whom the letter was first sent. However, there are certain allusions in the epistle which best adapt themselves to the Hebrew Christians of Palestine, and, perhaps, to other

Jewish believers of the East. They were in danger of returning to Judaism through the pressure of outward trial, not so much to the Law as to the ritual; they had been early converts, and had received the gospel from its earliest preachers; they were under severe persecution, and were in deep sympathy with others who were being persecuted. (See Heb. 2:1; 3:12; 4:1, 11; 5:12; 6:6, 10; 10:23-25, 29, 34.)

The epistle is a magnificent setting forth of the great high priest of all believers, Jesus Christ, whose ministry and sacrifice provided for man the only way of redemption from sin.

The great "Faith Chapter" is one of the loftiest flights of sustained eloquence in literature, with its catalogue of the heroes of Hebrew history, culminating in the masterful appeal: "Wherefore, seeing we also are compassed about with so great a cloud of witnesses, let us lay aside every weight, and the sin which doth so easily beset us, and let us run with patience the race that is set before us, looking unto Jesus, the author and finisher of our faith; who for the joy that was set before him endured the cross, despising the shame, and is set down at the right hand of the throne of God."

GOD, who at sundry times and in divers manners spake in time past unto the fathers by the prophets, hath in these last days spoken unto us by his Son, whom he hath appointed heir of all things, by whom also he made the worlds; who being the brightness of his glory, and the express image of his person, and upholding all things by the word of his power, when he had by himself purged our sins, sat down on the right hand of the Majesty on high; being made so much better than the angels, as he hath by inheritance obtained a more excellent name than they. For unto which of the angels said he at any time,

"Thou art my Son,
· This day have I begotten thee"?

And again,

"I will be to him a Father,
And he shall be to me a Son"?

And again, when he bringeth in the first begotten into the world, he saith, "And let all the angels of God worship him." And of the angels he saith,

"Who maketh his angels spirits,
And his ministers a flame of fire."

But unto the Son he saith,

"Thy throne, O God, is forever and ever:
A sceptre of righteousness is the sceptre of thy kingdom.
Thou hast loved righteousness, and hated iniquity;
Therefore God, even thy God, hath anointed thee
With the oil of gladness above thy fellows."

And,

"Thou, Lord, in the beginning hast laid the foundation of the earth,
And the heavens are the works of thine hands:
They shall perish; but thou remainest;
And they all shall wax old as doth a garment;
And as a vesture shalt thou fold them up,
And they shall be changed:
But thou art the same,
And thy years shall not fail."

But to which of the angels said he at any time,

"Sit on my right hand,
Until I make thine enemies thy footstool"?

Are they not all ministering spirits, sent forth to minister for them who shall be heirs of salvation?

— Hebrews 1:1–14.

"IF THE WORD SPOKEN BY ANGELS WAS STEADFAST, HOW SHALL WE ESCAPE IF WE NEGLECT SO GREAT SALVATION?"

Therefore we ought to give the more earnest heed to the things which we have heard, lest at any time we should let them slip. For if the word spoken by angels was steadfast, and every transgression and disobedience received a just recompence of reward; how shall we escape, if we neglect so great salvation; which at the first began to be spoken by the Lord, and was confirmed unto us by them that heard him; God also bearing them witness, both with signs and wonders, and with divers miracles, and gifts of the Holy Ghost, according to his own will?

For unto the angels hath he not put in subjection the world to come, whereof we speak. But one in a certain place testified, saying,

"What is man, that thou art mindful of him?
Or the son of man, that thou visitest him?
Thou madest him a little lower than the angels;
Thou crownedst him with glory and honour,
And didst set him over the works of thy hands:
Thou hast put all things in subjection under his feet."

For in that he put all in subjection under him, he left nothing that is not put under him. But now we see not yet all things put under him. But we see Jesus, who was made a little lower than the angels for the suffering of death, crowned with glory and honour; that he by the grace of God should taste death for every man.

— Hebrews 2:1–9.

"THE CAPTAIN OF OUR SALVATION"

For it became him, for whom are all things, and by whom are all things, in bringing many sons unto glory,

BIBLICAL VILLAGE OF ANCIENT NAIN, NEAR NAZARETH

to make the captain of their salvation perfect through sufferings. For both he that sanctifieth and they who are sanctified are all of one: for which cause he is not ashamed to call them brethren, saying,

"I will declare thy name unto my brethren,
In the midst of the church will I sing praise unto thee."

And again,

"I will put my trust in him."

And again,

"Behold I and the children which God hath given me."

Forasmuch then as the children are partakers of flesh and blood, he also himself likewise took part of the same; that through death he might destroy him that had the power of death, that is, the devil; and deliver them who through fear of death were all their lifetime subject to bondage. For verily he took not on him the nature of angels; but he took on him the seed of Abraham. Wherefore in all things it behoved him to be made like unto his brethren, that he might be a merciful and faithful high priest in things pertaining to God, to make reconciliation for the sins of the people. For in that he himself hath suffered being tempted, he is able to succour them that are tempted.

Wherefore, holy brethren, partakers of the heavenly calling, consider the Apostle and High Priest of our profession, Christ Jesus; who was faithful to him that appointed him, as also Moses was faithful in all his house. For this man was counted worthy of more glory than Moses, inasmuch as he who hath builded the house hath more honour than the house. For every house is builded by some man; but he that built all things is God. And

Moses verily was faithful in all his house as a servant, for a testimony of those things which were to be spoken after; but Christ as a son over his own house; whose house are we, if we hold fast the confidence and the rejoicing of the hope firm unto the end. Wherefore, as the Holy Ghost saith,

"To-day if ye will hear his voice,
Harden not your hearts, as in the provocation,
In the day of temptation in the wilderness:
When your fathers tempted me, proved me,
And saw my works forty years.
Wherefore I was grieved with that generation,
And said, 'They do alway err in their heart;
And they have not known my ways.'
So I sware in my wrath,
'They shall not enter into my rest.'"

Take heed, brethren, lest there be in any of you an evil heart of unbelief, in departing from the living God. But exhort one another daily, while it is called To-day; lest any of you be hardened through the deceitfulness of sin. For we are made partakers of Christ, if we hold the beginning of our confidence steadfast unto the end; while it is said,

"To-day if ye will hear his voice,
Harden not your hearts, as in the provocation."

For some, when they had heard, did provoke: howbeit not all that came out of Egypt by Moses. But with whom was he grieved forty years? Was it not with them that had sinned, whose carcasses fell in the wilderness? And to whom sware he that they should not enter into his rest, but to them that believed not? So we see that they could not enter in because of unbelief.

— Hebrews 2:10–18; 3:1–19.

"LET US FEAR, LEST WE COME SHORT OF HIS REST"

Let us therefore fear, lest, a promise being left us of entering into his rest, any of you should seem to come short of it. For unto us was the gospel preached, as well as unto them: but the word preached did not profit them, not being mixed with faith in them that heard it. For we which have believed do enter into rest, as he said,

> "As I have sworn in my wrath,
> If they shall enter into my rest":

although the works were finished from the foundation of the world. For he spake in a certain place of the seventh day on this wise, "And God did rest the seventh day from all his works." And in this place again, "If they shall enter into my rest." Seeing therefore it remaineth that some must enter therein, and they to whom it was first preached entered not in because of unbelief: again, he limiteth a certain day, saying in David,

> "To-day," after so long a time; as it is said,
> "To-day if ye will hear his voice,
> Harden not your hearts."

For if Jesus had given them rest, then would he not afterward have spoken of another day. There remaineth therefore a rest to the people of God. For he that is entered into his rest, he also hath ceased from his own works, as God did from his. Let us labour therefore to enter into that rest, lest any man fall after the same example of unbelief.　　　　　—Hebrews 4:1–11.

"THE WORD OF GOD IS QUICK, AND POWERFUL,
SHARPER THAN ANY TWO-EDGED SWORD"

For the word of God is quick, and powerful, and sharper than any two-edged sword, piercing even to the dividing asunder of soul and spirit, and of the joints and marrow, and is a discerner of the thoughts and intents of the heart. Neither is there any creature that is not manifest in his sight: but all things are naked and opened unto the eyes of him with whom we have to do.

Seeing then that we have a great high priest, that is passed into the heavens, Jesus, the Son of God, let us hold fast our profession.   — Hebrews 4:12-14.

"OUR HIGH PRIEST, TEMPTED LIKE AS WE ARE, YET WITHOUT SIN"

For we have not an high priest which cannot be touched with the feeling of our infirmities; but was in all points tempted like as we are, yet without sin. Let us therefore come boldly unto the throne of grace, that we may obtain mercy, and find grace to help in time of need.

For every high priest taken from among men is ordained for men in things pertaining to God, that he may offer both gifts and sacrifices for sins: who can have compassion on the ignorant, and on them that are out of the way; for that he himself also is compassed with infirmity. And by reason hereof he ought, as for the people, so also for himself, to offer for sins. And no man taketh this honour unto himself, but he that is called of God, as was Aaron. So also Christ glorified not himself to be made an high priest; but he that said unto him,

> "Thou art my Son,
> To-day have I begotten thee."

As he saith also in another place,

> "Thou art a priest forever
> After the order of Melchisedec."

APOSTLE JUDE THADDEUS
A painting by Anthony Gruerio

Who in the days of his flesh, when he had offered up
prayers and supplications with strong crying and tears
unto him that was able to save him from death, and was
heard in that he feared; though he were a Son, yet
learned he obedience by the things which he suffered;
and being made perfect, he became the author of eternal
salvation unto all them that obey him; called of God an
high priest after the order of Melchisedec.

Of whom we have many things to say, and hard to
be uttered, seeing ye are dull of hearing. For when for
the time ye ought to be teachers, ye have need that one
teach you again which be the first principles of the
oracles of God; and are become such as have need of
milk, and not of strong meat. For every one that useth
milk is unskilful in the word of righteousness: for he is a
babe. But strong meat belongeth to them that are of
full age, even those who by reason of use have their
senses exercised to discern both good and evil.

— Hebrews 4:15–5:14.

"LEAVING THE DOCTRINE, LET US GO ON UNTO PERFECTION"

Therefore leaving the principles of the doctrine of
Christ, let us go on unto perfection; not laying again
the foundation of repentance from dead works, and of
faith toward God, of the doctrine of baptisms, and of
laying on of hands, and of resurrection of the dead, and
of eternal judgment. And this will we do, if God permit.
For it is impossible for those who were once enlightened,
and have tasted of the heavenly gift, and were made
partakers of the Holy Ghost, and have tasted the good
word of God, and the powers of the world to come, if
they shall fall away, to renew them again unto repentance; seeing they crucify to themselves the Son of God
afresh, and put him to an open shame. For the earth

which drinketh in the rain that cometh oft upon it, and bringeth forth herbs meet for them by whom it is dressed, receiveth blessing from God: but that which beareth thorns and briers is rejected, and is nigh unto cursing; whose end is to be burned.

But, beloved, we are persuaded better things of you, and things that accompany salvation, though we thus speak. For God is not unrighteous to forget your work and labour of love, which ye have showed toward his name, in that ye have ministered to the saints, and do minister. And we desire that every one of you do show the same diligence to the full assurance of hope unto the end: that ye be not slothful, but followers of them who through faith and patience inherit the promises.

For when God made promise to Abraham, because he could swear by no greater, he sware by himself, saying, "Surely blessing I will bless thee, and multiplying I will multiply thee." And so, after he had patiently endured, he obtained the promise. For men verily swear by the greater: and an oath for confirmation is to them an end of all strife. Wherein God, willing more abundantly to show unto the heirs of promise the immutability of his counsel, confirmed it by an oath: that by two immutable things, in which it was impossible for God to lie, we might have a strong consolation, who have fled for refuge to lay hold upon the hope set before us: which hope we have as an anchor of the soul, both sure and steadfast, and which entereth into that within the veil; whither the forerunner is for us entered, even Jesus, made an high priest forever after the order of Melchisedec.　　　　　　　　　　　　　　— Hebrews 6.

"THE PRIESTHOOD OF MELCHISEDEC"

Melchisedec stands for a permanent priest, appointed personally by God, and superior to the Hebrew priesthood.

For this Melchisedec, King of Salem, priest of the most high God, who met Abraham returning from the slaughter of the kings, and blessed him; to whom also Abraham gave a tenth part of all; first being by interpretation King of righteousness, and after that also King of Salem, which is, King of peace; without father, without mother, without descent, having neither beginning of days, nor end of life; but made like unto the Son of God; abideth a priest continually.

Now consider how great this man was, unto whom even the patriarch Abraham gave the tenth of the spoils. And verily they that are of the sons of Levi, who receive the office of the priesthood, have a commandment to take tithes of the people according to the law, that is, of their brethren, though they come out of the loins of Abraham: but he whose descent is not counted from them received tithes of Abraham, and blessed him that had the promises. And without all contradiction the less is blessed of the better. And here men that die receive tithes; but there he receiveth them, of whom it is witnessed that he liveth. And as I may so say, Levi also, who receiveth tithes, payed tithes in Abraham. For he was yet in the loins of his father, when Melchisedec met him.

If therefore perfection were by the Levitical priesthood, (for under it the people received the law,) what further need was there that another priest should rise after the order of Melchisedec, and not be called after the order of Aaron? For the priesthood being changed, there is made of necessity a change also of the law. For he of whom these things are spoken pertaineth to another tribe, of which no man gave attendance at the altar. For it is evident that our Lord sprang out of Judah; of which tribe Moses spake nothing concerning priesthood.

And it is yet far more evident: for that after the similitude of Melchisedec there ariseth another priest, who is made, not after the law of a carnal commandment, but after the power of an endless life. For he testifieth,

> "Thou art a priest forever
> After the order of Melchisedec."

For there is verily a disannulling of the commandment going before for the weakness and unprofitableness thereof. For the law made nothing perfect, but the bringing in of a better hope did; by the which we draw nigh unto God. And inasmuch as not without an oath he was made priest: for those priests were made without an oath; but this with an oath by him that said unto him,

> "The LORD sware and will not repent,
> Thou art a priest forever
> After the order of Melchisedec":

by so much was Jesus made a surety of a better testament. And they truly were many priests, because they were not suffered to continue by reason of death: but this man, because he continueth ever, hath an unchangeable priesthood. Wherefore he is able also to save them to the uttermost that come unto God by him, seeing he ever liveth to make intercession for them.

For such an high priest became us, who is holy, harmless, undefiled, separate from sinners, and made higher than the heavens; who needeth not daily, as those high priests, to offer up sacrifice, first for his own sins, and then for the people's: for this he did once, when he offered up himself. For the law maketh men high priests which have infirmity; but the word of the oath, which was since the law, maketh the Son, who is consecrated forevermore. — Hebrews 7.

"WE HAVE SUCH AN HIGH PRIEST IN THE HEAVENS"

Now of the things which we have spoken this is the sum: We have such an high priest, who is set on the right hand of the throne of the Majesty in the heavens; a minister of the sanctuary, and of the true tabernacle, which the Lord pitched, and not man. For every high priest is ordained to offer gifts and sacrifices: wherefore it is of necessity that this man have somewhat also to offer. For if he were on earth, he should not be a priest, seeing that there are priests that offer gifts according to the law: who serve unto the example and shadow of heavenly things, as Moses was admonished of God when he was about to make the tabernacle: for, "See," saith he, "that thou make all things according to the pattern showed to thee in the mount." But now hath he obtained a more excellent ministry, by how much also he is the mediator of a better covenant, which was established upon better promises. — Hebrews 8:1-6.

THE OLD COVENANT

For if that first covenant had been faultless, then should no place have been sought for the second. For finding fault with them, he saith,

"'Behold, the days come,' saith the Lord,
'When I will make a new covenant with the house of Israel and with the house of Judah:
Not according to the covenant that I made with their fathers
In the day when I took them by the hand to lead them out of the land of Egypt;

Because they continued not in my covenant,
And I regarded them not,' saith the Lord.
'For this is the covenant that I will make with the
    house of Israel
After those days,' saith the Lord;
'I will put my laws into their mind,
And write them in their hearts:
And I will be to them a God,
And they shall be to me a people:
And they shall not teach every man his neighbour,
And every man his brother, saying, "Know the Lord":
For all shall know me,
From the least to the greatest.
For I will be merciful to their unrighteousness,
And their sins and their iniquities will I remember no
    more.'"

In that he saith, "A new covenant," he hath made the first old. Now that which decayeth and waxeth old is ready to vanish away.

Then verily the first covenant had also ordinances of divine service, and a worldly sanctuary. For there was a tabernacle made; the first, wherein was the candlestick, and the table, and the shewbread; which is called the sanctuary. And after the second veil, the tabernacle which is called the Holiest of all; which had the golden censer, and the ark of the covenant overlaid round about with gold, wherein was the golden pot that had manna, and Aaron's rod that budded, and the tables of the covenant; and over it the cherubim of glory shadowing the mercyseat; of which we cannot now speak particularly. Now when these things were thus ordained the priests went always into the first tabernacle, accomplishing the service of God. But into the second went the high priest alone once every year, not without blood, which he offered for himself, and for the errors of the people: the Holy Ghost this signifying, that the way into the holiest of all was not yet made manifest, while as the first tabernacle was yet standing: which was a figure for the time then present, in which were offered both gifts and sacrifices, that could not make him that did the service perfect, as pertaining to the conscience; which stood only in meats and drinks, and divers washings, and carnal ordinances, imposed on them until the time of reformation. — Hebrews 8:7–9:10.

THE NEW COVENANT

"NOT BY THE BLOOD OF GOATS BUT BY HIS OWN BLOOD"

But Christ being come an high priest of good things to come, by a greater and more perfect tabernacle, not made with hands, that is to say, not of this building; neither by the blood of goats and calves, but by his own blood he entered in once into the holy place, having obtained eternal redemption for us. For if the blood of bulls and of goats, and the ashes of an heifer sprinkling the unclean, sanctifieth to the purifying of the flesh: how much more shall the blood of Christ, who through the eternal Spirit offered himself without spot to God, purge your conscience from dead works to serve the living God? And for this cause he is the mediator of the new testament, that by means of death, for the redemption of the transgressions that were under the first testament, they which are called might receive the promise of eternal inheritance. For where a testament is, there must also of necessity be the death of the testator. For a testament is of force after men are dead: otherwise it is of no strength at all while the testator liveth. Where-

MOSES
A sculpture by Anthony Tantardini

upon neither the first testament was dedicated without blood. For when Moses had spoken every precept to all the people according to the law, he took the blood of calves and goats, with water, and scarlet wool, and hyssop, and sprinkled both the book, and all the people, saying, "This is the blood of the testament which God hath enjoined unto you." Moreover he sprinkled with blood both the tabernacle, and all the vessels of the ministry. And almost all things are by the law purged with blood; and without shedding of blood is no remission.

It was therefore necessary that the patterns of things in the heavens should be purified with these; but the heavenly things themselves with better sacrifices than these. For Christ is not entered into the holy places made with hands, which are the figures of the true; but into heaven itself, now to appear in the presence of God for us: nor yet that he should offer himself often, as the high priest entereth into the holy place every year with blood of others; for then must he often have suffered since the foundation of the world: but now once in the end of the world hath he appeared to put away sin by the sacrifice of himself. And as it is appointed unto men once to die, but after this the judgment: so Christ was once offered to bear the sins of many; and unto them that look for him shall he appear the second time without sin unto salvation. — Hebrews 9:11–28.

"THE LAW A SHADOW OF GOOD THINGS TO COME"

For the law having a shadow of good things to come, and not the very image of the things, can never with those sacrifices which they offered year by year continually make the comers thereunto perfect. For then would they not have ceased to be offered because that the worshipers once purged should have had no more conscience of sins? But in those sacrifices there is a remembrance again made of sins every year. For it is not possible that the blood of bulls and of goats should take away sins. Wherefore when he cometh into the world, he saith,

"Sacrifice and offering thou wouldest not,
But a body hast thou prepared me:
In burnt offerings and sacrifices for sin thou hast had
  no pleasure.
Then said I, 'Lo, I come
(In the volume of the book it is written of me,)
To do thy will, O God.'"

Above when he said, "Sacrifice and offering and burnt offerings and offering for sin thou wouldest not, neither hadst pleasure therein; which are offered by the law"; then said he, "Lo, I come to do thy will, O God." He taketh away the first, that he may establish the second. By the which will we are sanctified through the offering of the body of Jesus Christ once for all. And every priest standeth daily ministering and offering oftentimes the same sacrifices, which can never take away sins: but this man, after he had offered one sacrifice for sins forever, sat down on the right hand of God; from henceforth expecting till his enemies be made his footstool. For by one offering he hath perfected forever them that are sanctified. Whereof the Holy Ghost also is a witness to us: for after that he had said before,

"'This is the covenant that I will make with them
  After those days,' saith the LORD,
 'I will put my laws into their hearts,
  And in their minds will I write them;
  And their sins and iniquities will I remember no
    more.'"

Now where remission of these is, there is no more offering for sin.

— Hebrews 10:1–18.

"HAVING BOLDNESS TO ENTER IN BY A NEW AND LIVING WAY: LET US HOLD FAST THE PROFESSION OF OUR FAITH"

Having therefore, brethren, boldness to enter into the holiest by the blood of Jesus, by a new and living way, which he hath consecrated for us, through the veil, that is to say, his flesh; and having an high priest over the house of God; let us draw near with a true heart in full assurance of faith, having our hearts sprinkled from an evil conscience, and our bodies washed with pure water. Let us hold fast the profession of our faith without wavering; (for he is faithful that promised;) and let us consider one another to provoke unto love and to good works: not forsaking the assembling of ourselves together, as the manner of some is, but exhorting one another: and so much the more, as ye see the day approaching. For if we sin wilfully after that we have received the knowledge of the truth, there remaineth no more sacrifice for sins, but a certain fearful looking for of judgment and fiery indignation, which shall devour the adversaries. He that despised Moses' law died without mercy under two or three witnesses: of how much sorer punishment, suppose ye, shall he be thought worthy, who hath trodden under foot the Son of God, and hath counted the blood of the covenant, wherewith he was sanctified, an unholy thing, and hath done despite unto the Spirit of grace? For we know him that hath said, "'Vengeance belongeth unto me, I will recompense,' saith the Lord." And again, "The Lord shall judge his people." It is a fearful thing to fall into the hands of the living God.

JACOB
A painting by James J. Tissot

But call to remembrance the former days, in which, after ye were illuminated, ye endured a great fight of afflictions; partly, whilst ye were made a gazingstock both by reproaches and afflictions; and partly, whilst ye became companions of them that were so used. For ye had compassion of me in my bonds, and took joyfully the spoiling of your goods, knowing in yourselves that ye have in heaven a better and an enduring substance. Cast not away therefore your confidence, which hath great recompence of reward. For ye have need of patience, that, after ye have done the will of God, ye might receive the promise.

For yet a little while,
And he that shall come will come, and will not tarry.
Now the just shall live by faith:
But if any man draw back, my soul shall have no
   pleasure in him.

But we are not of them who draw back unto perdition; but of them that believe to the saving of the soul.
— Hebrew 10:19–39.

The Muster Roll of the Men and Women of Faith

Now faith is the substance of things hoped for, the evidence of things not seen. For by it the elders obtained a good report. Through faith we understand that the worlds were framed by the word of God, so that things which are seen were not made of things which do appear.

ABEL

By faith Abel offered unto God a more excellent sacrifice than Cain, by which he obtained witness that he was righteous, God testifying of his gifts: and by it he being dead yet speaketh.

ENOCH

By faith Enoch was translated that he should not see death; and was not found, because God had translated him: for before his translation he had this testimony, that he pleased God. But without faith it is impossible to please him: for he that cometh to God must believe that he is, and that he is a rewarder of them that diligently seek him.

NOAH

By faith Noah, being warned of God of things not seen as yet, moved with fear, prepared an ark to the saving of his house; by the which he condemned the world, and became heir of the righteousness which is by faith.

ABRAHAM

By faith Abraham, when he was called to go out into a place which he should after receive for an inheritance, obeyed; and he went out, not knowing whither he went. By faith he sojourned in the land of promise, as in a strange country, dwelling in tabernacles with Isaac and Jacob, the heirs with him of the same promise: for he looked for a city which hath foundations, whose builder and maker is God.

SARA

Through faith also Sara herself received strength to conceive seed, and was delivered of a child when she was past age, because she judged him faithful who had promised. Therefore sprang there even of one, and him as good as dead, so many as the stars of the sky in multitude, and as the sand which is by the seashore innumerable.

These all died in faith, not having received the promises, but having seen them afar off, and were

A PATRIARCH ON HIS WAY TO MARKET

persuaded of them, and embraced them, and confessed that they were strangers and pilgrims on the earth. For they that say such things declare plainly that they seek a country. And truly, if they had been mindful of that country from whence they came out, they might have had opportunity to have returned. But now they desire a better country, that is, an heavenly: wherefore God is not ashamed to be called their God: for he hath prepared for them a city.

ABRAHAM

By faith Abraham, when he was tried, offered up Isaac: and he that had received the promises offered up his only begotten son, of whom it was said, "In Isaac shall thy seed be called": accounting that God was able to raise him up, even from the dead; from whence also he received him in a figure.

ISAAC

By faith Isaac blessed Jacob and Esau concerning things to come. By faith Jacob, when he was a dying, blessed both the sons of Joseph; and worshiped, leaning upon the top of his staff.

JOSEPH

By faith Joseph, when he died, made mention of the departing of the children of Israel; and gave commandment concerning his bones.

MOSES

By faith Moses, when he was born, was hid three months of his parents, because they saw he was a proper child; and they were not afraid of the king's commandment. By faith Moses, when he was come to years,

refused to be called the son of Pharaoh's daughter;
choosing rather to suffer affliction with the people of
God, than to enjoy the pleasures of sin for a season;
esteeming the reproach of Christ greater riches than
the treasures in Egypt: for he had respect unto the
recompence of the reward. By faith he forsook Egypt,
not fearing the wrath of the king: for he endured, as
seeing him who is invisible. Through faith he kept the
passover, and the sprinkling of blood, lest he that destroyed the firstborn should touch them. By faith they
passed through the Red Sea as by dry land: which the
Egyptians assaying to do were drowned.

JOSHUA

By faith the walls of Jericho fell down, after they were
compassed about seven days.

RAHAB

By faith the harlot Rahab perished not with them
that believed not, when she had received the spies with
peace.

THE LONG LINE OF HEROES; NAMED AND UNNAMED

And what shall I more say? For the time would fail
me to tell of Gideon, and of Barak, and of Samson, and
of Jephthah; of David also, and Samuel, and of the
prophets: who through faith subdued kingdoms, wrought
righteousness, obtained promises, stopped the mouths
of lions, quenched the violence of fire, escaped the edge
of the sword, out of weakness were made strong, waxed
valiant in fight, turned to flight the armies of the aliens.
Women received their dead raised to life again: and
others were tortured, not accepting deliverance; that
they might obtain a better resurrection: and others had

trial of cruel mockings and scourgings, yea, moreover of bonds and imprisonment: they were stoned, they were sawn asunder, were tempted, were slain with the sword: they wandered about in sheepskins and goatskins; being destitute, afflicted, tormented; (of whom the world was not worthy:) they wandered in deserts, and in mountains, and in dens and caves of the earth. And these all, having obtained a good report through faith, received not the promise: God having provided some better thing for us, that they without us should not be made perfect.   — Hebrews 11.

"Let Us Run with Patience the Race that Is Set Before Us"

Wherefore seeing we also are compassed about with so great a cloud of witnesses, let us lay aside every weight, and the sin which doth so easily beset us, and let us run with patience the race that is set before us, looking unto Jesus, the author and finisher of our faith; who for the joy that was set before him endured the cross, despising the shame, and is set down at the right hand of the throne of God.

For consider him that endured such contradiction of sinners against himself, lest ye be wearied and faint in your minds. Ye have not yet resisted unto blood, striving against sin. And ye have forgotten the exhortation which speaketh unto you as unto children,

"My son, despise not thou the chastening of the Lord,
Nor faint when thou art rebuked of him:
For whom the Lord loveth he chasteneth,
And scourgeth every son whom he receiveth."

If ye endure chastening, God dealeth with you as with sons; for what son is he whom the father chasteneth not?

But if ye be without chastisement, whereof all are partakers, then are ye bastards, and not sons. Furthermore we have had fathers of our flesh which corrected us, and we gave them reverence: shall we not much rather be in subjection unto the Father of spirits, and live? For they verily for a few days chastened us after their own pleasure; but he for our profit, that we might be partakers of his holiness. Now no chastening for the present seemeth to be joyous, but grievous: nevertheless afterward it yieldeth the peaceable fruit of righteousness unto them which are exercised thereby. Wherefore lift up the hands which hang down, and the feeble knees; and make straight paths for your feet, lest that which is lame be turned out of the way; but let it rather be healed.

Follow peace with all men, and holiness, without which no man shall see the Lord: looking diligently lest any man fail of the grace of God; lest any root of bitterness springing up trouble you, and thereby many be defiled; lest there be any fornicator, or profane person, as Esau, who for one morsel of meat sold his birthright. For ye know how that afterward, when he would have inherited the blessing, he was rejected: for he found no place of repentance, though he sought it carefully with tears.

For ye are not come unto the mount that might be touched, and that burned with fire, nor unto blackness, and darkness, and tempest, and the sound of a trumpet, and the voice of words; which voice they that heard intreated that the word should not be spoken to them any more: for they could not endure that which was commanded, "And if so much as a beast touch the mountain, it shall be stoned, or thrust through with a dart": and so terrible was the sight, that Moses said,

"I exceedingly fear and quake": but ye are come unto
Mount Sion, and unto the city of the living God, the
heavenly Jerusalem, and to an innumerable company of
angels, to the general assembly and church of the firstborn, which are written in heaven, and to God the Judge
of all, and to the spirits of just men made perfect, and to
Jesus, the mediator of the new covenant, and to the blood
of sprinkling, that speaketh better things than that of
Abel. See that ye refuse not him that speaketh. For
if they escaped not who refused him that spake on earth,
much more shall not we escape, if we turn away from
him that speaketh from heaven: whose voice then shook
the earth: but now he hath promised, saying, "Yet once
more I shake not the earth only, but also heaven." And
this word, "Yet once more," signifieth the removing of
those things that are shaken, as of things that are made,
that those things which cannot be shaken may remain.
Wherefore we receiving a kingdom which cannot be
moved, let us have grace, whereby we may serve God
acceptably with reverence and godly fear: for our God
is a consuming fire.

Let brotherly love continue. Be not forgetful to
entertain strangers: for thereby some have entertained
angels unawares. Remember them that are in bonds,
as bound with them; and them which suffer adversity,
as being yourselves also in the body. Marriage is honourable in all, and the bed undefiled: but whoremongers
and adulterers God will judge. Let your conversation be
without covetousness; and be content with such things
as ye have: for he hath said, "I will never leave thee, nor
forsake thee." So that we may boldly say,

"The Lord is my helper, and I will not fear
What man shall do unto me."

Remember them which have the rule over you, who have spoken unto you the word of God: whose faith follow, considering the end of their conversation.

— Hebrews 12; 13:1-7.

"JESUS CHRIST THE SAME YESTERDAY, TO-DAY, AND FOREVER"

Jesus Christ the same yesterday, and to-day, and forever. Be not carried about with divers and strange doctrines. For it is a good thing that the heart be established with grace; not with meats, which have not profited them that have been occupied therein. We have an altar, whereof they have no right to eat which serve the tabernacle. For the bodies of those beasts, whose blood is brought into the sanctuary by the high priest for sin, are burned without the camp. Wherefore Jesus also, that he might sanctify the people with his own blood, suffered without the gate. Let us go forth therefore unto him without the camp, bearing his reproach. For here have we no continuing city, but we seek one to come. By him therefore let us offer the sacrifice of praise to God continually, that is, the fruit of our lips giving thanks to his name. But to do good and to communicate forget not: for with such sacrifices God is well pleased. Obey them that have the rule over you, and submit yourselves: for they watch for your souls, as they that must give account, that they may do it with joy, and not with grief: for that is unprofitable for you.

Pray for us: for we trust we have a good conscience, in all things willing to live honestly. But I beseech you the rather to do this, that I may be restored to you the sooner.

Now the God of peace, that brought again from the dead our Lord Jesus, that great shepherd of the sheep, through the blood of the everlasting covenant, make you perfect in every good work to do his will, working in you that which is wellpleasing in his sight, through Jesus Christ; to whom be glory forever and ever. Amen.

And I beseech you, brethren, suffer the word of exhortation: for I have written a letter unto you in few words. Know ye that our brother Timothy is set at liberty; with whom, if he come shortly, I will see you.

Salute all them that have the rule over you, and all the saints. They of Italy salute you.

Grace be with you all. Amen. — Hebrews 13:8–25.

NORTH SHORE OF LAKE OF GALILEE

Along this shore, east of Capernaum, Jesus must often have passed in a boat, and perhaps on foot, along the shore.

Letters of Leaders

Of the Early Church

The Epistle of James

*For as the body without the spirit is dead, so faith
without works is dead also.*

The important place which this epistle held in the early church
it has continued to occupy. It ranks with the great Pauline letters.
It was written by James the Apostle, "the brother of Jesus." It is
addressed to the "twelve tribes which are scattered abroad," the
Jewish Christians in the cities along the Mediterranean coast and
on the far-flung boundaries of the empire. These Jewish churches
did not escape the apostolic censure of James. He was as frank as
Paul. It was very plain speaking which he addressed to them, not
eloquent, but straight to the point, delivered with a directness and a
precision which cuts through all deceit and evasion. Many of the
terse epigrammatic expressions remind the reader of similar expressions in the teaching of Jesus and remain fixed in the memory—
"Every good gift and every perfect gift is from above"; ". . . let
every man be swift to hear, slow to speak, slow to wrath"; "Draw
nigh to God and He will draw nigh to you"; that perfect definition
of religion, "Pure religion and undefiled before God and the Father
is this, to visit the fatherless and widows in their affliction, and to
keep himself unspotted from the world." Who can forget the description of the rich man with the "gold ring" and the "gay apparel," who enters the church, pompously and is given the chief
place while the poor man in "vile apparel" is told to "stand there or
sit here under my footstool" or the little sermon on the dangers of
the evil use of speech with its figures of the ship and the rudder, and
the horse and the bridle, sweet waters and bitter, and the tongue as
a fire? The epistle throughout is a masterly setting forth of the
intensely practical nature of the Christian life.

James, a servant of God and of the Lord Jesus Christ, to the twelve tribes which are scattered abroad, greeting.

MY brethren, count it all joy when ye fall into divers temptations; knowing this, that the trying of your faith worketh patience. But let patience have her perfect work, that ye may be perfect and entire, wanting nothing.

If any of you lack wisdom, let him ask of God, that giveth to all men liberally, and upbraideth not; and it shall be given him. But let him ask in faith, nothing wavering. For he that wavereth is like a wave of the sea driven with the wind and tossed. For let not that man think that he shall receive anything of the Lord. A double-minded man is unstable in all his ways.

Let the brother of low degree rejoice in that he is exalted: but the rich, in that he is made low: because as the flower of the grass he shall pass away. For the sun is no sooner risen with a burning heat, but it withereth the grass, and the flower thereof falleth, and the grace of the fashion of it perisheth: so also shall the rich man fade away in his ways.　　　— James 1:1-11.

"BLESSED IS THE MAN WHO ENDURETH TEMPTATION"

Blessed is the man that endureth temptation: for when he is tried, he shall receive the crown of life, which the Lord hath promised to them that love him. Let no man say when he is tempted, "I am tempted of God": for God cannot be tempted with evil, neither tempteth he any man: but every man is tempted, when he is drawn away of his own lust, and enticed. Then when lust hath conceived, it bringeth forth sin: and sin, when it is finished, bringeth forth death. Do not err, my beloved brethren. Every good gift and every perfect gift is from above, and cometh down from the Father of lights, with whom is no variableness, neither shadow of turning. Of his own will begat he us with the word of truth, that we should be a kind of firstfruits of his creatures.

Wherefore, my beloved brethren, let every man be swift to hear, slow to speak, slow to wrath: for the wrath of man worketh not the righteousness of God. Wherefore lay apart all filthiness and superfluity of naughtiness, and receive with meekness the engrafted word, which is able to save your souls. — James 1:12–21.

"DOERS NOT HEARERS"

But be ye doers of the word, and not hearers only, deceiving your own selves. For if any be a hearer of the word, and not a doer, he is like unto a man beholding his natural face in a glass: for he beholdeth himself, and goeth his way, and straightway forgetteth what manner of man he was. But whoso looketh into the perfect law of liberty, and continueth therein, he being not a forgetful hearer, but a doer of the work, this man shall be blessed in his deed. If any man among you seem to be religious, and bridleth not his tongue, but deceiveth his own heart, this man's religion is vain. Pure religion and undefiled before God and the Father is this, to visit the fatherless and widows in their affliction, and to keep himself unspotted from the world. — James 1:22–27.

"BE NOT RESPECTERS OF PERSONS"

My brethren, have not the faith of our Lord Jesus Christ, the Lord of glory, with respect of persons. For if there come unto your assembly a man with a gold ring, in goodly apparel, and there come in also a poor man in vile raiment; and ye have respect to him that weareth the gay clothing, and say unto him, "Sit thou here in a good place"; and say to the poor, "Stand thou there, or sit here under my footstool": are ye not then partial in yourselves, and are become judges of evil thoughts?   Hearken, my beloved brethren, hath not God chosen the poor of this world rich in faith, and heirs of the kingdom which he hath promised to them that love him?   But ye have despised the poor.   Do not rich men oppress you, and draw you before the judgment seats?   Do not they blaspheme that worthy name by the which ye are called?   If ye fulfil the royal law according to the Scripture, "Thou shalt love thy neighbour as thyself," ye do well: but if ye have respect to persons, ye commit sin, and are convinced of the law as transgressors.   For whosoever shall keep the whole law, and yet offend in one point, he is guilty of all.   For he that said, "Do not commit adultery," said also, "Do not kill."   Now if thou commit no adultery, yet if thou kill, thou art become a transgressor of the law.   So speak ye, and so do, as they that shall be judged by the law of liberty.   For he shall have judgment without mercy, that hath showed no mercy; and mercy rejoiceth against judgment.   — James 2:1–13.

"FAITH WITHOUT WORKS IS DEAD"

What doth it profit, my brethren, though a man say he hath faith, and have not works? Can faith save him? If a brother or sister be naked, and destitute of daily food, and one of you say unto them, "Depart in peace, be ye warmed and filled"; notwithstanding ye give them not those things which are needful to the body; what doth it profit?   Even so faith, if it hath not works, is dead, being alone.   Yea, a man may say, "Thou hast

APOSTLE MATTHIAS
A painting by Anthony Gruerio

faith, and I have works: show me thy faith without thy works, and I will show thee my faith by my works. Thou believest that there is one God; thou doest well: the devils also believe, and tremble." But wilt thou know, O vain man, that faith without works is dead? Was not Abraham, our father, justified by works, when he had offered Isaac, his son, upon the altar? Seest thou how faith wrought with his works, and by works was faith made perfect? And the Scripture was fulfilled which saith, "Abraham believed God, and it was imputed unto him for righteousness: and he was called the Friend of God." Ye see then how that by works a man is justified, and not by faith only. Likewise also was not Rahab the harlot justified by works, when she had received the messengers, and had sent them out another way? For as the body without the spirit is dead, so faith without works is dead also. — James 2:14–26.

"THE TONGUE IS A FIRE"

My brethren, be not many masters, knowing that we shall receive the greater condemnation. For in many things we offend all. If any man offend not in word, the same is a perfect man, and able also to bridle the whole body. Behold, we put bits in the horses' mouths, that they may obey us; and we turn about their whole body. Behold also the ships, which though they be so great, and are driven of fierce winds, yet are they turned about with a very small helm, whithersoever the governor listeth. Even so the tongue is a little member, and boasteth great things. Behold, how great a matter a little fire kindleth! And the tongue is a fire, a world of iniquity: so is the tongue among our members, that it defileth the whole body, and setteth on fire the course of nature; and it is set on fire of hell. For every kind of beasts, and of birds, and of serpents, and of things in the sea, is tamed, and hath been tamed of mankind: but the tongue can no man tame; it is an unruly evil, full of deadly poison. Therewith bless we God, even the Father; and therewith curse we men, which are made after the similitude of God. Out of the same mouth proceedeth blessing and cursing. My brethren, these things ought not so to be. Doth a fountain send forth at the same place sweet water and bitter? Can the fig-tree, my brethren, bear olive berries, either a vine, figs? So can no fountain both yield salt water and fresh.

Who is a wise man and endued with knowledge among you? Let him show out of a good conversation his works with meekness of wisdom. But if ye have bitter envying and strife in your hearts, glory not, and lie not against the truth. This wisdom descendeth not from above, but is earthly, sensual, devilish. For where envying and strife is, there is confusion and every evil work. But the wisdom that is from above is first pure, then peaceable, gentle, and easy to be intreated, full of mercy and good fruits, without partiality, and without hypocrisy. And the fruit of righteousness is sown in peace of them that make peace.

From whence come wars and fightings among you? Come they not hence, even of your lusts that war in your members? Ye lust, and have not: ye kill, and desire to have, and cannot obtain: ye fight and war, yet ye have not, because ye ask not. Ye ask, and receive not, because ye ask amiss, that ye may consume it upon your lusts. Ye adulterers and adulteresses, know ye not that the friendship of the world is enmity with God? Whosoever therefore will be a friend of the world is the enemy of God. Do ye think that the Scripture saith in vain, "The spirit that dwelleth in us lusteth to envy"? But

he giveth more grace. Wherefore he saith, "God resisteth the proud, but giveth grace unto the humble."
Submit yourselves therefore to God. Resist the devil,
and he will flee from you.   — James 3; 4:1-7.

"DRAW NIGH TO GOD, AND HE WILL DRAW NIGH TO YOU"

Draw nigh to God, and he will draw nigh to you.
Cleanse your hands, ye sinners; and purify your hearts,
ye double-minded. Be afflicted, and mourn, and weep:
let your laughter be turned to mourning, and your joy
to heaviness. Humble yourselves in the sight of the
Lord, and he shall lift you up.

Speak not evil one of another, brethren. He that
speaketh evil of his brother, and judgeth his brother,
speaketh evil of the law, and judgeth the law: but if
thou judge the law, thou art not a doer of the law, but a
judge. There is one lawgiver, who is able to save and
to destroy: who art thou that judgest another?

Go to now, ye that say, "To-day or to-morrow we
will go into such a city, and continue there a year, and
buy and sell, and get gain": whereas ye know not what
shall be on the morrow. For what is your life? It is
even a vapour, that appeareth for a little time, and then
vanisheth away. For that ye ought to say, "If the
Lord will, we shall live, and do this, or that." But now
ye rejoice in your boastings: all such rejoicing is evil.
Therefore to him that knoweth to do good, and doeth it
not, to him it is sin.   — James 4:8-17.

"YE RICH MEN, WEEP"

Go to now, ye rich men, weep and howl for your
miseries that shall come upon you. Your riches are
corrupted, and your garments are motheaten. Your

gold and silver is cankered; and the rust of them shall be a witness against you, and shall eat your flesh as it were fire. Ye have heaped treasure together for the last days. Behold, the hire of the labourers who have reaped down your fields, which is of you kept back by fraud, crieth: and the cries of them which have reaped are entered into the ears of the Lord of sabaoth. Ye have lived in pleasure on the earth, and been wanton; ye have nourished your hearts, as in a day of slaughter. Ye have condemned and killed the just; and he doth not resist you. — James 5:1–6.

"BE YE PATIENT—FOLLOW THE EXAMPLE OF JOB AND OF THE PROPHETS"

Be patient therefore, brethren, unto the coming of the Lord. Behold, the husbandman waiteth for the precious fruit of the earth, and hath long patience for it, until he receive the early and latter rain. Be ye also patient; stablish your hearts: for the coming of the Lord draweth nigh. Grudge not one against another, brethren, lest ye be condemned: behold, the judge standeth before the door. Take, my brethren, the prophets, who have spoken in the name of the Lord, for an example of suffering affliction, and of patience. Behold, we count them happy which endure. Ye have heard of the patience of Job, and have seen the end of the Lord; that the Lord is very pitiful, and of tender mercy.

But above all things, my brethren, swear not, neither by heaven, neither by the earth, neither by any other oath: but let your yea be yea; and your nay, nay; lest ye fall into condemnation.

Is any among you afflicted? Let him pray. Is any merry? Let him sing psalms. — James 5:7–13.

"THE PRAYER OF FAITH SHALL SAVE THE SICK"

Is any sick among you? Let him call for the elders of the church; and let them pray over him, anointing him with oil in the name of the Lord: and the prayer of faith shall save the sick, and the Lord shall raise him up; and if he have committed sins, they shall be forgiven him. Confess your faults one to another, and pray one for another, that ye may be healed. The effectual fervent prayer of a righteous man availeth much. Elias was a man subject to like passions as we are, and he prayed earnestly that it might not rain: and it rained not on the earth by the space of three years and six months. And he prayed again, and the heaven gave rain, and the earth brought forth her fruit. Brethren, if any of you do err from the truth, and one convert him; let him know, that he which converteth the sinner from the error of his way shall save a soul from death, and shall hide a multitude of sins. — James 5:14–20.

SYNAGOGUE AT CAPERNAUM

The Synagogue is closely connected with our Lord's life and ministry. In them he worshipped in his youth and in his manhood.

Letters of Leaders
Of the Early Church

The First Epistle of Peter
Casting all your care upon him, for he careth for you.

We have been told much of the life and ministry of the apostle Peter during his years of training and leadership with Jesus. He was the most ardent, the most outspoken, the most pronounced leader of the twelve apostles. The earlier chapters of the Acts of the Apostles tell the story of his bold and capable leadership of the church during the first ten or fifteen years after the ascension. Then the leadership of the church in Jerusalem passed into the hands of James, the converted "brother of the Lord Jesus"; Paul became the great leader in Christian missions among the Gentiles, and Peter's name almost disappears from the pages of Christian history. He quite evidently took a subordinate place in humble labors to extend the gospel of Christ, and, as the apostle to the Hebrews, preached the Saviour wherever Jews could be found, in Antioch, in Rome, possibly at Corinth and in missionary journeys, accompanied by his wife, (see Acts 12:17; 15; 21:18; I Cor. 1:12; 9:5; Gal. 2:7-12).

However, these two epistles written by Peter, probably near the close of his earthly life, give us glimpses into his labors, sufferings, fortunes, and successes as a humble missionary of the cross. In these letters Peter's personality is revealed in singular and beautiful humility, in glowing loyalty to the faith of the gospel, and in deep concern for his brethren who were suffering under the strain of persecution. Peter's letters are strikingly marked by his lack of personal claims to leadership or preeminence in ecclesiastical authority, and by a recognition of the superlative leadership of Paul and other brethren.

The "farewell" of Peter found in the second epistle clearly indicates his sense of approaching death; it is similar in many respects to Paul's farewell to Timothy in his second letter to "his son in the

430

gospel". According to tradition, Peter was martyred soon after the death of Paul.

Peter, an apostle of Jesus Christ, to the strangers scattered throughout Pontus, Galatia, Cappadocia, Asia, and Bithynia, elect according to the foreknowledge of God the Father, through sanctification of the Spirit; unto obedience and sprinkling of the blood of Jesus Christ:
Grace unto you, and peace, be multiplied.

"KEPT BY THE POWER OF GOD UNTO SALVATION"

BLESSED be the God and Father of our Lord Jesus Christ, which according to his abundant mercy hath begotten us again unto a lively hope by the resurrection of Jesus Christ from the dead, to an inheritance incorruptible, and undefiled, and that fadeth not away, reserved in heaven for you, who are kept by the power of God through faith unto salvation ready to be revealed in the last time. Wherein ye greatly rejoice, though now for a season, if need be, ye are in heaviness through manifold temptations: that the trial of your faith, being much more precious than of gold that perisheth, though it be tried with fire, might be found unto praise and honour and glory at the appearing of Jesus Christ: whom having not seen, ye love; in whom, though now ye see him not, yet believing, ye rejoice with joy unspeakable and full of glory: receiving the end of your faith, even the salvation of your souls. Of which salvation the prophets have enquired and searched diligently, who prophesied of the grace that should come unto you: searching what, or what manner of time the Spirit of Christ which was in them did signify, when it testified before-

ST. PAUL'S JOURNEY—CAPPADOCIA

hand the sufferings of Christ, and the glory that should follow. Unto whom it was revealed, that not unto themselves, but unto us they did minister the things, which are now reported unto you by them that have preached the gospel unto you with the Holy Ghost sent down from heaven; which things the angels desire to look into.

—I Peter 1:1–12.

"GIRD UP THE LOINS OF YOUR MIND; BE SOBER AND HOPE FOR GRACE"

Wherefore gird up the loins of your mind, be sober, and hope to the end for the grace that is to be brought unto you at the revelation of Jesus Christ; as obedient children, not fashioning yourselves according to the former lusts in your ignorance: but as he which hath called you is holy, so be ye holy in all manner of conversation; because it is written, "Be ye holy; for I am holy."

—I Peter 1:13–16.

"YE WERE REDEEMED WITH THE PRECIOUS BLOOD OF CHRIST"

And if ye call on the Father, who without respect of persons judgeth according to every man's work, pass the time of your sojourning here in fear; forasmuch as ye know that ye were not redeemed with corruptible things, as silver and gold, from your vain conversation received by tradition from your fathers; but with the precious blood of Christ, as of a lamb without blemish and without spot: who verily was foreordained before the foundation of the world, but was manifest in these last times for you, who by him do believe in God, that raised him up from the dead, and gave him glory; that your faith and hope might be in God. Seeing ye have purified your souls in obeying the truth through the Spirit unto unfeigned love of the brethren, see that ye love one another with a pure heart fervently: being born again, not of corruptible seed, but of incorruptible, by the word of God, which liveth and abideth forever. For

"All flesh is as grass,
    And all the glory of man as the flower of grass.
The grass withereth, and the flower thereof falleth
    away:
But the word of the LORD endureth forever."

And this is the word which by the gospel is preached unto you.   — I Peter 1:17–25.

"AS NEWBORN BABES, DESIRE THE MILK OF THE WORD"

Wherefore laying aside all malice, and all guile, and hypocrisies, and envies, and all evil speakings, as newborn babes, desire the sincere milk of the word, that ye may grow thereby: if so be ye have tasted that the Lord is gracious. To whom coming, as unto a living stone, disallowed indeed of men, but chosen of God, and precious,   — I Peter 2:1–4.

YE ARE LIVELY STONES IN A SPIRITUAL HOUSE

Ye also, as lively stones, are built up a spiritual house, an holy priesthood, to offer up spiritual sacrifices, acceptable to God by Jesus Christ. Wherefore also it is contained in the Scripture,

"Behold, I lay in Sion a chief corner stone, elect, precious:
    And he that believeth on him shall not be confounded."

Unto you therefore which believe he is precious: but unto them which be disobedient,

"The stone which the builders disallowed,
    The same is made the head of the corner,"

and

"A stone of stumbling, and a rock of offence,"

even to them which stumble at the word, being disobedient: whereunto also they were appointed.

— I Peter 2:5-8

"YE ARE A ROYAL PRIESTHOOD"

But ye are a chosen generation, a royal priesthood, an holy nation, a peculiar people; that ye should show forth the praises of him who hath called you out of darkness into his marvelous light: which in time past were not a people, but are now the people of God: which had not obtained mercy, but now have obtained mercy.

— I Peter 2:9, 10.

"ABSTAIN FROM FLESHLY LUSTS, AS STRANGERS AND PILGRIMS"

Dearly beloved, I beseech you as strangers and pilgrims, abstain from fleshly lusts, which war against the soul; having your conversation honest among the Gentiles: that, whereas they speak against you as evildoers, they may by your good works, which they shall behold, glorify God in the day of visitation.   — I Peter 2:11, 12.

"SUBMIT YOURSELVES TO EVERY ORDINANCE OF MAN"

Submit yourselves to every ordinance of man for the Lord's sake: whether it be to the king, as supreme; or unto governors, as unto them that are sent by him for the punishment of evildoers, and for the praise of them that do well. For so is the will of God, that with well doing ye may put to silence the ignorance of foolish men: as free, and not using your liberty for a cloak of maliciousness, but as the servants of God. Honour all men. Love the brotherhood. Fear God. Honour the king.

THE STONE CUTTER

Servants, be subject to your masters with all fear; not only to the good and gentle, but also to the froward. For this is thankworthy, if a man for conscience toward God endure grief, suffering wrongfully. For what glory is it, if, when ye be buffeted for your faults, ye shall take it patiently? But if, when ye do well, and suffer for it, ye take it patiently, this is acceptable with God.

— I Peter 2:13–20.

"BY WHOSE STRIPES YE WERE HEALED"

For even hereunto were ye called: because Christ also suffered for us, leaving us an example, that ye should follow his steps: who did no sin, neither was guile found in his mouth: who, when he was reviled, reviled not again; when he suffered, he threatened not; but committed himself to him that judgeth righteously: who his own self bare our sins in his own body on the tree, that we, being dead to sins, should live unto righteousness: by whose stripes ye were healed. For ye were as sheep going astray; but are now returned unto the Shepherd and Bishop of your souls. — I Peter 2:21–25.

"BE YE ALL OF ONE MIND"

Likewise, ye wives, be in subjection to your own husbands; that, if any obey not the word, they also may without the word be won by the conversation of the wives; while they behold your chaste conversation coupled with fear. Whose adorning let it not be that outward adorning of plaiting the hair, and of wearing of gold, or of putting on of apparel; but let it be the hidden man of the heart, in that which is not corruptible, even the ornament of a meek and quiet spirit, which is in the sight of God of great price. For after this manner in the old time the holy women also, who trusted in God, adorned themselves, being in subjection unto their own husbands: even as Sara obeyed Abraham, calling him lord: whose daughters ye are, as long as ye do well, and are not afraid with any amazement.

Likewise, ye husbands, dwell with them according to knowledge, giving honour unto the wife, as unto the weaker vessel, and as being heirs together of the grace of life; that your prayers be not hindered.

Finally, be ye all of one mind, having compassion one of another, love as brethren, be pitiful, be courteous: not rendering evil for evil, or railing for railing: but contrariwise blessing; knowing that ye are thereunto called, that ye should inherit a blessing. For

"He that will love life,
And see good days,
Let him refrain his tongue from evil,
And his lips that they speak no guile:
Let him eschew evil,
And do good;
Let him seek peace, and ensue it.
For the eyes of the Lord are over the righteous,
And his ears are open unto their prayers:
But the face of the Lord is against them that do evil."

And who is he that will harm you, if ye be followers of that which is good? But and if ye suffer for righteousness' sake, happy are ye: and be not afraid of their terror, neither be troubled; but sanctify the Lord God in your hearts: and be ready always to give an answer to every man that asketh you a reason of the hope that is in you with meekness and fear: having a good conscience; that, whereas they speak evil of you, as of evildoers, they may be ashamed that falsely accuse your good conversation in Christ. For it is better, if the will of God be so, that ye suffer for well doing, than for evil doing. For Christ also hath once suffered for sins, the just for the unjust, that he might bring us to God, being put to death in the flesh, but quickened by the Spirit: by which also he went and preached unto the spirits in prison; which sometime were disobedient, when once the longsuffering of God waited in the days of Noah, while the ark was a preparing, wherein few, that is, eight souls were saved by water. The like figure whereunto even baptism doth also now save us (not the putting away of the filth of the flesh, but the answer of a good conscience toward God,) by the resurrection of Jesus Christ: who is gone into heaven, and is on the right hand of God; angels and authorities and powers being made subject unto him.　　　— I Peter 3.

ARM YOURSELVES FOR SUFFERING AND LIVE IN THE SPIRIT

Forasmuch then as Christ hath suffered for us in the flesh, arm yourselves likewise with the same mind: for he that hath suffered in the flesh hath ceased from sin; that he no longer should live the rest of his time in the flesh to the lusts of men, but to the will of God. For the time past of our life may suffice us to have wrought the will of the Gentiles, when we walked in lasciviousness, lusts, excess of wine, revellings, banquetings, and abominable idolatries: wherein they think it strange that ye run not with them to the same excess of riot, speaking evil of you: who shall give account to him that is ready to judge the quick and the dead. For this cause was the gospel preached also to them that are dead, that they might be judged according to men in the flesh, but live according to God in the spirit.　　　— I Peter 4:1-6.

APOSTLE PETER

A painting by Anthony Gruerio

"ABOVE ALL THINGS, HAVE CHARITY"

But the end of all things is at hand: be ye therefore sober, and watch unto prayer. And above all things have fervent charity among yourselves: for charity shall cover the multitude of sins. Use hospitality one to another without grudging. As every man hath received the gift, even so minister the same one to another, as good stewards of the manifold grace of God. If any man speak, let him speak as the oracles of God; if any man minister, let him do it as of the ability which God giveth: that God in all things may be glorified through Jesus Christ, to whom be praise and dominion forever and ever. Amen.   — I Peter 4:7-11.

REJOICE TO BE PARTAKERS OF CHRIST'S SUFFERINGS

Beloved, think it not strange concerning the fiery trial which is to try you, as though some strange thing happened unto you: but rejoice, inasmuch as ye are partakers of Christ's sufferings; that, when his glory shall be revealed, ye may be glad also with exceeding joy. If ye be reproached for the name of Christ, happy are ye; for the spirit of glory and of God resteth upon you: on their part he is evil spoken of, but on your part he is glorified. But let none of you suffer as a murderer, or as a thief, or as an evildoer, or as a busybody in other men's matters. Yet if any man suffer as a Christian, let him not be ashamed; but let him glorify God on this behalf. For the time is come that judgment must begin at the house of God: and if it first begin at us, what shall the end be of them that obey not the gospel of God? And if the righteous scarcely be saved, where shall the ungodly and the sinner appear? Wherefore let them that suffer according to the will of God commit the keeping

of their souls to him in well doing, as unto a faithful
Creator.   — I Peter 4:12–19.

YOUTH AND AGE

The elders which are among you I exhort, who am also
an elder, and a witness of the sufferings of Christ, and also
a partaker of the glory that shall be revealed: feed the
flock of God which is among you, taking the oversight
thereof, not by constraint, but willingly; not for filthy
lucre, but of a ready mind; neither as being lords over
God's heritage, but being ensamples to the flock. And
when the chief Shepherd shall appear, ye shall receive a
crown of glory that fadeth not away. Likewise, ye younger, submit yourselves unto the elder. Yea, all of you be
subject one to another, and be clothed with humility:
for God resisteth the proud, and giveth grace to the
humble.   — I Peter 5:1–5.

"CASTING ALL YOUR CARE UPON HIM"

Humble yourselves therefore under the mighty hand
of God, that he may exalt you in due time: casting all
your care upon him; for he careth for you. Be sober, be
vigilant; because your adversary the devil, as a roaring
lion, walketh about, seeking whom he may devour:
whom resist stedfast in the faith, knowing that the same
afflictions are accomplished in your brethren that are in
the world.

But the God of all grace, who hath called us unto his
eternal glory by Christ Jesus, after that ye have suffered a while, make you perfect, stablish, strengthen,
settle you. To him be glory and dominion forever and
ever. Amen.

By Silvanus, a faithful brother unto you, as I suppose, I have written briefly, exhorting, and testifying

that this is the true grace of God wherein ye stand. The church that is at Babylon, elected together with you, saluteth you; and so doth Marcus, my son.

Greet ye one another with a kiss of charity.

Peace be with you all that are in Christ Jesus. Amen.

— I Peter 5:6–14.

NEWER JERUSALEM

Inside the old walls of the Holy City, the streets and life are Oriental. But outside the walls, a brand new city has grown up with apartments, moving picture houses, beauty parlors, shops, and other western innovations.

But tucked away in this modern section, are historic remains from Roman and even more ancient days. Here we see (left, center of photograph) a part of a large reservoir called today the Mamilla pool, but in old days probably the Upper Pool of Gihon.

Near this pool, Titus, Roman General besieging and taking Jerusalem in 70 A.D., had a camp overlooking the Holy City.

This may have been four years after the writing of the Second Epistle of Peter.

Letters of Leaders

Of the Early Church

The Second Epistle of Peter

Simon Peter, a servant and an apostle of Jesus Christ, to them that have obtained like precious faith with us through the righteousness of God and our Saviour Jesus Christ:

Grace and peace be multiplied unto you through the knowledge of God, and of Jesus our Lord, according as his divine power hath given unto us all things that pertain unto life and godliness, through the knowledge of him that hath called us to glory and virtue: whereby are given unto us exceeding great and precious promises: that by these ye might be partakers of the divine nature, having escaped the corruption that is in the world through lust.

A SUM IN ADDITION

AND beside this, giving all diligence, add to your faith virtue; and to virtue knowledge; and to knowledge temperance; and to temperance patience; and to patience godliness; and to godliness brotherly kindness; and to brotherly kindness charity. For if these things be in you, and abound, they make you that ye shall neither be barren nor unfruitful in the knowledge of our Lord Jesus Christ. But he that lacketh these things is blind, and cannot see afar off, and hath forgotten that he was purged from his old sins. Wherefore the rather, brethren, give diligence to make your calling and election sure: for if ye do these things,

444

ye shall never fall: for so an entrance shall be ministered unto you abundantly into the everlasting kingdom of our Lord and Saviour Jesus Christ.   — II Peter 1:1-11.

"I THINK IT MEET TO STIR YOU UP"

Wherefore I will not be negligent to put you always in remembrance of these things, though ye know them, and be established in the present truth. Yea, I think it meet, as long as I am in this tabernacle, to stir you up by putting you in remembrance; knowing that shortly I must put off this my tabernacle, even as our Lord Jesus Christ hath showed me. Moreover I will endeavour that ye may be able after my decease to have these things always in remembrance. For we have not followed cunningly devised fables, when we made known unto you the power and coming of our Lord Jesus Christ, but were eyewitnesses of his majesty. For he received from God the Father honour and glory, when there came such a voice to him from the excellent glory, "This is my beloved Son, in whom I am well pleased." And this voice which came from heaven we heard, when we were with him in the holy mount. We have also a more sure word of prophecy; whereunto ye do well that ye take heed, as unto a light that shineth in a dark place, until the day dawn, and the day star arise in your hearts: knowing this first, that no prophecy of the Scripture is of any private interpretation. For the prophecy came not in old time by the will of man: but holy men of God spake as they were moved by the Holy Ghost.

— II Peter 1:12-21.

"THERE WERE FALSE PROPHETS";
THEY WHO FOLLOW THEM ARE PUNISHED

But there were false prophets also among the people, even as there shall be false teachers among you, who

privily shall bring in damnable heresies, even denying
the Lord that bought them, and bring upon themselves
swift destruction. And many shall follow their per-
nicious ways; by reason of whom the way of truth shall
be evil spoken of. And through covetousness shall they
with feigned words make merchandise of you: whose
judgment now of a long time lingereth not, and their
damnation slumbereth not. For if God spared not the
angels that sinned, but cast them down to hell, and
delivered them into chains of darkness, to be reserved
unto judgment; and spared not the old world, but saved
Noah, the eighth person, a preacher of righteousness,
bringing in the flood upon the world of the ungodly; and
turning the cities of Sodom and Gomorrha into ashes
condemned them with an overthrow, making them an
ensample unto those that after should live ungodly;
and delivered just Lot, vexed with the filthy conversation of the wicked: for that righteous man dwelling
among them, in seeing and hearing, vexed his righteous
soul from day to day with their unlawful deeds; the
Lord knoweth how to deliver the godly out of temptations, and to reserve the unjust unto the day of judgment
to be punished: but chiefly them that walk after the
flesh in the lust of uncleanness, and despise government.
Presumptuous are they, selfwilled, they are not afraid
to speak evil of dignities. Whereas angels, which are
greater in power and might, bring not railing accusation
against them before the Lord. But these, as natural
brute beasts, made to be taken and destroyed, speak
evil of the things that they understand not; and shall
utterly perish in their own corruption; and shall receive
the reward of unrighteousness, as they that count it
pleasure to riot in the daytime. Spots they are and
blemishes, sporting themselves with their own deceivings

while they feast with you; having eyes full of adultery, and that cannot cease from sin; beguiling unstable souls: an heart they have exercised with covetous practices; cursed children: which have forsaken the right way, and are gone astray, following the way of Balaam, the son of Bosor, who loved the wages of unrighteousness; but was rebuked for his iniquity: the dumb ass speaking with man's voice forbad the madness of the prophet. — II Peter 2:1–16.

"THESE ARE WELLS WITHOUT WATER"

These are wells without water, clouds that are carried with a tempest; to whom the mist of darkness is reserved forever. For when they speak great swelling words of vanity, they allure through the lusts of the flesh, through much wantonness, those that were clean escaped from them who live in error. While they promise them liberty, they themselves are the servants of corruption: for of whom a man is overcome, of the same is he brought in bondage. For if after they have escaped the pollutions of the world through the knowledge of the Lord and Saviour Jesus Christ, they are again entangled therein, and overcome, the latter end is worse with them than the beginning. For it had been better for them not to have known the way of righteousness, than, after they have known it, to turn from the holy commandment delivered unto them. But it is happened unto them according to the true proverb, "The dog is turned to his own vomit again; and the sow that was washed to her wallowing in the mire." — II Peter 2:17–22.

"THERE SHALL BE SCOFFERS IN THE LAST DAYS"

This second epistle, beloved, I now write unto you; in both which I stir up your pure minds by way of remembrance: that ye may be mindful of the words which were spoken before by the holy prophets, and of the commandment of us, the apostles of the Lord and Saviour: knowing this first, that there shall come in the last days scoffers, walking after their own lusts, and saying, "Where is the promise of his coming? For since the fathers fell asleep, all things continue as they were from the beginning of the creation." — II Peter 3:1–4.

"THEY WILLINGLY ARE IGNORANT"

For this they willingly are ignorant of, that by the word of God the heavens were of old, and the earth standing out of the water and in the water: whereby the world that then was, being overflowed with water, perished: but the heavens and the earth, which are now, by the same word are kept in store, reserved unto fire against the day of judgment and perdition of ungodly men. — II Peter 3:5–7.

"BE NOT IGNORANT THAT ONE DAY IS WITH THE LORD AS A THOUSAND YEARS"

But, beloved, be not ignorant of this one thing, that one day is with the Lord as a thousand years, and a thousand years as one day. The Lord is not slack concerning his promise, as some men count slackness; but is longsuffering to us-ward, not willing that any should perish, but that all should come to repentance. But the day of the Lord will come as a thief in the night; in the which the heavens shall pass away with a great noise, and the elements shall melt with fervent heat, the earth also and the works that are therein shall be burned up. Seeing then that all these things shall be dissolved, what manner of persons ought ye to be in all holy conversation and godliness, looking for and hasting unto the coming of the day of God, wherein the heavens being on fire shall be dissolved, and the elements shall melt with fervent heat?   – II Peter 3:8–12.

"WE LOOK FOR NEW HEAVENS AND A NEW EARTH"

Nevertheless we, according to his promise, look for new heavens and a new earth, wherein dwelleth righteousness.

Wherefore, beloved, seeing that ye look for such things, be diligent that ye may be found of him in peace, without spot, and blameless. And account that the long-suffering of our Lord is salvation; even as our beloved brother Paul also according to the wisdom given unto him hath written unto you; as also in all his epistles, speaking in them of these things; in which are some things hard to be understood, which they that are unlearned and unstable wrest, as they do also the other Scriptures, unto their own destruction.

Ye therefore, beloved, seeing ye know these things before, beware lest ye also, being led away with the error of the wicked, fall from your own steadfastness. But grow in grace, and in the knowledge of our Lord and Saviour Jesus Christ. To him be glory both now and forever. Amen.   — II Peter 3:13–18.

Letters of Leaders

Of the Early Church

The First Epistle of John

The three Epistles of John are full of that spirit of love which pervades the Gospel of John. There is a story to the effect that John when he was an old, old man used to be carried to the church on a litter, and that he would say over and over again in his feeble voice, "Little children, love one another; little children, love one another."

These Epistles were probably all written at Ephesus between A. D. 90 and 95.

THAT which was from the beginning, which we have heard, which we have seen with our eyes, which we have looked upon, and our hands have handled, of the Word of life; (for the life was manifested and we have seen it, and bear witness, and show unto you that eternal life, which was with the Father, and was manifested unto us;) that which we have seen and heard declare we unto you, that ye also may have fellowship with us: and truly our fellowship is with the Father, and with his Son Jesus Christ. And these things write we unto you, that your joy may be full. — I John 1:1-4.

"GOD IS LIGHT"

This then is the message which we have heard of him, and declare unto you, that God is light, and in him is no darkness at all. If we say that we have fellowship with him, and walk in darkness, we lie, and do not the

APOSTLE JOHN
A painting by Anthony Gruerio

truth: but if we walk in the light, as he is in the light, we have fellowship one with another, and the blood of Jesus Christ his Son cleanseth us from all sin.   —I John 1:5-7.

"IF WE CONFESS OUR SINS, HE IS FAITHFUL AND JUST TO FORGIVE US OUR SINS"

If we say that we have no sin, we deceive ourselves, and the truth is not in us. If we confess our sins, he is faithful and just to forgive us our sins, and to cleanse us from all unrighteousness. If we say that we have not sinned, we make him a liar, and his word is not in us.

My little children, these things write I unto you, that ye sin not. And if any man sin, we have an advocate with the Father, Jesus Christ the righteous: and he is the propitiation for our sins: and not for ours only, but also for the sins of the whole world. And hereby we do know that we know him, if we keep his commandments. He that saith, "I know him," and keepeth not his commandments, is a liar, and the truth is not in him. But whoso keepeth his word, in him verily is the love of God perfected: hereby know we that we are in him. He that saith he abideth in him ought himself also so to walk, even as he walked.   —I John 1:8–2:6.

AN OLD COMMANDMENT

Brethren, I write no new commandment unto you, but an old commandment which ye had from the beginning. The old commandment is the word which ye have heard from the beginning. Again, a new commandment I write unto you, which thing is true in him and in you: because the darkness is past, and the true light now shineth. He that saith he is in the light, and hateth his brother, is in darkness even until now. He that loveth his brother abideth in the light, and there is none occa-

sion of stumbling in him. But he that hateth his brother is in darkness, and walketh in darkness, and knoweth not whither he goeth, because that darkness hath blinded his eyes.
— I John 2:7-11.

"YOUR SINS ARE FORGIVEN FOR HIS NAME'S SAKE"

I write unto you, little children, because your sins are forgiven you for his name's sake. I write unto you, fathers, because ye have known him that is from the beginning. I write unto you, young men, because ye have overcome the wicked one. I write unto you, little children, because ye have known the Father. I have written unto you, fathers, because ye have known him that is from the beginning. I have written unto you, young men, because ye are strong, and the word of God abideth in you, and ye have overcome the wicked one.
— I John 2:12-14.

"LOVE NOT THE WORLD"

Love not the world, neither the things that are in the world. If any man love the world, the love of the Father is not in him. For all that is in the world, the lust of the flesh, and the lust of the eyes, and the pride of life, is not of the Father, but is of the world. And the world passeth away, and the lust thereof: but he that doeth the will of God abideth forever.

Little children, it is the last time: and as ye have heard that antichrist shall come, even now are there many antichrists; whereby we know that it is the last time. They went out from us, but they were not of us; for if they had been of us, they would no doubt have continued with us: but they went out, that they might be made manifest that they were not all of us. But ye have an unction from the Holy One, and ye know all things. I have not written unto you because ye know not the truth, but because ye know it, and that no lie is of the truth. Who is a liar but he that denieth that Jesus is the Christ? He is antichrist, that denieth the Father and the Son. Whosoever denieth the Son, the same hath not the Father: but he that acknowledgeth the Son hath the Father also. Let that therefore abide in you, which ye have heard from the beginning. If that which ye have heard from the beginning shall remain in you, ye also shall continue in the Son, and in the Father. And this is the promise that he hath promised us, even eternal life. These things have I written unto you concerning them that seduce you. But the anointing which ye have received of him abideth in you, and ye need not that any man teach you: but as the same anointing teacheth you of all things and is truth, and is no lie, and even as it hath taught you, ye shall abide in him. And now, little children, abide in him; that, when he shall appear, we may have confidence, and not be ashamed before him at his coming. If ye know that he is righteous, ye know that every one that doeth righteousness is born of him.

— I John 2:15–29.

"NOW ARE WE THE SONS OF GOD"

Behold, what manner of love the Father hath bestowed upon us, that we should be called the sons of God: therefore the world knoweth us not, because it knew him not. Beloved, now are we the sons of God, and it doth not yet appear what we shall be: but we know that, when he shall appear, we shall be like him; for we shall see him as he is. And every man that hath this hope in him purifieth himself, even as he is pure. Whosoever committeth sin transgresseth also the law: for sin is the transgression of the law. And ye know that he was manifested to take away our sins; and in him is no sin.

Whosoever abideth in him sinneth not: whosoever sinneth hath not seen him, neither known him. Little children, let no man deceive you: he that doeth righteousness is righteous, even as he is righteous. He that committeth sin is of the devil; for the devil sinneth from the beginning. For this purpose the Son of God was manifested, that he might destroy the works of the devil. Whosoever is born of God doth not commit sin; for his seed remaineth in him: and he cannot sin, because he is born of God. In this the children of God are manifest, and the children of the devil: whosoever doeth not righteousness is not of God, neither he that loveth not his brother. For this is the message that ye heard from the beginning, that we should love one another. Not as Cain, who was of that wicked one, and slew his brother. And wherefore slew he him? Because his own works were evil, and his brother's righteous.

—I John 3:1-12.

BROTHERLY LOVE

Marvel not, my brethren, if the world hate you. We know that we have passed from death unto life, because we love the brethren. He that loveth not his brother abideth in death. Whosoever hateth his brother is a murderer: and ye know that no murderer hath eternal life abiding in him. Hereby perceive we the love of God, because he laid down his life for us: and we ought to lay down our lives for the brethren. But whoso hath this world's good, and seeth his brother have need, and shutteth up his bowels of compassion from him, how dwelleth the love of God in him? My little children, let us not love in word, neither in tongue; but in deed and in truth. And hereby we know that we are of the truth, and shall assure our hearts before him. For if our heart condemn

JESUS CHRIST
A painting by Anthony Gruerio

us, God is greater than our heart, and knoweth all things. Beloved, if our heart condemn us not, then have we confidence toward God. And whatsoever we ask, we receive of him, because we keep his commandments, and do those things that are pleasing in his sight. And this is his commandment, that we should believe on the name of his Son Jesus Christ, and love one another, as he gave us commandment. And he that keepeth his commandments dwelleth in him, and he in him. And hereby we know that he abideth in us, by the Spirit which he hath given us. — I John 3:13–24.

"GOD IS LOVE"

Beloved, believe not every spirit, but try the spirits whether they are of God: because many false prophets are gone out into the world. Hereby know ye the Spirit of God: every spirit that confesseth that Jesus Christ is come in the flesh is of God: and every spirit that confesseth not that Jesus Christ is come in the flesh is not of God: and this is that spirit of antichrist, whereof ye have heard that it should come; and even now already is it in the world. Ye are of God, little children, and have overcome them: because greater is he that is in you, than he that is in the world. They are of the world: therefore speak they of the world, and the world heareth them. We are of God: he that knoweth God heareth us; he that is not of God heareth not us. Hereby know we the spirit of truth, and the spirit of error.

Beloved, let us love one another: for love is of God; and every one that loveth is born of God, and knoweth God. He that loveth not knoweth not God; for God is love. In this was manifested the love of God toward us, because that God sent his only begotten Son into the world, that we might live through him. Herein is

love, not that we loved God, but that he loved us, and
sent his Son to be the propitiation for our sins. Beloved,
if God so loved us, we ought also to love one another.
No man hath seen God at any time. If we love one
another, God dwelleth in us, and his love is perfected
in us. Hereby know we that we dwell in him, and he in
us, because he hath given us of his Spirit. And we have
seen and do testify that the Father sent the Son to be
the Saviour of the world. Whosoever shall confess that
Jesus is the Son of God, God dwelleth in him, and he in
God. And we have known and believed the love that
God hath to us. God is love; and he that dwelleth in
love dwelleth in God, and God in him. Herein is our
love made perfect, that we may have boldness in the
day of judgment: because as he is, so are we in this world.
— I John 4:1–17.

"PERFECT LOVE CASTETH OUT FEAR"

There is no fear in love; but perfect love casteth out
fear: because fear hath torment. He that feareth is not
made perfect in love. We love him, because he first
loved us. If a man say, "I love God," and hateth his
brother, he is a liar: for he that loveth not his brother
whom he hath seen, how can he love God whom he hath
not seen? And this commandment have we from him,
"That he who loveth God love his brother also."
— I John 4:18–21.

"THIS IS THE LOVE OF GOD, THAT WE KEEP HIS COMMANDMENTS: AND THESE ARE NOT GRIEVOUS"

Whosoever believeth that Jesus is the Christ is born
of God: and every one that loveth him that begat loveth
him also that is begotten of him. By this we know that
we love the children of God, when we love God, and keep
his commandments. For this is the love of God, that

we keep his commandments: and his commandments are not grievous. For whatsoever is born of God overcometh the world: and this is the victory that overcometh the world, even our faith. Who is he that overcometh the world, but he that believeth that Jesus is the Son of God? This is he that came by water and blood, even Jesus Christ; not by water only, but by water and blood. And it is the Spirit that beareth witness, because the Spirit is truth. For there are three that bear record in heaven, the Father, the Word, and the Holy Ghost: and these three are one. And there are three that bear witness in earth, the Spirit, and the water, and the blood: and these three agree in one. If we receive the witness of men, the witness of God is greater: for this is the witness of God which he hath testified of his Son. He that believeth on the Son of God hath the witness in himself: he that believeth not God hath made him a liar; because he believeth not the record that God gave of his Son. And this is the record, that God hath given to us eternal life and this life is in his Son. He that hath the Son hath life; and he that hath not the Son of God hath not life.

— I John 5:1–12.

"THAT YE MAY KNOW THAT YE HAVE ETERNAL LIFE"

These things have I written unto you that believe on the name of the Son of God; that ye may know that ye have eternal life, and that ye may believe on the name of the Son of God. And this is the confidence that we have in him, that, if we ask anything according to his will, he heareth us: and if we know that he hear us, whatsoever we ask, we know that we have the petitions that we desired of him. If any man see his brother sin a sin which is not unto death, he shall ask, and he shall give him life for them that sin not unto death. There is a sin unto death: I do not say that he shall pray for it. All unrighteousness is sin: and there is a sin not unto death.

We know that whosoever is born of God sinneth not; but he that is begotten of God keepeth himself, and that wicked one toucheth him not. And we know that we are of God, and the whole world lieth in wickedness. And we know that the Son of God is come, and hath given us an understanding, that we may know him that is true, and we are in him that is true, even in his Son Jesus Christ. This is the true God, and eternal life.

Little children, keep yourselves from idols. Amen.

— I John 5:13–21.

BETHLEHEM

Letters of Leaders

Of the Early Church

The Second Epistle of John

The elder unto the elect lady and her children, whom I love in the truth; and not I only, but also all they that have known the truth; for the truth's sake, which dwelleth in us, and shall be with us forever.

Grace be with you, mercy, and peace, from God the Father, and from the Lord Jesus Christ, the Son of the Father, in truth and love.

I REJOICED greatly that I found of thy children walking in truth, as we have received a commandment from the Father. And now I beseech thee, lady, not as though I wrote a new commandment unto thee, but that which we had from the beginning, that we love one another. And this is love, that we walk after his commandments. This is the commandment, that, as ye have heard from the beginning, ye should walk in it. For many deceivers are entered into the world, who confess not that Jesus Christ is come in the flesh. This is a deceiver and an antichrist. Look to yourselves, that we lose not those things which we have wrought, but that we receive a full reward Whosoever transgresseth, and abideth not in the doctrine of Christ, hath not God. He that abideth in the doctrine of Christ, he hath both the Father and the Son. If there come any unto you, and bring not this doctrine, receive him not into your house,

neither bid him God speed: for he that biddeth him
God speed is partaker of his evil deeds. Having many
things to write unto you, I would not write with paper
and ink: but I trust to come unto you, and speak face
to face, that our joy may be full.

The children of thy elect sister greet thee. Amen.
— II John.

SAREPTA OF SIDON

He carries his plow slung on the donkey's back, as he rides toward Barafand
on its hillside in Syria.

The ruins of Sarepta of Sidon are here, called in Old Testament times
Zarephath. Here at the command of the Lord came Elijah the Tishbite, while a
famine raged in the land, for neither dew nor rain had fallen for a long time.

Letters of Leaders

Of the Early Church

The Third Epistle of John

The elder unto the wellbeloved Gaius, whom I love in the truth.

BELOVED, I wish above all things that thou mayest prosper and be in health, even as thy soul prospereth. For I rejoiced greatly, when the brethren came and testified of the truth that is in thee, even as thou walkest in the truth. I have no greater joy than to hear that my children walk in truth. Beloved, thou doest faithfully whatsoever thou doest to the brethren, and to strangers; which have borne witness of thy charity before the church: whom if thou bring forward on their journey after a godly sort, thou shalt do well: because that for his name's sake they went forth, taking nothing of the Gentiles. We therefore ought to receive such, that we might be fellow-helpers to the truth.

I wrote unto the church: but Diotrephes, who loveth to have the pre-eminence among them, receiveth us not. Wherefore, if I come, I will remember his deeds which he doeth, prating against us with malicious words: and not content therewith, neither doth he himself receive the brethren, and forbiddeth them that would, and casteth them out of the church. Beloved, follow not that which is evil, but that which is good. He that doeth good is of God: but he that doeth evil hath not seen God. Demetrius hath good report of all men, and of the truth itself: yea, and we also bear record; and ye know that our record is true.

I had many things to write, but I will not with ink and pen write unto thee: but I trust I shall shortly see thee, and we shall speak face to face.

Peace be to thee. Our friends salute thee. Greet the friends by name.
— III John.

BURDEN BEARERS

In Palestine we see burden bearers carrying enormous packs on the back, even large pieces of furniture and unbelievably heavy goods.

These remind us of the Saviour's comforting words, "Come unto me all ye that labor and are heavy laden, and I will give you rest. Take my yoke upon you, and learn of me; for I am gentle and lowly in heart, and ye shall find rest unto your souls. For my yoke is easy, and my burden is light."

Read Matthew 11:28-30, Volume 7:118.

Letters of Leaders

Of the Early Church

The Epistle of Jude

This little letter about which almost nothing is known is "dedicated to them that are called" by "Judas, a servant of Jesus Christ and brother of James." An interesting incident is connected with the quotation from the "Book of Enoch" by the writer. This book was supposed to have been lost beyond any hope of recovery, but in 1773, an English traveler, Bruce, found three copies of the manuscript in Abyssinia. Scholars are always hoping that in some out-of-the-way place manuscripts will be discovered, like those of the recent Isaiah Scrolls (Volume 5:145), which will bring us much nearer the actual date of the writing of the books of the New Testament.

Jude, the servant of Jesus Christ, and brother of James, to them that are sanctified by God the Father, and preserved in Jesus Christ, and called:
Mercy unto you, and peace, and love, be multiplied.

BELOVED, when I gave all diligence to write unto you of the common salvation, it was needful for me to write unto you, and exhort you that ye should earnestly conte d for the faith which was once delivered unto the saints. For there are certain men crept in unawares, who were before of old ordained to this condemnation, ungodly men, turning the grace of our God into lasciviousness, and denying the only LORD God, and our Lord Jesus Christ.

I will therefore put you in remembrance, though ye once knew this, how that the LORD, having saved the people out of the land of Egypt, afterward destroyed them that believed not. And the angels which kept not their first estate, but left their own habitation, he hath reserved in everlasting chains under darkness unto the judgment of the great day. Even as Sodom and Gomorrha, and the cities about them in like manner, giving themselves over to fornication, and going after strange flesh, are set forth for an example, suffering the vengeance of eternal fire. Likewise also these filthy dreamers defile the flesh, despise dominion, and speak evil of dignities. Yet Michael, the archangel, when contending with the devil he disputed about the body of Moses, durst not bring against him a railing accusation, but said, "The LORD rebuke thee." But these speak evil of those things which they know not: but what they know naturally, as brute beasts, in those things they corrupt themselves. Woe unto them! For they have gone in the way of Cain, and ran greedily after the error of Balaam for reward, and perished in the gainsaying of Core. These are spots in your feasts of charity, when they feast with you, feeding themselves without fear: clouds they are without water, carried about of winds; trees whose fruit withereth, without fruit, twice dead, plucked up by the roots; raging waves of the sea, foaming out their own shame; wandering stars, to whom is reserved the blackness of darkness forever. And Enoch also, the seventh from Adam, prophesied of these, saying, "Behold, the Lord cometh with ten thousands of his saints, to execute judgment upon all, and to convince all that are ungodly among them of all their ungodly deeds which they have ungodly committed, and of all their hard speeches which ungodly sinners have spoken against him." These are murmurers, complainers, walking after their own lusts; and their mouth speaketh great swelling words, having men's persons in admiration because of advantage.

But, beloved, remember ye the words which were spoken before of the apostles of our Lord Jesus Christ; how that they told you there should be mockers in the last time, who should walk after their own ungodly lusts. These be they who separate themselves, sensual, having not the Spirit. But ye, beloved, building up yourselves on your most holy faith, praying in the Holy Ghost, keep yourselves in the love of God, looking for the mercy of our Lord Jesus Christ unto eternal life. And of some have compassion, making a difference: and others save with fear, pulling them out of the fire; hating even the garment spotted by the flesh.

Now unto him that is able to keep you from falling, and to present you faultless before the presence of his glory with exceeding joy, to the only wise God our Saviour, be glory and majesty, dominion and power, both now and ever. Amen.   — Jude.

THE JORDAN RIVER

This is taken from the bridge over the Jordan near Jericho. The low hills in the background are the banks of the broader Jordan valley.

TEMPLE OF JUNO

The Revelation of Saint John the Divine

THIS great book, which is also known as The Apocalypse from its Greek title, is believed to have been written at the end of the first Christian century, after the severe persecutions of the church had begun. It is a strange, splendid book, glowing with color, full of moving symbols, difficult now to understand or to interpret. In these vivid pages depicted by the hand of a prophet, we find "The Wild Beast from the Sea;" "The Wild Beast from the Land;" "The Red Dragon;" "The Seven Seals;" "The Son of Man on the Cloud;" "The Seven Trumpets;" "The Seven Vials;" "The Four Horsemen;" "Abaddon and Apollyon;" "Michael and his Angels;" "The Woman with the Wings of an Eagle;" "The Devil Chained for a Thousand Years."

Saint John foretold the breaking up of a great empire, the coming of wars and tumults. Persecution would arise; the members of the Christian church must face death in a hundred forms; but that great empire, those imperial beasts who occupied the throne, their doom was also sealed; the angels of wrath and destruction were on the wing; the great "Babylon," which was op-

pressing the world would go down into the
dust; but the church would live on a "thousand years the same."

The prediction was given; the cup of iniquity was full; it would soon overflow.

Why was Revelation written in this way?
Why did not John use plain language? Why
did he use symbols? There were perhaps
many reasons and one of these we may know
with certainty was that it would not have
been safe to use plain language about the
downfall of the Roman Empire, its sins and
its unspeakable corruption. The people of
the church to whom the letter was addressed
would know perfectly what was meant. For
another reason we all know that vivid symbols, dramatizing ideas and thoughts, help
to insure that they will be remembered and
more certainly acted upon. Finally John
gives his reason as follows: "I was in the
Spirit on the Lord's Day, and heard behind
me a great voice as of a trumpet saying,
'I am Alpha and Omega, the first and the
last': and, 'What thou seest, write in a book,
and send it unto the seven Churches which
are in Asia.' "

One of the greatest classics of the English
language is John Bunyan's Pilgrim's Progress.
Bunyan peoples his pages with symbolic
figures: "Christian"; "The Giant Despair";
"The Interpreter"; "Great Heart". The
Bible we know was Bunyan's inspiration.

Revelation in the New Testament and

Daniel in the Old Testament belong to that portion of sacred literature in which the thoughts and messages are expressed by use of symbols and visions. Especially in times of stress and trouble they bring comfort, and furnish hope in days of discouragement. The enemies of God are strong, but God is stronger and in His own time He will triumph. We read with wonder, admiration and awe; we are uplifted and exalted.

The symbols of The Apocalypse are by no means all that the book of Revelation contains. It opens with a series of warning and prophetic messages to the Seven Churches of Asia, and it closes with the sweetest, the most serene pictures of the future life which have ever been written. These, too, glow with color, not now the angry light of battle, the lurid flames from the pit; they are bright, instead, with the radiance of the celestial day, streets of gold, gates of pearl and walls of jasper. And it is full of immortal tenderness—"God shall wipe away all tears."

"A NEW HEAVEN AND A NEW EARTH"

"And I saw a new heaven and a new earth: for the first heaven and the first earth were passed away; and there was no more sea. And I, John, saw the holy city, new Jerusalem, coming down from God out of heaven, prepared as a bride adorned for her husband. And I heard a great voice out of heaven saying, 'Behold, the tabernacle of God is with

JOHN ON THE ISLE OF PATMOS
A molding by D. Mastroianni

men, and he will dwell with them, and they shall be his people, and God himself shall be with them, and be their God. And God shall wipe away all tears from their eyes; and there shall be no more death, neither sorrow, nor crying, neither shall there be any more pain: for the former things are passed away.'

"And he that sat upon the throne said, 'Behold, I make all things new.' And he said unto me, 'Write: for these words are true and faithful.' And he said unto me, 'It is done. I am Alpha and Omega, the beginning and the end. I will give unto him that is athirst of the fountain of the water of life freely. He that overcometh shall inherit all things; and I will be his God, and he shall be my son.' "

Even though the mystical and mysterious visions of this Book may be difficult to understand, and interpretations may be varied and diverse, The Revelation of Saint John the Divine is a prophetic message to the whole church. The humblest reader, if devout and spiritually minded, will find herein comfort, encouragement, renewed faith, hope and strength. "Blessed is he that readeth."

The Revelation of Saint John the Divine

The Revelation of Jesus Christ, which God gave unto him, to show unto his servants things which must shortly come to pass; and he sent and signified it by his angel unto his servant John: who bare record of the word of God, and of the testimony of Jesus Christ, and of all things that he saw. Blessed is he that readeth, and they that hear the words of this prophecy, and keep those things which are written therein: for the time is at hand.

John to the seven churches which are in Asia: Grace be unto you, and peace, from him which is, and which was, and which is to come; and from the seven Spirits which are before his throne; and from Jesus Christ, who is the faithful witness, and the first begotten of the dead, and the prince of the kings of the earth. Unto him that loved us, and washed us from our sins in his own blood, and hath made us kings and priests unto God and his Father; to him be glory and dominion forever and ever. Amen.

BEHOLD, he cometh with clouds; and every eye shall see him, and they also which pierced him: and all kindreds of the earth shall wail because of him. Even so. Amen.

I am Alpha and Omega, the beginning and the ending, saith the Lord, which is, and which was, and which is to come, the Almighty. — Revelation 1:1-8.

"I, JOHN, WAS IN THE SPIRIT ON THE LORD'S DAY, AND I HEARD A GREAT VOICE"

I, John, who also am your brother, and companion in tribulation, and in the kingdom and patience of Jesus Christ, was in the isle that is called Patmos, for the word of God, and for the testimony of Jesus Christ. I was in the Spirit on the Lord's day, and heard behind me a great voice, as of a trumpet, saying, "I am Alpha and Omega, the first and the last": and, "What thou seest, write in a book, and send it unto the seven churches which are in Asia; unto Ephesus, and unto Smyrna, and unto Pergamos, and unto Thyatira, and unto Sardis, and unto Philadelphia, and unto Laodicea."

And I turned to see the voice that spake with me. And being turned, I saw seven golden candlesticks; and in the midst of the seven candlesticks one like unto the Son of man, clothed with a garment down to the foot, and girt about the paps with a golden girdle. His head and his hairs were white like wool, as white as snow; and his eyes were as a flame of fire; and his feet like unto fine brass, as if they burned in a furnace; and his voice as the sound of many waters. And he had in his right hand seven stars: and out of his mouth went a sharp two-edged sword: and his countenance was as the sun shineth in his strength. And when I saw him, I fell at his feet as dead. And he laid his right hand upon me, saying unto me, "Fear not; I am the first and the last: I am he that liveth, and was dead; and, behold, I am alive for evermore, Amen; and have the keys of hell and of death. Write the things which thou hast seen, and the things which are, and the things which shall be hereafter; the mystery of the seven stars which thou sawest in my right hand, and the seven golden candlesticks. The seven stars are the angels of the seven

THE BURNING OF SMYRNA BY THE TURKS
AFTER THE MASSACRE OF CHRISTIANS

A UNIQUE photograph, taken aboard H. M. S. "Iron Duke," showing the gigantic fire which virtually wiped out Smyrna; the fire was said to have been started by Kemal's Turkish soldiers to conceal the horrors of the massacre and looting which followed the taking of the city.

From the sea the spectacle presented an unbroken line of fire two miles in length, in which twenty distinct volcanoes of raging flames threw up ragged, writhing tongues and thick coils of oily black smoke, to the accompaniment of violent explosions and the frantic screams of terror stricken refugees huddled on the narrow quays. Smyrna is one of the oldest Christian cities in the world and it has many times suffered destruction. "Unto the angel of the church in Smyrna write: 'Be thou faithful unto death and I will give thee a crown of life.'" —*Revelation 8a, 10b.* Many times in the past and now in this late age nearly twenty centuries since these words were written, the church of Smyrna has been "faithful unto death."

churches: and the seven candlesticks which thou sawest
are the seven churches.   — Revelation 1: 9–20.

TO THE CHURCH AT EPHESUS

"Unto the angel of the church of Ephesus write:
'These things saith he that holdeth the seven stars in
his right hand, who walketh in the midst of the seven
golden candlesticks; "I know thy works, and thy labour,
and thy patience, and how thou canst not bear them which
are evil: and thou hast tried them which say they are
apostles, and are not, and has found them liars: and
hast borne, and hast patience, and for my name's sake
hast laboured, and hast not fainted. Nevertheless I
have somewhat against thee, because thou hast left thy
first love. Remember therefore from whence thou art
fallen, and repent, and do the first works; or else I will
come unto thee quickly, and will remove thy candlestick out of his place, except thou repent. But this
thou hast, that thou hatest the deeds of the Nicolaitanes,
which I also hate. He that hath an ear, let him hear
what the Spirit saith unto the churches: 'To him that
overcometh will I give to eat of the tree of life, which is
in the midst of the paradise of God.'"

— Revelation 2:1–7.

TO THE CHURCH AT SMYRNA

"And unto the angel of the church in Smyrna write:
'These things saith the first and the last, which was
dead, and is alive; "I know thy works, and tribulation,
and poverty, (but thou art rich) and I know the blasphemy of them which say they are Jews, and are not,
but are the synagogue of Satan. Fear none of those
things which thou shalt suffer: behold, the devil shall
cast some of you into prison, that ye may be tried;

and ye shall have tribulation ten days: be thou faithful unto death, and I will give thee a crown of life. He that hath an ear, let him hear what the Spirit saith unto the churches: 'He that overcometh shall not be hurt of the second death.''''
— Revelation 2:8-11.

TO THE CHURCH AT PERGAMOS

"And to the angel of the church in Pergamos write: 'These things saith he which hath the sharp sword with two edges; "I know thy works, and where thou dwellest, even where Satan's seat is: and thou holdest fast my name, and hast not denied my faith, even in those days wherein Antipas was my faithful martyr, who was slain among you, where Satan dwelleth. But I have a few things against thee, because thou hast there them that hold the doctrine of Balaam, who taught Balac to cast a stumblingblock before the children of Israel, to eat things sacrificed unto idols, and to commit fornication. So hast thou also them that hold the doctrine of the Nicolaitanes, which thing I hate. Repent; or else I will come unto thee quickly, and will fight against them with the sword of my mouth. He that hath an ear, let him hear what the Spirit saith unto the churches: 'To him that overcometh will I give to eat of the hidden manna, and will give him a white stone, and in the stone a new name written, which no man knoweth saving he that receiveth it.''''
— Revelation 2:12-17.

TO THE CHURCH AT THYATIRA

"And unto the angel of the church in Thyatira write: These things saith the Son of God, who hath his eyes like unto a flame of fire, and his feet are like fine brass: "I know thy works, and charity, and service, and faith, and thy patience, and thy works; and the last to be more

PHILADELPHIA

than . the first. Notwithstanding I have a few things against thee, because thou sufferest that woman Jezebel, which calleth herself a prophetess, to teach and to seduce my servants to commit fornication, and to eat things sacrificed unto idols. And I gave her space to repent of her fornication; and she repented not. Behold, I will cast her into a bed, and them that commit adultery with her into great tribulation, except they repent of their deeds. And I will kill her children with death; and all the churches shall know that I am he which searcheth the reins and hearts: and I will give unto every one of you according to your works. But unto you I say, and unto the rest in Thyatira, as many as have not this doctrine, and which have not known the depths of Satan, as they speak; I will put upon you none other burden. But that which ye have already hold fast till I come. And he that overcometh, and keepeth my works unto the end, to him will I give power over the nations: and he shall rule them with a rod of iron; as the vessels of a potter shall they be broken to shivers: even as I received of my Father. And I will give him the morning star. He that hath an ear, let him hear what the Spirit saith unto the churches.'' '   — Revelation 2:18–29.

TO THE CHURCH AT SARDIS

"And unto the angel of the church in Sardis write: 'These things saith he that hath the seven Spirits of God, and the seven stars: "I know thy works, that thou hast a name that thou livest, and art dead. Be watchful, and strengthen the things which remain, that are ready to die: for I have not found thy works perfect before God. Remember therefore how thou hast received and heard, and hold fast, and repent. If therefore thou shalt not watch, I will come on thee as a thief, and thou shalt

not know what hour I will come upon thee. Thou hast
a few names even in Sardis which have not defiled their
garments; and they shall walk with me in white: for
they are worthy. He that overcometh, the same shall
be clothed in white raiment; and I will not blot out his
name out of the book of life, but I will confess his name
before my Father, and before his angels. He that hath
an ear, let him hear what the Spirit saith unto the
churches.'''   — Revelation 3:1–6.

TO THE CHURCH AT PHILADELPHIA

"And to the angel of the church in Philadelphia
write: 'These things saith he that is holy, he that is
true, he that hath the key of David, he that openeth,
and no man shutteth; and shutteth, and no man openeth: "I know thy works: behold, I have set before thee
an open door, and no man can shut it: for thou hast a
little strength, and hast kept my word, and hast not
denied my name. Behold, I will make them of the synagogue of Satan, which say they are Jews, and are not,
but do lie; behold, I will make them to come and worship before thy feet, and to know that I have loved
thee. Because thou hast kept the word of my patience, I
also will keep thee from the hour of temptation, which
shall come upon all the world, to try them that dwell upon
the earth. Behold, I come quickly: hold that fast which
thou hast, that no man take thy crown. Him that overcometh will I make a pillar in the temple of my God,
and he shall go no more out: and I will write upon him
the name of my God, and the name of the city of my God,
which is new Jerusalem, which cometh down out of
heaven from my God: and I will write upon him my new
name. He that hath an ear, let him hear what the Spirit
saith unto the churches.'''   — Revelation 3:7–13.

TO THE CHURCH AT LAODICEA

"And unto the angel of the church of the Laodiceans write: 'These things saith the Amen, the faithful and true witness, the beginning of the creation of God: "I know thy works, that thou art neither cold nor hot: I would thou wert cold or hot. So then because thou are lukewarm, and neither cold nor hot, I will spue thee out of my mouth. Because thou sayest, 'I am rich, and increased with goods, and have need of nothing'; and knowest not that thou art wretched, and miserable, and poor, and blind, and naked: I counsel thee to buy of me gold tried in the fire, that thou mayest be rich; and white raiment, that thou mayest be clothed, and that the shame of thy nakedness do not appear; and anoint thine eyes with eyesalve, that thou mayest see. As many as I love, I rebuke and chasten: be zealous therefore, and repent. Behold, I stand at the door, and knock: if any man hear my voice, and open the door, I will come in to him, and will sup with him, and he with me. To him that overcometh will I grant to sit with me in my throne, even as I also overcame, and am set down with my Father in his throne. He that hath an ear, let him hear what the Spirit saith unto the churches.""'"

— Revelation 3:14–22.

THE DOOR WHICH OPENED AND REVEALED
THE THRONE IN HEAVEN

After this I looked, and, behold, a door was opened in heaven: and the first voice which I heard was as it were of a trumpet talking with me; which said, "Come up hither, and I will show thee things which must be hereafter."

And immediately I was in the spirit: and, behold, a throne was set in heaven, and one sat on the throne.

And he that sat was to look upon like a jasper and a sardine stone: and there was a rainbow round about the throne, in sight like unto an emerald. And round about the throne were four and twenty seats: and upon the seats I saw four and twenty elders sitting, clothed in white raiment; and they had on their heads crowns of gold. And out of the throne proceeded lightnings and thunderings and voices: and there were seven lamps of fire burning before the throne, which are the seven Spirits of God. And before the throne there was a sea of glass like unto crystal: and in the midst of the throne, and round about the throne, were four beasts full of eyes before and behind. And the first beast was like a lion, and the second beast like a calf, and the third beast had a face as a man, and the fourth beast was like a flying eagle. And the four beasts had each of them six wings about him; and they were full of eyes within: and they rest not day and night, saying, "Holy, holy, holy, Lord God Almighty, which was, and is, and is to come." And when those beasts give glory and honour and thanks to him that sat on the throne, who liveth forever and ever, the four and twenty elders fall down before him that sat on the throne, and worship him that liveth forever and ever, and cast their crowns before the throne, saying, "Thou art worthy, O Lord, to receive glory and honour and power: for thou hast created all things, and for thy pleasure they are and were created."

— Revelation 4:1–11.

THE BOOK WITH THE SEVEN SEALS

And I saw in the right hand of him that sat on the throne a book written within and on the backside, sealed with seven seals. And I saw a strong angel proclaiming with a loud voice, "Who is worthy to open the book, and to loose the seals thereof?" And no man in heaven, nor in earth, neither under the earth, was able to open the book, neither to look thereon. And I wept much, because no man was found worthy to open and to read the book, neither to look thereon.

— Revelation 5:1–4.

THE LION OF THE TRIBE OF JUDAH WILL LOOSE THE SEVEN SEALS

And one of the elders saith unto me, "Weep not: behold, the Lion of the tribe of Juda, the Root of David, hath prevailed to open the book, and to loose the seven seals thereof." And I beheld, and, lo, in the midst of the throne and of the four beasts, and in the midst of the elders, stood a Lamb as it had been slain, having seven horns and seven eyes, which are the seven Spirits of God sent forth into all the earth. And he came and took the book out of the right hand of him that sat upon the throne. And when he had taken the book, the four beasts and four and twenty elders fell down before the Lamb, having every one of them harps, and golden vials full of odours, which are the prayers of saints. And they sang a new song, saying, "Thou art worthy to take the book, and to open the seals thereof: for thou wast slain, and hast redeemed us to God by thy blood out of every kindred, and tongue, and people, and nation; and hast made us unto our God kings and priests: and we shall reign on the earth." And I beheld, and I heard the voice of many angels round about the throne and the beasts and the elders: and the number of them was ten thousand times ten thousand, and thousands of thousands; saying with a loud voice, "Worthy is the Lamb that was slain to receive power, and riches, and wisdom, and strength, and honour, and glory, and blessing." And every creature which is in heaven, and on the earth, and under the earth, and such as are in the sea, and all that are in them, heard I saying, "Blessing, and honour, and glory, and power, be unto him that sitteth upon the throne, and unto the Lamb forever and ever." And the four beasts said, "Amen." And the four and twenty elders fell down and worshiped him that liveth forever and ever.

— Revelation 5:5–14.

THE WHITE HORSE AND THE CONQUEROR

And I saw when the Lamb opened one of the seals, and I heard, as it were the noise of thunder, one of the four beasts saying, "Come and see." And I saw, and behold a white horse: and he that sat on him had a bow; and a crown was given unto him: and he went forth conquering, and to conquer. And when he had opened the second seal, I heard the second beast say, "Come and see."

— Revelation 6:1–3.

THE RIDER OF THE RED HORSE WITH THE GREAT SWORD

And there went out another horse that was red: and power was given to him that sat thereon to take peace from the earth, and that they should kill one another: and there was given unto him a great sword.

— Revelation 6:4.

THE RIDER OF THE BLACK HORSE

And when he had opened the third seal, I heard the third beast say, "Come and see." And I beheld, and, lo, a black horse; and he that sat on him had a pair of balances in his hand. And I heard a voice in the midst of the four beasts say, "A measure of wheat for a penny, and three measures of barley for a penny; and see thou hurt not the oil and the wine." And when he had

THE FOUR HORSEMEN OF THE APOCALYPSE
A molding by D. Mastroianni

opened the fourth seal, I heard the voice of the fourth
beast say, "Come and see."   — Revelation 6:5–7.

THE PALE HORSE AND HIS RIDER, DEATH

And I looked, and behold a pale horse: and his
name that sat on him was Death, and Hell followed
with him. And power was given unto them over the fourth
part of the earth, to kill with sword, and with hunger,
and with death, and with the beasts of the earth.

— Revelation 6:8.

THOSE WHO WERE SLAIN FOR THE WORD OF GOD

And when he had opened the fifth seal, I saw under
the altar the souls of them that were slain for the word
of God, and for the testimony which they held: and
they cried with a loud voice, saying, "How long, O
Lord, holy and true, dost thou not judge and avenge
our blood on them that dwell on the earth?" And white
robes were given unto every one of them; and it was said
unto them, that they should rest yet for a little season,
until their fellowservants also and their brethren, that
should be killed as they were, should be fulfilled. And
I beheld when he had opened the sixth seal, and, lo,
there was a great earthquake; and the sun became black
as sackcloth of hair, and the moon became as blood;
and the stars of heaven fell unto the earth, even as a fig-
tree casteth her untimely figs, when she is shaken of a
mighty wind.   — Revelation 6:9–13.

THE HEAVENS ARE ROLLED AS A SCROLL

And the heaven departed as a scroll when it is rolled
together; and every mountain and island were moved
out of their places. And the kings of the earth, and the
great men, and the rich men, and the chief captains.

and the mighty men, and every bondman, and every free man, hid themselves in the dens and in the rocks of the mountains; and said to the mountains and rocks, "Fall on us, and hide us from the face of him that sitteth on the throne, and from the wrath of the Lamb: for the great day of his wrath is come; and who shall be able to stand?" — Revelation 6:14–17.

THE FOUR ANGELS AT THE FOUR CORNERS
OF THE EARTH

And after these things I saw four angels standing on the four corners of the earth, holding the four winds of the earth, that the wind should not blow on the earth, nor on the sea, nor on any tree. And I saw another angel ascending from the east, having the seal of the living God: and he cried with a loud voice to the four angels, to whom it was given to hurt the earth and the sea, saying, "Hurt not the earth, neither the sea, nor the trees, till we have sealed the servants of our God in their foreheads." And I heard the number of them which were sealed: and there were sealed an hundred and forty and four thousand of all the tribes of the children of Israel.

Of the tribe of Judah were sealed twelve thousand.
Of the tribe of Reuben were sealed twelve thousand.
Of the tribe of Gad were sealed twelve thousand.
Of the tribe of Aser were sealed twelve thousand.
Of the tribe of Nepthalim were sealed twelve thousand.
Of the tribe of Manasses were sealed twelve thousand.
Of the tribe of Simeon were sealed twelve thousand.
Of the tribe of Levi were sealed twelve thousand.
Of the tribe of Issachar were sealed twelve thousand.
Of the tribe of Zabulon were sealed twelve thousand.

Of the tribe of Joseph were sealed twelve thousand.
Of the tribe of Benjamin were sealed twelve thousand.

After this I beheld, and, lo, a great multitude, which
no man could number, of all nations, and kindreds, and
people, and tongues, stood before the throne, and before
the Lamb, clothed with white robes, and palms in their
hands; and cried with a loud voice, saying, "Salvation
to our God which sitteth upon the throne, and unto the
Lamb." And all the angels stood round about the throne,
and about the elders and the four beasts, and fell before
the throne on their faces, and worshiped God, saying,
"Amen: Blessing, and glory, and wisdom, and thanksgiving, and honour, and power, and might, be unto our
God forever and ever. Amen."

And one of the elders answered, saying unto me,
"What are these which are arrayed in white robes? And
whence came they?"

And I said unto him, "Sir, thou knowest."

— Revelation 7:1–14a.

"THESE ARE THEY WHICH CAME OUT OF GREAT TRIBULATION"

And he said to me, "These are they which came out
of great tribulation, and have washed their robes, and
made them white in the blood of the Lamb. Therefore
are they before the throne of God, and serve him day
and night in his temple: and he that sitteth on the throne
shall dwell among them. They shall hunger no more,
neither thirst any more; neither shall the sun light on
them, nor any heat. For the Lamb which is in the midst
of the throne shall feed them, and shall lead them unto
living fountains of waters: and God shall wipe away
all tears from their eyes." — Revelation 7:14b–17.

THE SEVEN ANGELS WHO STAND BEFORE GOD

And when he had opened the seventh seal, there was silence in heaven about the space of half an hour. And I saw the seven angels which stood before God; and to them were given seven trumpets.

And another angel came and stood at the altar, having a golden censer; and there was given unto him much incense, that he should offer it with the prayers of all saints upon the golden altar which was before the throne. And the smoke of the incense, which came with the prayers of the saints, ascended up before God out of the angel's hand. And the angel took the censer, and filled it with fire of the altar, and cast it into the earth: and there were voices, and thunderings, and lightnings, and an earthquake.

And the seven angels which had the seven trumpets prepared themselves to sound. — Revelation 8:1–6.

THE SOUNDING OF THE FIRST TRUMPET. HAIL
AND FIRE MINGLED WITH BLOOD

The first angel sounded, and there followed hail and fire mingled with blood, and they were cast upon the earth: and the third part of trees was burnt up, and all green grass was burnt up. — Revelation 8:7.

THE SOUNDING OF THE SECOND TRUMPET. THE
BURNING MOUNTAIN CAST INTO THE SEA

And the second angel sounded, and as it were a great mountain burning with fire was cast into the sea: and the third part of the sea became blood; and the third part of the creatures which were in the sea, and had life, died: and the third part of the ships were destroyed.

— Revelation 8:8, 9.

A BRANCH OF THE EUPHRATES

THE SOUNDING OF THE THIRD TRUMPET. A GREAT STAR FALLS FROM HEAVEN

And the third angel sounded, and there fell a great star from heaven, burning as it were a lamp, and it fell upon the third part of the rivers, and upon the fountains of waters; and the name of the star is called Wormwood: and the third part of the waters became wormwood; and many men died of the waters, because they were made bitter. —Revelation 8:10, 11

THE SOUNDING OF THE FOURTH TRUMPET. THE SUN, THE MOON, AND THE STARS ARE SMITTEN

And the fourth angel sounded, and the third part of the sun was smitten, and the third part of the moon, and the third part of the stars; so as the third part of them was darkened and the day shone not for a third part of it, and the night likewise. And I beheld, and heard an angel flying through the midst of heaven, saying with a loud voice, "Woe, woe, woe, to the inhabiters of the earth by reason of the other voices of the trumpet of the three angels, which are yet to sound!" —Revelation 8:12, 13.

THE SOUNDING OF THE FIFTH TRUMPET. THE OPENING OF THE BOTTOMLESS PIT

And the fifth angel sounded, and I saw a star fall from heaven unto the earth: and to him was given the key of the bottomless pit. And he opened the bottomless pit; and there arose a smoke out of the pit, as the smoke of a great furnace; and the sun and the air were darkened by reason of the smoke of the pit. And there came out of the smoke locusts upon the earth: and unto them was given power, as the scorpions of the earth have power. And it was commanded them that they should not hurt the grass of the earth, neither any green thing, neither any tree; but only those men which have not the seal of God in their foreheads. And to them it was given that they should not kill them, but that they should be tormented five months: and their torment was as the torment of a scorpion, when he striketh a man. And in those days shall men seek death, and shall not find it; and shall desire to die, and death shall flee from them. And the shapes of the locusts were like unto horses prepared unto battle; and on their heads were as it were crowns like gold, and their faces were as the faces of men. And they had hair as the hair of women, and their teeth were as the teeth of lions. And they had breastplates, as it were breastplates of iron; and the sound of their wings was as the sound of chariots of many horses running to battle. And they had tails like unto scorpions, and there were stings in their tails: and their power was to hurt men five months. And they had a king over them, which is the angel of the bottomless pit, whose name in the Hebrew tongue is Abaddon, but in the Greek tongue hath his name Apollyon.

One woe is past; and, behold, there come two woes more hereafter.   — Revelation 9:1–12.

THE SOUNDING OF THE SIXTH TRUMPET. THE ARMY OF THE EUPHRATES IS LOOSED

And the sixth angel sounded, and I heard a voice from the four horns of the golden altar which is before God, saying to the sixth angel which had the trumpet, "Loose the four angels which are bound in the great river Euphrates." And the four angels were loosed, which were prepared for an hour, and a day, and a month, and a year, for to slay the third part of men. And the number of the army of the horsemen were two hundred thousand thousand: and I heard the number of them. And thus I saw the horses in the vision, and them that sat on them, having breastplates of fire, and of jacinth, and brimstone: and the heads of the horses were as the heads of lions; and out of their mouths issued fire and smoke and brimstone. By these three was the third part of men killed, by the fire, and by the smoke, and by the brimstone, which issued out of their mouths. For their power is in their mouth, and in their tails: for their tails were like unto serpents, and had heads, and with them they do hurt. And the rest of the men which were not killed by these plagues yet repented not of the works of their hands, that they should not worship devils, and idols of gold, and silver, and brass, and stone, and of wood: which neither can see, nor hear, nor walk: neither repented they of their murders, nor of their sorceries, nor of their fornication, nor of their thefts.

And I saw another mighty angel come down from heaven, clothed with a cloud: and a rainbow was upon his head, and his face was as it were the sun, and his feet as pillars of fire: and he had in his hand a little book open: and he set his right foot upon the sea, and his left foot on the earth, and cried with a loud voice, as when a lion roareth: and when he had cried, seven thunders uttered their voices. And when the seven thunders had uttered their voices, I was about to write: and I heard a voice from heaven saying unto me, "Seal up those things which the seven thunders uttered, and write them not." — Revelation 9:13–10:4.

THE MYSTERY OF GOD SHALL BE FINISHED WITH THE SOUNDING OF THE SEVENTH TRUMPET

And the angel which I saw stand upon the sea and upon the earth lifted up his hand to heaven, and sware by him that liveth forever and ever, who created heaven, and the things that therein are, and the earth, and the things that therein are, and the sea, and the things which are therein, that there should be time no longer: but in the days of the voice of the seventh angel, when he shall begin to sound, the mystery of God should be finished, as he hath declared to his servants, the prophets. And the voice which I heard from heaven spake unto me again, and said, "Go and take the little book which is open in the hand of the angel which standeth upon the sea and upon the earth." — Revelation 10:5–8.

THE LITTLE BOOK THAT WAS SWEET AS HONEY
TO THE TASTE

And I went unto the angel, and said unto him, "Give me the little book."

And he said unto me, "Take it, and eat it up; and it shall make thy belly bitter, but it shall be in thy mouth sweet as honey."

And I took the little book out of the angel's hand, and ate it up; and it was in my mouth sweet as honey: and as soon as I had eaten it, my belly was bitter. And he said unto me, "Thou must prophesy again before many peoples, and nations, and tongues, and kings."

THE SECOND WOE IS PAST AND THE THIRD
COMETH QUICKLY

And there was given me a reed like unto a rod: and one said, "Rise, and measure the temple of God, and the altar, and them that worship therein. And the court which is without the temple leave without, and measure it not; for it hath been given unto the nations: and the holy city shall they tread under foot forty and two months. And I will give power unto my two witnesses, and they shall prophesy a thousand two hundred and threescore days, clothed in sackcloth. These are the two olive-trees and the two candlesticks, standing before the Lord of the earth. And if any man desireth to hurt them, fire proceedeth out of their mouth, and devoureth their enemies: and if any man shall desire to hurt them, in this manner must he be killed. These have the power to shut the heaven, that it rain not during the days of their prophecy: and they have power over the waters to turn them into blood, and to smite the earth with every plague, as often as they shall desire. And when they shall have finished their testimony, the beast that cometh up out of the abyss shall make war with them, and overcome them, and kill them. And their dead bodies lie in the street of the great city, which spiritually is called Sodom and Egypt, where also their Lord was crucified. And from among the peoples and tribes and tongues and nations do men look upon their dead bodies three days and a half, and suffer not their dead bodies to be laid in a tomb. And they that dwell on the earth rejoice over them, and make merry; and they shall send gifts one to another; because these two prophets tormented them that dwell on the earth. And after the three days and a half the breath of life from God entered into them, and they stood upon their feet; and great fear fell upon them which beheld them. And they heard a great voice from heaven saying unto them, 'Come up hither.' And they went up into heaven in a cloud; and their enemies beheld them. And the same hour was there a great earthquake, and the tenth part of the city fell, and in the earthquake were slain of men seven thousand: and the remnant were affrighted, and gave glory to the God of heaven.''

The second woe is past; and behold, the third woe cometh quickly.   — Revelation 10:9-11:14.

The Archangel Michael

By Fra Angelico da Fiesole (1387-1455)
In the Museum of the Monastery of San Marco, Florence
Photograph by Alinari Brothers, Florence, Italy

THIS figure is a detail from the frame of the large picture, THE DESCENT FROM THE CROSS also in Florence. It shows Fra Angelico's skillful rendering of form and feeling.

Fra Angelico was a famous artist monk of the Dominican order who lived in the early Renaissance. He was born in Vicchio, Italy, in 1387, and was christened Guido. At the age of twenty, he was admitted to the Dominican order at nearby Fiesole. He was given the name of Fra Giovanni, but soon, by virtue of his sweet character, was nicknamed Fra Angelico, by which name he is best known to the world. His life was spent in various monasteries of his order in Cortona, Fiesole, Florence and Rome. He soon distinguished himself as a painter, giving rise to the supposition that his early youth had been spent in some artist's shop with the idea of making painting his vocation. In those days, some field in art was by far the most attractive career for a boy. If a lad wished to become a painter, he was apprenticed at a very early age to a master, and under his guidance, learned to grind colors, prepare panels, copy designs and paint.

Fra Angelico was gifted with a supreme talent for pictorial representation and he lived at a time when art and all branches of learning were making rapid advances. As a person of the Renaissance, he shared the new interest in man and nature, and kept abreast of technical advances in art. As a devout monk, he held to the medieval traditions of the Church, and loved best to paint stories from sacred history and legend. Thus, in his work and in his life, the new and the old were in perfect harmony, and we understand why he is called the artist saint.

THE SOUNDING OF THE SEVENTH TRUMPET. "THE KING-
DOMS OF THE WORLD ARE BECOME THE KING-
DOMS OF OUR LORD AND OF HIS CHRIST"

And the seventh angel sounded; and there were great voices in heaven, saying, "The kingdoms of this world are become the kingdoms of our Lord, and of his Christ; and he shall reign forever and ever. And the four and twenty elders, which sat before God on their seats, fell upon their faces, and worshiped God, saying, "We give thee thanks, O Lord God Almighty, which art, and wast, and art to come; because thou hast taken to thee thy great power, and hast reigned. And the nations were angry, and thy wrath is come, and the time of the dead, that they should be judged, and that thou should-est give reward unto thy servants the prophets, and to the saints, and them that fear thy name, small and great; and shouldest destroy them which destroy the earth."

And the temple of God was opened in heaven, and there was seen in his temple the ark of his testament: and there were lightnings, and voices, and thunderings, and an earthquake, and great hail.

And there appeared a great wonder in heaven: a woman clothed with the sun, and the moon under her feet, and upon her head a crown of twelve stars: and she being with child cried, travailing in birth, and pained to be delivered. And there appeared another wonder in heaven; and behold a great red dragon, hav-ing seven heads and ten horns, and seven crowns upon his heads. And his tail drew the third part of the stars of heaven, and did cast them to the earth: and the dragon stood before the woman which was ready to be delivered, for to devour her child as soon as it was born. And she brought forth a man child, who was to rule all nations with a rod of iron: and her child was caught up unto God, and to his throne. And the woman fled into the wilderness, where she hath a place prepared of God, that they should feed her there a thousand two hundred and threescore days. — Revelation 11:15-12:6.

MICHAEL AND HIS ANGELS FIGHT THE DRAGON

And there was war in heaven: Michael and his angels fought against the dragon; and the dragon fought and his angels, and prevailed not; neither was their place found any more in heaven. And the great dragon was cast out, that old serpent, called the Devil, and Satan, which deceiveth the whole world: he was cast out into the earth, and his angels were cast out with him.

And I heard a loud voice saying in heaven, "Now is come salvation and strength, and the kingdom of our God, and the power of his Christ: for the accuser of our brethren is cast down, which accused them before our God day and night. And they overcame him by the blood of the Lamb, and by the word of their testimony; and they loved not their lives unto the death. Therefore rejoice, ye heavens, and ye that dwell in them. Woe to the inhabiters of the earth and of the sea! For the devil is come down unto you, having great wrath, because he knoweth that he hath but a short time."

And when the dragon saw that he was cast unto the earth, he persecuted the woman which brought forth the man child. And to the woman were given two wings of a great eagle, that she might fly into the wilderness, into her place, where she is nourished for a time, and times, and half a time, from the face of the serpent. And the serpent cast out of his mouth water as a flood after the woman, that he might cause her to be carried away of the flood. And the earth helped the woman, and the earth opened her mouth, and swallowed up the flood which the dragon cast out of his mouth. And the dragon was wroth with the woman, and went to make war with the remnant of her seed, which keep the commandments of God, and have the testimony of Jesus Christ.   — Revelation 12:7–17.

THE BEAST WHICH ROSE FROM THE SEA

And I stood upon the sand of the sea, and saw a beast rise up out of the sea, having seven heads and ten horns, and upon his horns ten crowns, and upon his heads the name of blasphemy. And the beast which I saw was like unto a leopard, and his feet were as the feet of a bear, and his mouth as the mouth of a lion: and the dragon gave him his power, and his seat, and great authority. And I saw one of his heads as it were wounded to death; and his deadly wound was healed: and all the world wondered after the beast. And they worshiped the dragon which gave power unto the beast: and they worshiped the beast, saying, "Who is like unto the beast? Who is able to make war with him?" And there was given unto him a mouth speaking great things and blasphemies; and power was given unto him to continue forty and two months. And he opened his mouth in blasphemy against God, to blaspheme his name, and his tabernacle, and them that dwell in heaven. And it was given unto him to make war with the saints, and to overcome them: and power was given him over all kindreds, and tongues, and nations. And all that dwell upon the earth shall worship him, whose names are not written in the book of life of the Lamb slain from the foundation of the world. If any man have an ear, let him hear. He that leadeth into captivity shall go into captivity: he that killeth with the sword must be killed with the sword. Here is the patience and the faith of the saints.   — Revelation 13:1–10.

THE BEAST WHICH CAME OUT OF THE EARTH

And I beheld another beast coming up out of the earth; and he had two horns like a lamb, and he spake as a dragon. And he exerciseth all the power of the first beast before him, and causeth the earth and them which dwell therein to worship the first beast, whose deadly wound was healed. And he doeth great wonders, so that he maketh fire come down from heaven on the earth in the sight of men, and deceiveth them that dwell on the earth by the means of those miracles which he had power to do in the sight of the beast; saying to them that dwell on the earth, that they should make an image to the beast, which had the wound by a sword, and did live. And he had power to give life unto the image of the beast, that the image of the beast should both speak, and cause that as many as would not worship the image of the beast should be killed. And he causeth all, both small and great, rich and poor, free and bond, to receive a mark in their right hand, or in their foreheads: and that no man might buy or sell, save he that had the mark, or the name of the beast, or the number of his name. Here is wisdom. Let him that hath understanding count the number of the beast: for it is the number of a man; and his number is six hundred threescore and six. — Revelation 13:11–18.

THE NEW SONG OF THE HARPERS HARPING WITH THEIR HARPS

And I looked, and, lo, a Lamb stood on the Mount Sion, and with him an hundred forty and four thousand, having his Father's name written in their foreheads. And I heard a voice from heaven, as the voice of many waters, and as the voice of a great thunder: and I heard the voice of harpers harping with their harps:

and they sang as it were a new song before the throne, and before the four beasts, and the elders: and no man could learn that song but the hundred and forty and four thousand, which were redeemed from the earth. These are they which were not defiled with women; for they are virgins. These are they which follow the Lamb whithersoever he goeth. These were redeemed from among men, being the firstfruits unto God and to the Lamb. And in their mouth was found no guile: for they are without fault before the throne of God.

And I saw another angel fly in the midst of heaven, having the everlasting gospel to preach unto them that dwell on the earth, and to every nation, and kindred, and tongue, and people, saying with a loud voice, "Fear God, and give glory to him; for the hour of his judgment is come: and worship him that made heaven, and earth, and the sea, and the fountains of waters."

And there followed another angel, saying, "Babylon is fallen, is fallen, that great city, because she made all nations drink of the wine of the wrath of her fornication."

And the third angel followed them, saying with a loud voice, "If any man worship the beast and his image, and receive his mark in his forehead, or in his hand, the same shall drink of the wine of the wrath of God, which is poured out without mixture into the cup of his indignation; and he shall be tormented with fire and brimstone in the presence of the holy angels, and in the presence of the Lamb: and the smoke of their torment ascendeth up forever and ever: and they have no rest day nor night, who worship the beast and his image, and whosoever receiveth the mark of his name. Here is the patience of the saints: here are they that keep the commandments of God, and the faith of Jesus."

— Revelation 14:1–12.

"BLESSED ARE THE DEAD WHICH DIE IN THE LORD"

And I heard a voice from heaven saying unto me, "Write, 'Blessed are the dead which die in the Lord from henceforth: Yea, saith the Spirit, that they may rest from their labours; and their works do follow them.'"

And I looked, and behold a white cloud, and upon the cloud one sat like unto the Son of man, having on his head a golden crown, and in his hand a sharp sickle.

And another angel came out of the temple, crying with a loud voice to him that sat on the cloud, "Thrust in thy sickle, and reap: for the time is come for thee to reap; for the harvest of the earth is ripe." And he that sat on the cloud thrust in his sickle on the earth; and the earth was reaped. And another angel came out of the temple which is in heaven, he also having a sharp sickle. And another angel came out from the altar, which had power over fire; and cried with a loud cry to him that had the sharp sickle, saying, "Thrust in thy sharp sickle, and gather the clusters of the vine of the earth; for her grapes are fully ripe." And the angel thrust in his sickle into the earth, and gathered the vine of the earth, and cast it into the great wine-press of the wrath of God. And the wine-press was trodden without the city, and blood came out of the wine-press, even unto the horse bridles, by the space of a thousand and six hundred furlongs. — Revelation 14:13-20.

THE SEVEN LAST PLAGUES

And I saw another sign in heaven, great and marvellous, seven angels having the seven last plagues; for in them is filled up the wrath of God.

And I saw as it were a sea of glass mingled with fire: and them that had gotten the victory over the

EMPEROR NERO

THIS is a greatly idealized portrait of the
emperor, who is characterized in history as
a monster of cruelty. This is the emperor
who condemned Paul to death.

Nero was born in 37 A.D. and died by his
own hand 68 A.D. Rome was destroyed by
fire 64 A.D. It is believed that Nero himself caused the fire to be started but the
blame was placed upon the Christians, and
the persecution of the new faith was begun.

MVN. PII. SEXTI. P.

beast, and over his image, and over his mark, and over the number of his name, stand on the sea of glass, having the harps of God. And they sing the song of Moses, the servant of God, and the song of the Lamb, saying, "Great and marvellous are thy works, Lord God Almighty; just and true are thy ways, thou King of saints. Who shall not fear thee, O Lord, and glorify thy name? For thou only art holy: for all nations shall come and worship before thee; for thy judgments are made manifest."

And after that I looked, and, behold, the temple of the tabernacle of the testimony in heaven was opened: and the seven angels came out of the temple, having the seven plagues, clothed in pure and white linen, and having their breasts girded with golden girdles. And one of the four beasts gave unto the seven angels seven golden vials full of the wrath of God, who liveth forever and ever. And the temple was filled with smoke from the glory of God, and from his power; and no man was able to enter into the temple, till the seven plagues of the seven angels were fulfilled. And I heard a great voice out of the temple saying to the seven angels, "Go your ways, and pour out the vials of the wrath of God upon the earth." And the first went, and poured out his vial upon the earth; and there fell a noisome and grievous sore upon the men which had the mark of the beast, and upon them which worshiped his image.

And the second angel poured out his vial upon the sea; and it became as the blood of a dead man: and every living soul died in the sea.

And the third angel poured out his vial upon the rivers and fountains of waters; and they became blood. And I heard the angel of the waters say, "Thou art righteous, O Lord, which art, and wast, and shalt be, because thou hast judged thus. For they have shed the blood of saints and prophets, and thou hast given them blood to drink; for they are worthy." And I heard another out of the altar say, "Even so, Lord God Almighty, true and righteous are thy judgments."

And the fourth angel poured out his vial upon the sun; and power was given unto him to scorch men with fire. And men were scorched with great heat, and blasphemed the name of God, which hath power over these plagues: and they repented not to give him glory.

And the fifth angel poured out his vial upon the seat of the beast; and his kingdom was full of darkness; and they gnawed their tongues for pain, and blasphemed the God of heaven because of their pains and their sores. and repented not of their deeds.

And the sixth angel poured out his vial upon the great river Euphrates; and the water thereof was dried up, that the way of the kings of the east might be prepared. And I saw three unclean spirits like frogs come out of the mouth of the dragon, and out of the mouth of the beast, and out of the mouth of the false prophet. For they are the spirits of devils, working miracles, which go forth unto the kings of the earth and of the whole world, to gather them to the battle of that great day of God Almighty. Behold, I come as a thief. Blessed is he that watcheth, and keepeth his garments, lest he walk naked, and they see his shame.   — Revelation 15; 16:1–15.

THE BATTLE OF ARMAGEDDON

And he gathered them together into a place called in the Hebrew tongue Armageddon.

And the seventh angel poured out his vial into the air; and there came a great voice out of the temple of heaven, from the throne, saying, "It is done." And there were voices, and thunders, and lightnings; and there was a great earthquake, such as was not since men were upon the earth, so mighty an earthquake, and so great. And the great city was divided into three parts, and the cities of the nations fell: and great Babylon came in remembrance before God, to give unto her the cup of the wine of the fierceness of his wrath. And every island fled away, and the mountains were not found. And there fell upon men a great hail out of heaven, every stone about the weight of a talent: and men blasphemed God because of the plague of the hail; for the plague thereof was exceeding great.

— Revelation 16:16–21.

BABYLON THE GREAT

And there came one of the seven angels which had the seven vials, and talked with me, saying unto me, "Come hither; I will shew unto thee the judgment of the great whore that sitteth upon many waters: with whom the kings of the earth have committed fornication, and the inhabitants of the earth have been made drunk with the wine of her fornication." So he carried me away in the spirit into the wilderness: and I saw a woman sit upon a scarlet coloured beast, full of names of blasphemy, having seven heads and ten horns. And the woman was arrayed in purple and scarlet colour, and decked with gold and precious stones and pearls, having a golden cup in her hand full of abominations and filthiness of her fornication: and upon her forehead was a name written, "MYSTERY, BABYLON THE GREAT, THE MOTHER OF HARLOTS AND ABOMINATIONS OF THE EARTH." And I saw the woman drunken with the blood of the saints, and with the blood of the martyrs of Jesus: and when I saw her, I wondered with great admiration. And the angel said unto me, "Wherefore

didst thou marvel? I will tell thee the mystery of the woman, and of the beast that carrieth her, which hath the seven heads and ten horns. The beast that thou sawest was, and is not; and shall ascend out of the bottomless pit, and go into perdition: and they that dwell on the earth shall wonder, whose names were not written in the book of life from the foundation of the world, when they behold the beast that was, and is not, and yet is. And here is the mind which hath wisdom. The seven heads are seven mountains, on which the woman sitteth. And there are seven kings: five are fallen, and one is, and the other is not yet come; and when he cometh, he must continue a short space. And the beast that was, and is not, even he is the eighth, and is of the seven, and goeth into perdition. And the ten horns which thou sawest are ten kings, which have received no kingdom as yet; but receive power as kings one hour with the beast. These have one mind, and shall give their power and strength unto the beast. These shall make war with the Lamb, and the Lamb shall overcome them: for he is Lord of lords, and King of kings: and they that are with him are called, and chosen, and faithful."

And he saith unto me, "The waters which thou sawest, where the whore sitteth, are peoples, and multitudes, and nations, and tongues. And the ten horns which thou sawest upon the beast, these shall hate the whore, and shall make her desolate and naked, and shall eat her flesh, and burn her with fire. For God hath put in their hearts to fulfill his will, and to agree, and give their kingdom unto the beast, until the words of God shall be fulfilled. And the woman which thou sawest is that great city, which reigneth over the kings of the earth." — Revelation 17:1–18.

MOUNT TABOR NEAR NAZARETH—THE SITE OF THE TRANSFIGURATION OF CHRIST

"BABYLON IS FALLEN, IS FALLEN!"

And after these things I saw another angel come down from heaven, having great power; and the earth was lightened with his glory. And he cried mightily with a strong voice, saying, "Babylon the great is fallen, is fallen, and is become the habitation of devils, and the hold of every foul spirit, and a cage of every unclean and hateful bird. For all nations have drunk of the wine of the wrath of her fornication, and the kings of the earth have committed fornication with her, and the merchants of the earth are waxed rich through the abundance of her delicacies."

And I heard another voice from heaven, saying, "Come out of her, my people, that ye be not partakers of her sins, and that ye receive not of her plagues. For her sins have reached unto heaven, and God hath remembered her iniquities. Reward her even as she rewarded you, and double unto her double according to her works: in the cup which she hath filled fill to her double. How much she hath glorified herself, and lived deliciously, so much torment and sorrow give her: for she saith in her heart, 'I sit a queen, and am no widow, and shall see no sorrow.' Therefore shall her plagues come in one day, death, and mourning, and famine; and she shall be utterly burned with fire: for strong is the Lord God who judgeth her. And the kings of the earth, who have committed fornication and lived deliciously with her, shall bewail her, and lament for her, when they shall see the smoke of her burning, standing afar off for the fear of her torment, saying, 'Alas, alas that great city Babylon, that mighty city! For in one hour is thy judgment come. And the merchants of the earth shall weep and mourn over her; for no man buyeth their merchandise any more: the merchandise of gold, and silver, and precious stones, and of pearls, and fine linen, and purple, and silk, and scarlet, and all thyine wood, and all manner vessels of ivory, and all manner vessels of most precious wood, and of brass, and iron, and marble, and cinnamon, and odours, and ointments, and frankincense, and wine, and oil, and fine flour, and wheat, and beasts, and sheep, and horses, and chariots, and slaves, and souls of men. And the fruits that thy soul lusted after are departed from thee, and all things which were dainty and goodly are departed from thee, and thou shalt find them no more at all. The merchants of these things, which were made rich by her, shall stand afar off for the fear of her torment, weeping and wailing, and saying, 'Alas, alas that great city, that was clothed in fine linen, and purple, and scarlet, and decked with gold, and precious stones, and pearls!' For in one hour so great riches is come to naught. And every shipmaster, and all the company in ships, and sailors, and as many as trade by sea, stood afar off, and cried when they saw the smoke of her burning, saying, 'What city is like unto this great city!' And they cast dust on their heads, and cried, weeping and wailing, saying, 'Alas, alas, that great city, wherein were made rich all that had ships in the sea by reason of her costliness! For in one hour is she made desolate. Rejoice over her, thou heaven, and ye holy apostles and prophets; for God hath avenged you on her.'

"And a mighty angel took up a stone like a great millstone, and cast it into the sea, saying, 'Thus with violence shall that great city Babylon be thrown down, and shall be found no more at all. And the voice of harpers, and musicians, and of pipers, and trumpeters, shall be heard no more at all in thee; and no craftsman of whatsoever craft he be, shall be found any more in thee; and the sound of a millstone shall be heard no more at all in thee; and the light of a candle shall shine no more at all in thee; and the voice of the bridegroom and of the bride shall be heard no more at all in thee: for thy merchants were the great men of the earth; for by thy sorceries were all nations deceived.' And in her was found the blood of prophets, and of saints, and of all that were slain upon the earth." — Revelation 18:1–24.

"SALVATION AND GLORY AND HONOR AND POWER UNTO THE LORD OUR GOD"

And after these things I heard a great voice of much people in heaven, saying, "Alleluia; Salvation, and glory, and honour, and power, unto the Lord our God: for true and righteous are his judgments: for he hath judged the great whore, which did corrupt the earth with her fornication, and hath avenged the blood of his servants at her hand."

And again they said, "Alleluia." And her smoke rose up forever and ever. And the four and twenty elders and the four beasts fell down and worshiped God that sat on the throne, saying, "Amen; Alleluia."

And a voice came out of the throne, saying, "Praise our God, all ye his servants, and ye that fear him, both small and great."

And I heard as it were the voice of a great multitude, and as the voice of many waters, and as the voice of mighty thunderings, saying, "Alleluia: for the Lord God omnipotent reigneth. Let us be glad and rejoice, and give honour to him: for the marriage of the Lamb is come, and his wife hath made herself ready." And to her was granted that she should be arrayed in fine linen, clean and white: for the fine linen is the righteousness of saints. And he saith unto me, "Write, 'Blessed are they which are called unto the marriage supper of the Lamb.'"

And he saith unto me, "These are the true sayings of God."

And I fell at his feet to worship him. And he said unto me, "See thou do it not: I am thy fellowservant, and of thy brethren that have the testimony of Jesus: worship God: for the testimony of Jesus is the spirit of prophecy."

And I saw heaven opened, and behold a white horse; and he that sat upon him was called Faithful and True, and in righteousness he doth judge and make war. His eyes were as a flame of fire, and on his head were many crowns; and he had a name written, that no man knew, but he himself. And he was clothed with a vesture dipped in blood: and his name is called The Word of God. And the armies which were in heaven followed him upon white horses, clothed in fine linen, white and clean. And out of his mouth goeth a sharp sword, that with it he should smite the nations: and he shall rule them with a rod of iron: and he treadeth the wine-press of the fierceness and wrath of Almighty God. And he hath on his vesture and on his thigh a name written, "KING OF KINGS, AND LORD OF LORDS."

And I saw an angel standing in the sun; and he cried with a loud voice, saying to all the fowls that fly in the midst of heaven, "Come and gather yourselves together unto the supper of the great God; that ye may eat the flesh of kings, and the flesh of captains, and the flesh of mighty men, and the flesh of horses, and of them that sit on them, and the flesh of all men, both free and bond, both small and great." And I saw the beast, and the kings of the earth, and their armies, gathered together to make war against him that sat on the horse, and against his army. And the beast was taken, and with him the false prophet that wrought miracles before him, with which he deceived them that had received the mark of the beast, and them that worshiped his image. These both were cast alive into a lake of fire burning with brimstone. And the remnant were slain with the sword of him that sat upon the horse, which sword proceeded out of his mouth: and all the fowls were filled with their flesh.

— Revelation 19:1–21.

THE CHAINING OF THE DRAGON

And I saw an angel come down from heaven, having the key of the bottomless pit and a great chain in his hand. And he laid hold on the dragon, that old serpent, which is the Devil, and Satan, and bound him a thousand years, and cast him into the bottomless pit, and shut him up, and set a seal upon him, that he should deceive the nations no more, till the thousand years should be fulfilled: and after that he must be loosed a little season.

And I saw thrones, and they sat upon them, and judgment was given unto them: and I saw the souls of them that were beheaded for the witness of Jesus, and for the word of God, and which had not worshiped the beast, neither his image, neither had received his mark upon their foreheads, or in their hands; and they lived and reigned with Christ a thousand years. But the rest of the dead lived not again until the thousand years were finished. This is the first resurrection. Blessed and holy is he that hath part in the first resurrection: on such the second death hath no power, but they shall be priests of God and of Christ, and shall reign with him a thousand years. And when the thousand years are expired, Satan shall be loosed out of his prison, and shall go out to deceive the nations which are in the four quarters of the earth, Gog and Magog, to gather them together to battle: the number of whom is as the sand of the sea. And they went up on the breadth of the earth, and compassed the camp of the saints about, and the beloved city: and fire came down from God out of heaven, and devoured them. And the devil that deceived them was cast into the lake of fire and brimstone, where the beast and the false prophet are, and shall be tormented day and night forever and ever.

And I saw a great white throne, and him that sat on it, from whose face the earth and the heaven fled away; and there was found no place for them.

And I saw the dead, small and great, stand before God; and the books were opened: and another book was opened, which is the book of life: and the dead were judged out of those things which were written in the books, according to their works. And the sea gave up the dead which were in it; and death and hell delivered up the dead which were in them: and they were judged every man according to their works. And death and hell were cast into the lake of fire. This is the second death. And whosoever was not found written in the book of life was cast into the lake of fire.   — Revelation 20:1-15.

A NEW HEAVEN AND A NEW EARTH

And I saw a new heaven and a new earth: for the first heaven and the first earth were passed away; and there was no more sea. And I, John, saw the holy city, new Jerusalem, coming down from God out of heaven, prepared as a bride adorned for her husband. And I heard a great voice out of heaven saying, "Behold, the tabernacle of God is with men, and he will dwell with them, and they shall be his people, and God himself shall be with them, and be their God. And God shall wipe away all tears from their eyes; and there shall be no more death, neither sorrow, nor crying, neither shall there be any more pain: for the former things are passed away."

And he that sat upon the throne said, "Behold, I make all things new." And he said unto me, "Write: for these words are true and faithful." And he said unto me, "It is done. I am Alpha and Omega, the beginning and the end. I will give unto him that is athirst of the fountain of the water of life freely. He that overcometh shall inherit all things; and I will be his God, and he shall be my son. But the fearful, and unbelieving and the abominable, and murderers, and whoremongers, and sorcerers, and idolaters, and all liars, shall have their part in the lake which burneth with fire and brimstone: which is the second death."

And there came unto me one of the seven angels which had the seven vials full of the seven last plagues, and talked with me, saying, "Come hither, I will show thee the bride, the Lamb's wife."   — Revelation 21:1-9.

THE NEW JERUSALEM DESCENDING OUT OF HEAVEN FROM GOD

And he carried me away in the spirit to a great and high mountain, and showed me that great city, the holy Jerusalem, descending out of heaven from God, having the glory of God: and her light was like unto a stone most precious, even like a jasper stone, clear as crystal; and had a wall great and high, and had twelve gates, and at the gates twelve angels, and names written thereon, which are the names of the twelve tribes of the children of Israel: on the east three gates; on the north three gates; on the south three gates; and on the west three gates. And the wall of the city had twelve foundations, and in them the names of the twelve apostles of the Lamb. And he that talked with me had a golden reed to measure the city, and the gates thereof, and the wall thereof. And the city lieth foursquare, and the length is as large as the breadth: and he measured the city with the reed, twelve thousand furlongs. The length and the breadth and the height of it are equal. And he measured the wall thereof, an hundred and forty and four cubits, according to the measure of a man, that is, of the angel. And the building of the wall of it was of jasper: and the city was pure gold, like unto clear glass. And the foundations of the wall of the city were garnished with all manner of precious stones. The first foundation was jasper; the second, sapphire; the third, a chalcedony; the fourth, an emerald; the fifth, sardonyx; the sixth, sardius; the seventh, chrysolyte; the eighth, beryl; the ninth, a topaz; the tenth, a chrysoprasus; the eleventh, a jacinth; the twelfth, an amethyst. And the twelve gates were twelve pearls; every several gate was of one pearl: and the street of the city was pure gold, as it were transparent glass. And I saw no temple therein: for the Lord God Almighty and the Lamb are the temple of it. And the city had no need of the sun, neither of the moon, to shine in it: for the glory of God did lighten it, and the Lamb is the light thereof. And the nations of them which are saved shall walk in the light of it: and the kings of the earth do bring their glory and honour into it. And the gates of it shall not be shut at all by day: for there shall be no night there. And they shall bring the glory and honour of the nations into it. And there shall in no wise enter into it anything that defileth, neither whatsoever worketh abomination, or maketh a lie: but they which are written in the Lamb's book of life.   — Revelation 21:10–27.

THE RIVER OF THE WATER OF LIFE

And he showed me a pure river of water of life, clear as crystal, proceeding out of the throne of God and of the Lamb. In the midst of the street of it, and on either side of the river, was there the tree of life, which bare twelve manner of fruits, and yielded her fruit every month: and the leaves of the tree were for the healing of the nations. And there shall be no more curse: but the throne of God and of the Lamb shall be in it; and his servants shall serve him: and they shall see his face; and his name shall be in their foreheads. And there shall be no night there; and they need no candle, neither light of the sun; for the Lord God giveth them light: and they shall reign forever and ever. And he said unto me, "These sayings are faithful and true: and the Lord God of the holy prophets sent his angel to shew unto his servants the things which must shortly be done. Behold, I come quickly: blessed is he that keepeth the sayings of the prophecy of this book."

And I, John, saw these things, and heard them. And when I had heard and seen, I fell down to worship before the feet of the angel which showed me these things. Then saith he unto me, "See thou do it not: for I am thy fellowservant, and of thy brethren, the prophets, and of them which keep the sayings of this book: worship God." And he saith unto me, "Seal not the sayings of the prophecy of this book: for the time is at hand. He that is unjust, let him be unjust still: and he which is filthy, let him be filthy still: and he that is righteous, let him be righteous still: and he that is holy, let him be holy still. And behold, I come quickly; and my reward is with me, to give every man according as his work shall be. — Revelation 22:1-12.

"I AM ALPHA AND OMEGA"

"I am Alpha and Omega, the beginning and the end, the first and the last. Blessed are they that do his commandments, that they may have right to the tree of life, and may enter in through the gates into the city. For without are dogs, and sorcerers, and whoremongers, and murderers, and idolaters, and whosoever loveth and maketh a lie. I, Jesus, have sent mine angel to testify unto you these things in the churches. I am the root and the offspring of David, and the bright and morning star." And the Spirit and the bride say, "Come." And let him that heareth say, "Come." And let him that is athirst come. And whosoever will, let him take the water of life freely. For I testify unto every man that heareth the words of the prophecy of this book, if any man shall add unto these things, God shall add unto him the plagues that are written in this book: and if any man shall take away from the words of the book of this prophecy, God shall take away his part out of the book of life, and out of the holy city, and from the things which are written in this book.

He which testifieth these things saith, "Surely I come quickly." Amen. Even so, come, Lord Jesus.

The grace of our Lord Jesus Christ be with you all. Amen.   — Revelation 22:13–21.

QUESTIONS

Give the salutation, the probable author, the argument, the main purpose of each of the epistles. Why were the epistles written? Did Paul write in his own hand? What was probably the first epistle? the occasion of writing? Upon what material were the epistles written? Who took Paul's epistle to the Romans to Rome? Which epistle was sent by a slave? Which epistle treats especially of the resurrection? What did Paul mean when he told the Galatians to stand fast in this liberty? Write down the persons mentioned in Paul's epistles. How did he happen to know so many people? What are the "pastoral epistles"? In what epistle does Paul ask for books and a cloak? In what epistles does Paul use the figure of the temple, the Greek games, the armor of the Roman soldier? What suggestions are made as to the authorship of Hebrews? What passages in the epistles are most inspiring to you? What ones present the following themes: faith, love, perseverance, the forward look, self-control, gentleness, helpfulness, tolerance, "unity of the spirit"?

For what purpose was Revelation written? What is the theme of the epistles of John? In what epistle is a church severely rebuked? What epistle teaches of faith and works? What is the theme of the epistles of Peter? of Jude?

NOTES ON PAUL'S LETTERS

ROMANS

I am debtor both to the Greeks and the Barbarians. "Barbarians" does not mean "savages," but those not speaking Greek. When used by Romans it meant those not speaking Greek or Latin.

It is the power of God . . . to everyone that believeth. This states the theme of the letter, which is "Salvation through Christ, and its results in life."

"What advantage then hath the Jew?" Paul remembers, as he writes this letter, the objections made to his positions, and he briefly states the objections and his answers to them: "If the Jewish religion does not always bring men to God, what is the advantage in being a Jew?"

"God has promised salvation; if he does not give it because men do not believe, does not that make his promise of no avail?"

"How can God justly punish, if the sin of man makes the glory of God plainer?"

Paul outlines his answer and pushes on in his argument.

I find then a law. Paul uses "law" in various meanings; the Old Testament law; the "law of God," general principles of righteousness; the law of the state; the controlling principles of life, whether good or evil. The last is the use in this passage.

More than conquerors. God gives even more strength than we need. See with what a shout of triumph this whole section of the letter closes in the sentences which follow!

O the depth of the riches! Another splendid close of a section of the letter. "How wonderful the wisdom of God, who can make the will of man work out his own great purposes!"

Your reasonable service. "Service" is "worship"; not, "the worship it is reasonable for you to offer," but, "which befits you as reasonable and spiritual persons." The chapter which this sentence opens has been called "Paul's description of a Christian gentleman."

Illyricum. The region northeast of Greece, corresponding roughly to modern Albania. The people of Albania are the descendants of the ancient Illyrians. Paul had never gone far into Illyria, but doubtless his disciples had, and he himself had approached the borders of the province.

I, Tertius, who wrote this letter. This seems strange, when Paul is the writer of Romans. But Paul usually employed an amanuensis to do the actual writing. Here the writer, who may have known many of those to whom Paul is sending the letter, adds his own greeting.

The First Letter to the Corinthians

Sosthenes. Acts 18:17 mentions a Sosthenes, ruler of the synagogue, at Corinth, who may be this man. If so, he had become a Christian leader and was now with Paul in Ephesus.

Things offered to idols. In a populous city like Corinth more animals were sometimes brought to the temples than could be used for sacrifice. The extra animals were killed and the meat sold in the market for the benefit of the temple. It is plain from Paul's writing that many regarded this meat which came from the temple as still connected in some measure with the idol. Two positions had arisen among the Christians. Some, whom Paul calls the "strong," said, "We no longer believe in idols. What difference does it make whether a piece of meat in the market has come from the temple or not?" Others, the "weak," could not forget that the meat had been offered to an idol, and thought they ought not to eat it. The church had written to Paul to ask which was right. Can you see what was Paul's decision?

We know that we all have knowledge. Perhaps this phrase is a quotation from the letter of the Corinthians to Paul, apologizing for asking about so simple a matter. He replies that knowledge is not sufficient; one needs love.

We know that an idol is nothing in the world. Another quotation from their letter, perhaps extending to "and we by him." Paul's answer follows: "There are some who can not think of the idol as nothing, and who seem to themselves to be worshiping it when they eat meat which has been offered to it."

The Lord Jesus the same night. Since the letters of Paul may be earlier than the gospels, this story of the last supper is perhaps the first record of an event of Jesus' life which has come down to us.

Spiritual gifts. All abilities and powers which help on the work of the church were considered by Paul to be gifts of the Spirit of God. The section about *charity* (Revised Version, love) is a sort of parenthesis. Love is not a spiritual gift, but it lies back of all spiritual gifts. "You are right," says Paul, "to seek the best gifts, but remember that better than any of the gifts is love." This section is one of the finest in all Paul's writing, and we should never have had it except for the quarreling of the Corinthian Christians.

Speaking with tongues was emotional utterance in words which had to be interpreted in order to be understood by others in the church.

The collection for the saints is more fully described in Romans 15:25–27. There were poor Christians at Jerusalem and Paul wished to show the unity of the Gentile and Jewish churches by taking a sum of money from the Gentile Christians for their impoverished Jewish brethren.

Winter with you. Paul planned to travel from Ephesus to Corinth, stay there through the winter, then go north to Macedonia and gather the collection from the churches of Thessalonica, Philippi, and elsewhere, and go from there to Jerusalem. This plan he carried out, though not in the order he expected. He went to Macedonia first, then to Corinth and back to Macedonia. See Acts 20:1–5.

SECOND CORINTHIANS

Our trouble which came to us in Asia. For the description of at least a part of the trouble see Acts 19.

Forty stripes save one. The Jews were careful to beat condemned prisoners with only 39 stripes, lest the 40 prescribed as the limit in the law should be exceeded. We know very few of the occasions mentioned in this list of Paul's sufferings; which illustrates how little after all we know of his whole life.

Once was I stoned. See Acts 14:19, 20.

Through a window . . . was I let down. See Acts 9:23-25.

GALATIANS

Conversation. Not "talk with others," but, as the Revised Version translates, "manner of life." So in Eph. 4:22, Phil. 1:27, 3:20 and other passages.

I went into Arabia. Nothing is said about this in Acts 9; nor do we know either to what part of Arabia he went, or what he did there. Two ideas have been current: (1) that he went into the desert to think through the position in which his new faith had placed him; (2) that he preached Christ in the towns of northern Arabia.

Then fourteen years after. This may be either after his conversation, or after his visit to Jerusalem.

Went up to Jerusalem. Probably the visit recorded in Acts 15, though some think it is that mentioned in Acts 11:30.

Barnabas. See Acts 13:1-3, 15:1-4.

Titus. Later a frequent traveling companion of Paul; II Corinthians 2:13; 7:6, etc. How he first came in contact with Paul is not known.

How large a letter. Better, as in the Revised Version, "with how large letters." Paul was accustomed to write a few words in his own hand at the close of the letters to attest them, like a signature on a typed letter. See II Thess. 3:17. Because of poor sight, or for some other reason, he writes here in a large hand, to which he calls attention.

EPHESIANS

Tychicus. Paul's messenger, who took from Rome this letter, Colossians and Philemon. See Col. 3:7-9.

PHILIPPIANS

In all the palace, and in all other places. Revised Version, "throughout the whole praetorian guard, and to all the rest." The

reference is not to a place, but to the imperial guard of ten thousand picked men stationed at Rome. One of these soldiers was constantly chained to Paul, and he had opportunity in this way to touch the lives of many men, not without result. There were Christians in Cæsar's household because Paul was prisoner in Rome. See Phil. 4:22.

Euodias and Syntyche. Two good women in the church who could not get on together; a situation still sometimes found in churches.

COLOSSIANS

COLOSSE. This is better known as Colossæ.

Thrones, dominions, principalities, powers. Names for the spiritual beings thought of as standing between God and man. A philosophy had come into Colossae which seemed to Paul dangerous to Christian faith, and he combats it strongly. It had two foundations: a theory about God and a theory about matter. God was placed so high that man could never hope to reach him. Between God and man is a long series of divine beings. Man can worship only these. Paul in 2:18 calls this hopelessness of reaching God a "false humility," and refers to the worship of the lesser beings as a "worship of angels."

The second theory was about matter: the world of matter is in itself evil. But if all matter is evil how did the good God come to create it? The theory said that he did not create it. The spiritual beings emanated in a chain, the first from God, then each from the preceding, and each was less pure than the one before. The final being in the series is so impure that he can create this impure material world. It follows that the creator of the world is not to be worshiped; man may not be able to reach very far up in the scale of divine beings, but he can at least reach beyond the creator. It follows also that the way to salvation lies in withdrawing from all contact, as far as possible, with the material world. This idea Paul condemns without hesitation in Col. 2:20–23. As to the spiritual beings,—"powers, principalities," whatever names they are called—he says that we do not need them; Christ is the only mediator needed between God and man (Col. 1:16, 17). They called the sum total of these beings the "fullness." Paul said that all the "fullness" was in Christ (Col. 1:19). This whole letter is filled with the terms of this philosophy, and with Paul's attempt to show that it is useless; Christianity is far better. Ephesians also contains references to this philosophy. though it does

RETAINING WALL—SEA OF GALILEE

not directly combat it. The philosophy is akin to what became known later as "Gnosticism," which in the second century was very attractive to many Christians.

Marcus, sister's son to Barnabas. The author of the Gospel of Mark, once refused by Paul as a companion (Acts 15:36—40), who now has proved his character and is highly esteemed by Paul.

Luke, the beloved physician. The author of the Gospel of Luke and of Acts.

Hebrews

Melchizedek, used in Hebrews as a type of "a priest forever," king of Salem and priest of the most High God, met Abraham after his victory over the five kings of the east, gave him bread and wine for himself and his men, bestowed upon Abraham the sacerdotal blessing of his high office, and received from Abraham the payment of tithes (Gen. 14:17—20). He held the dual office of king and priest; but his priesthood was not of the Levitical order, since he lived long before the establishment of the Hebrew priesthood. As a priest he was without a predecessor or successor. In all these facts he was a peculiar type of Christ, who is both King and Priest and who is without predecessor or successor, superior to, and abrogator of, the Aaronic priesthood; King and Priest, not of the Hebrew race, but of the whole redeemed family of God of every race and nation. (See Ps. 110:4; Heb. 5:6; 6:20; 7:3.)

Where a testament is. The same Greek word meant both a "covenant," in the sense of a binding promise, and a will, as in the phrase "last will and testament." In this chapter the writer passes from one use to the other, for both help his argument. When he speaks of "the ark of the covenant" he uses one meaning; when he says that a testament is of no value without the death of the testator, he uses the other. In both cases he is trying to show that a "covenant" is confirmed by a death; whether of a sacrificial animal or of the testator.

CHRONOLOGICAL TABLE OF THE LIFE OF PAUL AND CONTEMPORARY EVENTS

BIOGRAPHY OF ST. PAUL	CONTEMPORARY EVENTS
36(?)St. Paul's conversion.	
37(?)At Damascus.	Death of Tiberius and accession of Caligula (March 16).
38(?)Flight from Damascus to Jerusalem, and thence to Tarsus.	
39(?) ⎱ During these years St. Paul 40(?) ⎰ preaches in Syria and Cilicia, making Tarsus his headquarters, and probably un- 41(?)dergoes some of the sufferings mentioned at II Cor. 11:24–26, viz., two of the Roman 42(?) and the five Jewish scourg- 43(?) ings, and three shipwrecks.	Death of Caligula, and accession of Claudius (Jan. 25). Judaea and Samaria given to Herod Agrippa I. Invasion of Britain by Aulus Plautius.
44 He is brought from Tarsus to Antioch (Acts 11:26) and stays there a year before the famine.	Death of Herod Agrippa I (Acts 11). Cuspius Fadus (as procurator) succeeds to the government of Judaea.
45 He visits Jerusalem with Barnabas to relieve the famine.	
46 At Antioch.	Tiberius Alexander made procurator of Judaea (about this time)
46–48 His "First Missionary Journey" from Antioch to Cyprus, Antioch in Pisidia, Iconium, Lystra, Derbe, and back through the same places to Antioch (except Cyprus).	Agrippa II (Acts 25) made king of Chalcis. Cumanus made procurator of Judaea (about this time).

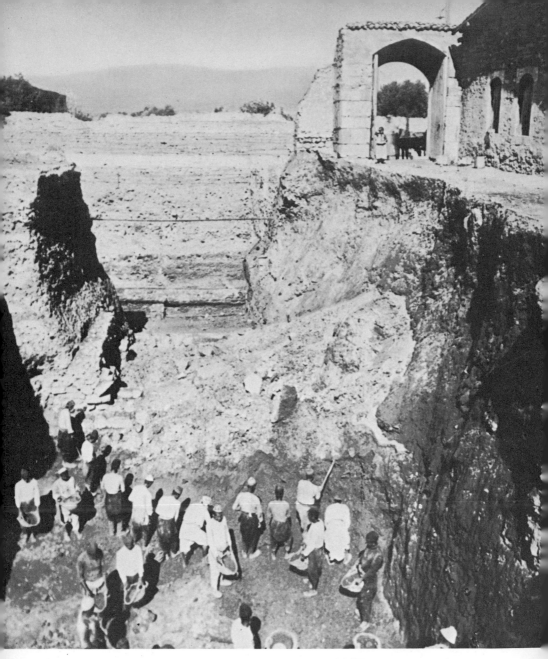

ANCIENT ANTIOCH

Digging down to the level of ancient Antioch, buried "three graves deep" by silt. The splendor of this once famous city is still in evidence. Capital of the Greek and Roman governors for nearly 1000 years. The first Gentile Church was founded here by the Apostle Paul and the disciples were here first called Christians. The birthplace of Chrysostom, A.D. 344.

49 St. Paul and Barnabas attend the "Council of Jerusalem."

Caractacus captured by the Romans in Britain;
Cogidunus (father of Claudia? II Tim. 4:21) assists the Romans in Britain.

49 His "Second Missionary Journey," from Antioch to Cilicia, Lycaonia, Galatia,

50 Troas, Philippi, Thessalonica, Berea and Athens.

Claudius expels the Jews from Rome (Acts 18:2).

51 At Corinth—Writes I Thess.
Corinth—Writes II Thess.

The tetrarchy of Trachonitis given to Agrippa II;
Felix made procurator of Judaea.

52 (Spring)—He leaves Corinth. and reaches (Summer)—Jerusalem at Pentecost, and thence goes to Antioch.

Death of Claudius and accession of Nero (Oct. 13).

53 (Autumn)—His "Third Missionary Journey."—He goes to Ephesus.

54 At Ephesus.

55 At Ephesus.

57 (Spring)—He writes I Cor.
(Summer)—Leaves Ephesus for Macedonia,
(Autumn)—where he writes II Cor., and thence
(Winter)—to Corinth, where he writes "Galatians."

58 (Spring)—He writes Romans, and leaves Corinth, going by Philippi and Miletus.
(Summer)—to Jerusalem (Pentecost), where he is arrested and sent to Cæsarea.

59 At Caesarea.

60 (Autumn)—Sent to Rome by Festus (about August).

61 (Spring)—He arrives at Rome.

Nero murders Agrippina.

Felix is recalled and succeeded by Festus. Embassy from Jerusalem to Rome, to petition about the wall.

62 At Rome. Philemon, Colossians.
(Spring)—Writes Ephesians.
(Autumn)—Writes Philippians.

63 (Spring)—He is acquitted, and goes to Macedonia (Phil. 2:24), and Asia Minor (Philemon 22).

64 He goes to Spain.(?)

65 In Spain.(?)

Burrus dies.

Albinus succeeds Festus as procurator; Nero marries Poppaea; Octavia is executed; Pallas put to death.

Poppaea's daughter Claudia born.

Great Fire at Rome (July 19), followed by persecution of Roman Christians; Gessius Florus made procurator of Judaea.

Conspiracy of Piso, and death of Seneca.

66 (Summer)—From Spain (?) to Asia Minor (I Tim. 1:3).

67 (Summer)—Writes I Tim. from Macedonia.
(Autumn)—Writes Titus from Ephesus.
(Winter)—At Nicopolis.

68 (Spring)—In prison at Rome. Writes II Tim.
(Summer)—Executed (May or June).

The Jewish war begins.

Death of Nero in the middle of June.

This table was compiled on the basis of the most comprehensive research work in the field, not only that of Conybeare and Howson, of Farrar, of Dobschuetz and of Weizsaecker, but especially on that of the epochal work of Ramsay and Deissmann, which has practically fixed the chronology of Paul's life.